# Workshop on Noisy User-generated Text 2015



**Co-located with ACL-IJCNLP 2015**

## Beijing, China
## 31 July 2015

ISBN: 978-1-5108-0953-6

**Printed from e-media with permission by:**

Curran Associates, Inc.
57 Morehouse Lane
Red Hook, NY 12571

**Some format issues inherent in the e-media version may also appear in this print version.**



Printed by Curran Associates, Inc. (2015)

For permission requests, please contact the Association for Computational Linguistics at the address below.

Association for Computational Linguistics
209 N. Eighth Street
Stroudsburg, Pennsylvania 18360

Phone: 1-570-476-8006
Fax: 1-570-476-0860

acl@aclweb.org

**Additional copies of this publication are available from:**

Curran Associates, Inc.
57 Morehouse Lane
Red Hook, NY 12571 USA
Phone: 845-758-0400
Fax: 845-758-2634
Email: curran@proceedings.com
Web: www.proceedings.com

ACL-IJCNLP 2015

# ACL 2015
# Workshop on Noisy User-generated Text

## Proceedings of the Workshop

July 31, 2015
Beijing, China

**Sponsors**

Microsoft Research

IBM Research

# Introduction

The WNUT 2015 workshop focuses on a core set of natural language processing tasks on top of noisy user-generated text, such as that found on social media, web forums and online reviews. Recent years have seen a significant increase of interest in these areas. The internet has democratized content creation leading to an explosion of informal user-generated text, publicly available in electronic format, motivating the need for NLP on noisy text to enable new data analytics applications. The workshop is an opportunity to bring together researchers interested in noisy text with different backgrounds and encourage crossover.

The workshop this year features two shared tasks, (a) Text Normalization and (b) Twitter Named Entity Recognition, to facilitate comparison of different approaches and help advance the state of the art. Because this is a fast-moving area, there is a lack of standardized datasets, and papers published in the same year may not compare against each other. By organizing these shared tasks we hope to help develop standardized evaluations and promote research on NLP in noisy text.

The program this year includes 8 papers in the main track, 8 system description papers in the Twitter Named Entity Recognition track, and 9 system description papers in the Text Normalization track. All the papers are presented as short talks and as well as posters. There are also 4 invited speakers, Tim Baldwin, Brendan O'Connor, Anders Søgaard and Joel Tetreault, with each of their talks covering a different aspect of NLP for user-generated text.

We would like to thank the Program Committee members who reviewed the papers this year. We would also like to thank the workshop participants. Last, a word of thanks also goes to our two sponsors: Microsoft Research and IBM Research.

Wei Xu, Bo Han and Alan Ritter
Co-Organizers

**Organizers:**

Wei Xu (University of Pennsylvania)
Bo Han (IBM Research)
Alan Ritter (The Ohio State University)

**Program Committee:**

David Bamman (Carnegie Mellon University)
Kalina Bontcheva (University of Sheffield)
Claire Cardie (Cornell University)
Colin Cherry (National Research Council Canada)
Grzegorz Chrupała (Tilburg University)
Leon Derczynski (University of Sheffield)
Jacob Eisenstein (Georgia Institute of Technology)
Jennifer Foster (Dublin City University)
Eric Fosler-Lussier (The Ohio State University)
Kevin Gimpel (Toyota Technological Institute at Chicago)
Weiwei Guo (Columbia University)
Dirk Hovy (University of Copenhagen)
Jing Jiang (Singapore Management University)
Emre Kiciman (Microsoft Research)
Wang Ling (Carnegie Mellon University)
Xiaohua Liu (University of Montreal)
Preslav Nakov (Qatar Computing Research Institute)
Miles Osborne (Bloomberg)
Kristen Parton (Facebook)
Ellie Pavlick (University of Pennsylvania)
Daniel Preoţiuc-Pietro (University of Pennsylvania)
Roi Reichart (Technion-IIT)
Alla Rozovskaya (Columbia University)
Nathan Schneider (University of Edinburgh)
Djamé Seddah (University Paris-Sorbonne)
Richard Sproat (Google)
Maosong Sun (Tsinghua University)
Oren Tsur (Harvard University)
Benjamin Van Durme (Johns Hopkins University)
Svitlana Volkova (Johns Hopkins University)
Lu Wang (Cornell University)
Jun-Ming Xu (University of Wisconsin-Madison)
Xiaojin Zhu (University of Wisconsin-Madison)

**Invited Speakers:**

Tim Baldwin (The University of Melbourne)
Brendan O'Connor (University of Massachusetts Amherst)
Anders Søgaard (University of Copenhagen)
Joel Tetreault (Yahoo! Research)

## Table of Contents

# Conference Program

**Friday, July 31, 2015**

**9:00–10:30** **Invited Talks**

9:00–9:45 *Text Mining of Social Media: Going beyond the Text and Only the Text*
Tim Baldwin

9:45–10:30 *Where is Language?*
Anders Søgaard

**10:30–11:00** ***Coffee Break***

**11:00–12:30** **Long Papers and Abstracts**

11:00–11:15 *Learning finite state word representations for unsupervised Twitter adaptation of POS taggers*
Julie Wulff and Anders Søgaard

11:15–11:30 *Towards POS Tagging for Arabic Tweets*
Fahad Albogamy and Allan Ramasy

11:30–11:45 *Minority Language Twitter: Part-of-Speech Tagging and Analysis of Irish Tweets*
Teresa Lynn, Kevin Scannell and Eimear Maguire

11:45–11:00 *Challenges of studying and processing dialects in social media*
Anna Jørgensen, Dirk Hovy and Anders Søgaard

12:00–12:15 *Toward Tweets Normalization Using Maximum Entropy*
Mohammad Arshi Saloot, Norisma Idris, Liyana Shuib, Ram Gopal Raj and AiTi Aw

12:15–12:30 *Five Shades of Noise: Analyzing Machine Translation Errors in User-Generated Text*
Marlies van der Wees, Arianna Bisazza and Christof Monz

**Friday, July 31, 2015 (continued)**

**12:30–14:00 Poster Session and Lunch**

*Learning finite state word representations for unsupervised Twitter adaptation of POS taggers*
Julie Wulff and Anders Søgaard

*Towards POS Tagging for Arabic Tweets*
Fahad Albogamy and Allan Ramasy

*Minority Language Twitter: Part-of-Speech Tagging and Analysis of Irish Tweets*
Teresa Lynn, Kevin Scannell and Eimear Maguire

*Challenges of studying and processing dialects in social media*
Anna Jørgensen, Dirk Hovy and Anders Søgaard

*Toward Tweets Normalization Using Maximum Entropy*
Mohammad Arshi Saloot, Norisma Idris, Liyana Shuib, Ram Gopal Raj and AiTi Aw

*Five Shades of Noise: Analyzing Machine Translation Errors in User-Generated Text*
Marlies van der Wees, Arianna Bisazza and Christof Monz

*A Normalizer for UGC in Brazilian Portuguese*
Magali Sanches Duran, Maria das Graças Volpe Nunes and Lucas Avanço

*USFD: Twitter NER with Drift Compensation and Linked Data*
Leon Derczynski, Isabelle Augenstein and Kalina Bontcheva

*Enhancing Named Entity Recognition in Twitter Messages Using Entity Linking*
Ikuya Yamada, Hideaki Takeda and Yoshiyasu Takefuji

*Improving Twitter Named Entity Recognition using Word Representations*
Zhiqiang Toh, Bin Chen and Jian Su

*NRC: Infused Phrase Vectors for Named Entity Recognition in Twitter*
Colin Cherry, Hongyu Guo and Chengbi Dai

*IITP: Multiobjective Differential Evolution based Twitter Named Entity Recognition*
Md Shad Akhtar, Utpal Kumar Sikdar and Asif Ekbal

**Friday, July 31, 2015 (continued)**

**Friday, July 31, 2015 (continued)**

**14:00–15:30 Shared Task Session**

14:00–14:30 *Shared Tasks of the 2015 Workshop on Noisy User-generated Text: Twitter Lexical Normalization and Named Entity Recognition*
Timothy Baldwin, Marie-Catherine de Marneffe, Bo Han, Young-Bum Kim, Alan Ritter and Wei Xu

14:30–14:45 *Enhancing Named Entity Recognition in Twitter Messages Using Entity Linking*
Ikuya Yamada, Hideaki Takeda and Yoshiyasu Takefuji

14:45–15:00 *Improving Twitter Named Entity Recognition using Word Representations*
Zhiqiang Toh, Bin Chen and Jian Su

15:00–15:15 *Multimedia Lab @ ACL WNUT NER Shared Task: Named Entity Recognition for Twitter Microposts using Distributed Word Representations*
Fréderic Godin, Baptist Vandersmissen, Wesley De Neve and Rik Van de Walle

15:15–15:30 *NCSU_SAS_SAM: Deep Encoding and Reconstruction for Normalization of Noisy Text*
Samuel Leeman-Munk, James Lester and James Cox

**15:30–16:00 *Coffee Break***

**16:00–17:30 Invited Talks**

16:00–16:45 *Automated Grammatical Error Correction for Language Learners: Where are we, and where do we go from there?*
Joel Tetreault

16:45–17:30 *Are Minority Dialects "Noisy Text"?: Implications of Social and Linguistic Diversity for Social Media NLP*
Brendan O'Connor

# Minority Language Twitter: Part-of-Speech Tagging and Analysis of Irish Tweets

**Teresa Lynn**[1,3], **Kevin Scannell**[2], and **Eimear Maguire**[1]
[1]ADAPT Centre, School of Computing, Dublin City University, Ireland
[2]Department of Mathematics and Computer Science, St. Louis University, USA
[3]Department of Computing, Macquarie University, Sydney, Australia
[1]{tlynn,emaguire}@computing.dcu.ie
[2]{kscanne}@gmail.com
[3]{teresa.lynn}@mq.edu.au,

## Abstract

Noisy user-generated text poses problems for natural language processing. In this paper, we show that this statement also holds true for the Irish language. Irish is regarded as a low-resourced language, with limited annotated corpora available to NLP researchers and linguists to fully analyse the linguistic patterns in language use in social media. We contribute to recent advances in this area of research by reporting on the development of part-of-speech annotation scheme and annotated corpus for Irish language tweets. We also report on state-of-the-art tagging results of training and testing three existing POS-taggers on our new dataset.

## 1 Introduction

The language style variation used on social media platforms, such as Twitter for example, is often referred to as noisy user-generated text. Tweets can contain typographical errors and ungrammatical structures that pose challenges for processing tools that have been designed for and tailored to high quality, well-edited text such as that found in newswire, literature and official documents. Previous studies, Foster et al. (2011) and Petrov and McDonald (2012) for example, have explored the effect that the style of language used in user-generated content has on the performance of standard NLP tools. Other studies by Gimpel et al. (2011), Owoputi et al. (2013), Avontuur et al. (2012), Rehbein (2013) and Derczynski et al. (2013) (POS-tagging), Ritter et al. (2011) (named entity recognition), Kong et al. (2014) and Seddah et al. (2012) (parsing) have shown that NLP tools and resources need to be adapted to cater for the linguistic differences present in such text.

When considering data-driven NLP tasks, a lack of resources can also produce additional challenges. We therefore examine the impact of noisy user-generated text on the existing resources for Irish, a low-resourced language. We also explore options for leveraging from existing resources to produce a new domain-adapted POS-tagger for processing Irish Twitter data. We achieve this by:

- defining a new POS tagset for Irish tweets
- providing a mapping from the PAROLE Irish POS-tagset to this new one
- manually annotating a corpus of 1537 Irish tweets
- training three statistical taggers on our data and reporting results

This paper is divided as follows: Section 2 gives a summary of Twitter and issues specific to the Irish Twitter data. Section 3 discusses the new part-of-speech tagged corpus of Irish tweets. Section 4 discusses our inter-annotator agreement study and the observations we note from annotator disagreements. Section 5 reports our tagging accuracy results on three state-of-the-art statistical taggers.

## 2 Irish Tweets

Irish, the official and national language of Ireland, is a minority language. While it is a second language for most speakers, everyday use outside of academic environments has seen a recent resurgence in social media platforms such as Facebook and Twitter. Twitter is a micro-blogging platform which allows users (*tweeters*) to create a social network through sharing or commenting on items of social interest such as ideas, opinions, events and news. Tweeters can post short messages called *tweets*, of up to 140 characters in length, that can typically be seen by the general public, including the user's *followers*. Tweets can be classified by topic by using *hashtags* (e.g. #categoryname)



*Proceedings of the ACL 2015 Workshop on Noisy User-generated Text*, pages 1–8,
Beijing, China, July 31, 2015. 

and linked to other tweeters through the use of *at-mentions* (e.g. @username).

The first tweets in Irish appeared not long after the launch of Twitter in 2006, and there have been more than a million tweets in Irish since then, by over 8000 tweeters worldwide[1].

The social nature of tweets can result in the use of informal text, unstructured or ungrammatical phrases, and a variety of typographical errors. The 140 character limit can also lead to truncated ungrammatical sentences, innovative spellings, and word play, such as those discussed by Eisenstein (2013) for English. From our analysis, this phenomenon appears to extend also to Irish tweets.

In Figure 1, we provide an example of an Irish tweet that contains some of these NLP challenges:

*Freezing i dTra Li,Ciarrai chun cinn le cuilin.*
Freezing i dTr**á** Lí, **tá** Ciarra**í** chun cinn le c**ú**il**í**n.
'Freezing in Tralee, Kerry (is) ahead by a point.'

Figure 1: Example of noisy Irish tweet

**Diacritics** Irish, in its standard orthography, marks long vowels with diacritics (á,é,í,ó,ú). Our analysis of Irish tweets revealed that these diacritics are often replaced with non-accented vowels (cúilín => cuilin). There are a number of word pairs that are differentiated only by the presence or absence of these diacritics (for example, *cead* 'permission' : *céad* 'hundred'). There are many possible reasons for omitting diacritics, including shortening the time required to tweet (this tweet is from a spectator at a Gaelic Football match), a lack of knowledge on how to find diacritics on a device's keyboard, carelessness, or uncertainty about the correct spelling.

**Code-switching** Alternating between English and Irish is common in our dataset. This is unsurprising as virtually all Irish speakers are fluent English speakers, and many use English as their first language in their daily lives. In the example given, there is no obvious reason why "Freezing" was used in place of various suitable Irish words (e.g. *Préachta*), other than perhaps seeking a more dramatic effect. Sometimes, however, English is understandably used when there is no suitable Irish term in wide use, for example 'hoodie' or 'rodeo-clown'. Aside from occurring at an intra-sentential level, code-switching at an inter-sentential level is also common in Irish: *an t-am seo an t7ain seo chugainn bei 2 ag partyáil le muintir Ráth Daingin! Hope youre not too scared #upthevillage*. In total, of the 1537 tweets in our gold-standard corpus, 326 (21.2%) contain at least one English word with the tag G[2].

**Verb drop** We can see in this example that the verb *tá* 'is' has been dropped. This is a common phenomenon in user-generated content for many languages. The verb is usually understood and can be interpreted through the context of the tweet.

**Spacing** Spacing after punctuation is often overlooked (i) in an attempt to shorten messages or (ii) through carelessness. In certain instances, this can cause problems when tokenizing tweets; Li,Ciarrai => Li, Ciarrai.

**Phonetic spelling** Linguistic innovations often result from tweeters trying to fit their message into the 140 character limit. Our dataset contains some interesting examples of this phenomenon occurring in Irish. For example *t7ain* is a shortened version of *tseachtain* 'week'. Here the word *seacht* 'seven' is shortened to its numeral form and the initial mutation *t* remains attached. Other examples are *gowil (go bhfuil), beidir (b'fhéidir), v (bhí)*.

**Abbreviations** Irish user-generated text has its own set of frequently used phrase abbreviations – referred to sometimes as text-speak. Forms such as *mgl:maith go leor*, 'fair enough' and *grma:go raibh maith agat* 'thank you' have been widely adopted by the Irish language community.

The linguistic variation of Irish that is used in social media is relatively unexplored, at least not in any scientific manner. We expect therefore that the part-of-speech tagged corpus and taggers that we have developed for Irish language tweets will contribute to further research in this area.

## 3 Building a corpus of annotated Irish tweets

Unlike rule-based systems, statistical data-driven POS-taggers require annotated data on which they can be trained. Therefore, we build a gold-standard corpus of 1537 Irish tweets annotated

[1] `http://indigenoustweets.com/ga/`

[2] The tag G is used for foreign words, abbreviations, items and unknowns, as shown in Table 1.

with a newly defined Twitter POS tagset. The following describes this development process.

### 3.1 New Irish Twitter POS tagset

The rule-based Irish POS-tagger (Uí Dhonnchadha and van Genabith, 2006) for standard Irish text is based on the PAROLE Morphosyntactic Tagset (ITÉ, 2002). We used this as the basis for our Irish Twitter POS tagset. We were also inspired by the English-tweet POS tagset defined by Gimpel et al. (2011), and have aimed to stay closely aligned to it in order to facilitate any future work on cross-lingual studies.

We started by selecting a random sample of 500 Irish tweets to carry out an initial analysis. From our analysis of these tweets we concluded that our new Twitter-specific POS tagset would not require the granularity of the original standard Irish POS set. For example we do not need to differentiate between a locative adverb and a temporal adverb, or between a vocative particle and an infinitive particle. While our tagset is also closely aligned with the English-tweet POS tagset, we introduce the following tags that the English set does not use:

- **`VN`: Verbal Noun** Progressive aspectual phrases in Irish are denoted by the preposition *ag* followed by a verbal noun (e.g. *ag rith* 'running'). We choose to differentiate between N and VN to avoid losing this verbal information in what would otherwise be a regular prepositional phrase.

- **`#MWE`: Multiword hashtag** These are hashtags containing strings of words used to categorise a text (e.g. #godhelpus). We retain information on the multi-word nature of these hashtags in order to facilitate future syntactic analysis efforts.

We also adapt the `T` particle to suit Irish linguistic features.

- **`T`: Particle** We extend the `T` tag to not only cover verb particles, but all other Irish particles: relative particles, surname particles, infinitive particles, numeric particles, comparative particles, the vocative particle, and adverbial particles.

We do not use the following tags from the English set: `S, Z, L, M, X, Y,` as the linguistic cases they apply to do not occur in either standard or non-standard Irish. The final set of 21 POS-tags is presented in Table 1.

Most of the tags in the tagset are intuitive to an Irish language speaker. However, some tags require specific explanation in the guidelines. Hashtags and at-mentions can be a syntactic part of a sentence or phrase within a tweet. When this is the case, we apply the relevant syntactic POS tag. For example, *Beidh mé ar chlár @SplancNewstalk*$_{\wedge}$ *anocht ag labhairt leis @AnRonanEile*$_{\wedge}$ *faoi #neknomination*$_{N}$ 'I will be on @SplancNewstalk tonight speaking to @AnRonanEile about #neknomination'. Otherwise if they are not part of the syntactic structure of the tweet (typically appended or prepended to the main tweet text), they are tagged as `@` and `#` (or `#MWE`). In our gold standard corpus, 554 out of 693 hashtags (79.9%), and 1604 out of 1946 at-mentions (82.4%) are of this non-syntactic type.

With some Twitter clients, if a tweet exceeds the 140 character limit, the tweet is truncated and an ellipsis is used to indicate that some text is missing. We leave this appended to the final (usually partial) token, which was often a URL. We marked these cases as `G`. For example *http://t.co/2nvQsxala7. . . .*

Some strings of proper nouns contain other POS elements, such as determiners and common nouns. Despite being a proper noun phrase syntactically, we tag each token as per its POS. For example, *Cú*$_{\wedge}$ *na*$_{D}$ *mBaskerville*$_{\wedge}$ 'The Hound of the Baskervilles'.

### 3.2 Tweet pre-processing pipeline

About 950,000 Irish language tweets were posted between Twitter's launch in 2006 and September 2014 by approximately 8000 users identified and tracked by the Indigenous Tweets web site. Non-Irish tweets from these users were filtered out using a simple character-trigram language identifier. We selected a random sample of 1550 tweets from these 950,000 tweets and processed them as follows:

(1) We tokenised the set with Owoputi et al. (2013)'s version of `twokenise`[3], which works well on web content features such as emoticons and URLs.

(2) Using a list of multiword units from Uí Dhonnchadha (2009)'s rule-based Xerox FST tokeniser[4], we rejoined multiword tokens that had

[3]Available to download from `http://www.ark.cs.cmu.edu/TweetNLP/#pos`

[4]Available to download from `https://github.com/stesh/apertium-gle/tree/master/dev/`

| Tag | Description (PAROLE TAGS) |
|---|---|
| N | common noun (Noun, Pron Ref, Subst) |
| ∧ | proper noun (Prop Noun) |
| O | pronoun (Pron Pers, Pron Idf, Pron Q, Pron Dem) |
| VN | verbal noun (Verbal Noun) |
| V | verb (Cop, Verb*) |
| A | adjective (Adj, Verbal Adj, Prop Adj) |
| R | adverb (Adv*) |
| D | determiner (Art, Det) |
| P | preposition, prep. pronoun (Prep*, Pron Prep) |
| T | particle (Part*) |
| , | punctuation (Punct) |
| & | conjunction (Conj Coord, Conj Subord) |
| $ | numeral, quantifier (Num) |
| ! | interjection (Itj) |
| G | foreign words, abbreviations, item (Foreign, Abr, Item, Unknown) |
| ~ | discourse marker |
| # | hashtag |
| #MWE | multi-word hashtag |
| @ | at-mention |
| E | emoticon |
| U | URL/email address/XML (Web) |

Table 1: Mapping of Irish Twitter tagset to PAROLE tagset. (* indicates all forms of the fine-grained set for that tag.)

been split by the language-independent tokenizer (e.g. the compound preposition *go_dtí*).

(3) Using regular expressions, we then split tokens with the contractions *b' (ba), d' (do), m' (mo)* prefixes. For example *b'fhéidir* 'maybe'; *d'ith* 'ate'; *m'aigne* 'my mind'.

(4) We took a bootstrapping approach by pre-tagging and lemmatising the data with the rule-based Irish POS-tagger first, and then mapped the tags to our new Twitter-specific tagset.

(5) In cases where the rule-based tagger failed to produce a unique tag, we used a simple bigram tag model (trained on the gold-standard POS-tagged corpus from Uí Dhonnchadha (2009) – see Section 5.1) to choose the most likely tag from among those output by the rule-based tagger.

(6) Finally, we manually corrected both the tags and lemmas to create a gold-standard corpus.

### 3.3 Annotation

The annotation task was shared between two annotators. Correction of the first 500 tweets formed a basis for assessing both the intuitiveness of our tagset and the usability of our annotation guide. Several discussions and revisions were involved at this stage before finalising the tagset. The next 1000 tweets were annotated in accordance with the guidelines, while using the first 500 as a reference. At this stage, we removed a small number of tweets that contained 100% English text (errors in the language identifier). All other tweets containing non-Irish text represented valid instances of code-switching.

The annotators were also asked to verify and correct the lemma form if an incorrect form was suggested by the morphological analyser. All other tokeniser issues, often involving Irish contractions, were also addressed at this stage. For example *Tá'n* $->$ *Tá an*.

## 4 Inter-Annotator Agreement

Inter-Annotator agreement (IAA) studies are carried out during annotation tasks to assess consistency, levels of bias, and reliability of the annotated data. For our study, we chose 50 random Irish tweets, which both annotators tagged from scratch. This differed from the rest of the annotation process, which was semi-automated. However, elimination of possible bias towards the pre-annotation output allowed for a more disciplined assessment of agreement level between the annotators. We achieved an agreement rate of 90% and a $\kappa$ score (Cohen, 1960) of 0.89.

Smaller tagsets make an annotation task easier due to the constraint on choices available to the annotator, and is certainly one reason for our high IAA score. This result also suggests that the tagging guidelines were clear and easy to understand. A closer comparison analysis of the IAA data explains some disagreements. The inconsistency of conflicts suggests that the disagreements arose from human error. Some examples are given below.

**Noun vs Proper Noun** The word *Gaeilge* 'Irish' was tagged on occasion as `N` (common noun) instead of ∧ (proper noun). This also applied

`irishfst`

to some proper noun strings such as *Áras an Uachtaráin* (the official name of the President of Ireland's residence).

**Syntactic at-mentions** A small number of at-mentions that were syntactically part of a tweet (e.g. *mar chuid de @SnaGaeilge* 'as a part of @SnaGaeilge') were incorrectly tagged as regular at-mentions (`@`).

**Retweet colons** One annotator marked ':' as punctuation at random stages rather than using the discourse tag ~.

## 5 Experiments

### 5.1 Data

We took the finalised set of Irish POS-tagged tweets and divided them into a test set (148 tweets), development set (147 tweets) and training set (1242 tweets). Variations of this data are used in our experiments where we normalise certain tokens (described further in Section 5.2.)

We also automatically converted Uí Dhonnchadha (2009)'s 3198 sentence (74,705 token) gold-standard POS-tagged corpus using our mapping scheme. This text is from the New Corpus for Ireland – Irish[5], which is a collection of text from books, newswire, government documents and websites. The text is well-structured, well-edited, and grammatical, and of course lacks Twitter-specific features like hashtags, at-mentions, and emoticons, thus differing greatly from our Twitter data. The average sentence length in this corpus is 27 tokens, diverging significantly from the average tweet length of 17.2 tokens. Despite this, and despite the fact the converted tags were not reviewed for accuracy, we were still interested in exploring the extent to which this additional training data could improve the accuracy of our best-performing model. We refer to this set as `NCII_3198`.

### 5.2 Taggers

We trained and evaluated three state-of-the-art POS-taggers with our data. All three taggers are open-source tools.

**Morfette** As Irish is an inflected language, inclusion of the lemma as a training feature is desirable in an effort to overcome data sparsity. Therefore we trained Morfette (Chrupala et al., 2008), a lemmatization tool that also predicts POS tags and uses the lemma as a training feature. We report on experiments both with and without an optional dictionary (`Dict`) information. We used the dictionary from Scannell (2003), which contains $350,418$ surface forms. Our baseline Morfette data (`BaseMorf`) contains the token, lemma and POS-tag. The lemmas of URLs and non-syntactic hashtags have been normalised as $< URL >$ and $< \# >$, respectively.

We then evaluated the tagger with (non-syntactic) $< \# >$, $< @ >$ and $< URL >$ normalisation of both token form and lemma (`NormMorf`). Both experiments are re-run with the inclusion of our dictionary (`BaseMorf+Dict,NormMorf+Dict`).

**ARK** We also trained the CMU Twitter POS-tagger (Owoputi et al., 2013), which in addition to providing pre-trained models, allows for re-training with new languages. The current release does not allow for the inclusion of the lemma as a feature in training, however. Instead, for comparison purposes, we report on two separate experiments, one using the surface tokens as features, and the other using only the lemmas as features (`ArkForm`, `ArkLemma`). We also tested versions of our data with normalised at-mentions, hashtags and URLs, as above.

**Stanford tagger** We re-trained the Stanford tagger (Toutanova et al., 2003) with our Irish data. We experimented by training models using both the surface form only (`BestStanForm`) and the lemma only (`BestStanLemma`). The best performing model was based on the feature set `left3words, suffix(4), prefix(3), wordshapes(-3,3), biwords(-1,1)`, using the `owlqn2` search option.[6]

**Baseline** Finally, to establish a baseline (`Baseline`), and more specifically to evaluate the importance of domain-adaptation in this context, we evaluated a slightly-enhanced version of the rule-based Irish tagger on the Twitter dataset. When the rule-based tagger produced more than one possible tag for a given token, we applied a bigram tag model to choose the most likely tag, as we did in creating the first

[5]New Corpus for Ireland - Irish. See `http://corpas.focloir.ie`

[6]All other default settings were used.

draft of the gold-standard corpus. In addition, we automatically assigned the tag `U` to all URLs, # to all hashtags, and @ to all at-mentions.

### 5.3 Results

| Training Data | Dev | Test |
|---|---|---|
| **Baseline** | | |
| Rule-Based Tagger | 85.07 | 83.51 |
| **Morfette** | | |
| BaseMorf | 86.77 | 88.67 |
| NormMorf | 87.94 | 88.74 |
| BaseMorf+Dict | 87.50 | 89.27 |
| NormMorf+Dict | 88.47 | 90.22 |
| **ARK** | | |
| BaseArkForm | 88.39 | 89.92 |
| ArkForm#@ | 89.36 | 90.94 |
| ArkForm#URL@ | 89.32 | 91.02 |
| BaseArkLemma#URL | 90.74 | 91.62 |
| ArkLemma#URL@ | 91.46 | 91.89 |
| **Stanford** | | |
| BestStanForm | 82.36 | 84.08 |
| BestStanLemma | 87.34 | 88.36 |
| **Bootstrapping Best Model** | | |
| ArkLemma#URL@+NCII | 92.60 | 93.02 |

Table 2: Results of evaluation of POS-taggers on new Irish Twitter corpus

The results for all taggers and variations of data-setup are presented in Table 2.

Firstly, our best performing single model (`ArkLemma#URL@`) on the test set achieves a score of 91.89%, which is 8 points above our rule-based baseline score of 83.51%. This confirms that tailoring training data for statistically-driven tools is a key element in processing noisy user-generated content, even in the case of minority languages. It is worth noting that the best-performing model learns from the lemma information instead of the surface form. This clearly demonstrates the effect that the inflectional nature of Irish has on data sparsity. The Twitter-specific tokens such as URLs, hashtags and at-mentions have been normalised which demonstrates the impact the relative uniqueness of these tokens has on the learner.

All of our results are comparable with state-of-the-art results produced by Gimpel et al. (2011) and Owoputi et al. (2013). This is interesting, given that in contrast to their work, we have not optimised our system with unsupervised word clusters due to the lack of sufficient Irish tweet data. Nor have we included a tag dictionary, distribution similarity or phonetic normalisation – also due to a lack of resources.

We carried out a closer textual comparison of Owoputi et al. (2013)'s English tweet dataset (`daily547`) and our new Irish tweet dataset. After running each dataset through a language-specific spell-checker, we could see that the list of highly ranked OOV (out of vocabulary) tokens in English are forms of text-speak, such as *lol* 'laugh out loud', *lmao* 'laugh my ass off' and *ur* 'your', for example. Whereas the most common OOVs in Irish are English words such as 'to', 'on', 'for', 'me', and words misspelled without diacritics. This observation shows the differences between textual challenges of processing these two languages. It may also suggest that Irish Twitter text may follow a more standard orthography than English Twitter text, and will make for an interesting future cross-lingual study of Twitter data.

Finally, we explored the possibility of leveraging from existing POS-tagged data by adding `NCII_3198` to our best performing model `ArkLemma#URL@`. We also duplicated the tweet training set to bring the weighting for both domains into balance. This brings our training set size to 5682 (117,273 tokens). However, we find that a significant increase in the training set size only results in just over a 1 point increase in POS-tagging accuracy. At a glance, we can see some obvious errors the combined model makes. For example, there is confusion when tagging the word *an*. This word functions as both a determiner and an interrogative verb particle. The lack of direct questions in the NCII corpus results in a bias towards the `D` (determiner) tag. In addition, many internal capitalised words (e.g. the beginning of a second part of a tweet) are mislabelled as proper nouns. This is a result of the differing structure of the two data sets – each tweet may contain one or more phrases or sentences, while the NCII is split into single sentences.

## 6 Future Work

Limited resources and time prevented exploration of some options for improving our POS-tagging results. One of these options is to modify the CMU (English) Twitter POS-tagger to allow for inclusion of lemma information as a feature. Another option, when there is more unlabelled data available (i.e. more Irish tweets online), would be to include Irish word cluster features in the training model. This approach has also been taken by Rehbein (2013) for POS tagging German tweets.

The resources we provide through this study are a valuable contribution to the Irish NLP community. Firstly, we expect that this new data resource (the POS-tagged Twitter corpus) will provide a solid basis for linguistic and sociolinguistic study of Irish on a social media platform. This new domain of Irish language use can be analysed in an empirical and scientific manner through corpus analysis by means of our data. The authors are currently working towards this follow-up study.

From a tool-development perspective, we expect this corpus and the derived POS-tagging models could be used in a domain-adaptation approach to parsing Irish tweets, similar to the work of Kong et al. (2014). This would involve adapting Lynn et al. (2012)'s Irish statistical dependency parser for use with social media text. Our corpus could provide the basis of a treebank for this work.

Following our discovery of the extent that code-switching is present our Irish Twitter data, we feel future studies on this phenomenon would be of interest to various research disciplines (e.g Solorio et al. (2014)). In order to do that, we suggest updating the corpus with a separate tag for English tokens (that is, a tag other than `G`, which is also used for abbreviations, items and unknowns) before carrying out further experiments in this area.

## 7 Conclusion

We present the first dataset of gold-standard POS-tagged Irish language tweets and we have produced training models for a selection of POS-taggers.[7] We have also shown how we have leveraged from existing work to build these resources for a low-resourced language, to achieve state-of-the-art results. We also confirm that the NLP challenges arising from noisy user-generated text can also apply to a minority language.

## 8 Acknowledgments

The authors would like to thank the three anonymous reviewers for their helpful feedback. We also would like to thank Kevin Gimpel for his support with using the CMU English Twitter POS tagger, Djamé Seddah for his support with Morfette, and Elaine Uí Dhonnchadha and Francis Tyers for their support with the Irish rule-based POS tagger. This work was funded by the Fulbright Commision of Ireland (Fulbright Enterprise-Ireland Award 2014-2015), and supported by Science Foundation Ireland through the CNGL Programme (Grant 12/CE/I2267) in the ADAPT Centre (www.adaptcentre.ie) at Dublin City University. The second author was partially supported by US NSF grant 1159174.

[7] Our data is available to download from `https://github.com/tlynn747/IrishTwitterPOS`

## References

Tetske Avontuur, Iris Balemans, Laura Elshof, Nanne van Noord, and Menno van Zaanen. 2012. Developing a part-of-speech tagger for dutch tweets. *Computational Linguistics in the Netherlands Journal*, 2:34–51, 12/2012.

Grzegorz Chrupala, Georgiana Dinu, and Josef van Genabith. 2008. Learning morphology with morfette. In *Proceedings of the International Conference on Language Resources and Evaluation, LREC 2008, 26 May - 1 June 2008, Marrakech, Morocco.*

J. Cohen. 1960. A Coefficient of Agreement for Nominal Scales. *Educational and Psychological Measurement*, 20(1):37.

Leon Derczynski, Alan Ritter, Sam Clark, and Kalina Bontcheva. 2013. Twitter part-of-speech tagging for all: Overcoming sparse and noisy data. In Galia Angelova, Kalina Bontcheva, and Ruslan Mitkov, editors, *RANLP*, pages 198–206. RANLP 2011 Organising Committee / ACL.

Jacob Eisenstein. 2013. What to do about bad language on the internet. In *Proceedings of the 2013 Conference of the North American Chapter of the Association for Computational Linguistics: Human Language Technologies*, pages 359–369. Association for Computational Linguistics.

J. Foster, Ö. Çetinoglu, J. Wagner, J. Le Roux, S. Hogan, J. Nivre, D. Hogan, J. Van Genabith, et al. 2011. # hardtoparse: Pos tagging and parsing the twitterverse. In *Proceedings of the Workshop On Analyzing Microtext (AAAI 2011)*, pages 20–25.

Kevin Gimpel, Nathan Schneider, Brendan O'Connor, Dipanjan Das, Daniel Mills, Jacob Eisenstein, Michael Heilman, Dani Yogatama, Jeffrey Flanigan, and Noah A. Smith. 2011. Part-of-speech tagging for Twitter: Annotation, features, and experiments. In *Proceedings of the 49th Annual Meeting of the Association for Computational Linguistics: Human Language Technologies: Short Papers - Volume 2*, HLT '11, pages 42–47, Stroudsburg, PA, USA. Association for Computational Linguistics.

ITÉ. 2002. PAROLE Morphosyntactic Tagset for Irish. Institiúid Teangeolaíochta Éireann.

Lingpeng Kong, Nathan Schneider, Swabha Swayamdipta, Archna Bhatia, Chris Dyer, and Noah A. Smith. 2014. A dependency parser for tweets. In *Proceedings of the 2014 Conference on Empirical Methods in Natural Language Processing (EMNLP)*, pages 1001–1012, Doha, Qatar, October. Association for Computational Linguistics.

Teresa Lynn, Jennifer Foster, Mark Dras, and Elaine Uí Dhonnchadha. 2012. Active learning and the Irish treebank. In *Proceedings of the Australasian Language Technology Workshop (ALTA)*, pages 23–32.

Olutobi Owoputi, Brendan O'Connor, Chris Dyer, Kevin Gimpel, Nathan Schneider, and Noah A. Smith. 2013. Improved part-of-speech tagging for online conversational text with word clusters. In *Proceedings of the 2013 Conference of the North American Chapter of the Association for Computational Linguistics: Human Language Technologies*, pages 380–390, Atlanta, Georgia, June. Association for Computational Linguistics.

Slav Petrov and Ryan McDonald. 2012. Overview of the 2012 Shared Task on Parsing the Web. In *First Workshop on Syntactic Analysis of Non-Canonical Language (SANCL)*.

Ines Rehbein. 2013. Fine-grained pos tagging of german tweets. In Iryna Gurevych, Chris Biemann, and Torsten Zesch, editors, *GSCL*, volume 8105 of *Lecture Notes in Computer Science*, pages 162–175. Springer.

Alan Ritter, Sam Clark, Mausam, and Oren Etzioni. 2011. Named entity recognition in tweets: An experimental study. In *Proceedings of the Conference on Empirical Methods in Natural Language Processing*, EMNLP '11, pages 1524–1534, Stroudsburg, PA, USA. Association for Computational Linguistics.

Kevin P. Scannell. 2003. Automatic thesaurus generation for minority languages: an Irish example. *Actes de la 10e conférence TALNa Batz-sur-Mer*, 2:203–212.

Djamé Seddah, Benoit Sagot, Marie Candito, Virginie Mouilleron, and Vanessa Combet. 2012. The French Social Media Bank: a treebank of noisy user generated content. In *Proceedings of COLING 2012*, pages 2441–2458.

Thamar Solorio, Elizabeth Blair, Suraj Maharjan, Steven Bethard, Mona Diab, Mahmoud Ghoneim, Abdelati Hawwari, Fahad AlGhamdi, Julia Hirschberg, Alison Chang, and Pascale Fung. 2014. *Proceedings of the First Workshop on Computational Approaches to Code Switching*, chapter Overview for the First Shared Task on Language Identification in Code-Switched Data, pages 62–72. Association for Computational Linguistics.

Kristina Toutanova, Dan Klein, Christopher D. Manning, and Yoram Singer. 2003. Feature-rich part-of-speech tagging with a cyclic dependency network. In *Proceedings of the 2003 Conference of the North American Chapter of the Association for Computational Linguistics on Human Language Technology - Volume 1*, NAACL '03, pages 173–180, Stroudsburg, PA, USA. Association for Computational Linguistics.

Elaine Uí Dhonnchadha and Josef van Genabith. 2006. A part-of-speech tagger for Irish using finite-state morphology and constraint grammar disambiguation. In *Proceedings of the 5th International Conference on Language Resources and Evaluation (LREC 2006)*.

Elaine Uí Dhonnchadha. 2009. *Part-of-Speech Tagging and Partial Parsing for Irish using Finite-State Transducers and Constraint Grammar*. Ph.D. thesis, Dublin City University.

# Challenges of studying and processing dialects in social media

**Anna Katrine Jørgensen, Dirk Hovy, and Anders Søgaard**
University of Copenhagen
Njalsgade 140
DK-2300 Copenhagen S
soegaard@hum.ku.dk

## Abstract

Dialect features typically do not make it into formal writing, but flourish in social media. This enables large-scale variational studies. We focus on three phonological features of African American Vernacular English and their manifestation as spelling variations on Twitter. We discuss to what extent our data can be used to falsify eight sociolinguistic hypotheses. To go beyond the spelling level, we require automatic analysis such as POS tagging, but social media language still challenges language technologies. We show how both newswire- and Twitter-adapted state-of-the-art POS taggers perform significantly worse on AAVE tweets, suggesting that large-scale dialect studies of language variation beyond the surface level are not feasible with out-of-the-box NLP tools.

## 1 Introduction

Dialectal and sociolinguistic studies are traditionally based on interviews of small sets of speakers of each variety. The *Atlas of North American English* (Labov et al., 2005) has been the reference point for American dialectology since its completion, but is based on only 762 speakers. Dallas is represented by four subjects, the New York City dialect by six, etc. Data is costly to collect, and, as a consequence, scarce.

Written language was traditionally used for formal purposes, and therefore differed in style from colloquial, spoken language. However, with the rise of social media platforms and the vast production of user generated content, differences between written and spoken language diminish. A number of recent papers have explored social media with respect to sociolinguistic and dialectological questions (Rao et al., 2010; Eisenstein, 2013; Volkova et al., 2013; Doyle, 2014; Hovy et al., 2015; Volkova et al., 2015; Johannsen et al., 2015; Hovy and Søgaard, 2015; Eisenstein, to appear). Emails, chats and social media posts serve purposes similar to those of spoken language, and consequently, features of spoken language, such as interjections, ellipses, and phonological variation, have found their way into this type of written language. Our work differs from most previous approaches by investigating several phonological spelling correlates of a specific language variety.

The 284 million active users on Twitter post more than half a billion tweets every day, and some fraction of these tweets are geo-located. Eisenstein (2013) and Doyle (2014) studied the effect of phonological variation across the US on spelling in Twitter posts, and both found some evidence that dialectal phonological variation has a direct impact on spelling



*Proceedings of the ACL 2015 Workshop on Noisy User-generated Text*, pages 9–18,
Beijing, China, July 31, 2015. 

on Twitter. Both authors note various methodological problems using Twitter as a source of evidence for dialectal and sociolinguistic studies, including what we refer to as USER POPULATION BIAS and TOPIC BIAS below.

In this paper, we collect Twitter data to test eight (8) research hypotheses originating in sociolinguistic studies of African-American Vernacular English (AAVE). The hypotheses relate to three phonological features of AAVE, namely derhotacization, interdental fricative mutation, and backing in /str/. Some of our findings shed an interesting light on existing hypotheses, but our main focus in this paper is to identify the methodological challenges in using social media for testing sociolinguistic hypotheses.

Almost all previous large-scale variational studies using social media have focused on *spelling variation* and *lexical markers* of dialect. Ours is no exception. However, dialectal variation also manifests itself at the morpho-syntactic level. To investigate this variation, we also annotate some data with part-of-speech (POS) tags, using two NLP systems. This approach reveals a severe methodological challenge: sentences containing AAVE features are associated with significant drops in tagger performance.

This result challenges large-scale variational studies on social media that require automated analyses. The observed drops in performance are prohibitive for studying syntactic and semantic variation, and we believe the NLP community should make an effort to provide better and more robust dialect-adapted models to researchers and industry interested in processing social media. The findings also raise the question of whether NLP technology systematically disadvantages groups of non-standard language users.

### 1.1 Contributions

- We identify eight (8) research hypotheses from the sociolinguistic literature. We test them in a study of the distribution of three phonological features typically associated with AAVE in Twitter data. We test the features' correlations with various demographic variables. Our results falsify the hypothesis that AAVE is male-dominated (but see §3.1).

- We identify five (5) methodological problems common to variational studies in social media and discuss to what extent they compromise the validity of results.

- Further, we show that state-of-the-art newswire and Twitter POS taggers perform much worse on tweets containing AAVE features. This suggests an additional limitation to large-scale sociolinguistic research using social media data, namely that it is hard to analyze variation beyond the lexical level with current tools.

### 1.2 Sociolinguistic hypotheses

AAVE is, in contrast to other North American dialects, not geographically restricted. Although variation in AAVE does exist, AAVE in urban settings has been established as a uniform system with suprasegmental norms (Ash and Myhill, 1986; Labov et al., 2005; Labov, 2006; Wolfram, 2004). This paper considers the following eight (8) hypotheses from the sociolinguistic literature about AAVE as a ethnolect:

H1: AAVE is an *urban* ethnolect (Rickford, 1999; Wolfram, 2004).

H2: AAVE features are more present in the Gulf states than in the rest of the United States (Rastogi et al., 2011).

H3: The likelihood of speaking AAVE correlates negatively with income and educational level, and AAVE is more frequently appropriated by men (Rickford, 1999; Rickford, 2010).

H4: Derhotacization is more frequent in African Americans than in European Americans (Labov et al., 2005; Rickford, 1999).

H5: Derhotacization is negatively correlated with income and educational level (Rickford, 1999).

H6: Interdental fricative mutation is more frequent in AAVE than in European American speech (Pollock et al., 1998; Thomas, 2007).

H7: Interdental fricative mutation is predominantly found in the Gulf states (Rastogi et al., 2011).

H8: Backing in /str/ (to /skr/) is unique to AAVE (Rickford, 1999; Thomas, 2007; Labov, 2006).

Hypotheses 1–8 are investigated by correlating the distribution of phonological variants in geo-located tweets with demographic information.

Our method is similar to those proposed by Eisenstein (2013) and Doyle (2014), lending statistical power to sociolinguistic analyses, and circumventing traditional issues with data collection such as the Observer's Paradox (Labov, 1972b; Meyerhof, 2006). Our work differs from previous work by studying phonological *rules* associated with specific dialects, as well as considering a wide range of actual sociolinguistic research hypotheses, but our main focus is the methodological problems doing this kind of work, as well as assessing the limitations of such work.

### 1.3 Methodological problems

One obvious challenge relating social media data to sociolinguistic studies is that there is generally not a one-to-one relationship between phonological variation and spelling variation. People, in other words, do not spell the way they pronounce. Eisenstein (2013) discusses this challenge ((1) WRITING BIAS), but shows that effects of the phonological environment carry over to social media, which he interprets as evidence that there is at least some causal link between pronunciation and spelling variation.

A related problem is that non-speakers of AAVE may cite known features of AAVE with specific purposes in mind. They may use it in citations, for example:

(1) My 5 year old sister texted me on my mums phone saying "why did you take a picher in da bafroom" lool okay b (Twitter, Feb 21 2015)

or in meta-linguistic discussions:

(2) Whenever I hear a black person inquire about the location of the "bafroom"... (Twitter, Jan 20 2015)

We refer to these phenomena as (2) META-USE BIAS. This bias is important with rare phenomena. With "bafroom", it seems that about 1 in 20 occurrences on Twitter are meta-uses. Meta-uses may also serve social functions. AAVE features are used as cultural markers by Latinos in North Carolina (Carter, 2013), for example.

Some of the research hypotheses considered (**H3** and **H5**) relate to demographic variables such as income and educational levels. While we do not have socio-economic information about the individual Twitter user, we can use the geo-located tweets to study the correlation between socio-economic variables and linguistic features at the level of cities or ZIP codes.[1]

Eisenstein et al. (2011) note that this level of abstraction introduces some noise. Since Twitter users do not form representative samples of the population, the mean income for a city or ZIP code is not necessarily the mean income for the Twitter users in that area. We refer to this problem as the (3) USER POPULATION BIAS.

Another serious methodological problem known as (4) GALTON'S PROBLEM (Naroll, 1961; Roberts and Winters, 2013), is the observation that cross-cultural associations are

[1]Unlike many others, we rely on physical locations rather than user-entered profile locations. See Graham et al. (2014) for discussion.

often explained by geographical diffusion. In other words, it is the problem of discriminating historical from functional associations in cross-cultural surveys. Briefly put, when we sample tweets and income-levels from US cities, there is little independence between the city data points. Linguistic features diffuse geographically and do not change at random, and we can therefore expect to see more spurious correlations than usual. Like with the famous example of chocolate and Nobel Prize winners, our positive findings may be explained by hidden background variables. A positive correlation between income-level and a phonological pattern may also have cultural, religious or geographical explanations.

Reasons to be less worried about GALTON'S PROBLEM in our case, include that a) we only consider standard hypotheses from the sociolinguistics literature and not a huge set of previously unexplored, automatically generated hypotheses, b) we sample data points at random from all across the US, giving us a very sparse distribution compared to country-level data, but more notably, c) location is an important, explicit variable in our study. GALTON'S PROBLEM is typically identified by clustering tests based on location (Naroll, 1961). Obviously, the phonological features considered here cluster geographically, as evidenced by our geographic correlations in Table 2, but since our studies explicitly test the influence of location, it is not the case for most of the hypotheses considered here that geographic diffusion is the underlying explanation for something else.

In §3, we discuss whether these four methodological problems compromise the validity of our findings. One other methodological problems that may be relevant for other studies of dialect in social media, is almost completely irrelevant for our study: It is often important to control for topic in dialectal and sociolinguistic studies (Bamman et al., 2014), e.g., when studying the lexical preferences of speakers of urban ethnolects. We call this problem (5) TOPIC BIAS. Using word pairs with equivalent meanings for our studies, we implicitly control for topic (but see §3.1).

| Feature | Positive | Negative | Total count |
|---|---|---|---|
| | brotha | brother | 9528 |
| | foreva | forever | 3673 |
| | hea | here | 4352 |
| | lova | lover | 1273 |
| /r/ ⟶ /Ø/ or /ə/ | motha | mother | 4668 |
| | ova | over | 3441 |
| | sista | sister | 5325 |
| | wateva | whatever | 2974 |
| | wea | where | 5153 |
| | total | | 40,387 |
| | skreet | street | 1226 |
| /str/ ⟶ /skr/ | skrong | strong | 1629 |
| | skrip | strip | 1101 |
| | total | | 3956 |
| | brova | brother | 3715 |
| | dat | that | 2610 |
| | deez | these | 4477 |
| /ð/ ⟶ /d/ or /v/ | dem | them | 3645 |
| | dey | they | 2434 |
| | dis | this | 2135 |
| | mova | mother | 2462 |
| | total | | 21,478 |
| | mouf | mouth | 3861 |
| | nuffin | nothing | 2861 |
| | souf | south | 1102 |
| /θ/ ⟶ /t/ or /f/ | teef | teeth | 1857 |
| | trough | through | 2804 |
| | trow | throw | 1090 |
| | total | | 13,575 |
| All tweets | | | 79,396 |

Table 1: Word pairs and counts

## 2 Data and Method

We focus on derhotacization, backing in /str/, and interdental fricative mutation. Specifically, we collect data to study the following four phonological variations (the latter two are both instances of interdental fricative mutation): *a)* derhotacization: /r/ ⟶ /Ø/ or /ə/, *b)* /str/ ⟶ /skr/, *c)* /ð/ ⟶ /d/ or /v/ and, *d)* /θ/ ⟶ /t/ or /f/.

In non-rhotic dialects, /r/ is either not pronounced or is approximated as a vocalization in the surface form, when /r/ is in a pre-vocalic position. This can result in an elongation of the preceding vowel or in an off-glide schwa /ə/, e.g., *guard* ⟶ /gɑ:d/, *car* ⟶ /ka:/, *fear* ⟶ /fiə/ (Thomas, 2007).

Backing in /skr/ denotes the substitution

of /str/ for /skr/ in word-initial positions resulting in pronunciations such as /skrit/ for *street*, /skrɑŋ/ for *strong* and /skrɪp/ for *strip*. Backing in /str/ has been reported to be a unique feature in AAVE, as it is unheard in other North American dialects (Rickford, 1999; Labov, 1972a; Thomas, 2007).

The two interdental fricative mutations relate to substitutions of /ð/ and /θ/ by /d/, /v/ and /t/, /f/ in words such as *that* and *mother* or *nothing* and *with*. It has been reported that mutations of /ð/ and /θ/ are more common among African Americans than among European Americans and that the frequency of the mutations is inversely correlated with socio-economic levels and formality of speaking (Rickford, 1999).

We follow Eisenstein (2013) and Doyle (2014) in assuming that spelling variation may be a result of phonological differences and select 25 word pairs for our study (Tabel 1). For each word pair, we collect positive (e.g., "skreet") and negative occurrences (e.g., "street"), resulting in a total number of 79,396 tweets. The word pairs were chosen based on the unambiguity, frequency and representability of the phonological variations. Uniquely, backing in /str/ is represented by three word pairs of high similarity, which is due to phonological restrictions on the variation of /str/ to /skr/ and to the fact that backing in /str/ is a very rare phenomena.

The Twitter data used in the experiments was gathered from May to August 2014 using TwitterSearch.[2] We only collected tweets with geo-locations in the contiguous United States, from users reporting to tweet in English, and which were also predicted to be in English using *langid.py*.[3] The demographic information was obtained from the 2012 American Community Survey from the United States Census Bureau, as was information about population sizes in US cities. We linked each tweet in our data to demographic information using the geo-coordinates of the tweet and its nearest city in the following way.

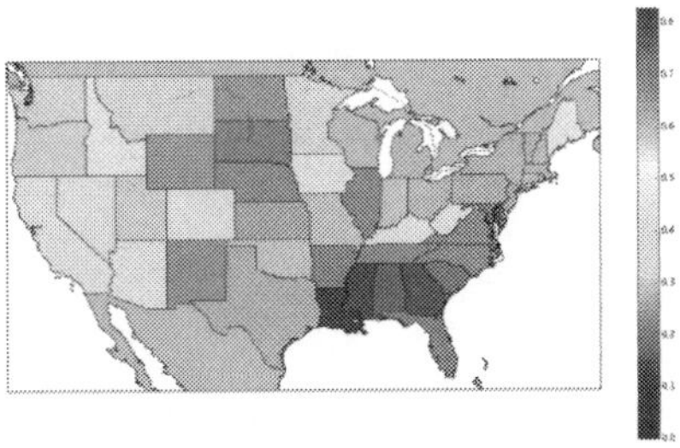

Figure 1: The ratio of AAVE examples over US states

For the 110 US cities of $\geq$ 200,000 inhabitants, we gathered information about: *a*) percentage high school graduates, *b*) percentage below poverty level, *c*) population size, *d*) median household income, *e*) percentage of males, *f*) percentage between 15 and 24 years old, *g*) percentage of African Americans and *h*) unemployment rate.

The overall geographical distribution of our data is shown in Figure 1. The map shows that we see more tweets with AAVE features in the Gulf states, in particular Louisiana, Mississippi and Georgia. This lends preliminary support to **H2**.

## 3 Results with phonological features

Occurrences of the phonological variations related to AAVE were correlated with the geographic and demographic variables using Spearman's $\rho$ (Table 2–3), at the level of individual tweets. From the correlation coefficients we see that the distributions of the three chosen AAVE rules are best explained by longitude, the distinction between the Gulf states and the rest of the US, and by the distribution

[2] https://pypi.python.org/pypi/TwitterSearch/

[3] https://pypi.python.org/pypi/langid

| Feature | word pairs | male | black | 15-24 | citysize | highschool | income | poverty | unemployment |
|---|---|---|---|---|---|---|---|---|---|
| /r/ → /Ø/ or /ə/ | brotha/brother | *** | ** | – | – | ** | – | – | – |
| | foreva/forever | ** | *** | – | – | – | – | ** | – |
| | hea/here | – | *** | ** | *** | *** | *** | *** | * |
| | lova/lover | – | – | – | – | *** | * | ** | – |
| | motha/mother | – | ** | – | * | – | ** | – | – |
| | ova/over | *** | *** | – | – | – | *** | *** | – |
| | sista/sister | * | *** | – | – | ** | – | – | – |
| | wateva/whatever | *** | *** | – | – | – | *** | *** | – |
| | wea/where | ** | *** | *** | *** | *** | *** | *** | * |
| | **total** | *** | *** | *** | *** | *** | *** | *** | – |
| /str/ → /skr/ | skreet/street | – | – | – | ** | * | ** | * | ** |
| | skrong/strong | ** | *** | – | * | ** | ** | ** | * |
| | skrip/strip | * | – | * | *** | *** | – | *** | *** |
| | **total** | *** | *** | – | *** | *** | *** | – | - |
| /ð/ → /d/ or /v/ | brova/brother | *** | *** | *** | *** | *** | – | *** | *** |
| | dat/that | – | *** | – | – | – | ** | ** | – |
| | deez/these | – | – | – | ** | *** | – | ** | *** |
| | dem/them | * | *** | ** | ** | *** | – | – | – |
| | dey/they | *** | *** | ** | * | ** | ** | *** | – |
| | dis/this | – | *** | ** | – | – | – | * | * |
| | mova/mother | *** | *** | *** | – | *** | *** | – | *** |
| | **total** | *** | *** | *** | – | *** | – | *** | *** |
| /θ/ → /t/ or /f/ | mouf/mouth | ** | – | – | – | – | – | – | – |
| | nuffin/nothing | *** | *** | *** | *** | *** | *** | – | *** |
| | souf/south | *** | – | ** | – | ** | – | *** | *** |
| | teef/teeth | – | – | – | – | ** | – | – | – |
| | trough/through | – | – | – | – | ** | – | * | * |
| | trow/throw | * | – | – | *** | ** | * | ** | ** |
| | **total** | *** | *** | *** | *** | – | ** | – | * |

– = $p \geq 0.05$, * = $0.05 > p \geq 0.01$, ** = $p \leq 0.01$, , *** = $p \leq 0.0005$

Shading corresponds to negative correlations

Table 3: Demographic correlations

of African Americans (with explained variances in the range of 0.03-0.05).

Our data suggests that **H2**, namely that AAVE is more prevalent in the Gulf states, is probably true. Hypothesis **H1**, that AAVE is an urban ethnolect, lends some support in our data, but the correlation with urbanicity is weaker (and negatively correlated or non-significant in half of the cases).

Our data only lends limited support to the first half of hypothesis **H3**. While derhotacization and /str/ correlate (negatively) significantly with income levels, we see no significant correlations within /ð/ and a positive correlation within /θ/. However, our data does not suggest that **H3** is false, either. Our data does lend support to the more specific hypothesis **H5**, namely that derhoticization is sensitive to income level, while the strong correlation with the distribution of African Americans lends support to **H4**.

More interestingly, our data suggests that *women use AAVE features more often than men*, i.e., there is a negative correlation between male gender and AAVE features, contrary to the second half of **H3**, namely that AAVE is more frequently appropriated by men. Note, however, that our gender ratios are aggregated for city areas, and with the demographic bias of Twitter, these correlations should be taken with a grain of salt. Considering the small gender ratio differences, we also compute correlations between our linguistic features and gender using the Rovereto Twitter N-gram Corpus (RTC) (Herdagdelen and Baroni, 2011).[4] The RTC corpus contains information about the gender of the tweeter associated with n-grams. While there is too little data in the corpus to correlate gender and backing in /str/, derhotacization and both interdental fricative mutations (/ð/ → /d/ or /v/ and /θ/ → /t/ or /f/) correlate significantly with women. Out of our words, 10 correlate sig-

[4] http://clic.cimec.unitn.it/amac/twitter_ngram/

| Feature | word pairs | latitude | longitude | urban | Gulf |
|---|---|---|---|---|---|
| /r/ | brotha/brother | *** | *** | *** | *** |
| | foreva/forever | *** | ** | – | *** |
| | hea/here | *** | *** | * | *** |
| | lova/lover | *** | *** | ** | *** |
| | motha/mother | – | – | *** | – |
| | ova/over | *** | – | – | *** |
| | sista/sister | – | *** | ** | *** |
| | wateva/whatever | *** | *** | ** | *** |
| | wea/where | *** | *** | – | *** |
| | **total** | *** | *** | *** | *** |
| /str/ | skreet/street | *** | – | *** | *** |
| | skrong/strong | *** | * | *** | *** |
| | skrip/strip | *** | – | *** | *** |
| | **total** | *** | ** | – | *** |
| /ð/ | brova/brother | *** | *** | *** | *** |
| | dat/that | *** | * | – | *** |
| | deez/these | * | *** | – | – |
| | dem/them | *** | *** | – | *** |
| | dey/they | *** | *** | – | *** |
| | dis/this | *** | – | – | *** |
| | mova/mother | * | *** | *** | *** |
| | **total** | *** | *** | *** | *** |
| /θ/ | mouf/mouth | *** | – | – | *** |
| | nuffin/nothing | *** | *** | *** | *** |
| | souf/south | *** | *** | *** | *** |
| | teef/teeth | ** | – | ** | *** |
| | trough/through | – | *** | – | – |
| | trow/throw | *** | ** | – | *** |
| | **total** | * | *** | *** | *** |

– = $p \geq 0.05$, * = $0.05 > p \geq 0.01$, ** = $p \leq 0.01$, *** = $p \leq 0.0001$

Shading corresponds to negative correlations

Table 2: Geographic correlations

nificantly with female speakers; seven with male. The correlations are found in Table 4. For each feature, certain words correlate significantly with female speakers, while others correlate significantly with male speakers. Consequently, neither our Twitter data not the Twitter data in the RTC suggest that AAVE is more often appropriated by men. We discuss whether our data provides a basis for falsifying the second half of **H3** in §3.1.

The high correlation between mutations of /ð/ and longitude supports the presence of these mutations of /ð/ in non-standard northern varieties (Rickford, 1999). The mutation of /θ/ is also correlated with longitude, and with latitude, suggesting an Eastern American feature rather than a distinct Southern feature (Rickford, 1999). The variation in mutations could possibly be explained by both geography as well as the distribution og African Americans.

There is evidence in our data that backing in /str/ (to /skr/) is appropriated more often by AAVE speakers than by speakers of other dialects (**H8**). There is also a negative correlation between latitude and backing in /str/ as well as a strong positive correlation with the Gulf states, suggesting that backing in /str/ is a feature primarily seen in this region. The data thereby suggests that the feature is appropriated significantly more by African Americans than by speakers of the Southern dialect.

In sum, while our data lends support to several of the common hypotheses from the sociolinguistics literature, we found one unexpected tendency, going against the second half of **H3**, namely that AAVE features were found more often with females. We now discuss this finding in light of the methodological problems discussed in §1.2.

| Feature | word pairs | male |
|---|---|---|
| /r/ ⟶ /Ø/ or /ə/ | brotha-brother | ** |
| | foreva-forever | ** |
| | hea-here | * |
| | lova-lover | – |
| | motha-mother | ** |
| | ova-over | ** |
| | sista-sister | – |
| | wateva-whatever | – |
| | wea-where | ** |
| ð ⟶ /d/ or /v/ | brova-brother | * |
| | dat-that | ** |
| | deez-these | ** |
| | dem-them | ** |
| | dey-they | ** |
| | dis-this | ** |
| | mova-mother | – |
| θ ⟶ /f/ or /t/ | mouf-mouth | ** |
| | nuffin-nothing | ** |
| | souf-south | ** |
| | teef-teeth | – |
| | trough-through | ** |
| | trow-throw | ** |

– = $p \geq 0.05$, * = $0.05 > p \geq 0.01$, ** = $p \leq 0.01$

Shading corresponds to negative correlations

Table 4: Gender correlations in RTC

### 3.1 Is AAVE *not* male-dominated?

We now discuss whether our data falsifies the second half of **H3**, one methodological problem at a time (see §1.3). If WRITTEN BIAS were to bias our conclusions, one gender should be more likely to exhibit more phonologically motivated spelling variation. This may actually be true, since it is well-established that women tend to be more linguistically creative and have larger vocabularies (Labov, 1990; Brizendine, 2006). Whether women are also more meta-linguistic (META-USE BIAS), has to the best of our knowledge not been studied. Since genders are almost equally geographically distributed, and since Twitter is generally considered gender-balanced, neither USER POPULATION BIAS nor GALTON'S PROBLEM is likely to bias our conclusions. TOPIC BIAS, on the other hand, may. While our semantically equivalent pairs control for topic, the pragmatics sometimes differ. Just like code-switching is a strategy for bilinguals, using the spelling *motha* instead of *mother* could mean something, say irony, which one gender is more prone for. In sum, while we do believe that our data should lead sociolinguists to question whether AAVE is male-dominated, our findings may be biased by WRITTEN BIAS.

## 4 POS tagging

We need automated syntactic analysis to study morpho-syntactic dialectal variation. We ran a state-of-the-art POS tagger trained on newswire[5] (STANFORD), as well as two state-of-the-art POS taggers adapted to Twitter, namely GATE[6] and ARK[7], on our data. We had one professional annotator manually annotate 100 positive (AAVE) and 100 negative (non-AAVE) sentences using the coarse-grained tags proposed by Petrov et al. (2011). We map the tagger outputs to those tags and report tagging accuracies. See Table 5 for results, with $\Delta(+,-)$ being the absolute difference in performance from non-AAVE to AAVE.

[5]http://nlp.stanford.edu/software/tagger.shtml

[6]https://gate.ac.uk/wiki/twitter-postagger.html

[7]http://www.ark.cs.cmu.edu/TweetNLP/

| | STANFORD | GATE | ARK |
|---|---|---|---|
| AAVE | 61.4 | **79.1** | 77.5 |
| non-AAVE | 74.5 | **83.3** | 77.9 |
| Δ(+,-) | 13.1 | 4.2 | 0.4 |

Table 5: POS tagging accuracies (%)

While GATE is certainly better than STANFORD on our data, performance is generally poor and prohibitive of many downstream applications and variational studies. We also note that both the best and worst tagger perform significantly worse on AAVE tweets than on non-AAVE tweets. What are the sources of error in the AAVE data? One example is the word *brotha*, which is tagged as a both an adverb, a verb, and as X (foreign words, mark-up, etc.). Contractions like *finna* ("fixing to" meaning "going to") and *gimme* ("give me") are often tagged as particles, but annotated as verbs or, as in the case of *witchu* ("with you"), as a preposition. Another interesting mistake is tagging adverbial *like* as a verb.

## 5 Conclusion

Large-scale variational studies of social media can be used to question received wisdom about dialects, lending support to some sociolinguistic research hypotheses and questioning others. However, we caution that our results were biased by several factors, including the representativity of the social media user bases. We also show how state-of-the-art POS taggers are more likely to fail on dialects in social media. The performance drops may be considered prohibitive of studying morph-syntactic patterns across dialects and as a challenge to us as a community.

## References

Sharon Ash and John Myhill. 1986. Linguistic correlates of inter-ethnic contact. In David

Sankoff, editor, *Diversity and Diachronyc*, pages 33–44, Amsterdam and Philadelphia. John Benjamins Publishing Co.

David Bamman, Jacob Eisenstein, and Tyler Schnoebelen. 2014. Gender identity and lexical variation in social media. *Journal of Sociolinguistics*, 18.

Louann Brizendine. 2006. *The Female Brain*. Morgan Road Books.

Phillip Carter. 2013. Shared spaces, shared structures: Latino social formation and African American English in the U.S. south. *Journal of Sociolinguistics*, 17:66–92.

Gabriel Doyle. 2014. Mapping dialectal variation by querying social media. In *EACL*, pages 98–106, Gothenburg, Sweden. Association for Computational Linguistics.

Jacob Eisenstein, Noah A. Smith, and Eric Xing. 2011. Discovering sociolinguistic associations with structured sparsity. In *ACL*.

Jacob Eisenstein. 2013. Phonological factors in social media writing. In *NAACL Workshop on Language Analysis in Social Media*, pages 11–19, Atlanta, Georgia. Association for Computational Linguistics.

Jacob Eisenstein. to appear. Systematic patterning in phonologically-motivated orthographic variation. *Journal of Sociolinguistics*.

Mark Graham, Scott Hale, and Devin Gaffney. 2014. Where in the world are you? Geolocation and language identification on Twitter. *The Professional Geographer*, 66(4).

Amac Herdagdelen and Marco Baroni. 2011. Stereotypical gender actions can be extracted from web text. *Journal of the American Society for Information Science and Technology*, 62:1741–1749.

Dirk Hovy and Anders Søgaard. 2015. Tagging performance correlates with author age. In *ACL*.

Dirk Hovy, Anders Johannsen, and Anders Søgaard. 2015. User review-sites as a source for large-scale sociolinguistic studies. In *WWW*.

Anders Johannsen, Dirk Hovy, and Anders Søgaard. 2015. Cross-lingual syntactic variation over age and gender. In *CoNLL*.

William Labov, Sharon Ash, and Charles Boberg. 2005. *The Atlas of North American English Phonetics, Phonology and Sound Change*. Mouton de Gruyter, New York, NY.

William Labov. 1972a. *Language in the Inner City: Studies in the Black English Vernacular*. University of Pennsylvania Press.

William Labov. 1972b. *Sociolingustic Patterns*. University of Pennsylvania Press, Philadelphia, PA.

William Labov. 1990. The intersection of sex and social class in the course of linguistic change. *Language Variation and Change*, 2:205–254, 7.

William Labov. 2006. Unendangered dialects, endangered people. In Natalie Schilling-Estes, editor, *GURT'06*.

Miriam Meyerhof. 2006. *Introducing Sociolinguistics*. Routledge.

R Naroll. 1961. Two solutions to Galton's problem. *Philosophy of Science*, 28.

Slav Petrov, Dipanjan Das, and Ryan McDonald. 2011. A universal part-of-speech tagset. CoRR abs/1104.2086.

K.E. Pollock, G. Bailey, M. Berni, D. Fletcher, L. Hinton, I. Johnson, J. Roberts, and R. Weaver. 1998. Phonological features of african american english. http://www.rehabmed.ualberta.ca/spa/phonology/features.htm.

Delip Rao, David Yarowsky, Abhishek Shreevats, and Manaswi Gupta. 2010. Classifying latent user attributes in twitter. In *Proceedings of the 2nd International Workshop on Search and Mining User-generated Contents*, pages 37–44. ACM.

Sonya Rastogi, Tallese D. Johnson, Elizabeth M. Hoeffel, and Malcolm P. Drewery Jr. 2011. The black population: 2010. Technical report, US Census, September.

John Rickford. 1999. *African American Vernacular English: Features, Evolution, Educational Implications*. Blackwell, Malden, MA.

John Rickford. 2010. Geographical diversity, residential segregation, and the vitality of african american vernacular english and its speakers. *Transforming Anthropology*, 18(1):28–34.

Sean Roberts and James Winters. 2013. Linguistic diversity and traffic accidents: lessons from statistical studies of cultural traits. *PLoS ONE*, 8(8).

Eric Thomas. 2007. Phonological and phonetic characteristics of african american vernacular english. *Language and Linguistic Compass*, 1(5):450–475.

Svitlana Volkova, Theresa Wilson, and David Yarowsky. 2013. Exploring demographic language variations to improve multilingual sentiment analysis in social media. In *EMNLP*.

Svitlana Volkova, Yoram Bachrach, Michael Armstrong, and Vijay Sharma. 2015. Inferring latent user properties from texts published in social media (demo). In *AAAI*.

Walt Wolfram. 2004. The grammar of urban african american vernacular english. In Kormann B. and E. Schneider, editors, *Handbook of Varieties of English*, pages 111–132, Berlin. Mouton de Gruyter.

# Toward Tweets Normalization Using Maximum Entropy

**Mohammad Arshi Saloot**
Department of Artificial Intelligence, University of Malaya, 50603, Malaysia
phd_siamak@yahoo.com

**Norisma Idris**
Department of Artificial Intelligence, University of Malaya, 50603, Malaysia
norisma@um.edu.my

**Liyana Shuib**
Department of Information System, University of Malaya, 50603, Malaysia
liyanashuib@um.edu.my

**Ram Gopal Raj**
Department of Artificial Intelligence, University of Malaya, 50603, Malaysia
ramdr@um.edu.my

**AiTi Aw***
Institute for Infocomm Research (I2R), A*STAR, Singapore
aaiti@i2r.a-star.edu.sg

*Corresponding author

## Abstract

The use of social network services and microblogs, such as Twitter, has created valuable text resources, which contain extremely noisy text. Twitter messages contain so much noise that it is difficult to use them in natural language processing tasks. This paper presents a new approach using the maximum entropy model for normalizing Tweets. The proposed approach addresses words that are unseen in the training phase. Although the maximum entropy needs a training dataset to adjust its parameters, the proposed approach can normalize unseen data in the training set. The principle of maximum entropy emphasizes incorporating the available features into a uniform model. First, we generate a set of normalized candidates for each out-of-vocabulary word based on lexical, phonemic, and morphophonemic similarities. Then, three different probability scores are calculated for each candidate using positional indexing, a dependency-based frequency feature and a language model. After the optimal values of the model parameters are obtained in a training phase, the model can calculate the final probability value for candidates. The approach achieved an 83.12 BLEU score in testing using 2,000 Tweets. Our experimental results show that the maximum entropy approach significantly outperforms previous well-known normalization approaches.

## 1 Introduction

The advent of Web 2.0 and electronic communications has enabled the extensive creation and dissemination of user-generated content (UGC). The UGC collections provide invaluable data sources in order to mine and extract beneficial information and knowledge, while, at the same time, resulting in less standardized language (Clark & Araki, 2011; Daugherty, Eastin, & Bright, 2008).

However, such content diverges from standard writing conventions. As shown by experts (Bieswanger, 2007; Thurlow & Brown, 2003), this divergence is due to the usage of a variety of coding strategies, including digit phonemes (*you too* → *you2*), phonetic transcriptions (*you* → *u*), vowel drops (*dinner* → *dnnr*), misspellings (*convenience* → *convineince*), and missing or incorrect punctuation marks (*If I were you, I'd probably go.* → *If I were you Id probably go*). These alterations are due to three main parameters: 1) The small allowance of characters, 2) the constraints of the small keypads, and 3) using UGC in informal communications between friends and relatives.

Whatever their causes, these alterations considerably affect any standard natural language processing (NLP) system, due to the presence of many out of vocabulary (OOV) words, also known as non-standard words (NSWs) and unknown words. Therefore, a text normalization process must be performed before any conven-



*Proceedings of the ACL 2015 Workshop on Noisy User-generated Text*, pages 19–27,
Beijing, China, July 31, 2015. ©2015 Association for Computational Linguistics

tional NLP process is implemented (Sproat et al., 2001). As defined by Liu, Weng, Wang, and Liu (2011), "Text message normalization aims to replace the non-standard tokens that carry significant meanings with the context-appropriate standard words."

This paper proposes a novel normalization approach for Twitter messages. Twitter is the most popular microblogging service in the world for news-casting, sharing thoughts, and staying in touch with friends. Since its initial founding in 2006, it has gathered hundreds of millions of registered users. Tweets refer to messages sent on Twitter, which is restricted to 140 characters, 20 characters less than the 160 allowed by SMS. Because of this limitation, users have to transcribe Tweets with as much brevity as possible.

The normalization bears a resemblance to spelling correction. The ultimate goal of which is the detection and correction of OOV words. The spelling correction methods only focus on misspelled words while normalization systems consider all forms of OOV words, such as representing sounds phonetically (e.g. *by the way* → *btw*) and shortened forms (e.g. *university* → *uni*). Thus, normalization approaches should address a higher volume of OOV words compared to spelling correction approaches that lead to more complexity.

To address this complexity, we use maximum entropy (Berger, Pietra, & Pietra, 1996; Och & Ney, 2002) for utilizing and incorporating more probability functions. Our approach is based on the hypothesis that integrating more probability functions will boost the performance of the method; however, the available information and number of probability functions for (*OOV word, standard word*) pairs are always limited. Maximum entropy (Maxent) provides a criterion for integrating probability distributions based on partial knowledge. The Maxent produces the lowest biased estimation on the given information, that is, it is maximally neutral regarding missing information. When defining some unknown events with a statistical model, we should always select the one that has maximum entropy. Although the Maxent has already been used in the normalization sphere (e.g. Pennell and Liu (2010) utilized Maxent to classify deletion-based abbreviations), this paper explains how to employ Maxent for selecting the best-normalized candidate.

We have developed a method that does not require annotated training data and it normalizes unseen data. Most of the normalization approaches substantially depend on the manually annotated data, while the labeled data is costly and time consuming to prepare. We generate normalized candidates for each detected OOV based on lexical, phonemic, and morphophonemic variations. In addition, since our target dataset encompasses Twitter messages from Singaporeans and code-switching between Malay and English is frequent in the dataset, a Malay-English dictionary is utilized to generate candidates for Malay words. Finally, maximum entropy presents a backbone to combine several conditional probabilities of normalized candidates.

The remainder of this paper is organized as follows: Section 2 gives a survey of different approaches of normalizing noisy text. Section 3 describes the preprocessing stage. Section 4 illustrates the candidate generation stage. The proposed candidate selection method is demonstrated in Section 5. Finally, Section 6 concludes this paper with a summary and future works.

## 2 Related work

The normalization approaches can be categorized into four groups. The first group is called statistical machine translation (SMT) paradigm that addresses the normalization problem as a statistical machine translation task. This paradigm was first introduced by Aw, Zhang, Xiao and Su (2006) to normalize SMS text that translates a source language (UGC) to a target language (standard language). This paradigm has since been re-examined, expanded and improved by other researchers (Lopez Ludeña, San Segundo, Montero, Barra Chicote, & Lorenzo, 2012). For example, Kaufmann and Kalita (2010) used the SMT-like approach to normalize English Tweets.

To normalize SMS language, a supervised noisy channel model was introduced by Choudhury, Saraf, Jain, Sarkar, and Basu (2007) that used a hidden Markov model (HMM). This approach mimics the spell checking task that tries to handle the normalization problem via noisy channel models that study the UGC text as a noisy version of standard language. This paradigm has been scrutinized and enhanced by other researchers (Liu et al., 2011; Xue, Yin, & Davison, 2011a). For example, Cook and Stevenson (2009) modified this approach to design an unsupervised method using probabilistic models for only three common abbreviation types: stylistic variation, prefix clipping, and subsequence abbreviation. In addition, Beaufort, Roekhaut, Cougnon, and Fairon (2010) merged the SMT-like and the spell checking approaches to normalize French SMSs.

The third group is the dictionary based normalization approach, which is an easy-to-use and fast solution. This approach requires a dictionary whose entries are OOV and standard form pairs. It has been proven that using a colloquial dictionary can outperform some state-of-the-art and complex approaches (Clark & Araki, 2011; Saloot, Idris, & Mahmud, 2014). However, its performance highly relies on the size of the dictionary. Therefore, Han, Cook, and Baldwin (2012) introduced a method to automatically compile a large dictionary. To address the shortcomings of the dictionary approach, Oliva, Serrano, Del Castillo, and Igesias (2013) introduced a special Spanish phonetic dictionary, in which each entry is formed by a coded consonant string, vowels strings, and their positions in the word, for normalizing Spanish SMS texts.

The fourth group resembles automatic speech recognition (ASR) systems. This paradigm consists of three steps: 1) converting the text to strings of phonemes via letter-to-phone rules, 2) converting the strings of phonemes to words via pronunciation dictionaries, and 3) choosing the most probable words. The ASR-like approach has been merged with other approaches to boost its performance. Kobus, Yvon, and Damnati (2008) combined ASR-like and SMT-like approaches to normalize French SMSs. Lin, Bilmes, Vergyri, and Kirchhoff (2007) used this approach to detect OOV words in switchboard data.

Han and Baldwin (2011) illustrated a lexical method for normalizing Twitter messages. After detecting OOVs, ill-formed words, and generating a set of candidates, the best candidate is selected using a variety of metrics: lexical edit distance, phonemic edit distance, longest common subsequence (LCS), affix substring, language model, and dependency-based frequency features. The method achieved a 93.4 BLEU score in normalizing 549 English Tweets. This inspired us to design a normalization method that has three major stages: preprocessing, candidate generation, and candidate selection.

## 3 Preprocessing

First, we perform some initial text refining on the tweets. For example, consecutive whitespace characters are trimmed to single whitespace, and extra whitespaces are removed from the beginning and end of Tweets. The initial stage of most NLP tasks is the tokenization. Existing tokenization methods can perform accurately when the text is thoroughly clean, such as news feeds and book datasets. For example, the PTB-Tokenizer is a fast, deterministic, and efficient tokenization method. On the other hand, UGC text demands special methods due to irregularities in its whitespaces and punctuation. As suggested by Lopez Ludeña et al. (2012), we employ a straightforward word separating method, which performs tokenization based on whitespace characters.

One of the most important primary steps in unsupervised normalization systems is to detect OOV words. Hanspell and GNU Aspell are two well-known spell checker systems, however, Aspell performance is more accurate on the noisy text (Clark & Araki, 2011). The Aspell dictionary is utilized to distinguish between OOV and standard English words. In addition, we used seven regular expression rules, which were introduced by Saloot, Idris, and Aw (2014). This helps to detect proper nouns, email and URL addresses, Twitter special symbols, and digits. The potential errors in the OOV word detection step would not affect the performance of the normalization system since the detected OOV word will be included in the candidate set.

## 4 Candidate generation

For each given OOV word, a set of normalized candidates is generated via four different modules. The first module executes a lexical candidate generation, which is extensively utilized in spell checker systems. It calculates candidates within a distance of $T$ edit operations of the detected OOV words. Han and Baldwin (2011) stated that when $T$ is less than or equal to two, the level of recall is high enough. The edit distance is the number of applied edits in changing one word to another. An edit could be a deletion, transposition, alteration, or insertion. Studies in spelling correction found that one lexical edit distance covers 80% to 95% of errors, and two lexical edit distances cover 98% of them. Therefore, here we use lexical variations with less than or equal to two edit distances.

For a word of length $n$ characters, $54n + 25$ combinations will be generated with one lexical edit distance using four reshaping strategies: 1) Deletion strategy eliminates characters in all possible positions (e.g. *aer* → *er*, *ar*, *ae*), which generates $n$ combinations. 2) Transposition strategy switches two adjacent characters (e.g. aer →

*ear*, *are*), which generates $n - 1$ combinations. 3) Alteration strategy substitutes each character with all English alphabets (e.g. *aer* → *ber*, *cer*, *der*, *eer*, *fer*, *ger*, *her*, etc.), which generates $26n$ combinations. 4) Insertion strategy presumes that a letter is dropped, thus adding all the alphabets between characters (e.g. *aer* → *aaer*, *baer*, *caer*, *daer*, *eaer*, *faer*, *gaer*, *haer*, etc.), which generates $26(n + 1)$ combinations. Finally, from the achieved combinations, standard words will be selected using the Aspell dictionary. However, many OOV words in Twitter are quite far from their target in term of edit distance especially in terms of deletions and substitutions. Therefore, we generated more candidates via three other methods.

Similar to the speech recognition systems, the second module generates candidates based on phoneme sounds. First, grapheme to phoneme conversion is performed using the Phonetisaurus tool (Novak, Yang, Minematsu, & Hirose, 2011). Phonetisaurus is an open-source phonetizer that is designed in the form of a weighted finite state transducer (WFST). After selecting the 10 best phoneme sequences, it looks up the phonemes in a pronouncing dictionary – Carnegie Mellon University (CMU) dictionary. The CMU is a machine-readable pronunciation dictionary that contains over 134,000 words including OOV words such as proper nouns and acronyms. Due to the existence of a large number of OOV words in the CMU dictionary, we filter out the OOVs using the Aspell dictionary.

The third module, as proposed by Saloot, Idris, and Aw (2014), is a combination of the two previous modules. First, it lexically generates candidates within one edit distance of the given OOV word, and then sends the candidates to the phoneme module. Since our testing dataset consists of English Tweets posted by Singaporeans, code-switching between Malay and English is frequent in the text. Therefore, our last module translates OOV words to English (if any). We searched for the tokens in the Smith Malay-English Dictionary (Smith & Padi, 2006), and inserted the meanings in the candidate set.

Table 1 displays the average number of generated candidates for each module. The lowest rate is associated with the Malay dictionary module. Two lexical edit operations generate the highest number of candidates, which indicates the highest recall and lowest precision. The rank of combination and phoneme modules are second and third, respectively.

| *No.* | *module* | *Average number of candidates* |
|---|---|---|
| 1. | Two lexical edit distance | 70 |
| 2. | Combination | 50 |
| 3. | Phoneme | 20 |
| 4. | Malay dictionary | 3 |

Table 1: The average number of generated candidates for five letter words.

## 5 Candidate selection

The main contribution of this work is to present a novel candidate selection method. The candidate selection stage consists of two steps: 1) assigning a variety of probability scores to candidates, and 2) integrating probability scores to select the best candidate. Our candidate selection method requires a training dataset. The training and testing datasets are collected from an extensive English Twitter corpus posted by Singaporeans (Saloot, Idris, Aw, & Thorleuchter, 2014). Three linguistic experts manually normalized 7,000 Tweets, while using inter-normalization agreement as an indicator. The experts were instructed to produce a text that is as close to standard English as possible, but leaves the Twitter special symbols (e.g. #topic and @username) as is. The dataset was split into two parts: 5,000 messages for the training phase, and 2,000 messages for the testing phase.

### 5.1 Calculation of probability scores

In order to select the most suitable candidates, we calculate their conditional probability scores using, positional indexing, a dependency-based frequency feature, and a language model (LM).

Inspired by work on a normalization dictionary (Han et al., 2012), the first method to calculate the probability score of the candidates is the positional indexing, which is widely used in information retrieval systems. The positional indexing deals with positional locations of term occurrences inside documents. To compile a positional index dataset, a method illustrated in Manning and Raghavan (2009) is applied on a cleansed portion of our Twitter corpus. Table 2 refers to an example of our achieved positional index dataset. Each Twitter message is considered as a single document, and, hence, a unique document ID is assigned to each document. The frequency value indicates the total number of appearances of a word in a document. The position values express the locations of the word in the document.

| *Vocab* | *Document ID.* | *Frequency* | *Position* |
|---|---|---|---|
| have | 1 | 2 | 4,9 |
| | 4 | 3 | 5, 11, 18 |
| are | 5 | 1 | 2 |
| | 12 | 2 | 2, 9 |
| | 14 | 2 | 2, 11 |

Table 2: An example of the positional indexes obtained.

A probability score is assigned to the normalized candidate according to a comparison between the position of the candidate and positional indexes in the dataset. We look for the candidate in the dataset where there is an occurrence of the candidate with its position index. After aggregating the number of occurrences, we normalize it between 0.0 and 1.0.

The next probability calculation method is the dependency-based frequency, which is an augmentation of the previous method. Inspired by a work on the lexical normalization of Tweets (Han & Baldwin, 2011), the noisy portion of our training dataset is parsed to obtain a dependency bank using our adapted version of the Stanford dependency parser (Marneffe, MacCartney, & Manning, 2006). Since our aim is not to perform actual dependency parsing, the dependency types are not extracted. A cleansed corpus is not utilized because the percentage of IV words is high enough in the corpus, and in the probability-measuring phase, OOV words are already detected. For example, from a sentence such as *"I will go to London by next week,"* (*next*, *go* +3) is obtained, indicating that *next* appears two words after *go*. The aggregations of all the dependency scores, which are called confidence scores, are stored in the dependency bank. A five-gram dependency bank is prepared without using a root node (head-word), that is, the process is iterated for all words in the sentence.

A probability score between 0.0 and 1.0 is assigned to each candidate. A relative position score in the form of (*candidate word*, *context word*, position) is calculated for each candidate within a context window of two words on either side. The obtained relative position of a candidate is compared with the existing confidence score in the dependency bank.

The third method of probability measurement calculates the probabilities based on a language model. The cleansed part of our training dataset, which consists of more than 55,000 words, is fed into SRILM (Stolcke, 2002) to compile a bidirectional trigram LM by employing the Kneser-Ney smoothing algorithm. To calculate the probability of each candidate, we used a beam search decoder through the Moses decoder (Koehn et al., 2007).

### 5.2 Selecting the most probable candidate

Previous works on spelling correction and normalization used the source channel model, which is also known as the noisy channel model and Naïve Bayes (Beaufort et al., 2010; Kernighan, Church, & Gale, 1990; Mays, Damerau, & Mercer, 1991; Toutanova & Moore, 2002; Xue, Yin, & Davison, 2011b). In the noisy channel approach, we observe the conversion of standard words to noisy words in a training phase in order to build a model. In the prediction phase, the decoder can select the most probable candidate based on the obtained model. The candidate selection is accomplished based on only two parameters: the LM and error model, which is computed as follows:

$$G = \arg\max\{P(T \mid O)\}$$
$$= \arg\max\left\{\sum_{m=1}^{M} \lambda_m \bullet f_m(T,O)\right\}$$

Where $T$ is a target word, $O$ is an observed word, $f_m(T,O)$ is a feature function, $M$ is a number of total feature functions, and $\lambda$ is a Lagrange multiplier of each function. In our case, $M$ equals three, in which $f_1$ is the positional indexing, $f_2$ is the dependency-based frequency feature, and $f_3$ is the LM probability. The Maxent requires $\lambda$ being determined in the training phase before the actual usage.

## 6 Experimental results and discussion

We evaluate our approach in terms of BLEU score (Papineni, Roukos, Ward, & Zhu, 2002), since BLEU has become a well-known and adequate evaluation metric in normalization studies (Contractor, Faruquie, & Subramaniam, 2010; Schlippe, Zhu, Gebhardt, & Schultz, 2010). The achieved baseline for the testing dataset is 42.01 BLEU score, that is, the volume of similarity between the testing text and the reference text (manually normalized text) in term of BLEU score.

In the training phase, we performed maximum likelihood training (Papineni, Roukos, & Ward, 1998; Streit & Luginbuhl, 1994) for $\lambda_1$, $\lambda_2$ and $\lambda_3$ between 0.0 and 1.0. Figure 1 shows the tolerance of the performance while transition of $\lambda_1$ and $\lambda_2$ (when $\lambda_3$ is fixed to 1.0). Figure 1 depicts that the value of performance achieves the highest when the $\lambda_1$ and $\lambda_2$ are close to 0.63 and 0.9, respectively. It is found that the best performance is achieved by 0.6, 0.9, and 1.0 values for $\lambda_1$, $\lambda_2$, and $\lambda_3$, respectively. This means that LM has the highest impact on the candidate selection, and that dependency-based frequency has a higher impact on candidate selection than positional.

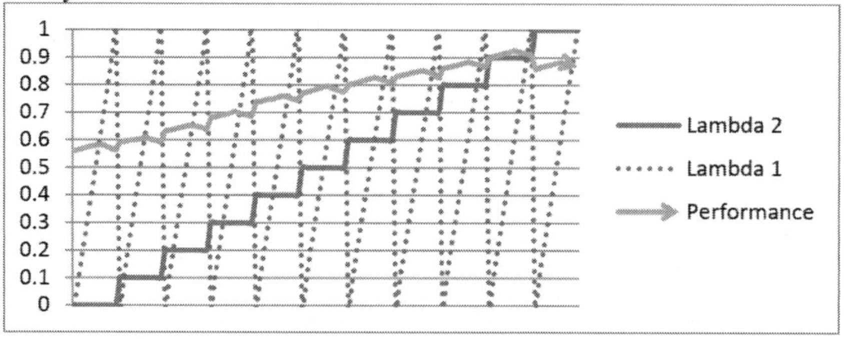


Figure 1: The training of Maxent for lambda settings.

We divided our dataset into six equal sets in order to perform 6-fold cross validation. As shown in Table 3, the average of the obtained BLEU scores in six evaluation rounds was 83.12. The evaluation proves that our approach boosts the BLEU score by 41.11 (i.e. from 42.01 to 83.12). Since previous normalization studies used different data sources in their experiments, a direct comparison between our accuracy values is not meaningful. Therefore, we re-examined one of the state-of-the-art approaches using our dataset.

| *6-fold cross validation* | *BLEU score* |
|---|---|
| Round 1 | 80.99 |
| Round 2 | 81.57 |
| Round 3 | 84.82 |
| Round 4 | 83.91 |
| Round 5 | 83.90 |
| Round 6 | 83.55 |
| Average | 83.12 |

Table 3: Normalization results for 6-fold cross validation test.

The statistical machine translation (SMT) is a cutting-edge approach that handles the normalization problem as a statistical machine translation task; it was first introduced by Aw, Zhang, Xiao, and Su (2006). The SMT-like approach translates a source language (UGC) to a target language (standard language). The experiment was performed using Moses (Koehn et al., 2007) for statistical translation, Giza++ (Och & Ney, 2003) for word alignment, and SRILM (Stolcke, 2002) for LM compiling. The SMT system is trained using our Twitter aligned dataset. The optimum results were achieved using a trigram LM and Backoff smoothing (Jelinek, 1990): 78.81 BLEU score.

Table 4 indicates some statistics about our testing dataset. The OOV words are those detected by our OOV detection module. The BLEU score of raw text is an important measure to analyze the difficulty of the task. It is important to note that the dataset used in our experiment contains an above average number of OOV words compared to the datasets in other related papers. The dataset used by Kobus et al. (2008) consists of 32% OOV words, which is slightly lower than 34% of our dataset. In addition, Aw et al. (2006) used a dataset with a baseline BLEU score of 57.84, which indicates that the raw text is much more similar to the manual translated text (reference text) than the ones used in our experiment.

| | |
|---|---|
| Avg. length of words (character) | 5 |
| Avg. number of words | 11 |
| Total No. of tokens | 19,759 |
| OOV words | 34.02% |
| BLEU score of raw text | 42.01 |

Table 4: Statistics of testing dataset.

As shown in Table 4, the average length of words is five characters, which makes the normalization task more difficult. For example, the candidate set for the OOV word "*yoor*" contains 59 words, as shown in Table 5. The large number of candidates causes difficulty for candidate selection because more options lead to more possibilities and more computational cost. Furthermore, the generated candidates are lexically, syntactically, and semantically very akin to each other. For example, for the OOV word "*yoor*", "*our*" might be mistakenly selected instead of "*your*". There are a smaller number of potential candidates for lengthy OOV words. As shown in Table 5, the number of candidates for the OOV word *"acessibility"* is only 14, which is less than average, thereby making candidate selection easier. Moreover, there is a distinct difference between the meanings of candidates, which is an easy situation for our context-based probability functions to select the correct one. Although our approach obtained promising results on this dataset, it works better on long words.

| *OOV word* | *Candidate set* | *No. of candidates* |
|---|---|---|
| acessibility | accessibility, accessibly, basicity, bicyclists, bicyclist, italicizes, abilities, bicyclist, sibilates, stabilize, silicates, celibacy, bicycles, and bicycle. | 14 |
| yoor | your, you, door, our, or, yoga, yak, yuck, yule, moon, tour, poor, ... | 59 |

Table 5: Example of candidate sets for OOV words.

Our approach and SMT-like system attained BLEU scores of 83.12 and 78.81, respectively. This result proves that if we integrate three probability scores via Maxent, promising normalization accuracy can be obtained. This result confirms that a normalization system constructed based on the Maxent principle can surpass state-of-the-art systems. However, several drawbacks of our method were disclosed by inspecting the output of the system. The most noticeable one is that the approach fails when tackling very noisy text, that is, ample usage of OOV words in a text. We altered our dataset to have higher levels of noise using an approach introduced by Gadde, Goutam, Shah, Bayyarapu, and Subramaniam (2011), which artificially generates OOV words. If the percentage of OOV words crosses 45%, the accuracy of the method drastically drops to a BLEU score of less than 65. Another shortcoming of our approach is that it is not able to address combined words and abbreviations (e.g. *alot* → *a lot*, *btw* → *by the way*) because candidate generation module forms only single words for each OOV.

## 7 Conclusion

In this paper, we have presented a normalization approach based on the maximum entropy model. This approach provides a unified layout for incorporating different sources of features to normalize Twitter messages. Our proposed approach consists of three stages: preprocessing, candidate generation, and candidate selection. The approach is robust to normalize unseen words since its candidate generation stage does not practice machine-learning methods. In the preprocessing stage, after trimming erroneous whitespaces and tokenization, OOV words are detected via the GNU Aspell dictionary. Normalized candidates are generated for each OOV word in the second stage regarding to lexical, phonemic, and morphophonemic similarities. Since code-switching between Malay and English is very common in our dataset, the potential English translation of OOV words is also added to the candidate set.

In the third stage, three conditional probability scores are assigned to each candidate: 1) positional indexing considers the probability of positional locations of term occurrences inside documents, 2) dependency-based frequency measures the probability of prevalence of the dependency relation of words to each other, and 3) the language model indicates the probability of distribution of the sequence of words. Finally, the best candidate is selected. Maximum entropy integrates the obtained probability scores to estimate the ultimate probability of each candidate.

The approach is examined using 7,000 parallel Twitter messages, which is split into 5,000 messages for training and 2,000 for testing. The result is promising whereby we achieve a BLEU score of 83.12 against the baseline BLEU, which scores 42.01. We have compared our approach with a SMT-like approach using the same dataset. The accuracy of the SMT-like was lower than our approach (i.e. 78.81 BLEU score for the SMT-like). For future work, we will examine the Maxent normalization approach with more probability functions, such as distributional clustering and semantic features.

## Acknowledgments

The research for this paper was financially supported by the University of Malaya FRGS Grant (FP021-2014B). We thank Asad Abdi for assistance with graphical illustrations.

## Reference


Aw, A., Zhang, M., Xiao, J., & Su, J. (2006). A Phrase-based Statistical Model for SMS Text Normalization. In Proceedings of the COLING/ACL on Main Conference Poster Sessions (pp. 33–40). Stroudsburg, PA, USA: Association for Computational Linguistics.

Beaufort, R., Roekhaut, S., Cougnon, L.-A., & Fairon, C. (2010). A Hybrid Rule/Model-based Finite-state Framework for Normalizing SMS Messages. In Proceedings of the 48th Annual Meeting of the Association for Computational Linguistics (pp. 770–779). Stroudsburg, PA, USA: Association for Computational Linguistics.

Berger, A. L., Pietra, V. J. Della, & Pietra, S. A. Della. (1996). A Maximum Entropy Approach to Natural Language Processing. Comput. Linguist., 22(1), 39–71.

Bieswanger, M. (2007). 2 abbrevi8 or not 2 abbrevi8: A Contrastive Analysis of Different Space- and Time-Saving Strategies in English and German Text Messages. Texas Linguistic Forum, Vol. 50.

Choudhury, M., Saraf, R., Jain, V., Sarkar, S., & Basu, A. (2007). Investigation and Modeling of the Structure of Texting Language, 63–70.

Clark, E., & Araki, K. (2011). Text Normalization in Social Media: Progress, Problems and Applications for a Pre-Processing System of Casual English. Procedia - Social and Behavioral Sciences, 27(0), 2–11.

Contractor, D., Faruquie, T. A., & Subramaniam, L. V. (2010). Unsupervised Cleansing of Noisy Text. In Proceedings of the 23rd International Conference on Computational Linguistics: Posters (pp. 189–196). Stroudsburg, PA, USA: Association for Computational Linguistics.

Cook, P., & Stevenson, S. (2009). An Unsupervised Model for Text Message Normalization. In Proceedings of the Workshop on Computational Approaches to Linguistic Creativity (pp. 71–78). Stroudsburg, PA, USA: Association for Computational Linguistics.

Daugherty, T., Eastin, M. S., & Bright, L. (2008). Exploring Consumer Motivations for Creating User-Generated Content. Journal of Interactive Advertising, 8(2).

Gadde, P., Goutam, R., Shah, R., Bayyarapu, H. S., & Subramaniam, L. V. (2011). Experiments with Artificially Generated Noise for Cleansing Noisy Text. In Proceedings of the 2011 Joint Workshop on Multilingual OCR and Analytics for Noisy Unstructured Text Data (pp. 4:1–4:8). New York, NY, USA: ACM. doi:10.1145/2034617.2034622

Han, B., & Baldwin, T. (2011). Lexical Normalisation of Short Text Messages: Makn Sens a #Twitter. In Proceedings of the 49th Annual Meeting of the Association for Computational Linguistics: Human Language Technologies - Volume 1 (pp. 368–378). Stroudsburg, PA, USA: Association for Computational Linguistics.

Han, B., Cook, P., & Baldwin, T. (2012). Automatically Constructing a Normalisation Dictionary for Microblogs. In Proceedings of the 2012 Joint Conference on Empirical Methods in Natural Language Processing and Computational Natural Language Learning (pp. 421–432). Stroudsburg, PA, USA: Association for Computational Linguistics.

Jelinek, F. (1990). Readings in Speech Recognition. In A. Waibel & K.-F. Lee (Eds.), (pp. 450–506). San Francisco, CA, USA: Morgan Kaufmann Publishers Inc.

Kaufmann, M., & Kalita, J. (2010). Syntactic normalization of Twitter messages. International Conference on Natural Language Processing, Kharagpur, India.

Kernighan, M. D., Church, K. W., & Gale, W. A. (1990). A Spelling Correction Program Based on a Noisy Channel Model. In Proceedings of the 13th Conference on Computational Linguistics - Volume 2 (pp. 205–210). Stroudsburg, PA, USA: Association for Computational Linguistics.

Kobus, C., Yvon, F., & Damnati, G. (2008). Normalizing SMS: Are Two Metaphors Better Than One? In Proceedings of the 22Nd International Conference on Computational Linguistics - Volume 1 (pp. 441–448). Stroudsburg, PA, USA: Association for Computational Linguistics.

Koehn, P., Hoang, H., Birch, A., Callison-Burch, C., Federico, M., Bertoldi, N., … Herbst, E. (2007). Moses: Open Source Toolkit for Statistical Machine Translation. In Proceedings of the 45th Annual Meeting of the ACL on Interactive Poster and Demonstration Sessions (pp. 177–180). Stroudsburg, PA, USA: Association for Computational Linguistics.

Lin, H., Bilmes, J., Vergyri, D., & Kirchhoff, K. (2007). OOV detection by joint word/phone lattice alignment. In Automatic Speech Recognition Understanding, 2007. ASRU. IEEE Workshop on (pp. 478–483). doi:10.1109/ASRU.2007.4430159

Liu, F., Weng, F., Wang, B., & Liu, Y. (2011). Insertion, Deletion, or Substitution?: Normalizing Text Messages Without Pre-categorization nor Supervision. In Proceedings of the 49th Annual Meeting of the Association for Computational Linguistics: Human Language Technologies: Short Papers - Volume 2 (pp. 71–76). Stroudsburg, PA, USA: Association for Computational Linguistics.

Lopez Ludeña, V., San Segundo, R., Montero, J. M., Barra Chicote, R., & Lorenzo, J. (2012). Architecture for Text Normalization using Statistical Machine Translation techniques. In IberSPEECH 2012 (pp. 112–122). Madrid, Spain: Springer.

Manning, C. D., & Raghavan, P. (2009). An Introduction to Information Retrieval. Online. doi:10.1109/LPT.2009.2020494

Marneffe, M.-C. de, MacCartney, B., & Manning, C. D. (2006). Generating typed dependency parses from phrase structure parses. In The International Conference on Language Resources and Evaluation (LREC) (pp. 449–454). Genova, Italy.

Mays, E., Damerau, F. J., & Mercer, R. L. (1991). Context based spelling correction. Information Processing & Management, 27(5), 517–522.

Novak, J., Yang, D., Minematsu, N., & Hirose, K. (2011). Phonetisaurus: A wfst-driven phoneticizer. The University of Tokyo, Tokyo Institute of Technology. Retrieved January 1, 2014, from http://code.google.com/p/phonetisaurus/

Och, F. J., & Ney, H. (2002). Discriminative Training and Maximum Entropy Models for Statistical Machine Translation. In Proceedings of the 40th Annual Meeting on Association for Computational Linguistics (pp. 295–302). Stroudsburg, PA, USA: Association for Computational Linguistics.

Och, F. J., & Ney, H. (2003). A Systematic Comparison of Various Statistical Alignment Models. Comput. Linguist., 29(1), 19–51.

Oliva, J., Serrano, J. I., Del Castillo, M. D., & Igesias, Á. (2013). A SMS Normalization System Integrating Multiple Grammatical Resources. Natural Language Engineering, 19(01), 121–141.

Papineni, K., Roukos, S., & Ward, T. (1998). Maximum likelihood and discriminative training of direct translation models. In Acoustics, Speech and Signal Processing, 1998. Proceedings of the 1998 IEEE International Conference on (Vol. 1, pp. 189–192 vol.1).

Papineni, K., Roukos, S., Ward, T., & Zhu, W.-J. (2002). BLEU: A Method for Automatic Evaluation of Machine Translation. In Proceedings of the 40th Annual Meeting on Association for Computational Linguistics (pp. 311–318). Stroudsburg, PA, USA: Association for Computational Linguistics.

Pennell, D. L., & Liu, Y. (2010). Normalization of text messages for text-to-speech. Acoustics Speech and Signal Processing (ICASSP), 2010 IEEE International Conference on.

Saloot, M. A., Idris, N., & Aw, A. (2014). Noisy Text Normalization Using an Enhanced Language Model. In Proceedings of the International Conference on Artificial Intelligence and Pattern Recognition (pp. 111–122). Kuala Lumpur, Malaysia: SDIWC.

Saloot, M. A., Idris, N., Aw, A., & Thorleuchter, D. (2014). Twitter corpus creation: The case of a Malay Chat-style-text Corpus (MCC). Digital Scholarship in the Humanities. Retrieved from http://dsh.oxfordjournals.org/content/early/2014/12/13/llc.fqu066.abstract

Saloot, M. A., Idris, N., & Mahmud, R. (2014). An architecture for Malay Tweet normalization. Information Processing & Management, 50(5), 621–633.

Schlippe, T., Zhu, C., Gebhardt, J., & Schultz, T. (2010). Text normalization based on statistical machine translation and internet user support. In T. Kobayashi, K. Hirose, & S. Nakamura (Eds.), INTERSPEECH (pp. 1816–1819). ISCA.

Smith, J., & Padi, P. (2006). Lets make a dictionary. In Proceedings of the the Eighth Biennial Conference of the Borneo Research Council (BRC) (pp. 515–520). Sarawak, Malaysia: Borneo Research Council (BRC).

Sproat, R., Black, A. W., Chen, S., Kumar, S., Ostendorf, M., & Richards, C. (2001). Normalization of non-standard words. Computer Speech & Language, 15(3), 287–333.

Stolcke, A. (2002). SRILM-an extensible language modeling toolkit. In Proceedings International Conference on Spoken Language Processing (pp. 257–286).

Streit, R. L., & Luginbuhl, T. E. (1994). Maximum likelihood training of probabilistic neural networks. Neural Networks, IEEE Transactions on, 5(5), 764–783. doi:10.1109/72.317728

Thurlow, C., & Brown, A. (2003). Generation Txt? The sociolinguistics of young people's text-messaging.

Toutanova, K., & Moore, R. C. (2002). Pronunciation Modeling for Improved Spelling Correction. In Proceedings of the 40th Annual Meeting on Association for Computational Linguistics (pp. 144–151). Stroudsburg, PA, USA: Association for Computational Linguistics.

Xue, Z., Yin, D., & Davison, B. D. (2011a). Normalizing Microtext. In Analyzing Microtext (Vol. WS-11-05). AAAI.

Xue, Z., Yin, D., & Davison, B. D. (2011b). Normalizing Microtext. In Analyzing Microtext: Papers from the 2011 AAAI Workshop (pp. 74–79). San Francisco, CA, USA: AAAI.

# Five Shades of Noise: Analyzing Machine Translation Errors in User-Generated Text

**Marlies van der Wees** **Arianna Bisazza** **Christof Monz**
Informatics Institute, University of Amsterdam
{m.e.vanderwees,a.bisazza,c.monz}@uva.nl

## Abstract

It is widely accepted that translating user-generated (UG) text is a difficult task for modern statistical machine translation (SMT) systems. The translation quality metrics typically used in the SMT literature reflect the overall quality of the system output but provide little insight into what exactly makes UG text translation difficult. This paper analyzes in detail the behavior of a state-of-the-art SMT system on five different types of informal text. The results help to demystify the poor SMT performance experienced by researchers who use SMT as an intermediate step of their UG-NLP pipeline, and to identify translation modeling aspects that the SMT community should more urgently address to improve translation of UG data.

## 1 Introduction

User-generated (UG) text such as found on social media and web forums poses different challenges to statistical machine translation (SMT) than formal text. This is reflected by poor translation quality for informal genres (see for example Figure 1), which is typically measured with automatic quality metrics such as BLEU (Papineni et al., 2002), METEOR (Banerjee and Lavie, 2005), or TER (Snover et al., 2006). These scores alone, however, only reflect the overall translation quality, and do not provide any insight in what exactly makes translating UG text hard. While such knowledge is crucial for improving SMT of UG text, surprisingly little work on error analysis for SMT of user-generated text has been reported.

Moreover, the notion of user-generated content only partially specifies the exact nature of documents. What all documents that can be classified as being UG have in common is the fact that they have been written by a lay-person, as opposed to a journalist or professional author, and that they have not undergone any editorial control. UG text also tends to express the writer's opinion to a larger degree than news articles which generally strive for balance and nuance. Within UG text, we can distinguish several subclasses, including (i) message and dialog-oriented content such as short message service (SMS) texts, Internet chat messages, and transcripts of conversational speech, (ii) commentaries to news articles, often expressing an opinion about the corresponding articles and relating the content to the reader's situation, and (iii) weblogs, which can bear some resemblance to editorial pieces published by news organizations.

| | |
|---|---|
| In (Arabic): | قالت عشان العيال متزعلش |
| Reference: | she said so the kids do not feel upset |
| MT output: | she said because of the sons |
| In (Chinese): | 你 路上 慢 点 |
| Reference: | take your time |
| MT output: | you are on the road to slow points |

Figure 1: SMS examples with poor SMT output.

While UG text processing tasks are becoming more and more common, the research in SMT is still mostly driven by formal translation tasks[1], and existing error analysis approaches are only partially useful for UG. In this work, we conduct a series of analyses on five different UG benchmark sets for two language pairs, Arabic-English and Chinese-English, with the goals of (i) explaining the typically poor SMT performance observed for UG texts, and (ii) identifying translation modeling

[1] One of the very few exceptions is NIST OpenMT 2015, which focusses entirely on translating informal genres.



*Proceedings of the ACL 2015 Workshop on Noisy User-generated Text*, pages 28–37,
Beijing, China, July 31, 2015. ©2015 Association for Computational Linguistics

aspects that should be addressed to improve translation of UG data. We not only contrast our observations with two news data sets, but we also show that SMT quality can vary significantly across different types of UG content, and that different UG types exhibit dissimilar error distributions. Specifically, we summarize our main findings as follows:

- The SMS and chat benchmarks are the most distant from formal text at all the analyzed levels. Errors in other types of UG are often more similar to news errors than to those in SMS and chat messages.
- SMT model coverage dramatically deteriorates for phrases of length 3 or longer in most of the UG benchmarks.
- Errors due to out-of-vocabulary (OOV) words in the *source* text substantially increase in number for UG data sets, but are considerably less common than errors due to *source-target* OOVs, i.e., phrase pairs that are not covered by the SMT models.

## 2 Related Work

Identifying and analyzing different types of SMT errors is an essential step towards the development of translation approaches that can achieve more robust performance, and has been the focus of earlier work. Popović and Ney (2011), for example, combine word error rates with morpho-syntactic information to classify errors into five categories; inflectional errors, reordering errors, lexical errors, word deletions, and word insertions. Irvine et al. (2013) use word alignment links to quantify incorrect lexical choices, and determine how such errors change when shifting domains. Other work on SMT error analysis studies the effect of domain adaptation on SMT, for example by examining in which stage of the SMT pipeline the available in-domain data can best be used (Duh et al., 2010), or whether it is more promising to improve either phrase extraction or scoring (Bisazza et al., 2011; Haddow and Koehn, 2012).

The vast majority of SMT research, including the above described work on error analysis, is evaluated on data containing *formal* language. Work on SMT of *informal* text mostly targets reduction of OOV words in the source text, for example by correcting spelling errors (Bertoldi et al., 2010), normalizing noisy text to more formal text (Banerjee et al., 2012; Ling et al., 2013a), or enhancing the training data with bilingual segments extracted from Twitter (Jehl et al., 2012; Ling et al., 2013b). Other work improves SMT of UG text by combining statistical and rule-based MT (Carrera et al., 2009), or models trained on formal and informal data (Banerjee et al., 2011). Finally, Roturier and Bensadoun (2011) conduct a comparative study to determine the ability of several SMT systems to translate UG text, but they do not examine what errors the systems make. To our knowledge, our work is the first that looks inside an SMT system to systematically inspect its behavior across a diverse spectrum of UG text types.

## 3 Experimental setup

We perform our error analysis on two language pairs, Arabic-English and Chinese-English.

### 3.1 Evaluation sets

For both language pairs we use evaluation sets for five types of user-generated text: SMS messages, chat messages, manual transcripts of phone conversations (called Conversational Telephone

| | Dev set | | Test set | | |
|---|---|---|---|---|---|
| Genre | Lines | Tokens | Lines | Tokens | Refs |
| SMS | 2.7K | 23.3K | 7.6K | 44.9K | 1 |
| Chat | 3.5K | 22.5K | 7.1K | 44.5K | 1 |
| CTS | 2.4K | 23.1K | 3.6K | 40.6K | 1 |
| Comments | 1.1K | 25.8K | 1.7K | 45.5K | 1 |
| Weblogs | 0.8K | 14.6K | 1.3K | 39.9K | 4 |
| News 1 | 1.0K | 26.9K | 1.6K | 46.3K | 1 |
| News 2 | 1.0K | 34.4K | 1.4K | 46.6K | 4 |

Table 1: Statistics of the Arabic-English UG (top) and contrastive news (bottom) evaluation sets. Tokens are counted on the Arabic side.

| | Dev set | | Test set | | |
|---|---|---|---|---|---|
| Genre | Lines | Tokens | Lines | Tokens | Refs |
| SMS | 1.8K | 15.3K | 4.2K | 36.3K | 1 |
| Chat | 4.0K | 25.6K | 6.0K | 45.7K | 1 |
| CTS | 2.2K | 25.1K | 2.9K | 44.8K | 1 |
| Comments | 1.0K | 26.5K | 1.5K | 41.0K | 1 |
| Weblogs | 0.5K | 8.8K | 0.7K | 14.4K | 4 |
| News 1 | 0.8K | 24.5K | 1.5K | 41.9K | 1 |
| News 2 | 1.2K | 29.4K | 0.7K | 17.7K | 4 |

Table 2: Statistics of the Chinese-English UG (top) and contrastive news (bottom) evaluation sets. Tokens are counted on the Chinese side.

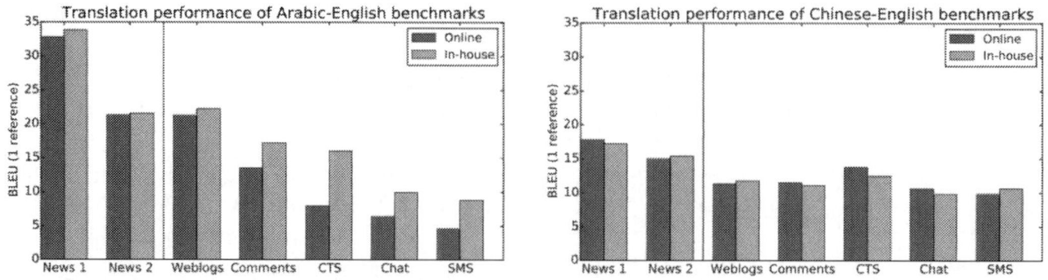


Figure 2: Translation performance of baseline experiments for various Arabic-English (left) and Chinese-English (right) data sets, measured in case-insensitive BLEU for one reference translation.

Speech (CTS)), weblogs, and readers' comments to news articles. The first four data sets originate from BOLT and NIST OpenMT, and are distributed by the Linguistic Data Consortium (LDC), while the last data set is crawled from the web. All UG experiments are contrasted with two news data sets; the news portions of NIST evaluation sets, and web-crawled news articles.

For Arabic-English, the web-crawled news articles and comments originate from the Gen&Topic data set (van der Wees et al., 2015), in which both genres cover the same distributions over various topics. Consequently, any observed differences between the news and UG portions of this data set can be entirely attributed to genre differences and not to potential topical variation.

We have created similar-sized benchmark sets as much as possible, however sometimes limited by availability. Tables 1 and 2 show the data specifications of the Arabic-English and Chinese-English evaluation sets, respectively.[2]

### 3.2 SMT systems

All experiments presented in this paper are performed with our in-house state-of-the-art system based on phrase-based SMT and similar to Moses (Koehn et al., 2007). Our Arabic-English system is built from 1.75M lines (52.9M source tokens) of parallel text, and our Chinese-English system from 3.13M lines (55.4M source tokens) of parallel text. We tokenize all Arabic data using MADA (Habash and Rambow, 2005), ATB scheme, and we segment the Chinese data following Tseng et al. (2005). Both systems use an adapted 5-gram English language model that linearly interpolates different English Gigaword subcorpora with the English side of our bitexts, containing both news and UG data.

While parallel data is scarce in general, the situation is much worse for UG data, where there are hardly any sizable parallel corpora for any language pair. As a consequence, the training data of both systems comprises 70-75% news data, mostly LDC-distributed, and 25-30% data in various other genres (weblogs, comments, editorials, speech transcripts, and small amounts of chat data), mostly harvested from the web. Per language pair, all experiments use the same SMT models, but we tune parameters separately for each benchmark set using pairwise ranking optimization (PRO) (Hopkins and May, 2011).

To put the results of our system into perspective, we also run a first series of experiments on a well-known and established online SMT system.

## 4 Error analysis and results

We perform four series of experiments, each with the goal of answering different questions about SMT for UG text:

1. How large is the gap in translation quality between news and different types of UG data? (§4.1). To answer this question, we measure the BLEU score of two state-of-the-art SMT system outputs on all our data sets.

2. What kind of translation choices does the SMT system make for UG data? To answer this question, we measure phrase lengths used during the translation (or decoding) process (§4.2).

3. What translation choices could have been made by the SMT system? To answer this question, we compute mono- and bilingual coverage of the SMT models (§4.3).

[2]Note that two evaluation sets contain four reference translations instead of one. To allow for fair comparison, we average the scores of the four references in all our analyses.

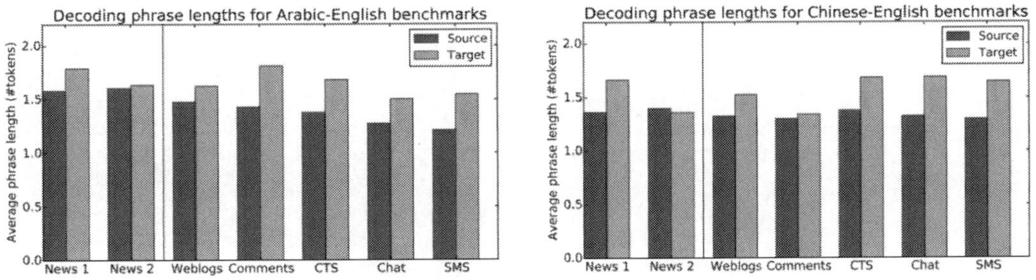


Figure 3: Average source-side and target-side phrase lengths used during decoding.

4. Why did the SMT system make the translation choices that it made? What errors are observed for each benchmark, and how often? To answer these questions, we reimplement the word-alignment driven error analysis approach by Irvine et al. (2013) and perform a qualitative analysis on the results (§4.4).

### 4.1 Overall translation quality

A first important indication of SMT quality across different genres can be given by translation quality measures that are based on the similarity between the SMT output and a reference human translation. To estimate the gap in translation quality between news and UG text, but also among various types of UG text, we measure the BLEU scores (1 reference) of our in-house SMT system and that of the online system on all our evaluation sets.

The results in Figure 2 (left) show that translation quality differs greatly between the Arabic-English data sets. In particular, the News 1 data set (from NIST) yields considerably higher BLEU scores than all other evaluation sets, including the News 2 (web-crawled) set, which represents the same genre but is visibly more difficult to translate. On the other end of the spectrum, we see that translation quality of the SMS and chat data sets is very poor. Note that our in-house system is optimized per genre, whereas the online system is optimized for general language and speed.

For Chinese-English (Figure 2, right) the differences in BLEU are less pronounced, both across the different data sets and between the two SMT systems. Still, translation quality is worse for the UG data sets than for news, indicating that also for this language pair translating UG text is more challenging than translating news.

As all subsequent analyses require system-internal information, we carry out the experiments with our in-house system only.

### 4.2 Translation phrase length analysis

Most state-of-the-art SMT systems, including our in-house system, are phrase-based, with translations being generated phrase by phrase rather than word by word (Koehn et al., 2003). An abundant use of small phrases during decoding indicates that the system is not taking advantage of the model's ability to memorize large contextual and possibly non-compositional translation blocks. It is therefore interesting to measure the average phrase length (i.e., number of tokens) used by the system, for the source as well as the target language (Figure 3). For Arabic-English we see that source-side phrases are noticeably longer for both news benchmarks than for the UG data sets. The average target-side phrase length, on the other hand, shows less correlation with the genres of the data sets. Similar trends are observed for Chinese-English, however differences are less extreme.

In general, SMT systems incur higher model costs when utilizing many small phrases rather than few large phrases. If, in spite of that, a system selects many short phrases, which is the case for most of our UG benchmarks, this can be due to (i) unreliable translation probabilities or (ii) to the mere lack of correct translation options in the models. We investigate both issues in the following analyses.

### 4.3 Model coverage analysis

Next, we examine the translation model coverage for each data set, which tells us what phrases the system *could have* used for decoding. For each of our test sets, we create automatic word alignments using GIZA++ (Och and Ney, 2003), and extract from these the set of all reference phrase pairs using Moses' phrase extraction algorithm (Koehn et al., 2007). By comparing this set of phrase pairs to the available phrases in the SMT models, which

| Genre | BLEU | LM PP | Source phrase recall 1 | 2 | 3 | 4 | Target phrase recall 1 | 2 | 3 | 4 | Phrase pair recall 1 | 2 | 3 | 4 |
|---|---|---|---|---|---|---|---|---|---|---|---|---|---|---|
| News 1 | 33.8 | 65 | 99.7 | 88.9 | 56.3 | 26.1 | 99.7 | 91.1 | 61.5 | 29.6 | 84.9 | 54.4 | 23.6 | 8.1 |
| News 2 | 21.5 | 86 | 99.6 | 88.1 | 53.7 | 21.8 | 99.5 | 88.1 | 53.4 | 23.6 | 77.4 | 46.9 | 18.8 | 5.9 |
| Weblogs | 22.3 | 152 | 99.2 | 80.5 | 40.6 | 13.5 | 99.5 | 86.3 | 48.9 | 17.8 | 78.4 | 41.5 | 12.9 | 2.9 |
| Comments | 17.2 | 117 | 97.7 | 80.2 | 43.0 | 15.3 | 99.7 | 89.8 | 55.3 | 21.9 | 59.1 | 33.2 | 11.1 | 2.8 |
| CTS | 16.0 | 103 | 97.4 | 66.3 | 25.1 | 6.4 | 99.8 | 90.8 | 54.3 | 21.5 | 66.7 | 25.7 | 6.1 | 1.0 |
| Chat | 10.0 | 179 | 94.1 | 56.0 | 19.4 | 4.7 | 98.6 | 86.1 | 47.3 | 16.7 | 60.8 | 21.3 | 4.5 | 0.8 |
| SMS | 8.8 | 196 | 93.7 | 57.8 | 17.5 | 3.3 | 99.1 | 86.3 | 47.0 | 14.6 | 62.0 | 21.1 | 3.7 | 0.4 |

Table 3: Target language model perplexity and translation model coverage of Arabic-English benchmarks. Phrase pair recall values are broken down by source phrase length. Intensities of the cell colors indicate relative recall values with respect to the best scoring benchmark (measured in BLEU).

| Genre | BLEU | LM PP | Source phrase recall 1 | 2 | 3 | 4 | Target phrase recall 1 | 2 | 3 | 4 | Phrase pair recall 1 | 2 | 3 | 4 |
|---|---|---|---|---|---|---|---|---|---|---|---|---|---|---|
| News 1 | 17.2 | 121 | 99.0 | 80.2 | 40.8 | 16.2 | 99.5 | 84.9 | 48.0 | 19.5 | 69.1 | 34.8 | 10.8 | 3.3 |
| News 2 | 15.4 | 118 | 98.8 | 84.2 | 44.3 | 16.0 | 99.4 | 83.8 | 44.2 | 14.7 | 63.1 | 32.4 | 10.7 | 3.3 |
| Weblogs | 11.8 | 153 | 98.6 | 76.6 | 33.8 | 11.1 | 99.3 | 81.6 | 40.8 | 12.4 | 59.0 | 27.0 | 7.3 | 1.7 |
| Comments | 11.1 | 195 | 98.7 | 78.3 | 35.2 | 8.7 | 97.9 | 77.9 | 35.1 | 10.2 | 53.5 | 21.6 | 5.0 | 1.0 |
| CTS | 12.5 | 135 | 98.7 | 80.7 | 40.1 | 10.5 | 99.8 | 86.3 | 47.4 | 16.4 | 70.0 | 33.5 | 9.3 | 1.7 |
| Chat | 9.9 | 221 | 98.0 | 71.9 | 27.5 | 6.1 | 99.4 | 82.6 | 43.2 | 13.0 | 62.3 | 24.8 | 5.4 | 0.6 |
| SMS | 10.7 | 234 | 97.3 | 68.5 | 24.9 | 4.8 | 99.0 | 80.4 | 40.5 | 12.5 | 62.6 | 24.6 | 5.1 | 0.5 |

Table 4: Target language model perplexity and translation model coverage of Chinese-English benchmarks. See Table 3 for explanation on colors and categories.

have been extracted using the same procedure, we can compute the following statistics:

1. *Source phrase recall*, defined as the fraction of reference phrase pairs whose *source* side is found in the SMT models.

2. *Target phrase recall*, defined as the fraction of reference phrase pairs whose *target* side is found in the SMT models.

3. *Phrase pair recall*, defined as the fraction of reference phrase pairs whose source and target side are jointly found in the SMT models.

Low recall values indicate that the models lack phrases or phrase pairs that match the test data, which can be addressed by adding additional relevant training data or by generating new phrases. In addition, we measure language model perplexity as an indication of how predictable each benchmark is for the language model. Note that high perplexity corresponds to lower coverage.

The model coverage results for Arabic-English and Chinese-English are shown in Tables 3 and 4, respectively. All recall scores are broken down by phrase length, up to phrases of four tokens.[3] We use cell color intensity to represent relative recall values with respect to the best scoring benchmark according to BLEU, i.e., News 1. The results show that source phrase recall is substantially lower for the UG benchmarks than for news, particularly for longer phrases. Regarding target phrase recall, differences between various data sets and genres are much smaller. This suggests that many of the reference phrases could potentially be generated by the system, even for the UG data. However, to be able to output the available target phrases, the system needs a match with the input source phrases, which is exactly what is being measured with phrase pair recall. Here, we see that for the majority of single-word source phrases, the expected target phrase is accessible by the system. For longer phrases, though, there is again a drastic decline in recall, with almost no phrases of length 4 or longer having the expected target covered by the models. Similar to source phrase recall, this decline is notably bigger for UG than for news.

[3]The source-target phrase pair recall (last four columns) is split by source phrase length rather than target phrase length since source phrases are the actual input to the SMT system.

Looking at the differences between the various types of UG data, we see that the SMS and chat benchmarks are most severely affected by overall poor model coverage. As for weblogs, the target phrase recall is similar to SMS and chat, whereas both source phrase and phrase pair recall are much higher. For CTS and web comments, there are notable differences between model coverage for the two language pairs, despite similar BLEU scores. While comments have better coverage in the Arabic-English models, CTS has higher recall values for Chinese-English.

Finally, we see that language model perplexity is on average lower for Arabic-English than for the Chinese-English benchmarks. This is somewhat surprising given that perplexity is measured on the English side, but it can partially explain the low BLEU scores on, for example, the Chinese-English News 1 benchmark. All news benchmarks have relatively low perplexities, which is expected since the language model covers more news than UG data. Of the UG benchmarks, CTS has a remarkably low perplexity value, suggesting that for this genre the language model can potentially compensate for low translation model coverage.

### 4.4 WADE: Word Alignment Driven Evaluation

Next, to gain a more fine-grained insight in *why* our SMT system makes its translation choices, we reimplement an evaluation approach proposed by Irvine et al. (2013), which analyzes SMT error types at the word alignment level. The analysis exploits automatic word alignments between (i) a given source sentence and its reference translation, and (ii) the same source sentence and its automatic translation. Each aligned source-reference word pair is examined for whether the alignment link is matched by the decoder. Formally, $f_i$ is a foreign word, $e_j$ is a reference word aligned to $f_i$, $a_{i,j}$ is the alignment link between $f_i$ and $e_j$, and $H_i$ is the set of output words that are aligned to $f_i$ by the decoder. If $e_j \in H_i$, the alignment link $a_{i,j}$ is marked as correct. Otherwise, $a_{i,j}$ is categorized with one of the following error types:

1. A SEEN error indicates an unseen source word, i.e., out-of-vocabulary (OOV) item. This error is assigned to $a_{i,j}$ if $f_i$ does not appear in the phrase table used for translation. This type of error inversely correlates with length-1 source phrase recall (§4.3).
2. A SENSE error indicates an unseen target word. This error is assigned to $a_{i,j}$ if $f_i$ does appear in the phrase table but never with translation candidate $e_j$.
3. A SCORE error indicates suboptimal scoring of translation options. This error is assigned to $a_{i,j}$ if $f_i$ exists in the phrase table with translation candidate $e_j$, but another translation candidate is preferred by the decoder.

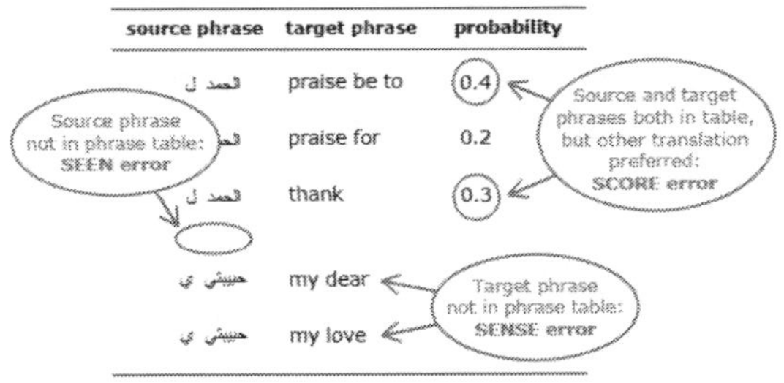


Figure 4: Graphical overview of SEEN, SENSE and SCORE errors in a toy phrase table.

Figure 4 shows a graphical representation of these error types and their 'location' in the phrase table. In addition to the listed error types, Irvine et al. define SEARCH errors as errors due to pruning in beam search, and refer to the complete set of errors as the $S^4$ *taxonomy*. For this analysis, however, SEARCH errors are indistinguishable from SCORE errors, and are therefore never assigned.

A final category that can be considered are *freebies*: OOVs that are copied over verbatim to the output sentence and accidentally match the reference translation (e.g., urls, proper nouns, etc.). For the language pairs that we study, they are very rare; at most 0.35% for Arabic-English (in CTS) and 0.63% for Chinese-English (in SMS). Manual inspection reveals that nearly all freebies are English words in the foreign source text. Since they are so rare, we omit freebies from our results.

As WADE errors are assigned at the fine-grained level of individual words, this analysis allows for (i) sentence-level visualization of errors, and (ii) collecting aggregate statistics of each error type for an entire evaluation set. By assembling the latter for various benchmarks, we can quantify global differences between genres or data sets. At the same time, by examining (i) we can gain insight in the nature of the different 'errors', which might be real mistakes, or, for instance, different lexical choices.

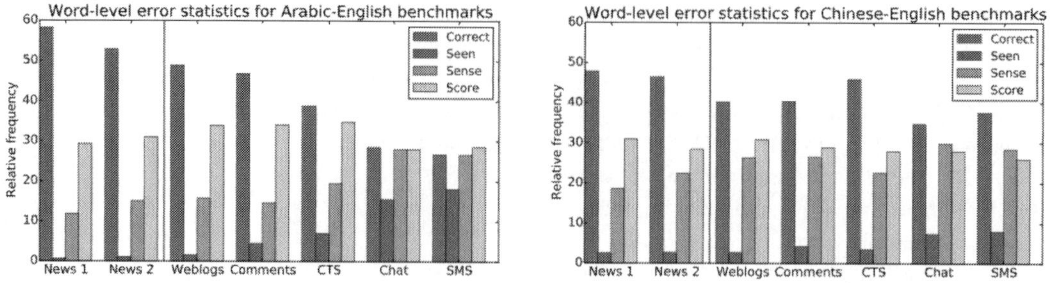


Figure 5: Aggregate error statistics for Arabic-English (left) and Chinese-English (right) benchmark sets.

**Quantitative results.** The aggregate error statistics for each data set are shown in Figure 5. To put our results into perspective, we recall the findings of Irvine et al. (2013). They find that for *formal* domains using a French-English system, 50–60% of the alignment links are correct, and SCORE errors are more common than SENSE errors, which in turn are more common than SEEN errors. While we observe a similar distribution for our Arabic-English news benchmarks, these numbers do not generalize to the Arabic-English UG benchmarks nor to any of the Chinese-English data sets.

First, the portion of SEEN errors increases dramatically for the Arabic-English UG translation tasks. For Chinese-English this trend is less pronounced yet also clearly observable. Next, SENSE errors also increase substantially for most of the UG data, making up the majority of the errors for Chinese-English SMS and chat. This indicates that a promising strategy for adapting SMT systems to translating UG data involves generating new target-side translation candidates that match the source phrases in the input sentences. Finally, we evaluate the fraction of SCORE errors. While this is the most commonly observed error type in most of the data sets, there seems to be very little correspondance with the genre or BLEU scores of the benchmarks. This is an interesting finding since most work in system adaptation for SMT focuses on better scoring of existing translation candidates (Matsoukas et al., 2009; Foster et al., 2010; Axelrod et al., 2011; Chen et al., 2013, among others). However, for UG translation tasks this does not appear as the most profitable approach.

**Qualitative results.** The generated sentence-level error annotations allow us to examine the various error types in detail. The first phenomenon that we repeatedly observe in the UG data are SEEN errors due to misspellings or, in the case of Arabic, dialectal forms. Two such examples are shown in Figures 6A and 6B: In the first, the SMT system does not recognize the dialectal form of verb negation 'mtzEl$', which is a morphologically complex word containing both a prefix and a suffix. In the second, the input word 'Almw**b**Ayl' ('mobile') is wrongly spelled 'Almw**y**Ayl'. It is interesting to note that 'b' and 'y' are very similar in the Arabic script. This type of errors is particularly frequent in chat and SMS, which can partly explain the different distribution of errors across the Arabic-English data sets (Figure 5).

Also frequently observed in the UG data are SMT lexical choices that are more formal than the reference translations. This is not surprising given the large amount of formal data in the SMT models, but it does illustrate the need for adaptation to UG data. Often, the optimal lexical choice is simply absent from the SMT models, resulting in SENSE errors. This can be observed in Figure 6A, where 'sons' is output instead 'kids', and in Figure 6C, where 'i understand' is output instead of the colloquial 'i got it'. In other situations, the annotated SCORE errors indicate that the correct choice was available to the SMT system without being selected for translation. For example in Figure 6D, the output 'my parents' is preferred to the more colloquial 'mom and dad' in the reference.

Another phenomenon, particularly common for Chinese-English UG translations, is that idioms are translated in small chunks, thereby losing their meaning as a phrase. In Figure 6D, the characters '说', '一', and '声' mean 'to say', 'one', and 'sound', respectively. The phrase '说一声' as a whole means 'talk a bit about something' but is not covered by the SMT models. Similarly, '你路上慢点' in Figure 6E literally means 'you on the road slow a bit', which, if covered by the models, could have been translated into 'be careful on

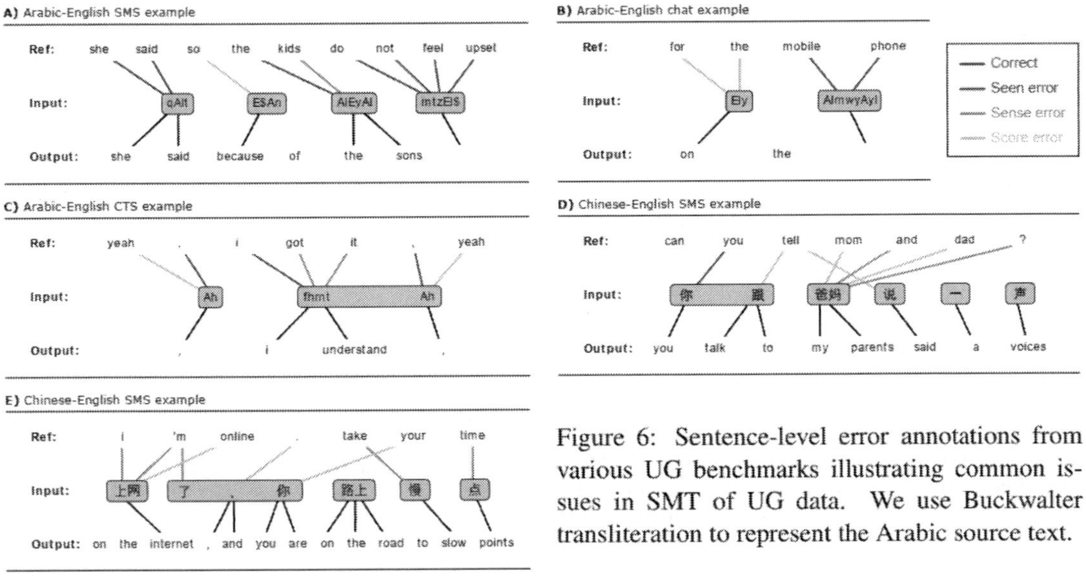


Figure 6: Sentence-level error annotations from various UG benchmarks illustrating common issues in SMT of UG data. We use Buckwalter transliteration to represent the Arabic source text.

your way' or 'take your time'. These examples illustrate that the low phrase pair recall for longer phrases severely complicates SMT of UG data.

A final recurring issue in SMS and chat messages is the omission of first person pronouns, see for example Figure 6E. The Chinese source phrase '上网了' literally means 'get online' (+ auxiliary word marking past tense). A native speaker understands that this concerns the sender, which is reflected by a first person pronoun in the reference. The SMT system, on the other hand, cannot infer the subject of this phrase and instead generates a translation without pronouns.

Other, less common, types of errors occurring in the UG data are due to inconsistent segmentation or tokenization of input text, which mostly affects rare words, emoticons, and repeating punctation. Finally, SEEN errors for named entities are overall rare but occur in both news and UG benchmarks.

## 5 Conclusions and future directions

Translating user-generated (UG) text is a difficult task for SMT. To explain the poor translation quality observed for UG data, we have performed a detailed error analysis on two language pairs (Arabic-English and Chinese-English) and five different types of UG data (SMS, chat, CTS, weblogs, and comments). Our quantitative results show among others that (i) UG data is translated with shorter source phrases than news, (ii) UG translation model coverage deteriorates substantially for longer phrases, and (iii) phrase-pair OOVs pose a bigger challenge to UG translation tasks than source OOVs. In our qualitative analysis we found that common issues in UG data include (i) OOVs due to misspellings or Arabic dialectal forms, (ii) lexical choices that do not reflect colloquial formulations, (iii) phrasal idioms being translated word by word, and (iv) omitted first person pronouns in SMS and chat.

Finally, different types of UG exhibit dissimilar error distributions, demanding diverse strategies to improve SMT quality. For example, SMS and chat data might benefit from text normalization (Bertoldi et al., 2010; Yvon, 2010; Ling et al., 2013a) or otherwise resolving source OOVs, which also has been the main focus of previous work on SMT for UG. On the other hand, while research in domain adaptation for SMT often aims at better scoring of existing translation candidates, we have shown that for many UG tasks the most promising direction involves increasing phrase pair recall of the SMT models (i.e., reducing phrase pair OOVs), for example by paraphrasing (Callison-Burch et al., 2006) or translation synthesis (Irvine and Callison-Burch, 2014).

## Acknowledgments

This research was funded in part by the Netherlands Organization for Scientific Research (NWO) under project number 639.022.213. We thank Rachel Cotterill, Nigel Dewdney, and the anonymous reviewers for their valuable comments.

## References

Amittai Axelrod, Xiaodong He, and Jianfeng Gao. 2011. Domain adaptation via pseudo in-domain data selection. In *Proceedings of the 2011 Conference on Empirical Methods in Natural Language Processing*, pages 355–362.

Satanjeev Banerjee and Alon Lavie. 2005. METEOR: an automatic metric for MT evaluation with improved correlation with human judgments. In *Proceedings of the ACL Workshop on Intrinsic and Extrinsic Evaluation Measures for Machine Translation*, pages 65–72.

Pratyush Banerjee, Sudip Kumar Naskar, Johann Roturier, Andy Way, and Josef van Genabith. 2011. Domain adaptation in statistical machine translation of user-forum data using component level mixture modelling. In *Proceedings of the XIII Machine Translation Summit*, pages 285–292.

Pratyush Banerjee, Sudip Kumar Naskar, Johann Roturier, Andy Way, and Josef van Genabith. 2012. Domain adaptation in SMT of user-generated forum content guided by OOV word reduction: Normalization and/or supplementary data. In *Proceedings of the 16th Conference of the European Association for Machine Translation*, pages 169–176.

Nicola Bertoldi, Mauro Cettolo, and Marcello Federico. 2010. Statistical machine translation of texts with misspelled words. In *Human Language Technologies: The 2010 Annual Conference of the North American Chapter of the Association for Computational Linguistics*, pages 412–419.

Arianna Bisazza, Nick Ruiz, and Marcello Federico. 2011. Fill-up versus interpolation methods for phrase-based SMT adaptation. In *Proceedings of the 8th International Workshop on Spoken Language Translation*, pages 136–143.

Chris Callison-Burch, Philipp Koehn, and Miles Osborne. 2006. Improved statistical machine translation using paraphrases. In *Proceedings of the Human Language Technology Conference of the NAACL, Main Conference*, pages 17–24.

Jordi Carrera, Olga Beregovaya, and Alex Yanishevsky. 2009. Machine translation for cross-language social media.

Boxing Chen, Roland Kuhn, and George Foster. 2013. Vector space model for adaptation in statistical machine translation. In *Proceedings of the 51st Annual Meeting of the Association for Computational Linguistics*, pages 1285–1293.

Kevin Duh, Katsuhito Sudoh, and Hajime Tsukada. 2010. Analysis of translation model adaptation in statistical machine translation. In *Proceedings of the 7th International Workshop on Spoken Language Translation (IWSLT 2010)*, pages 243–250.

George Foster, Cyril Goutte, and Roland Kuhn. 2010. Discriminative instance weighting for domain adaptation in statistical machine translation. In *Proceedings of the 2010 Conference on Empirical Methods in Natural Language Processing*, pages 451–459.

Nizar Habash and Owen Rambow. 2005. Arabic tokenization, part-of-speech tagging and morphological disambiguation in one fell swoop. In *Proceedings of the 43rd Annual Meeting on Association for Computational Linguistics*, pages 573–580.

Barry Haddow and Philipp Koehn. 2012. Analysing the effect of out-of-domain data on SMT systems. In *Proceedings of the Seventh Workshop on Statistical Machine Translation*, pages 422–432.

Mark Hopkins and Jonathan May. 2011. Tuning as ranking. In *Proceedings of the 2011 Conference on Empirical Methods in Natural Language Processing*, pages 1352–1362. Association for Computational Linguistics.

Ann Irvine and Chris Callison-Burch. 2014. Hallucinating phrase translations for low resource MT. In *Proceedings of the Eighteenth Conference on Computational Natural Language Learning*, pages 160–170.

Ann Irvine, John Morgan, Marine Carpuat, Hal Daumé III, and Dragos Stefan Munteanu. 2013. Measuring machine translation errors in new domains. *Transactions of the Association for Computational Linguistics*, 1:429–440.

Laura Jehl, Felix Hieber, and Stefan Riezler. 2012. Twitter translation using translation-based cross-lingual retrieval. In *Proceedings of the Seventh Workshop on Statistical Machine Translation*, pages 410–421.

Philipp Koehn, Franz Josef Och, and Daniel Marcu. 2003. Statistical phrase-based translation. In *Proceedings of the 2003 Conference of the North American Chapter of the Association for Computational Linguistics on Human Language Technology*, pages 48–54.

Philipp Koehn, Hieu Hoang, Alexandra Birch, Chris Callison-Burch, Marcello Federico, Nicola Bertoldi, Brooke Cowan, Wade Shen, Christine Moran, Richard Zens, Chris Dyer, Ondrej Bojar, Alexandra Constantin, and Evan Herbst. 2007. Moses: Open source toolkit for statistical machine translation. In *Proceedings of the 45th Annual Meeting of the Association for Computational Linguistics Companion Volume Proceedings of the Demo and Poster Sessions*, pages 177–180.

Wang Ling, Chris Dyer, Alan W Black, and Isabel Trancoso. 2013a. Paraphrasing 4 microblog normalization. In *Proceedings of the 2013 Conference on Empirical Methods in Natural Language Processing*, pages 73–84.

Wang Ling, Guang Xiang, Chris Dyer, Alan Black, and Isabel Trancoso. 2013b. Microblogs as parallel corpora. In *Proceedings of the 51st Annual Meeting of the Association for Computational Linguistics (Volume 1: Long Papers)*, pages 176–186.

Spyros Matsoukas, Antti-Veikko I. Rosti, and Bing Zhang. 2009. Discriminative corpus weight estimation for machine translation. In *Proceedings of the 2009 Conference on Empirical Methods in Natural Language Processing*, pages 708–717.

Franz Josef Och and Hermann Ney. 2003. A systematic comparison of various statistical alignment models. *Computational Linguistics*, 29(1):19–51.

Kishore Papineni, Salim Roukos, Todd Ward, and Wei-Jing Zhu. 2002. BLEU: a method for automatic evaluation of machine translation. In *Proceedings of the 40th Annual Meeting of the Association for Computational Linguistics*, pages 311–318.

Maja Popović and Hermann Ney. 2011. Towards automatic error analysis of machine translation output. *Computational Linguistics*, 37(4):657–688.

Johann Roturier and Anthony Bensadoun. 2011. Evaluation of MT systems to translate user generated content. In *Proceedings of the XIII Machine Translation Summit*, pages 244–251.

Matthew Snover, Bonnie Dorr, Richard Schwartz, Linnea Micciulla, and John Makhoul. 2006. A study of translation edit rate with targeted human annotation. In *Proceedings of the Seventh Conference of the Association for Machine Translation in the Americas*, pages 223–231.

Huihsin Tseng, Pichuan Chang, Galen Andrew, Daniel Jurafsky, and Christopher Manning. 2005. A conditional random field word segmenter. In *Proceedings of the fourth SIGHAN workshop on Chinese language Processing*, volume 171, pages 168–171.

Marlies van der Wees, Arianna Bisazza, Wouter Weerkamp, and Christof Monz. 2015. What's in a domain? Analyzing genre and topic differences in statistical machine translation. In *Proceedings of the Joint Conference of the 53th Annual Meeting of the ACL and the 7th International Joint Conference on Natural Language Processing of the AFNLP*.

François Yvon. 2010. Rewriting the orthography of SMS messages. *Natural Language Engineering*, 16(2):133–159.

# A Normalizer for UGC in Brazilian Portuguese

**Magali Sanches Duran**
NILC - Center for Computational Linguistics
São Paulo University (USP)
São Carlos-SP, Brazil
magali.duran@uol.com.br

**Lucas Avanço**
NILC - Center for Computational Linguistics
São Paulo University (USP)
São Carlos-SP, Brazil
avanco89@gmail.com

**M. Graças Volpe Nunes**
NILC- Center for Computational Linguistics
São Paulo University (USP)
São Carlos-SP, Brazil
gracan@icmc.usp.br

## Abstract

User-generated contents (UGC) represent an important source of information for governments, companies, political candidates and consumers. However, most of the Natural Language Processing tools and techniques are developed from and for texts of standard language, and UGC is a type of text especially full of creativity and idiosyncrasies, which represents noise for NLP purposes. This paper presents UGCNormal, a lexicon-based tool for UGC normalization. It encompasses a tokenizer, a sentence segmentation tool, a phonetic-based speller and some lexicons, which were originated from a deep analysis of a corpus of product reviews in Brazilian Portuguese. The normalizer was evaluated in two different data sets and carried out from 31% to 89% of the appropriate corrections, depending on the type of text noise. The use of UGCNormal was also validated in a task of POS tagging, which improved from 91.35% to 93.15% in accuracy and in a task of opinion classification, which improved the average of F1-score measures (F1-score positive and F1-score negative) from 0.736 to 0.758.

## 1. Introduction

The increasing volume of text posted by users on the web is regarded as an extremely useful opportunity to reveal public opinion on many issues. For a variety of reasons, governments, companies, political candidates, and consumers want to explore such web content. This type of text is referred to in the literature as UGC (user-generated content) or EWoM (electronic word-of-mouth). However, due to the large amount of data available, it is impossible for humans to analyze all available UGC for most issues. As a result, processing and analyzing UGC became a task of NLP (Natural Language Processing). The problem is that, until now, almost all NLP tools and techniques were developed from, and for, standard language text, but UGC displays a range of creative and idiosyncratic differences, which represent noise for NLP purposes. In order to reuse the NLP tools to process UGC, the normalization or standardization of this genre of text became an essential preprocessing step, aiming to make UGC as close as possible to standard language.

The level of noise in UGC varies depending on the social media in which it is posted. Short messages (SMS and microblogs, such as Twitter) tend to be much noisier than texts posted in blogs and sites of reviews, as users need to be creative to deal with character limitations (140 characters for Twitter and 160 for SMS). The challenge for NLP is to determine the aspects in which UGC deviates from standard language and develop strategies to deal with the normalization of these aspects.

Many of UGC's deviations from standard language are motivated by wordplay (U=you, 4=for), by the need to save space (short messages have a limited length), by the influence of pronunciation, or even by a low level of literacy. Regardless of the causes of UGC deviations from standard language, if they are recurrent, they need to be addressed by normalization processes.

Some characteristics of UGC are language-independent, as the long vowels used to express emphasis (Goooooooooooooood) and the unconventional use of lower and upper cases (proper names in lowercase and common words in uppercase). Other characteristics are language-dependent, such as the apostrophe suppression in English (wont=won't) and the omission of



*Proceedings of the ACL 2015 Workshop on Noisy User-generated Text*, pages 38–47,
Beijing, China, July 31, 2015. 

diacritics and cedilla under "c" in Portuguese (eleicao=eleição).

UGC differs from the standard language mainly in the lexical level. For this reason, the normalization problem is approached by strategies of word correction (the lexical items of the UGC are treated as "errors") and strategies for machine translation (the UGC is treated as source language and the standard language as target language).

We address herein the normalization process as a set of procedures that deal with different types of deviation. The input consists of consumer reviews on electronic products. The main purpose is to convert such texts, as closely as possible, into the form expected by NLP tools trained on corpora of standard language.

This work was preceded by the detection and analysis of out-of-vocabulary[1] (OOV) words in a corpus of product reviews (Hartmann et al. 2014). In another preliminary investigation, we have found other different types of deviations and their impact on a tagging task (Duran et al., 2014). Such diagnosis has resulted in the procedures that integrate the normalization system proposed here.

The remainder of this paper is organized as follows. Section 2 presents related works. Section 3 describes the characteristics of the product review corpus and the problems they pose to normalization. Section 4 reports the methodology used to construct the normalization tool. Section 5 describes and discusses the evaluation and validation results. Finally, in Section 6, we make some final remarks and outline future work.

## 2. Related works

Text normalization is a term used to convey the idea of converting the format of a text to meet the requirements of a given purpose. There are many text normalization processes reported in the NLP literature and they vary in: i) the genre of the input text; ii) the desired output format; iii) the purpose of the normalization, and iv) the method used to perform the task. It is important to take into account such characteristics to clearly define what "text normalization" means in each context.

The input text may or may not be well-written. The task of normalizing text from a newspaper (as in Schlippe et al., 2012) is quite different from normalizing texts produced by non-professional internet users, i.e. UGC. In addition, the normalization of UGC may depend on the social media used. For example, there are substantial differences between short message texts (SMS and microblogs), on-line chats and users' reviews. Short messages and chats deviate much more from the standard language than users' reviews and are commonly regarded as "noisy texts". The normalization processes of short messages, such as SMS and Twitter messages (Contractor et. al. 2010; Liu et al. 2011; Han et al., 2013; Bali, 2013; Chrupała, 2014) and longer UGC texts, such as reviews and blogs, have much in common, but the differences are sufficiently significant to justify addressing them separately.

Different normalization purposes may require the use of substantially different normalization procedures For example, converting text-to-speech requires the expansion of acronyms and abbreviations, as well as the conversion of numeric or mathematical expressions into words (Boros et al., 2012, Schlippe et al. 2012); conversely, normalization for purpose of storing data may perform the reduction of word forms into their stems. Even a "noisy text" of UGC may be normalized for different purposes. For example, while Mosquera et al. (2012) use normalization to improve the accessibility of web content, Aw et al. (2006) and Contractor et al. (2010) see the normalization as a prerequisite for other automatic processing tasks.

Approaches to text normalization may be roughly divided into two groups: those that "translate" non-standard language into standard language using contextual information (based on language models), and those that replace OOV words (lexical-based) by suitable forms in the standard language. For the latter, lexical information is essential; for the former, parallel corpora of non-standard and standard language are required. Lexical-based approaches are commonly used to normalize general texts, whereas machine-translation approaches are usually an option to tackle SMS normalization.

Aw et al. (2006) first proposed to regard SMS normalization as a machine translation problem. Many other studies have followed this approach

[1] "Out-of-vocabulary (OOV) words are unknown words that appear in the testing speech but not in the recognition vocabulary. They are usually important content words such as names and locations, which contain information crucial to the success of many speech recognition tasks. However, most speech recognition systems are closed-vocabulary recognizers that only recognize words in a fixed finite vocabulary." IN: Long Qin. 2013. Learning Out-of-Vocabulary Words in Automatic Speech Recognition. Phd Thesis. Carnegie Mellon University. 2013.

(Contractor et al., 2010; Schlippe et al., 2012; Bali, 2013, to cite just a few). They differ in the machine translation technique adopted or in the method used to obtain the parallel corpus for training and evaluation. Aw et al. (2006) constructed a parallel corpus with 5,000 SMS, Contractor et al. (2010) generated artificial "clean" sentences in a statistical machine translation approach, and Schlippe et al. (2012) constructed a web interface to receive suggestions of clean versions of noisy sentences.

Many studies have adopted a lexical approach to normalization. For example, Liu et al., 2011, aiming to tackle SMS normalization, proposed the generation of nonstandard tokens by performing letter transformation on the dictionary words. Han et al. (2013) observed that most ill-formed tokens in Twitter are morphophonemically similar to the respective correct forms. Based on this evidence, they proposed an automatic approach to constructing a set of word variants by using edit distance and phonemic transcription; finally, they ranked the candidates using a trigram language model. Mosquera et al. (2012) developed a multilingual lexical-based approach (English and Spanish) to normalize general text from a news corpus. The approaches of Ringlstetter et al. (2006), Clark and Araki (2011), and Bildhauer and Schäfer (2013) are similar to ours, as they regard normalization as a number of subproblems to be solved in sequence. In lexical-based approaches to normalization of web content, lexicons play an important role and require constant updating to keep pace with UGC innovations.

## 3. Characteristics of User-Generated Content in product reviews

The characteristics we describe in this Section have been observed in the corpus of product reviews Buscapé, built by Hartmann et al. (2014). The corpus is the result of crawling an e-commerce search engine of same name, where users can post comments about several products. This corpus consists of 85,910 reviews, 4,097,905 tokens and 90,513 types. After removing stop words, numbers and punctuation, it has 63,917 types, from which 34,774 are OOV words. To find OOV words, we used Unitex-PB, a Brazilian Portuguese lexicon (Muniz et. al. 2005). Words that miss a diacritic (3,652 or 10.2%) were automatically corrected. From the remaining 31,123 OOV words, we analyzed 5,775, which correspond to words with more than two occurrences in the corpus. Such OOV words were classified in a double-blind annotation task, which obtained 0.752 of inter-annotator agreement (Kappa statistics, Carletta, 1996). The analysis showed that such OOV words encompass misspellings, named entities written in lowercase, foreign loan words and recurrent non-standard words in UGC (Internet slang), for which an equivalent exists in the standard language. The normalization of OOV words, therefore, depends on distinguishing these categories, as they require different procedures: misspellings require spelling correction, named entities require conversion to uppercase, foreign loan words need to be incorporated to the lexicon, and non-standard words require substitution for words from the standard language.

An in-depth analysis of the 1,323 cases classified as misspellings by both annotators (100% of inter-annotator agreement) revealed that 791 were typos, 451 were phonetically-motivated errors, 64 were misused diacritics and 14 were problems related to the recent Portuguese orthographical rules, mostly associated with the use of hyphen in compounds. As open-source Portuguese spellers do not tackle phonetically-motivated misspellings, we undertook the development of a phonetic-based speller (Avanço et al., 2014), which achieved 65.46% of first hit accuracy, against 46.94% of the open-source speller Aspell[2].

Further analysis of the corpus led us to verify that many words that require normalization were not included among the OOV words, a phenomenon known as "real-word errors". In Portuguese there are around 25,000 pairs of words that are distinguished only by diacritics and, due to the systematic absence of diacritics in UGC, such pairs of words remain indistinguishable without contextual information, as the homographs (eg: "varias" (=to vary in the second person singular in the present tense) and "várias" (=several)). There are also some non-conventional words from Internet slang (eg. "vai testa"="vai testar"=will test)) and named entities (eg. the companies Oi, Claro and Sadia), which match existing words ("testa"=forehead; "oi"=hi; "claro"=light, clear; "sadia"=healthy). Therefore, if such words are identical to other words that belong to the lexicon, they are not identified as OOV words. For this reason, the identification of

[2] http://aspell.net/

tokens that require normalization is more complex in UGC than in the standard language.

The unconventional use of case is another characteristic of UGC observed in product reviews. Frequently, capital letters are not used after punctuation as well as for proper nouns. Conversely, common words are written in capital letters to emphasize an opinion (eg. "MUITO BOM" = VERY GOOD). There are also whole reviews written in uppercase or in lowercase or even a mix as: "Fiz Contato com o Vendedor, no qual ele De forma Discarada informa ser um produto ORIGINAL!" (literally: Make Contact with a Seller and he informs In a Shameless manner to be an ORIGINAL product!"). These phenomena cause problems for the recognition of named entities and for the segmentation of sentences since both tasks use capital letters as a clue. Lexical-based strategies can help to identify named entities written in lowercase. However, as proper names and acronyms are in open classes, it is infeasible to construct a comprehensive lexicon for them. Fortunately, the product reviews have metadata that contain most of the named entities found in the respective texts, which help to construct a domain-dependent lexicon of named entities. The opposite problem also exists, that is, to decide whether a word written in uppercase is a named entity or not.

Missing punctuation is another common characteristic of product reviews, which jeopardize sentence and clause segmentations. Some reviews reproduce a kind of uninterrupted stream of consciousness, making it difficult to punctuate the text, even for a human. In addition, most product reviews consist of three sections: Pros, Cons, and General Opinion. General Opinion usually is a plain text, but Pros and Cons may present single words (Pros: inexpensive), noun phrases (Pros: battery life), bulleted lists of words and noun phrases, or complete sentences. For this reason, it is challenging to punctuate the Pros and Cons sections, and the solutions sometimes require arbitrary decisions.

In the corpus of product reviews, unlike in short messages, word abbreviations, agglutination of several tokens into a single one, and suppression of grammatical words rarely occur .

## 4. A lexicon-based approach to UGC normalization

The nature of the deviations described in Section 3 have motivated us to develop a normalization tool tailored for product reviews. The goal is to normalize the deviations due to: 1) the case use, in what concerns the use of lowercase instead of uppercase; 2) the correction of misspellings, except for those cases that depend on contextual clues to disambiguate two existing words in Portuguese; 3) the substitution of Internet slang by standard language words, and 4) the insertion of missing periods (other punctuation marks will be addressed in future work).

One of the challenges of building a normalization tool refers to how to combine different normalization procedures in such a way that the effect of a procedure does not jeopardize the subsequent ones. For example, there are non-standard words from Internet slang as well as named entities written in lowercase among the OOV words. They need to be identified and protected from spelling correction.

The proposed pipeline architecture of the UGC Normalizer Tool (UCGNormal) is presented in Fig. 1.

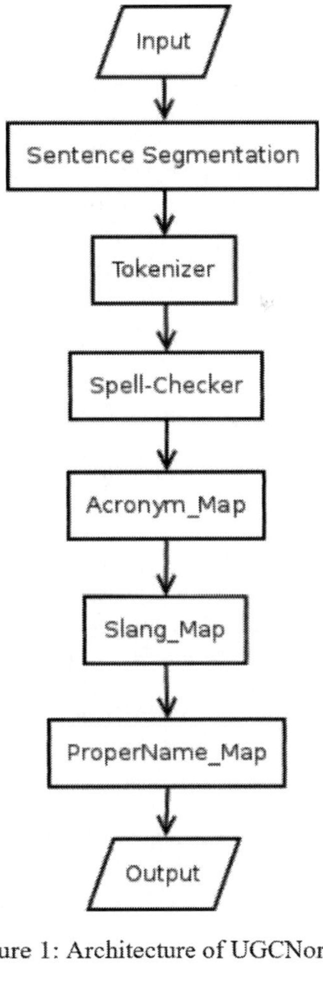


Figure 1: Architecture of UGCNormal

The input is a UGC text written in Brazilian Portuguese. The first step consists in applying the sentence segmentation tool proposed in Condori and Pardo (2015), which is a machine learning-based system trained in a journalistic corpus. It allows us to insert periods where they are missing and, consequently, to properly convert the initial words to uppercase. When evaluated in the Buscapé corpus, it achieved 0.953 for precision; 0.895 for recall; and 0.921 for F-Measure.

Subsequently, the sentences are tokenized, specifically accounting for the nature of UGC texts. Usually, tokenizers consider only blank spaces, punctuation, and few special symbols. However, when processing UGC, it is necessary to consider the occurrence of more complex tokens, like emoticons ( ' :) ', ' :-) ', ' :( ', etc.), units of measurement ('1GB', '100Kb', '2mb', etc.), and URL's. In order to properly identify and split tokens like those, we have developed a tokenizer using GNU-Flex lexical analyzer tool.

The lexicon-based Spell-Checker developed by Avanço et al. (2014) does the major part of the normalization process. It was specially developed to tackle phonetically-motivated misspellings, i.e. words written as they are pronounced. Another important characteristic of this speller is the automatic correction, as it does not presuppose user interaction. Therefore, instead of suggesting some candidates for correction, it automatically replaces the misspelled word with the best-ranked candidate. In such a scenario, the accuracy of the first hit is essential.

In short, the algorithm consists of (a) identifying misspelt words, using the UNITEX-PB[3] lexicon; b) generating candidates for the substitute word by using the edit distance (Levenshtein, 1966); (c) ranking the candidates by considering corpus-based frequency information; (d) looking for phonetic similarities by using several specific rules for Portuguese and using a variation of the Soundex[4] algorithm.

For UGCNormal, we made major improvements to the original algorithm of the speller, as well as adapting it to fit in the pipeline. As many misspellings are related to the omission of diacritics and cedilla under "c", we have incorporated some heuristics to correct this kind of error before the generation of candidates.

As the correction of real-word errors is a hard context-dependent problem, this phonetic-based speller cannot handle them well. In order to overcome this limitation, we applied a simple strategy that enables the correction of some real-word errors without contextual information. For this, we have compiled, from the lexicon Unitex-PB, a list of 25,722 pairs of words that differ from each other by a single diacritic. From this list, we analyzed the pairs that differ in morphological tags (2,877), and selected 561 pairs of a highly frequent word and a highly infrequent word (eg. "óbvio" (=obvious) and "obvio" (an inflection of "obviar"=to obviate). The infrequent word was then excluded from the lexicon in order to enable the speller to eventually correct the more frequent one.

The remaining pairs are not addressed by the tool since the frequency of the words is similar. The most serious problem is related to pairs of frequent words, like "e" (=and) and "é" (=is); "da" (=of the) and "dá" (third person of the verb "dar"=to give).

Another modification was made in the speller to prevent the correction of acronyms and Internet slang. Foreign loan words and proper nouns have been incorporated to the lexicon, which is used to identify misspelled words and to generate candidates for misspelling correction. This decision was motivated by the high frequency of misspelled technology jargon in the domain of product reviews (eg. "desing" instead of "design" and "Blutoth" instead of "Bluetooth").

The lexical resources, created especially for this, comprise: Internet slang (420 items), foreign loan words (248 items), proper nouns (20,730 items), and acronyms (156 items). These sets of items were partially compiled by Hartmann et al., (2014) and further complemented during the analysis of the corpus.

The module Acronym_Map sets all letters to uppercase whenever it detects an acronym (the detection of acronyms is based on the lexicon). The module Slang_Map substitutes some frequent slang words by their equivalent in standard language and normalizes long vowels by using regular expressions. There are two types of Internet slangs: 1) those that can be identified in a lexical-based approach (eg. "vc"="você"; "tb"= "também"), and 2) those that have a homonym in the standard language, as "fala" in "vo fala" (="vou falar"=I will speak) and "fala" (=he/she speaks; speech). Here we deal only with the correction of the first kind, as the second kind requires context knowledge to be identified and

[3] http://www.nilc.icmc.usp.br/nilc/projects/unitex-pb/web/dicionarios.html

[4] http://www.archives.gov/research/census/soundex.html

corrected. All these modules use their own lexicons as well as a set of regular expressions for recognizing the items.

The last module, ProperName_Map, uses a lexicon of named entities, which consists of 8,465 proper nouns from the NILC Lexicon (Nunes et al., 1996). We have also added a further 12,265 proper nouns, consisting of product names including brands and models. These were extracted from the metadata available in the Buscapé corpus, and the addition of these resulted in 20,730 lexical items. When a proper noun is recognized, this module capitalizes it. However, detection of proper nouns written in lowercase is far from a simple task, because many proper nouns are also common words in the language lexicon, as mentioned in Section 3. Although there are some named entity recognizer (NER) systems for Portuguese, they do not perform well for UGC, since they heavily rely on the occurrence of a capital letter starting the proper nouns, and the problem is in discovering proper nouns that are not capitalized. That is why we have adopted a domain and lexical-based approach.

## 5. UGCNormal Evaluation

We evaluated the normalization tool intrinsically, in two corpus, and extrinsically, in a POS tag task and in an Opinion Classifier.

### 5.1. Intrinsic Evaluation

In the intrinsic evaluation we used two samples, one from the Buscapé corpus, and one from another corpus of the same genre, extracted from the e-commerce website Mercado Livre, which constitutes unseen data. In both cases, a sample of 60 product reviews was manually annotated with respect to punctuation errors, case use, and misspellings.

Our two samples (random selection from both corpora) are described in Table 1.

Table 1: Samples' statistics

| | **Buscapé Sample** | **Mercado Livre Sample** |
|---|---|---|
| reviews | 60 | 60 |
| tokens | 3,179 | 3,897 |
| tokens without stop-words | 2,061 | 2,732 |
| tokens without stop-words and punctuation marks | 1,563 | 1,967 |
| types | 887 | 1,096 |

Table 2 shows the recall figures of UGCNormal in both samples. The second and third columns contain X/Y=Z, where X shows the number of items to be normalized, Y shows the number of correctly normalized items, and Z shows the corresponding accuracy rate. As expected, the results in the Buscapé corpus (used for diagnosis) are better than in Mercado Livre, because some lexical resources were constructed from analysis of OOV words in Buscapé. In spite of both samples having the same number of reviews, the Mercado Livre sample contains proportionally more items to be normalized than the Buscapé sample, that is, the reviews from Mercado Livre deviate more from standard language than those from Buscapé.

For the misspellings whose corrections are context-free, UGCNormal achieved a recall of 89% in Buscapé corpus and 80% in Mercado Livre corpus. This difference may be due to the small size of both samples and the number of misspellings (in Mercado Livre there are almost twice as many misspellings as in Buscapé).

Table 2: Distribution of errors and corrections for each UGC sample, and the recall values for each error type.

| **Error type** | **Buscapé** | **Mercado Livre** | **Average** |
|---|---|---|---|
| common misspellings | **50/56 = 0.89** | **87/108 = 0.80** | **0.84** |
| real-word misspellings | **15/39 = 0.38** | **24/76 = 0.31** | **0.34** |
| internet slang | **4/6 = 0.67** | **15/25 = 0.60** | **0.61** |
| case use (proper names and acronyms) | **11/12 = 0.92** | **13/19 = 0.68** | **0.77** |
| case use (start of sentence) | **14/14 = 1.00** | **7/12 = 0.58** | **0.81** |
| glued words | **0/2 = 0** | **2/6 = 0.33** | **0.25** |
| punctuation | **44/47 = 0.94** | **58/79 = 0.73** | **0.81** |

We evaluated the task noise removal in a single pass, identifying and correcting errors simultaneously. Therefore, cases where errors were identified but not corrected were taken to be failures just like unidentified errors.

However, it is worth mentioning that the normalizer failed to correct 6 true errors identified in the Buscapé sample and 14 true errors identified in the Mercado Livre sample. The other non-corrected errors were not even identified.

The normalization tool corrected 66% (138 of 209) of the manually annotated errors in the Buscapé sample, and 63% (206 of 325) in the Mercado Livre sample.

Misspellings whose correction depends on contextual information were not expected to be corrected, as the speller is based only on lexical information. However, thanks to the strategy of excluding highly infrequent words that are homographs of frequent words without diacritics, some such errors were corrected (38% of the annotated errors of such category in Buscapé and 31% in Mercado Livre).

The case use in the start of sentences and the punctuation are treated by the sentence segmentation tool. These procedures are simultaneous: if a punctuation mark is not inserted, the initial word after a period is consequently not converted into uppercase. In the Mercado Livre corpus, the use of uppercase and lowercase is far more unconventional than in the Buscapé corpus and this explains the deterioration of results in case use and punctuation. For example, in Mercado Livre, unlike in Buscapé, we found reviews completely written in uppercase.

The conversion of proper nouns and acronyms to uppercase, as well as the conversion of Internet slangs to the standard language, are two issues that depend on the respective lexicons. As such, lexicons resulting from the analysis of the Buscapé corpus are not sufficient to identify all the proper nouns, acronyms and Internet slangs from the Mercado Livre corpus.

Finally, the glued words are normalized by the tokenizer only in cases where numbers are followed by units of measurement. Glued words are rare in both evaluated corpora, but we need to tackle them in the future if we want to address other categories of UGC, such as chats and short messages.

UGCNormal made 149 corrections in the Buscapé sample, of which 138 were true positives and 11 were false positives (well-formed words that were incorrectly modified), representing a precision of 93%. In the Mercado Livre sample, UGCNormal made 220 corrections, of which 206 were true positives and 14 were false positives, also representing a precision of 93%.

From the 82 OOV words in the Buscapé sample, UGCNormal corrected 65 (79%), and the remaining 17 words are constituted of 6 (7.3%) true errors and 11 (13.4%) real words.

In the Mercado Livre sample, UGCNormal identified 145 OOV words and appropriately corrected 117 (80.6%). From the remaining 28 OOV words, 14 (9.6%) are true errors and 14 (9.6%) are real words.

The false positives (real words identified as errors) are mainly foreign loan words, proper nouns, acronyms and Internet slang absent from the UGCNormal's lexicons.

### 5.2. Extrinsic Evaluation

To validate the normalization tool, we evaluated its impact as a preprocessing step in two NLP tasks: POS tagging and opinion classification.

For the first task, we used the tagger MXPOST (Ratnaparkhi, 1996), trained in the MAC-Morpho corpus (1.2 million tokens, Aluisio et al., 2003). The better reported results of MXPOST are around 97%, for journalistic texts, the same genre used to train the tagger.

For this experiment, we first randomly selected a sample of ten reviews from the Buscapé corpus. Then we tagged the sample with MXPOST and performed a linguistic revision of the POS tags, in order to create a gold-standard POS-tagged version of the sample. Subsequently, we POS-tagged three different versions of the same sample: 1) the original one; 2) a version manually normalized, and 3) a version automatically normalized by UGCNormal. The results of the three versions evaluated against the gold-standard version are presented in the Table 3.

Table 3: The number of correct tags produced by the tagger, for each sample version.

| | Without Normaliz. | After Human Normaliz. | After Automatic Normaliz. |
|---|---|---|---|
| Correct tags | 1120 | 1145 | 1142 |
| Accuracy - MXPOST | 91.35% | 93.39% | 93.15% |

The accuracy values are the ratio between the number of correct tags and the total number of tags (1226). The result achieved by the automatically normalized version (UGCNormal) is almost the same as that achieved by the human normalized version.

We have also made a test of statistical significance to evaluate the probability that such improvement in the tagger precision could have been obtained by chance. Given the sample size and some relevant considerations while evaluating NLP tasks (Sogaard et al., 2014), we opted for the non-parametric test Wilcoxon Signed-Rank. We observed a significance of 0.05, the p-value being equal to 0.02249.

The other extrinsic evaluation is based on a lexicon-based opinion classifier (Avanço and Nunes, 2014), which assigns polarity to texts (positive, negative or neutral). We applied the classifier on a sample of 13,685 reviews (6,812 positives and 6,873 negatives) extracted from the Buscapé corpus, before and after normalization by UGCNormal. The average of F1-score measures (F1-score positive and F1-score negative) was 0.736 for non-normalized texts, and 0.758 for normalized texts.

The performance of a lexicon-based opinion classifier is highly dependent of the recognition of sentiment words in the text. As errors like "exelente" (excelente=excellent) and "otimo" (ótimo=great) are very frequent, such improvement in the precision, after normalization, was expected.

### 5.3 Some limitations of the normalization tool

The UGCNormal corrects a few real-word misspellings thanks to the strategy of extracting from UNITEX-PB those infrequent words that are homographs (except by the diacritics) of frequent words. However, many real-word misspellings remain unsolved, as those corrections would require contextual information. This problem is more serious when the homographs are very frequent words, such as "esta" (=this) and "está" (=is). Besides homographs, we also have to deal with the homophone words (those with identical pronunciation), which also frequently cause real-word misspellings, such as "segmento" (=segment) and "seguimento" (=follow up).

The normalization of acronyms, Internet slang, and proper names is dependent on their respective lexicons, which are not only domain-dependent, but also corpus-dependent, as we observed in the evaluation. The lexicons have been constructed with data from the Buscapé corpus and this justifies the best performance of the normalizer in such corpus.

The normalization of punctuation presupposes a plain text. For this reason, some product reviews that consist of simple items or noun phrases are difficult to normalize. If each item starts with uppercase, the sentence segmentation tool inserts a period after each item. Conversely, if an item starts in lower case and there is another item in the sequence, the sentence segmentation tool does not insert periods.

Another problem that remains unsolved is related to common words written in uppercase. We only convert uppercase to lowercase when the whole review is in uppercase. Otherwise, we maintain the uppercase, because it may indicate an acronym or a proper noun.

## 6. Final remarks and future work

The UGCNormal performance ranges from an average of 25% (for glued words) to 84% (for common misspellings). The validation of the tool shows that the results of both POS tagging and opinion classification tasks improved around by two percentage points after normalization.

Although there is no all-purpose normalization process, it is possible to reuse some modules of a normalization pipeline, assembling them differently in order to suit another purpose. The proposed normalization tool will certainly be useful for the development of UGC normalization tools that encompass short messages normalization. In order to be suitable for short messages normalization, this tool needs to address some problems related to word agglutination and informal abbreviations of nouns with stem preservation.

This normalizer evolved from a phonetic-based speller aimed at tackling common errors in UGC (words written as they are pronounced). Our approach is largerly dependent on lexical resources, incurring a high maintenance cost. In addition, this normalizer does not perform well with real-word errors. We believe that machine learning approaches will enable us to overcome these shortcomings. We have, indeed, made some preliminary experiments with language models, but the high occurrence of false positives (well-written words wrongly corrected) remains as a challenge.

## Acknowledgements

Part of the results presented in this paper were obtained through research activity in the project entitled "Semantic Processing of Texts in Brazilian Portuguese", sponsored by Samsung Eletrônica da Amazônia Ltda. under the terms of Brazilian federal law number 8.248/91.

## References


Aluísio, S. M.; Pelizzoni, J. M.; Marchi, A. R.; Oliveira, L. H.; Manenti, R.; Marquivafável, V. (2003). An account of the challenge of tagging a reference corpus of Brazilian Portuguese. In: *Proceedings of PROPOR'2003*. Springer Verlag, 2003, pp. 110-117.

Avanço, L. V., Duran, M. S.; Nunes, M. G. V. (2014) Towards a Phonetic Brazilian Portuguese Spell Checker. *TorPorEsp - Workshop on Tools and Resources for Automatically Processing Portuguese and Spanish.* Available at: http://www.lbd.dcc.ufmg.br/bdbcomp/servlet/Evento?id=755.).

Avanço, L. V.; Nunes, M. G. V. (2014). Lexicon-based sentiment analysis for reviews of products in Brazilian Portuguese. *Proceedings of the Brazilian Conference on Intelligent Systems* (BRACIS) - 2014, October 18-23, 2014, in São Carlos, SP, Brazil, pp. 277–281.

Aw, A.; Zhang, M.; Xiao, J.;Su, J. (2006) A phrase-based statistical model for SMS text normalization. In *Proceedings of COLING 2006*. ACL.

Bali, R. (2013) A Theoretical Review on SMS Normalization using Hidden Markov Models (HMMs). *International Journal of Computer Trends and Technology* (IJCTT), V.4 (7):2388-2387 July Issue 2013 .ISSN 2231-2803.www.ijcttjournal.org. Published by Seventh Sense Research Group.

Bildhauer, F.; Schäfer, R. (2013) Token-level noise in large Web corpora and non-destructive normalization for linguistic applications. In: *Proceedings of Corpus Analysis with Noise in the Signal* (CANS 2013).

Boros, T.; Stefănescu, D.; Ion, R. (2012) Bermuda, a data-driven tool for phonetic transcription of words info. *Proceedings of Natural Language Processing for Improving Textual Accessibility* (NLP4ITA) Workshop.

Carletta, J. (1996). Assessing Agreement on Classification Tasks: The Kappa Statistic. *Computational Linguistics*, vol. 22, n. 2, pp. 249--254.

Chrupała, G. (2014). Normalizing tweets with edit scripts and recurrent neural embeddings. In *Proceedings of the 52nd Annual Meeting of the Association for Computational Linguistics* (Volume 2: Short Papers), pp. 680-686

Clark, E., & Araki, K. (2011). Text normalization in social media: progress, problems and applications for a pre-processing system of casual English. *Procedia-Social and Behavioral Sciences*, 27, 2-11.

Condori, R. E. L.; Pardo, T. A. S. (2015) Experiments on Sentence Boundary Detection in User-Generated Web Content. In: 16th International Conference on Intelligent Text Processing and Computational Linguistics, 2015, Cairo. *Proceedings of the 16th International Conference on Intelligent Text Processing and Computational Linguistics*, 2015. v. 9041. p. 227-237.

Contractor, D.; Faruquie, T. A.; Subramaniam, V. (2010) Unsupervised cleansing of noisy text. *Coling 2010: Poster Volume*, pages 189–196, Beijing, August 2010.

Duran, M. S.; Avanço, L. V., Pardo, T. A. S.; Aluísio, S. M.; Nunes, M. G. V. Some issues on the normalization of a corpus of products reviews in Portuguese. In: Felix Bildhauer & Roland Schäfer (eds.), *Proceedings of the 9th Web as Corpus Workshop* (WaC-9) EACL 2014, pages 22–28, Gothenburg, Sweden, April 26 2014. 2014 Association for Computational Linguistics.

Han, B.;Cook, P.; Baldwin, T. (2013) Lexical Normalisation of Short Text Messages. *ACM Transactions on Intelligent Systems and Technology* 4(1), pp. 5:15:27.

Hartmann, N. S.; Avanço. L.; Balage, P. P.; Duran, M. S.; Nunes, M. G. V.; Pardo, T.; Aluísio, S. (2014). A Large Opinion Corpus in Portuguese - Tackling Out-Of-Vocabulary Words. In: *Proceedings of the Ninth International Conference on Language Resources and Evaluation* (LREC 2014).

Levenshtein, V. I. (1966) Binary codes capable of correcting deletions, insertions, and reversals. *Soviet Physics Doklady*, 1966.

Liu, F.; Weng, F.; Wang, B.; Liu, Y. (2011) Insertion, Deletion, or Substitution? Normalizing Text Messages without Pre-categorization nor Supervision. *Proceedings of the 49th Annual Meeting of the Association for Computational Linguistics*:shortpapers, pages 71–76, Portland, Oregon, June 19-24, 2011. Association for Computational Linguistics.

Mosquera, A.;Lloret, E.; Moreda, P. (2012) Towards Facilitating the Accessibility of Web 2.0 Texts through Text Normalisation. *Proceedings of Natural Language Processing for Improving Textual Accessibility* (NLP4ITA) Workshop.

Muniz, M.C.M.; Nunes, M.G.V.; Laporte. E. (2005) "UNITEX-PB, a set of flexible language resources for Brazilian Portuguese", *Proceedings of the Workshop on Technology of Information and Human Language* (TIL), São Leopoldo (Brazil): Unisinos.

Nunes, M.G.V.; Vieira, F. M. C.; Zavaglia, C.; Sossolote, C. R. C.; Hernandez, J. (1996) (In Portuguese) The design of a Lexicon for Brazilian Portuguese: Lessons learned and Perspectives. *Proceedings of the II Workshop on Computational Processing of Written and Speak Portuguese.* CEFET-PR, Curitiba, October 23-25, p. 61-70.

Ratnaparkhi, A. (1996). A maximum entropy model for part-of-speech tagging. In: *Proceedings of the conference on empirical methods in natural language processing* (Vol. 1, pp. 133-142).

Ringlstetter, C.; Schulz, K. U.; Mihov, S. (2006). Orthographic Errors in Web Pages: Toward Cleaner Web Corpora. In: *Computational Linguistics* Volume 32, Number 3, p. 295-340.

Schlippe, T.; Zhu, C.; Gebhardt, J.; Schultz, T. (2010). Text normalization based on statistical machine translation and internet user support. *Interspeech*, 2010, pp. 1816-1819.

Søgaard, A., Johannsen, A., Plank, B., Hovy, D., & Martinez, H. (2014). What's in a p-value in NLP? In: *Proceedings of the eighteenth conference on computational natural language learning* (CONLL'14), pp. 1-10.

# USFD: Twitter NER with Drift Compensation and Linked Data

**Leon Derczynski**
University of Sheffield, UK
leon@dcs.shef.ac.uk

**Isabelle Augenstein**
University of Sheffield, UK
isabelle@dcs.shef.ac.uk

**Kalina Bontcheva**
University of Sheffield, UK
kalina@dcs.shef.ac.uk

**Abstract**

This paper describes a pilot NER system for Twitter, comprising the USFD system entry to the W-NUT 2015 NER shared task. The goal is to correctly label entities in a tweet dataset, using an inventory of ten types. We employ structured learning, drawing on gazetteers taken from Linked Data, and on unsupervised clustering features, and attempting to compensate for stylistic and topic drift – a key challenge in social media text. Our result is competitive; we provide an analysis of the components of our methodology, and an examination of the target dataset in the context of this task.

## 1 Introduction

Social media is a very challenging genre for Natural Language Processing (NLP) (Derczynski et al., 2013a), providing high-volume linguistically idiosyncratic text rich in latent signals, the correct interpretation of which requires diverse contextual and author-based information. Consequently, this noisy content renders NLP systems trained on more consistent, longer documents, such as newswire, mostly impotent (Derczynski et al., 2015b). Suffering from a sustained dearth of annotated Twitter datasets, it may be useful to understand what makes this genre tick, and how our existing techniques and resources can be generalised better to fit such a challenging text source.

This paper has focused on introducing our Named Entity Recognition (NER) entry to the WNUT evaluation challenge (Baldwin et al., 2015), which builds on our earlier experiments with Twitter and news NER (Derczynski and Bontcheva, 2014; Bontcheva et al., 2013; Cunningham et al., 2002). In particular, we push data sources and representations, using what is know about Twitter so far to construct a model that informs our choices. Specifically, we attempt to compensate for entity drift; to harness unsupervised word clustering in a principled fashion; to bring in large-scale gazetteers; to attenuate the impact of terms frequent in this text type; and to pick and choose targeted gazetteers for specific entity types.

## 2 Datasets

The training and development sets provided with the challenge were drawn from the Ritter et al. (2011) corpus. This was a set of 2394 tweets from late 2010, annotated with ten entity types, including the "other" type. A later release in the challenge gave a set of 420 tweets from 2015, annotated in the same way (*dev_2015*). As no other tweet corpora use this 10-class entity model, we stuck with this data for the supervised parts of our approach.

For language modelling, we used a set of 250 million tweets drawn from the Twitter garden hose, which is a fair 10% sample of all tweets (Kergl et al., 2014). These were reduced to just English tweets using langid.py (Lui and Baldwin, 2012), and then tokenized using the twokenizer tool (Connor et al., 2010), which gives the same tokenization as used in the input and evaluation corpora.

In addition, we used three sources of gazetteers. The first two were manually created, and covered named temporal expressions (Brucato et al., 2013) and first person names (Cunningham et al., 2002). The last comprised more recent data, drawn automatically from Freebase as part of a distant supervision approach to entity detection and relation annotation (Augenstein et al., 2014).

## 3 Method

The WNUT Twitter NER task required us to address many data sparsity challenges. Firstly, the datasets involved are simply very small, making it hard to generalise in supervised learning, and meaning that effect sizes cannot be reliably measured. Secondly, Twitter language is arguably one of the noisiest and idiosyncratic text genres, which manifests as a large number of word types, and very large vocabularies due to lexical variation (Eisenstein, 2013). Thirdly, the language and especially entities found in tweets change over time, which is commonly referred to as *drift*. The majority of the WNUT training data is from 2010, and only a small amount from 2015, leading to a sparsity in examples of modern language. Therefore, in our machine learning approach, many of the features we introduce are there to combat sparsity.



*Proceedings of the ACL 2015 Workshop on Noisy User-generated Text*, pages 48–53,
Beijing, China, July 31, 2015. 

### 3.1 Unsupervised Clustering

We use an unsupervised clustering of terms to generate word type features. The goal of this is to gain a progressive reduction in the profusion of word types intrinsic to the text type. 250 million tweets from 2010-2012 were used to generate 2,000 word classes using Brown clustering (Brown et al., 1992). Typically 1,000 or fewer are used; the larger number of classes was chosen because it helpfully increased the expressivity of the representation (Derczynski et al., 2015a), while retaining a useful sparsity reduction. These hierarchical classes were represented using bit depths of 3-10 inclusive, and then 12, 14, 16, 18 and 20, one feature per depth. The typical levels are 4, 6, 10 and 20, though selection of bit depths to use often yields brittle feature sets (Koo et al., 2008), and so we leave it to the classifier to decide which ones are useful. These choices are examined in our post-exercise investigations into the model, Section 5.1, and the clusters provided with this paper. Finally, we also include the Brown class paths for the previous token.

To aid in filtering out common tokens and reducing the impact they may have as e.g. spurious gazetteer matches, we incorporate a term frequency from our language model. This is applied to terms that are in the top 50,000 found in our garden hose sample, and represented as a feature having a value scaled in proportion to the term's relative frequency, multiplied by 100 to reduce underflows and ensure it has an effective impact.

### 3.2 Morpho-Syntactic Features

To model context, we used reasonably conventional features: the token itself, the uni- and bigrams in a $[-2, 2]$ offset window from the current token, and both wordshape (e.g. *London* becomes *Xxxxxx*) and reduced wordshape (*London* to *Xx*) features.

We also included a part-of-speech tag for each token. These were automatically generated by a custom tweet PoS tagger using an extension of the PTB tagset (Derczynski et al., 2013b).

To capture orthographic information, we take suffix and prefix features of length $[1..3]$.

Capitalisation is notoriously unreliable in tweets, and also often overfitted to by newswire systems trained on more canonical forms of text. To wean these systems away from capitals while trying to minimise false negatives, we used case-insensitive gazetteers to generate gazetteer features.

### 3.3 Gazetteers

While we collected and experimented with a variety of gazetteers, the most helpful ones were:

- Freebase gazetteers mined for distant supervision (Augenstein et al., 2014);
- ANNIE first name lists (Cunningham et al., 2002);
- First name trigger terms (Derczynski and Bontcheva, 2014);
- Lists of named temporal expressions (Brucato et al., 2013), used due to the prevalence of festival and event names in the *other* category.

| NE type | Freebase type |
|---|---|
| company | /business/business_operation, /organization/organization |
| facility | /architecture/building, /architecture/structure, /travel/tourist_attraction |
| geo-loc | /location/location |
| movie | /film/film |
| musicartist | music/artist |
| other | /education/university, /time/holiday, /time/recurring_event |
| person | /people/person |
| product | /business/consumer_product, /business/brand, /computer/software, /computer/operating_system, /computer/programming_language, /digicams/digital_camera, /cvg/computer_videogame, /cvg/cvg_platform, /food/food, /food/beverage, /food/tea, /food/beer, /food/brewery_brand_of_beer, /food/candy_bar, /food/cheese, /food/dish, /wine/wine /distilled_spirits/distilled_spirit |
| sportsteam | /sports/sports_team |
| tvshow | /tv/tv_program |

Table 1: NE types and corresponding Freebase types used for creating gazetteers

Freebase (Bollacker et al., 2008) is a large knowledge base consisting of around 3 billion facts[1]. As such, it has been used extensively as background knowledge for NLP tasks such as entity and relation extraction (Augenstein et al., 2014). Gazetteers for the 10 entity types were retrieved from Freebase semi-automatically. Some of the types correspond to Freebase types directly, e.g. person corresponds to /people/*person*, but for other types such as *product* there are no directly corresponding types. To build gazetteers, we therefore retrieved all Freebase types for all entities in the training corpus and selected the most prominent Freebase types per entity type in the gold standard. The list of Freebase types corresponding to each entity type in the gold standard is listed in Table 1.

For each Freebase type, separate gazetteers were created for entity names and alternative names (aliases), since the latter tend to be of lower quality.

There were several other gazetteer sources that we tried but which did not work very well: IMDb dumps,[2] Ritter's LabeledLDA lists (Ritter et al., 2011) (duplicated in the baseline system), and ANNIE's other

[1] The Freebase project is being discontinued as of May 2015, however, the data is being integrated with Wikidata (Vrandečić and Krötzsch, 2014). `https://plus.google.com/109936836907132434202/posts/3aYFVNf92A1`

[2] See http://www.imdb.com/interfaces

| Entity type | P | R | F1 |
|---|---|---|---|
| company | 28.07 | 41.03 | 33.33 |
| facility | 25.00 | 23.68 | 24.32 |
| geo-loc | 53.91 | 53.45 | 53.68 |
| movie | 20.00 | 6.67 | 10.00 |
| musicartist | 14.29 | 2.44 | 4.17 |
| other | 45.78 | 28.79 | 35.35 |
| person | 54.63 | 65.50 | 59.57 |
| product | 27.78 | 13.51 | 18.18 |
| sportsteam | 42.86 | 25.71 | 32.14 |
| tvshow | 0.00 | 0.00 | 0.00 |
| Overall | 45.72 | 39.64 | 42.46 |
| No types | 63.81 | 56.28 | 59.81 |

Table 2: Results of the USFD W-NUT 2015 system.

gazetteers (largely consisting of organisations, locations, and date entities) en masse. Each of these introduced a drop in performance or an unstable performance, possibly due to the increased ambiguity. This is a known problem with discriminative learning – only a certain amount of gazetteers may be used as features in this way before performance of a discriminative learner drops (Smith and Osborne, 2006).

### 3.4 Learning Models and Representation

As BIO NE chunking is readily framed as a sequence labeling problem, we experimented with structured learning. Out of CRF using L-BFGS updates, CRF with passive-aggressive updates to combat Twitter noise (Derczynski and Bontcheva, 2014), and structured perceptron (also useful on Twitter noise (Johannsen et al., 2014)), CRF L-BFGS provided the best performance on our dataset for the ten-types task.

### 3.5 Training Data

In our final system, we included the dev_2015 data, to combat drift present in the corpus. We anticipated that the test set would be from 2015. The original dataset was harvested in 2010, long enough ago to be demonstrably disadvantaged when compared with modern data (Fromreide et al., 2014), and so it was critical to include something more. The compensate for the size imbalance – the dev_2015 data is 0.175 the size of the 2010 data – we weighted down the older dataset to by 0.7, as suggested by (Cherry and Guo, 2015), implemented by uniformly scaling individual feature values on older instances. This successfully reduced the negative impact of the inevitable drift.

## 4 Performance

Our results are given in Table 2. As can be seen, the best results were achieved for the person and geo-loc entity types. It is also worth noting that performance on the notypes task is significantly better across all metrics, which indicates that the system is capable of identifying entities correctly, but encounters issues with their type classification.

We found that the biggest contributions to our system's performance were the Freebase gazetteer features, and using Brown clusters with high values of $m$ (the number of classes) and large amounts of recent input data. This led our computational efforts in the last week to be based around running the biggest Brown clustering task that we could in time.

We also noted during testing that, while passive-aggressive CRF updates helped with single-type entity recognition in tweets (Derczynski and Bontcheva, 2014), it was detrimental to an all-types system. It was also not helpful for the no-types task, where L-BFGS updates again gave better performance. This is rational: the all-types and multiple-types tasks are effectively similar when contrasted with the single-types task, in that they require the recognition of many different kinds of named entity.

Finally, we found that other gazetteer types were not helpful to performance; taking for example all of the ANNIE gazetteers, gazetteers from IMDb dumps, entity names extracted from other Twitter NER corpora, or entities generated through LLDA (Ritter et al., 2011) all decreased performance. We suspect this is due to their swamping already-small input dataset with too great a profusion of information, c.f. Smith and Osborne (2006).

In addition, we tried generating semi-supervised data using vote-constrained bootstrapping, but this was not helpful either – presumably due to the initially low performance of machine-learning based tools on Twitter NER making it hard to develop semi-supervised bootstrapped training data, no matter how stringent the filtering of autogenerated examples.

For the final run, we were faced with a decision about fitting. We could either choose a configuration that minimised training loss on all the available training data (train + dev + dev_2015), but risked overfitting to it. Alternatively, we could choose a configuration that fit less well, in order to avoid overfitting. In the end, we decided to adopt the above principled approach, assuming that final data would be from 2015, and therefore down-weighting training data from prior years. We also evaluated the system while including the dev_2015 data in the training set, to see how well we would match it.

## 5 Analysis

### 5.1 Features

In terms of features, we looked at the strongest-weighted observations in the notypes model, to see what the general indicators are of named entities in tweets. The largest of these are shown in Table 3. Of note is that features indicating URLs, hashtags and usernames indicate against an entity; lowercase words including punctuation, or comprising only punctuation, are not entities; being proceeded by *at* indicates being in an entity (+ve B weight and -ve O weight); being preceded by *of*, *and* or *with* suggests an entity; short words and hashtag-shaped words are not entities; being followed by *tonight* suggests being inside an entity;

| Features | Label | Weight |
| --- | --- | --- |
| pref=@ | O | 3.368445 |
| pref=htt | O | 2.049354 |
| pref=# | O | 1.979034 |
| shapeshort-x.x | O | 1.688033 |
| shapeshort-. | O | 1.552530 |
| w[-1]=at | B | 1.519609 |
| p14x11110011111011 | O | 1.326481 |
| w[-1]=at | O | -1.285570 |
| w[-1]=of | O | -1.244912 |
| length-2 | O | 1.196777 |
| length-3 | O | 1.177138 |
| shapeshort-x. | O | 1.172663 |
| in_gaz=Freebase_ videogameplatform | O | -1.152093 |
| w[-1]=and | O | -1.143885 |
| length-1 | B | -1.132128 |
| shapeshort-Xx | O | -1.128341 |
| w[-1]=with | O | -1.093224 |
| w[1]=tonight | O | -1.077982 |
| shapeshort-0 | B | -1.051406 |

Table 3: Largest weighted features in notypes model

| Features | Label Weight | Terms |
| --- | --- | --- |
| prev_p3x011 | B-geo-loc | -0.571505 |
| p14x11110011111001 | B-other | -0.585369 |
| prev_p6x111100 | B-company | -0.604976 |
| p12x111100111110 | B-geo-loc | -0.620909 |
| prev_p4x0100 | B-person | -0.655420 |
| prev_p18x0000111110 | B-facility | 0.699101 |
| prev_p20x0000111110 | B-facility | 0.699101 |
| prev_p3x010 | B-sportsteam | 0.709865 |
| p10x0110011010 | B-tvshow | 0.714127 |
| p3x011 | B-person | -0.717037 |
| p14x11110011111001 | B-product | 0.747492 |
| prev_p8x11110110 | B-other | 0.774895 |
| p14x11110011111100 | B-geo-loc | 0.804635 |
| prev_p3x010 | B-person | -0.894333 |
| p12x111100111111 | B-geo-loc | 0.895203 |
| p14x11110011110110 | B-person | 0.950866 |
| p14x11110011111000 | B-company | 1.044984 |

Table 4: Largest-weighted Brown cluster features in 10-types task

numbers rarely start entities; and being matched by an entry in the video games gazetteer suggests being an entity.

One cluster prefix was indicative of being outside an entity. This cluster prefix contained four subclusters, each dominated by lot of frequently-occurring dates (e.g. *September* with 12368 mentions in the source data) and less-frequent date spellings like *Wedneaday* or rarer occasions *Pentecost*, but also a lot of less-frequent noise entries, some of which were potentially named entities (e.g. *#ITV3*, *Buggati*, *Katja*). The noise present suggests that, while the clustering is working well, there are not enough clusters; for 250M tweets, we should use $m > 2000$ (Derczynski et al., 2015a).

We also looked at the Brown clusters most indicative of entity starts in the typed task, to get an idea of how these clusters helped. Results are shown in Table 4. Without going into too much detail – the cluster paths are distributed with this work, and on the web,[3] for further examination – some top-level observations can be made. Firstly, the preceding word is often influential; note the large number of *prev_* features. Secondly, the clusters prefixed 111100- contained words often used as the first term in many kinds of entity, suggesting distributional similarities in the first words of named entities. As Brown clustering is based on bigram distributionality, this finding aligns with the existence of highly-weighted common preceding tokens seen in the model weights for the notypes task. Thirdly, Brown clusters are more useful for some entity types than others; there are more features for person, company and geo-loc types than others.

Note the large-weighted shallow-depth features for entities. One is for the terms found before a sportsteam entity (but not a person, note the -ve weight): *prev_p3x010*. This cluster subtree contains many adjectives, possessive pronouns and determiners (*the*, *ur*, *dis*, *each*, *mah*, *his* etc.). The terms helpful when not preceding geo-locs were close to this subtree, differing only in its least-significant bit: *prev_p3x011*. This other large-weighted shallow-depth feature was also useful for avoiding first terms of person entities. Its cluster subtree contains common nouns and qualifiers (*one*, *people*, *good*, *shit*, *day*, *great*, *little*), though it is not immediately clear how these terms were helpful; perhaps the prominence of this subtree feature is due to its frequency alone, and better regularisation is needed to handle it.

### 5.2 Gold standard

When developing the system, we encountered several problems and inconsistencies in the gold standard. These issues are partly a general problem of developing gold standards, i.e. the more complicated the task is, the more humans tend to disagree on correct answers (Tissot et al., 2015). For Twitter NERC with 10 types, some of the tokens are very difficult to label because the context window is very small (140 characters), which then also leads to acronyms being used very frequently to save space, and because world knowledge about sports, music etc. is required.

In particular, the following groups of problems in the gold standard training corpus were identified:

**Broad categories:** While some of the NE types are well-defined (e.g. person, geo-loc), other types are very broad and therefore pose a big challenge. This is already evident by the number of gazetteers created per type (see Table 1), i.e. those broad categories consist of many different subtypes. Since the training set is very small, only a handfull of examples are observed for each subtype (e.g. video game), which makes training a classifier for those types very challenging. One of the most challenging types was products, as many different things can be products.

[3]See http://derczynski.com/sheffield/resources/gha.250M-c2000.tar

**Overlapping types:** Some NEs belong to more than one type, which makes the classification task even more difficult. For example, it is difficult to distinguish between companies and their products with the same name. There are also inconsistent examples of this in the gold standard, e.g. "*I*: O *just*: O *bought*: O *Dior*: B-product *mascara*: O". In this example, "*Dior*" should be annotated as a company, but "*Dior mascara*" as a product from that company.

**The type *other*:** Since annotation guidelines are not available for the gold standard, we rely entirely on examples in the training set to identify what subtypes belong to the type "other". While most examples seem to be public holidays and events, the type also seems to be used for overlapping or otherwise unclear tokens. Examples for this are "*Radio 1*" (a broadcasting organisation), "*UMASS*" (a university), "*Edmonton Journal*" (a broadcasting organisation), "*Dems*" (democrats, a group of people or a policical party). The type "other" is also one for which annotation guidelines differ heavily – meaning performance does not increase if we try to aggregate the gold standard corpus with over available Twitter NER gold standards.

**Inconsistent annotation for hashtags:** Important words in tweets are often preceded by a hashtag to emphasise them, e.g. "*#JenniferAniston quote of the day*". Despite the fact that many of the 327 tokens starting with hashtags were named entities, only 5 of them are annotated with NE types (#Vh1: B-other, #Astros: B-sportsteam, #Denver: B-geo-loc, #Padres: B-sportsteam, #BB11: B-tvshow). The false negatives belong to different NE types and are mostly easy to spot (e.g. #BROOKLYN, #lindsaylohan). A related problem is the annotation of direct mentions of Twitter accounts with @ in sentences, e.g in "*All*: O *caught*: O *up*: O *with*: O *@SHO_weeds*: O *!*: O". In that sentence, "*@SHO_weeds*" refers to the Showtime TV series "*Weeds*" and should be annotated as *tvshow*. However, all tokens starting with @ are annotated as O, so even though this is not neccessarily correct, it is consistent within the gold standard.

## 6 Conclusion

This paper has described the USFD system entered in W-NUT 2015. It achieves performance through unsupervised feature generation, through Freebase gazetteers, and through weighting input data according to its origin date in order to account for drift. This lead to state-of-the-art Twitter NER performance.


## Acknowledgments

This work was partially supported by the European Union under grant agreement No. 611233 PHEME,[4] and the UK EPSRC grant No. EP/K017896/1 uComp.[5]


[4]http://www.pheme.eu

[5]http://www.ucomp.eu

## References


I. Augenstein, D. Maynard, and F. Ciravegna. 2014. Relation extraction from the web using distant supervision. In *Knowledge Engineering and Knowledge Management*, pages 26–41. Springer.

T. Baldwin, B. Han, M. M. C. de Marneffe, Y.-B. Kim, A. Ritter, and W. Xu. 2015. Findings of the 2015 Workshop on Noisy User-generated Text. In *Proceedings of the Workshop on Noisy User-generated Text (WNUT 2015)*. Association for Computational Linguistics.

K. Bollacker, C. Evans, P. Paritosh, T. Sturge, and J. Taylor. 2008. Freebase: a collaboratively created graph database for structuring human knowledge. In *Proceedings of the 2008 ACM SIGMOD international conference on Management of data*, pages 1247–1250. ACM.

K. Bontcheva, L. Derczynski, A. Funk, M. A. Greenwood, D. Maynard, and N. Aswani. 2013. TwitIE: An Open-Source Information Extraction Pipeline for Microblog Text. In *Proceedings of the International Conference on Recent Advances in Natural Language Processing*. Association for Computational Linguistics.

P. Brown, V. Della Pietra, P. de Souza, J. Lai, and R. Mercer. 1992. Class-based n-gram models of natural language. *Computational Linguistics*, 18:467–479.

M. Brucato, L. Derczynski, H. Llorens, K. Bontcheva, and C. S. Jensen. 2013. Recognising and interpreting named temporal expressions. In *RANLP*, pages 113–121.

C. Cherry and H. Guo. 2015. The unreasonable effectiveness of word representations for Twitter named entity recognition. In *Proc. NAACL*.

B. O. Connor, M. Krieger, and D. Ahn. 2010. TweetMotif: Exploratory Search and Topic Summarization for Twitter. In *Proceedings of the Fourth AAAI Conference on Weblogs and Social Media (ICWSM)*, pages 384–385.

H. Cunningham, D. Maynard, K. Bontcheva, and V. Tablan. 2002. GATE: an Architecture for Development of Robust HLT Applications. In *Proceedings of the 40th Annual Meeting on Association for Computational Linguistics*, pages 168–175.

L. Derczynski and K. Bontcheva. 2014. Passive-aggressive sequence labeling with discriminative post-editing for recognising person entities in tweets. In *Proceedings of the 14th Conference of the European Chapter of the Association for Computational Linguistics*, volume 2, pages 69–73.

L. Derczynski, D. Maynard, N. Aswani, and K. Bontcheva. 2013a. Microblog-Genre Noise and Impact on Semantic Annotation Accuracy. In *Proceedings of the 24th ACM Conference on Hypertext and Social Media*. ACM.

L. Derczynski, A. Ritter, S. Clark, and K. Bontcheva. 2013b. Twitter Part-of-Speech Tagging for All: Overcoming Sparse and Noisy Data. In *Proceedings of Recent Advances in Natural Language Processing (RANLP)*. Association for Computational Linguistics.

L. Derczynski, S. Chester, and K. S. Bøgh. 2015a. Extrinsic impact of tuning Brown clustering. In *To appear*.

L. Derczynski, D. Maynard, G. Rizzo, M. van Erp, G. Gorrell, R. Troncy, and K. Bontcheva. 2015b. Analysis of named entity recognition and linking for tweets. *Information Processing and Management*, 51:32–49.

J. Eisenstein. 2013. What to do about bad language on the internet. In *Proceedings of NAACL-HLT*, pages 359–369.

H. Fromreide, D. Hovy, and A. Søgaard. 2014. Crowdsourcing and annotating NER for Twitter #drift. In *Proc. LREC*.

A. Johannsen, D. Hovy, H. M. Alonso, B. Plank, and A. Søgaard. 2014. More or less supervised supersense tagging of twitter. *Proc. *SEM*, pages 1–11.

D. Kergl, R. Roedler, and S. Seeber. 2014. On the endogenesis of Twitter's Spritzer and Gardenhose sample streams. In *Proc. ASONAM*, pages 357–364. IEEE.

T. Koo, X. Carreras, and M. Collins. 2008. Simple semi-supervised dependency parsing. In *Proc. ACL*, page 595.

M. Lui and T. Baldwin. 2012. langid.py: An off-the-shelf language identification tool. In *Proceedings of the 50th Annual Meeting of the Association for Computational Linguistics (ACL)*.

A. Ritter, S. Clark, Mausam, and O. Etzioni. 2011. Named entity recognition in tweets: An experimental study. In *Proc. of Empirical Methods for Natural Language Processing (EMNLP)*, Edinburgh, UK.

A. Smith and M. Osborne. 2006. Using gazetteers in discriminative information extraction. In *Proceedings of the Tenth Conference on Computational Natural Language Learning (CoNLL-X)*, pages 133–140. Association for Computational Linguistics.

H. Tissot, A. Roberts, L. Derczynski, G. Gorrell, and M. Didonet Del Fabro. 2015. Analysis of temporal expressions annotated in clinical notes. In *Proceedings of 11th Joint ACL-ISO Workshop on Interoperable Semantic Annotation*, pages 93–102, London, UK. ACL.

D. Vrandečić and M. Krötzsch. 2014. Wikidata: A Free Collaborative Knowledge Base. *Communications of the ACM*.

# NRC: Infused Phrase Vectors for Named Entity Recognition in Twitter

**Colin Cherry** and **Hongyu Guo** and **Chengbi Dai**
National Research Council Canada
first.last@nrc-cnrc.gc.ca

**Abstract**

Our submission to the W-NUT Named Entity Recognition in Twitter task closely follows the approach detailed by Cherry and Guo (2015), who use a discriminative, semi-Markov tagger, augmented with multiple word representations. We enhance this approach with updated gazetteers, and with infused phrase embeddings that have been adapted to better predict the gazetteer membership of each phrase. Our system achieves a typed F1 of 44.7, resulting in a third-place finish, despite training only on the official training set. A post-competition analysis indicates that also training on the provided development data improves our performance to 54.2 F1.

## 1 Introduction

Named entity recognition (NER) is the task of finding rigid designators as they appear in free text and assigning them to coarse types such as *person* or *geo-location* (Nadeau and Sekine, 2007). NER is the first step in many information extraction tasks, but in social media, this task is extremely challenging. The text to be analyzed is unedited and noisy, and covers a much more diverse set of topics than one might expect in newswire. As such, we are quite interested in the W-NUT Named Entity Recognition in Twitter task (Baldwin et al., 2015) as a platform to benchmark and drive forward work on NER in social media.

Our submission to this competition closely follows Cherry and Guo (2015), who advocate the use of a semi-Markov tagger trained online with standard discriminative tagging features, gazetteer matches, Brown clusters, and word embeddings. We augment this approach with updated gazetteers, phrase embeddings, and *infused embeddings* that have been adapted to better predict gazetteer membership. Our novel infusion technique allows us to adapt existing vectors to NER regardless of their source, by training a type-level auto-encoder whose hidden layer must predict the corresponding phrase's gazetteer memberships while also recovering the original vector.

Our submitted system achieved a typed F1 of 44.7, placing third in the competition, while training only on the provided training data. The competition organizers provided two development sets, one (dev) that is close to the training data, with both train and dev being drawn from the year 2010, and another (dev_2015) that is close to the test data, with both dev_2015 and test being drawn from the winter of 2014–2015. We present a post-competition system that achieves an F1 of 54.2 using the same features and hyper-parameters as our submitted system, except that our tagger is also trained on all provided development data. We close with an analysis of dev_2015's relation to the test set, and argue that these results may overestimate the impact that a small, in-domain training set can have on NER performance.

## 2 Data Resources

We make use of two external data resources: gazetteers and unlabeled tweets. For gazetteers, we begin with the word lists provided with the W-NUT baseline system, which appear to be mostly derived from Freebase. We treat each file in the lexicon directory as a distinct word list. We update and augment these lists with our own Freebase queries in Section 3.2.

We use unannotated tweets to build various word representations (see Section 3.1). Our unannotated corpus collects 98M tweets (1,995M tokens) from between May 2011 and April 2012. The same corpus is used by Cherry and Guo (2015). These tweets have been tokenized and post-processed to remove many special Unicode



*Proceedings of the ACL 2015 Workshop on Noisy User-generated Text*, pages 54–60,
Beijing, China, July 31, 2015. ©2015 Association for Computational Linguistics

characters; they closely resemble those that appear in the provided training and development sets. Furthermore, the corpus consists only of tweets in which the NER system of Ritter et al. (2011) detects at least one entity. The automatic NER tags are used only to select tweets for inclusion in the corpus, after which the annotations are discarded. Filtering our tweets in this way has two immediate effects: first, each tweet is very likely to contain an entity mention. Second, the tweets are very long, with an average of 20.4 tokens per Tweet.

As the test data is drawn from the winter of 2014–2015, we attempted to augment our corpus with more recent data: 13M unannotated English tweets drawn from Twitter's public stream, from between April 24 and May 6, 2015. As we had very little recent data, we made no attempt to bias the corpus to be entity-rich. This corpus of recent tweets has an average tweet length of only 13.8 tokens. Our attempts to use this data to build word representations did not improve NER performance on the 2015 development set, regardless of whether we used the data on its own or in combination with our larger corpus.

## 3 Methods

### 3.1 Base Tagger

We first summarize the approach of Cherry and Guo (2015), which we build upon for our system.

*Tagger:* We tag each tweet independently using a semi-Markov tagger (Sarawagi and Cohen, 2004), which tags phrasal entities using a single operation, as opposed to traditional word-based entity tagging schemes. An example tag sequence, drawn from the 2010 development data, is shown in Figure 1. Semi-Markov tagging gives us the freedom to design features at either the phrase or the word level, while also simplifying our tag set. Furthermore, with our semi-Markov tags, we find we have no need for Markov features that track previous tag assignments, as our entity labels cohere naturally. This speeds up tagging dramatically. Semi-Markov tagging also introduces a hyper-parameter $P$, the maximum entity length in tokens.

*Training:* Our tagger is trained online with large-margin updates, following a structured variant of the passive aggressive (PA) algorithm (Crammer et al., 2006). We regularize the model both with a fixed number of epochs $E$ through the data, and using PA's regularization term $C$, which is similar to that of an SVM. We also have the capacity to deploy example-specific $C$-parameters, allowing us to assign some examples more weight during training, which we use only in post-competition analysis.

*Lexical Features:* Recall that our semi-Markov model allows for both word and phrase-level features. The vast majority of our features are word-level, with the representation for a phrase being the sum of the features of its words. Our word-level features closely follow the set proposed by Ratnaparkhi (1996), covering word identity, the identities of surrounding words within a window of 2 tokens, and prefixes and suffixes up to three characters in length. Each word identity feature has three variants, with the first reporting the original word, the second reporting a lowercased version, and the third reporting a summary of the word's shape ("Mrs." becomes "Aa.") All word-level features also have a variant that appends the word's Begin/Inside/Last/Unique position within its entity. Our phrase-level features report phrase identity, with lowercased and word shape variants, along with a bias feature that is always on. Phrase identity features allow us to memorize tags for common phrases explicitly. Following the standard discriminative tagging paradigm, all features have the tag identity appended to them.

*Representation Features:* We also produce word-level features corresponding to a number of external representations: gazetteer membership, Brown clusters (Brown et al., 1992) and word embeddings. For gazetteers, we first segment the tweet into longest matching gazetteer phrases, resolving overlapping phrases with a greedy left-to-right walk through the tweet. Each word then generates a set of features indicating which gazetteers (if any) contain its phrase. For cluster representations, we train Brown clusters on our unannotated corpus, using the implementation by Liang (2005) to build 1,000 clusters over types that occur with a minimum frequency of 10. Following Miller et al. (2004), each word generates indicators for bit prefixes of its binary cluster signature, for prefixes of length 2, 4 8 and 12. For word embeddings, we use an in-house Java re-implementation of word2vec (Mikolov et al., 2013a) to build 300-dimensional vector representations for all types that occur at least 10 times in our unannotated corpus. Each word then reports a real-valued feature (as opposed to an indicator) for each of the 300

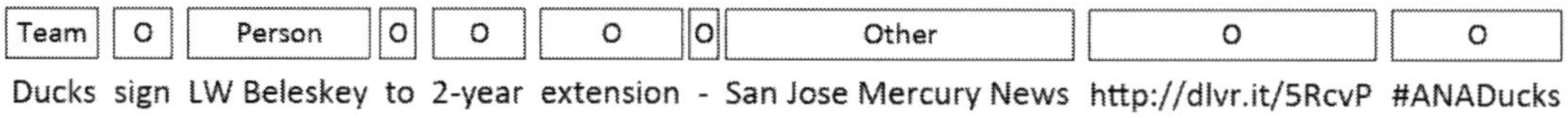


Figure 1: An example of semi-Markov tagging.

dimensions in its vector representation. A single random vector is created to represent all out-of-vocabulary words. Our vectors and clusters cover 2.5 million types. Note that we do not include part-of-speech tags as features, as they were not found to be useful by Cherry and Guo (2015).

### 3.2 Updated Gazetteers

During development, we found that features involving gazetteers were having a larger impact on dev than on dev_2015. Therefore, we enhanced the gazetteers provided with the W-NUT baseline system with our own Freebase queries, issued between May 6–7, 2015. These updates are summarized in Table 1. The baseline lexicons for which we could infer Freebase categories were replaced with updated queries, indicated with *new=no*. We also added a number of entirely new queries (*new=yes*). Any baseline lexicon that is not mentioned in Table 1 was left untouched, and remains included in our updated gazetteers.

### 3.3 Phrase Embeddings

The work of Passos et al. (2014) suggests that embeddings built over phrases may be more useful to NER than those built over words. To test this for our tagger, we use the phrase finding tool provided with word2vec to segment our unannotated corpus into phrases up to 4 tokens in length (Mikolov et al., 2013b). Their software uses a simple statistic similar to pointwise mutual information to assess whether two tokens should be combined into a phrase. Token-pairs passing a threshold are segmented into phrases, creating a new corpus. Phrases longer than 2 tokens can be generated by running this process repeatedly, allowing, for example, *Toronto* to merge with *Maple_Leafs* on the second pass. Once the phrasal corpus has been created, we run word2vec as usual. There is no reason the same procedure could not be applied to Brown clustering, only time constraints prevented us from doing so.

The resulting phrase embeddings are used in place or word embeddings, mostly for efficiency considerations. We assign each word in the tweet to its longest embedded phrase that matches the tweet, resolving conflicts with a greedy, left-to-right matching process. Each word is then assigned a vector corresponding to its matched phrase, meaning that the same vector will be repeated for each token in its phrase. This has the property of having words receive different representations, depending on their context. Otherwise, the embedding features are identical to those described in Section 3.1. Phrase embeddings enable more gazetteer matches for gazetteer-infused vectors, which we discuss next.

### 3.4 Gazetteer-Infused Phrase Vectors

We employ an auto-encoder to leverage knowledge derived from domain-specific gazetteers to make the distributed phrase representations more relevant to our NER task. In recent years, two sources of information have been found to be valuable to boost the performance for NER: distributed representation learned from a large corpus and domain-specific lexicons (Turian et al., 2010; Cherry and Guo, 2015). Research has also shown that merging these two forms of information can result in further predictive improvement for an NER system (Passos et al., 2014). A similar strategy for enhancing word embeddings has also been demonstrated for sentiment analysis (Tang et al., 2014). Following this line of research, we aim to tailor (post-process) the unsupervised phrase embeddings, created in Section 3.3, for our NER task, using an auto-encoder.

The auto-encoder eliminates the need to have access to the original training data and the vector training model, requiring only the trained distributed vectors. In this sense, it can be considered computationally lighter than the above mentioned information fusion methods.[1] Our approach is inspired by Ngiam et al. (2011) and Glorot et al. (2011), where auto-encoders are efficiently deployed to generate improved features for domains or modalities that are different from those of its inputs. Here, we employ an auto-encoder to inject

[1]In practice, a number of popular sets of pre-trained embedding vectors, trained with very large corpora, are made available online to the research community, but without the original training data; such as some sets from http://nlp.stanford.edu/projects/glove/ and https://code.google.com/p/word2vec/

| Gazetteer | # | new |
|---|---|---|
| architecture.museum | 9k | no |
| architecture.structure | 111k | yes |
| broadcast.tv_channel | 1k | no |
| business.brand | 9k | no |
| business.consumer_company | 2k | no |
| business.consumer_product | 439k | no |
| business.employer | 282k | yes |
| business.sponsor | 2k | no |
| business.company | 393k | yes |
| location.location | 1,336k | no |
| location.citytown* | 189k | yes |
| location.country | 1k | no |
| location.state_province_region* | 66k | yes |
| film.film | 262k | yes |
| music.artist | 613k | yes |
| music.musical_group | 195k | yes |
| people.family_name | 6k | no |
| people.person | 3,200k | no |
| business.product_line | 439k | no |
| sports.professional_sports_team | 1k | yes |
| sports.school_sports_team | 2k | yes |
| sports.sports_facility | 7k | yes |
| sports.sports_league | 4k | no |
| sports.sports_team | 33k | no |
| tv.tv_network | 3k | no |
| tv.tv_program | 74k | no |
| tv.tv_series_episode | 1,316k | yes |

Table 1: The Freebase gazetteers we either updated (*new=no*) or added (*new=yes*) to the baseline gazetteers. Freebase categories can be recovered by replacing "." with "/". Gazetteers marked with a * were extracted from /location/mailing_address using the indicated property name.

relevant entity type information derived from our gazetteers into the pre-trained phrase representations.

Using learned phrase vectors as input, the auto-encoder's goal is to reconstruct both the provided input vector $V$ and its entity types, as derived from the collected gazetteers. In our experiments, we assume the entity membership vector has a 0-1 encoding. That is, if there are $G$ lexicon types, then it has length $G$, where a 1 indicates membership in the corresponding gazetteer. We implement the squared error as the reconstruction cost criterion for the auto-encoder training:

$$[V;G] = f(W_d f(W_e V + b_e) + b_d)$$

where $f$ denotes the hyperbolic *tanh* function, while $b_e$ and $b_d$ are the biases for the encoder and decoder, respectively. We initialize the parameters, namely the decoder matrix $W_d$ and encoder matrix $W_e$, by randomly sampling each value from a uniform distribution [-0.1, +0.1]. Our experiments use a learning rate of 0.001 and a moment of 0.9. We found the optimal size for the hidden encoding layer to be 200 nodes. The auto-encoder is trained using Stochastic Gradient Descent (SGD) with 100 iterations, which converges very well for our data.

With the above experimental settings, our Gazetteer-Infused phrase vectors are created with two stages. During the initial phase, we select the 69,329 phrases that are shared by both the phrase vectors and the collected gazetteers. The resulting set of phrases is a very small fraction of the total of 4.5M vector entries created in Section 3.3. Consequently, the overwhelming number of negative examples causes a highly imbalanced class distribution problem for the gazetteer membership component of our auto-encoder (Guo and Viktor, 2004). To cope with this skewed class challenge, we randomly down-sample the negative training data to balance the negative and positive instances. These rebalanced data are then fed into the auto-encoder to optimize the parameter matrices. In the second stage, the trained auto-encoder is used to generate a new vector $[V;G]$ for every phrase created in Section 3.3. These gazetteer-infused phrase vectors include a decoded version of the original embedding $V$, as well as explicit soft predictions of gazetteer membership in $G$. Note that we apply this process for all 45 of our gazetteers, and not just those that correspond directly to the types tagged in this task.

## 4 Results

We have collected results for our submitted system, along with some salient pre- and post- competition variants in Table 2. We discuss these results in detail below.

### 4.1 Competition Results

Our submitted system is shown as $[A]+[U]$, and includes all of the features described in Section 3. It achieves our highest results on both dev_2015 and the average of dev and dev_2015, and its performance on test was sufficient to place third in the competition.

| System | dev P | dev R | dev F | dev_2015 P | dev_2015 R | dev_2015 F | Avg F | test P | test R | test F | Rnk |
|---|---|---|---|---|---|---|---|---|---|---|---|
| Baseline | 57.0 | 44.4 | 49.9 | 38.5 | 30.9 | 34.3 | 42.1 | 35.6 | 29.1 | 32.0 | - |
| Our Baseline | 64.6 | 38.5 | 48.2 | 47.7 | 27.2 | 34.7 | 41.5 | 44.4 | 23.3 | 30.6 | 8 |
| C&G 2015 | 68.6 | 50.3 | 58.0 | 56.4 | 41.9 | 48.1 | 53.1 | 49.8 | 36.5 | 42.1 | 5 |
| Inc. Regularization | 70.7 | 50.8 | 59.2 | 57.2 | 42.3 | 48.6 | 53.9 | 51.4 | 36.8 | 42.9 | 4 |
| [P]hrase vectors | 69.4 | 50.8 | 58.7 | 58.0 | 42.7 | 49.2 | 53.9 | 52.6 | 37.8 | 44.0 | 3 |
| [A]dapted vectors | 70.0 | 51.7 | 59.5 | 59.9 | 42.3 | 49.6 | 54.5 | 52.2 | 37.5 | 43.7 | 4 |
| [U]pdated gazetteers | 68.5 | 51.4 | 58.8 | 57.4 | 42.7 | 49.0 | 53.9 | 52.0 | 37.4 | 43.5 | 4 |
| [P]+[U] | 73.7 | 54.2 | **62.5** | 59.7 | 44.1 | 50.7 | 56.6 | 53.2 | 38.9 | 44.9 | 3 |
| [A]+[U] (**Submitted**) | 72.8 | 53.4 | 61.6 | 62.4 | 44.5 | **51.9** | **56.8** | 53.2 | 38.6 | 44.7 | 3 |
| + dev | - | - | - | 59.0 | 44.5 | 50.7 | - | 54.9 | 41.0 | 46.9 | 3 |
| + dev + dev_2015 | - | - | - | - | - | - | - | 62.5 | 47.8 | **54.2** | 2 |

Table 2: Experimental results for variants of our system, reporting **P**recision, **R**ecall and balanced **F**-measure. The **Avg F** column lists the average F-measure across dev and dev_2015, which was our model selection criterion. The **Rnk** column lists the retro-active rank of each system in the competition.

### 4.2 Ablation

The systems above *[A]+[U]* are intended to demonstrate our development process. *Our baseline* is our attempt to re-implement the provided baseline in our code base, and includes all lexical features and the baseline gazetteers.

*C&G 2015* adds Brown clusters and word embeddings to create a complete re-implementation of Cherry and Guo (2015). We can see that these representations have a huge impact on NER performance for all dev and test sets.

We then performed a careful hyper-parameter sweep using the two provided development sets, resulting in the *Inc. Regularization* system. The hyper-parameters suggested by Cherry and Guo (2015) (E=10, C=0.01, P=10) were selected to work well with and without representations. We found that once we have committed to using representations, the tagger benefits from increased regularization, so long as we allow the model to converge (E=30, C=0.001, P=8). Although we revisited these settings periodically, these hyper-parameters have proved to be quite stable, and we use them for all remaining experiments.

The next three systems test the three extensions described in Section 3. Neither *[P]hrase vectors* nor *[U]pdated gazetteers* were able to improve both dev and dev_2015 when applied alone, while the *[A]dapted vectors* did boost performance on both sets, increasing average F-measure by 0.6. In particular, the adapted vectors improved the rare entity types such as *movie* and *sports team*. Unfortunately, these improvements do not seem to carry over to the test set.

As we combine the ideas with *[P]+[U]* and *[A]+[U]*, we see even larger improvements on both development sets. Note that adapted vectors implicitly include phrase vectors, as those are the vectors that have been adapted. These ideas may work better in combination because both our phrase vectors and our updated gazetteers include many noisy phrasal entries, but their sources of noise are independent, allowing one to compensate for the other.

### 4.3 Post-Competition Results

All systems discussed thus far have been trained only on the official training data. The final two systems in Table 2 test the impact of adding dev (599 tweets from 2010) and dev_2015 (420 tweets from 2014–2015) to the 1,795 training tweets. When training with dev_2015, we take advantage of our system's data-weighting capabilities to assign these examples twice as much weight; this hyper-parameter was selected only based on dev_2015's relatively small size, and we did not test any other values for it. As one can see, both development sets have a significant impact on test performance, with dev_2015 producing a 7.3 point improvement in F-measure, eclipsing the impact of all other enhancements to our system.

We chose not to include dev in our final system because it did not appear to have a positive impact on dev_2015. We chose not to include dev_2015 in our final system because cross validation experiments, where we train including half of dev_2015 and then test on the other half, indicated that its impact would be minimal (less than 1 point of F-measure), and we did not want to discard the safety net that a held-out development set provides when selecting a final system. In retrospect, this was a fairly large mistake.

### 4.4 Dev-Test Data Analysis

Does this mean that 420 examples drawn from a time period close to that of the test set will consistently provide 7 points of F-measure? We do not believe so, for at least two reasons: time overlap and Twitter bots.

*Time overlap:* dev_2015 and test appear to have both been drawn from overlapping periods of time. Though the tweets provided for development and test were not dated, we can infer the date spans from various bots that tweet the date, producing tweets like:

> @ABCD http://t.co/MA3WYTR72Q February 02 , 2015 at 10:57 PM

throughout both sets. Using the regular expression "(December|(Jan|Febr)uary) [0-9]+ , 201[4-5] at" we were able to find tweets between December 11, 2014 and February 4, 2015 in dev_2015, and between December 12, 2014 and February 5, 2015 in test. This means that both sets contain the same major holidays, such as Christmas, and sporting events, such as Super Bowl 49. Accordingly, our post-competition system sees its largest improvements in the types *sports team* and *other* (which covers many event names). These sorts of improvements are not necessarily indicative of how a system trained on data from the past will perform on new data, which is a common use case for NER. This also highlights the importance of having an NER system's training data be drawn from throughout the year. The official training data has no mention of the Super Bowl and very few of Christmas, despite these being yearly events.

*Twitter bots:* bots are common in both dev_2015 and test, but much less prominent in train and dev, perhaps reflecting an overall change in twitter traffic between 2010 and 2015. For the most part, bots are harmless, and a system should be tested in terms of its ability to ignore these sources of noise. However, some bots tweet entities in an extremely formulaic manner, and a discriminative NER system needs to see very few tweets from such a bot in order to tag it consistently. One such example from this competition is the horoscope bot, which produces tweets that look like:

> Your boss may be critical of your easy-going attitude at work t ... More for Cancer http://t.co/74bwPzVbiB

This bot can be detected reliably with the regular expression "[.][.][.] More for [A-Z]". In the gold-standard annotations, tweets from this bot consistently have the astrological sign (Cancer in this case) tagged as *other*. While this bot appears only 4 times in dev_2015, it appears 23 times in test. If we remove these 23 tweets from the test set, our submitted system increases is performance to a Precision / Recall / F-measure of 53.5 / 40.0 / 45.8, while our best post-competition system decreases to 61.0 / 46.2 / 52.6, narrowing the gap in F-measure by 2.6 points. The ability to extract entities from formulaic bots such as this one could be useful, but the core purpose of NER technology is to enable the extraction of information from human-written text.

## 5 Conclusion

We have summarized our entry to the first W-NUT Named Entity Recognition in Twitter task. Our entry extends the work of Cherry and Guo (2015) with updated lexicons, phrase embeddings, and gazetteer-infused phrase embeddings. Our gazetteer infusion technique is novel in that it allows us to adapt existing vectors, regardless of their source. Taken together with improved hyper-parameters, these extensions improve the approach of Cherry and Guo (2015) by 2.6 F-measure on a completely blind test. Our final submission achieves a test F-measure of 44.7, placing third in the competition, and could have achieved an F-measure of 54.2 had we included all development data as training data. We have also presented a discussion of how the most recent development set relates to the test set, arguing that these results likely over-estimate the impact of a small, in-domain training set on NER performance.

## References

Timothy Baldwin, Marie Catherine de Marneffe, Bo Han, Young-Bum Kim, Alan Ritter, and Wei Xu. 2015. Shared tasks of the 2015 workshop on noisy user-generated text: Twitter lexical normalization and named entity recognition. In *Proceedings of the Workshop on Noisy User-generated Text (WNUT 2015)*, Beijing, China.

Peter F Brown, Peter V Desouza, Robert L Mercer, Vincent J Della Pietra, and Jenifer C Lai. 1992. Class-based n-gram models of natural language. *Computational linguistics*, 18(4):467–479.

Colin Cherry and Hongyu Guo. 2015. The unreasonable effectiveness of word representations for Twitter named entity recognition. In *HLT-NAACL*.

Koby Crammer, Ofer Dekel, Joseph Keshet, Shai Shalev-Shwartz, and Yoram Singer. 2006. Online passive-aggressive algorithms. *Journal of Machine Learning Research*.

Xavier Glorot, Antoine Bordes, and Yoshua Bengio. 2011. Domain adaptation for large-scale sentiment classification: A deep learning approach. In *ICML*, pages 513–520.

Hongyu Guo and Herna L. Viktor. 2004. Learning from imbalanced data sets with boosting and data generation: the databoost-im approach. *SIGKDD Explorations*, 6(1):30–39.

Percy Liang. 2005. *Semi-supervised learning for natural language*. Ph.D. thesis, Massachusetts Institute of Technology.

Tomas Mikolov, Kai Chen, Greg Corrado, and Jeffrey Dean. 2013a. Efficient estimation of word representations in vector space. In *ICLR Workshop*.

Tomas Mikolov, Ilya Sutskever, Kai Chen, Greg S Corrado, and Jeff Dean. 2013b. Distributed representations of words and phrases and their compositionality. In *Advances in Neural Information Processing Systems*, pages 3111–3119.

Scott Miller, Jethran Guinness, and Alex Zamanian. 2004. Name tagging with word clusters and discriminative training. In *HLT-NAACL*, pages 337–342.

David Nadeau and Satoshi Sekine. 2007. A survey of named entity recognition and classification. *Lingvisticae Investigationes*, 30(1):3–26.

Jiquan Ngiam, Aditya Khosla, Mingyu Kim, Juhan Nam, Honglak Lee, and Andrew Y. Ng. 2011. Multimodal deep learning. In *ICML*, pages 689–696.

Alexandre Passos, Vineet Kumar, and Andrew McCallum. 2014. Lexicon infused phrase embeddings for named entity resolution. In *CoNLL*, pages 78–86.

Adwait Ratnaparkhi. 1996. A maximum entropy model for part-of-speech tagging. In *EMNLP*, pages 133–142.

Alan Ritter, Sam Clark, Mausam, and Oren Etzioni. 2011. Named entity recognition in tweets: An experimental study. In *EMNLP*, pages 1524–1534, Edinburgh, Scotland, UK.

Sunita Sarawagi and William W Cohen. 2004. Semi-markov conditional random fields for information extraction. In *NIPS*, pages 1185–1192.

Duyu Tang, Furu Wei, Nan Yang, Ming Zhou, Ting Liu, and Bing Qin. 2014. Learning sentiment-specific word embedding for twitter sentiment classification. In *ACL*, pages 1555–1565.

Joseph Turian, Lev Ratinov, and Yoshua Bengio. 2010. Word representations: a simple and general method for semi-supervised learning. In *ACL*, pages 384–394.

# IITP: Multiobjective Differential Evolution based Twitter Named Entity Recognition

**Md Shad Akhtar, Utpal Kumar Sikdar and Asif Ekbal**
Dept of Computer Science and Engineering
IIT Patna
Patna, India
(shad.pcs15,utpal.sikdar,asif)@iitp.ac.in

## Abstract

In this paper we propose a differential evolution (DE) based named entity recognition (NER) system in twitter data. In the first step, we develop various NER systems using different combinations of the features. We implemented these features without using any domain-specific features and/or resources. As a base classifier we use Conditional Random Field (CRF). In the second step, we propose a DE based feature selection approach to determine the most relevant set of features and its context information. The optimized feature set applied to the training set yields the precision, recall and F-measure values of 60.68%, 29.65% and 39.84%, respectively for the fine-grained named entity (NE) types. When we consider only the coarse-grained NE types, it shows the precision, recall and F-measure values of 63.43%, 51.44% and 56.81%, respectively.

## 1 Introduction

During the last few years there has been a phenomenal growth in the number of users that make use of different social networking platforms to share their opinions and views. Twitter now has upto over 500 million users with approx 302 million active users [1]. One can easily imagine that amount of tweets generated per day would be enormous i.e. almost 500 million tweets per day [2]. These information are usually unstructured and noisy in nature. The reason behind its unstructured nature is that tweets are rather short messages (constitute upto 140 characters only), contains several grammatical & spelling mistakes etc. The size limitation bounds a user to invent several short forms (*e.g. 2mrw, tmrw for tomorrow*) of a valid word which a human mind can interpret easily but, on the other hand, becomes very difficult to come up with an accurate system for solving any problem related to natural language processing (NLP). Also in order to show their emotions, users sometime put extra emphasis by elongating a valid word (*e.g. yeeesssss!! for yes*).

Named entity recognition (NER) can be seen as one of the important and foremost tasks for many natural language processing (NLP) tasks such as machine translation, information extraction, question-answering etc. The task of NER can be thought of as a two-step process that involves identifying proper names from the text and classifying them into some predefined categories such as person, organization, location etc. Although the techniques (Bikel et al., 1999; Ekbal and Bandyopadhyay, 2008a; Ekbal and Bandyopadhyay, 2008b; Sikdar et al., 2012) for recognizing named entities (NEs) in newswire and other well-formatted traditional corpus has already matured but it is still a challenging task to perform in unstructured and noisy twitter data.

The concept of NER in twitter has recently drawn the attention of researchers worldwide. Very few authors have reported their works (Liu et al., 2011; Ramage et al., 2009; Li et al., 2012) for NER in twitter. A semi-supervised model for NER has been reported in (Liu et al., 2011) where K-nearest neighbour classifier is combined with CRF. Application of LabeledLDA (Ramage et al., 2009) in supervised environment can be found in (Ritter et al., 2011). Their method classifies NEs into fine-grained types of 10 classes (as in our case). In another work (Li et al., 2012), authors have used random walk model to build an unsupervised approach to NER. They modelled their system on local(*tweets*) and global (*www*) context without employing any of the linguistic features.

[1]http://en.wikipedia.org/wiki/Twitter

[2]http://www.cnet.com/news/report-twitter-hits-half-a-billion-tweets-a-day/



*Proceedings of the ACL 2015 Workshop on Noisy User-generated Text*, pages 61–67,
Beijing, China, July 31, 2015. 

Few more related works can be found in (Derczynski et al., 2015) and (Locke and Martin, 2009).

Due to several challenges it pose, recently there has been a huge interest to identify NE in twitter data. In compliance with this a shared task "ACL2015 W-NUT: Named Entity Recognition in Twitter"[3] was organized. The work that we report here is a part of this shared task. The main objective of the shared task was to efficiently identify various coarse-grained and fine-grained named entities. Fine-grained NE types include 10 different categories namely, person, product, company, geo-loc, movie, musicartist, tvshow, facility, sportsteam and other. We have used a rich feature set based on lexical and syntactic properties of a tweet as discussed in Section 3.9. Our proposed work uses Conditional Random Field (CRF) (Lafferty et al., 2001) as learning algorithm, which is very efficient as a sequence learner. Subsequently we have applied Differential Evolution (DE), a stochastic, population based optimization algorithm, introduced by Storn and Prince in 1996 (Storn and Price, 1997), to obtain the optimal feature set for NER in twitter data.

The organization of the paper is as follows. Section 2 provides a very brief theoretical discussion of DE. Feature set and methodology used in the proposed work are discussed in Section 3. Experimental result and analysis can be found in Section 4. We conclude the paper in Section 5.

## 2 MultiObjective Differential Evolution (DE)

Differential Evolution (DE) (Storn and Price, 1997) is a heuristic search optimization technique and it provides near optimal solution for an optimization problem. Within a search space the parameters are encoded in the form of string, which is called chromosome/vector. A chromosome is, therefore, nothing but of D number of real values. A collection of such types of chromosomes is called population. A fitness value is associated with each chromosome. For single objective optimization the fitness value depends upon the these D number of real parameters. For multiobjective optimization, more than one fitness value is associated with each chromosome. The fitness value denotes the goodness of the chromosome. DE generates new vector by adding the weighted difference between two vectors to the third vector. This operation is called the mutation. In the next step, the mutant vector parameters are mixed with the parameters of the predefined vector. The new vector is termed as the trial vector, and the parameter mixing process is called crossover. The best vectors are selected from the trial vectors. The process of selecting new vectors from the current population is known as selection. The algorithm that we follow for this is known as the crowding distance sorting algorithm. The processes of mutation, crossover and selection continue for a fixed number of generation.

[3]http://noisy-text.github.io/

## 3 Methods

The proposed system is consisting of two steps. In the very first step we generate many models based on the best fitting feature sets. Following this heuristic based approach we select the best model by fine-tuning on the development data. In the second step we develop a multiobjective DE based feature selection approach to find out the best feature combinations and its contextual information from the selected feature set. Schematic diagram of the proposed system is depicted in figure 1.

### 3.1 Problem Formulation

Suppose there are D features available, and these are denoted by $F_1, \ldots, F_D$, where $\mathcal{A} = \{F_i : i = 1; D\}$ Determine the subset of features $\mathcal{A}' \subseteq \mathcal{A}$ such that we learn a classifier with these subset of features and optimize some metrics. In our proposed multiobjective DE, we optimize two functions, namely precision and recall.

### 3.2 Problem Representation and Population Initialization

All the chromosomes are initialized with the binary values of either 0 or 1, where 1 denotes that the corresponding feature is present and 0 denotes that the corresponding feature is off. Total number of available features denote the length of the chromosome, and we set this as D. A classifier learns with the available set of features. One example of chromosome representation is shown in Figure 2.

### 3.3 Fitness Computation

The fitness computation corresponds to determining the values precision and recall as two objective functions. If M number of features are present in the chromosome, a classifier is trained with these

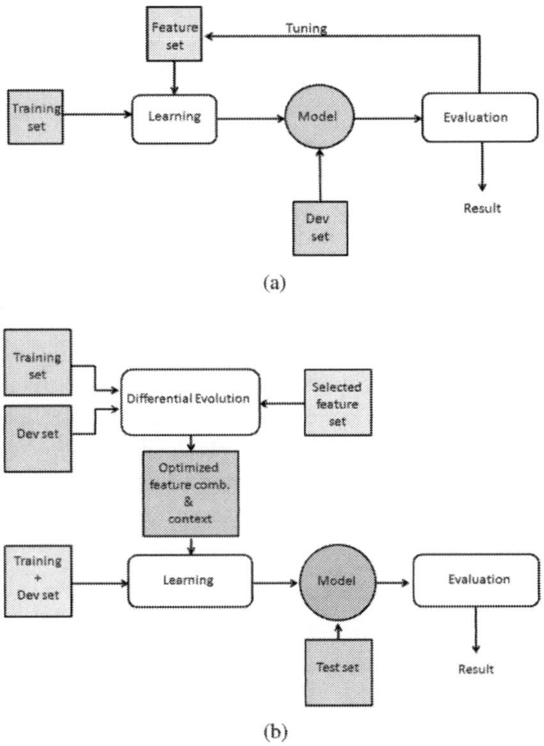


Figure 1: Proposed methodology (a) Step 1 (b) Step 2.

Figure 2: Chromosome representation: Here #available features = 15 and #features present = 8

M number of features. The classifier is then evaluated on the development data. We calculate precision and recall as the two objective functions. The goal is to maximize these two functions.

### 3.4 Mutation

In mutation process, a mutant vector $V_{i,G+1}$ is generated for each target vector $X_{i,G}$; $i = 1, 2, 3, \ldots, NP$, according to

$$V_{i,G+1} = x_{r1,G} + F \times (x_{r2,G} - x_{r3,G}), \quad (1)$$

where $r1$, $r2$, $r3$ are generated randomly with different indices, not equals to current index $i$ and belong to $\{1, 2, \ldots, NP\}$, $G$ is the generation number and F is the mutant factor which is set to 0.5. If the parameters of mutant vector $v_{i,j,G+1} > 1$, then the parameter values are set to 1. If the parameters of mutant vector $v_{i,j,G+1} < 0$, then the parameter values are set to 0.

### 3.5 Crossover

To generate better solutions (represented by the chromosomes) to the next generation population, crossover is needed. The parameter mixing of the target vector $X_{i,G}$ and mutant vector $V_{i,G+1}$ is called crossover. Crossover generates a trial vector as follows:

$$U_{i,G+1} = (u_{1,i,G+1}, u_{2,i,G+1}, \ldots, u_{D,i,G+1}) \quad (2)$$

where

$$u_{j,i,G+1} = v_{j,i,G+1} \text{ if } (r_j \leq CR) \text{ or } j = i_r \quad (3)$$
$$= x_{j,i,G} \text{ if } (r_j > CR) \text{ and } j \neq i_r \quad (4)$$

for $j = 1, 2, \ldots, D$, where $r_j$ is an uniform random number of the $j$th evaluation which belongs to $[0, 1]$ and CR is crossover constant which is set to 0.5. The index value $i_r$ belongs to $\{1, 2, \ldots, D\}$ that ensures that at least one parameter of trial vectors $U_{i,G+1}$ gets one parameter from the mutant vector $V_{i,G+1}$.

### 3.6 Selection

In selection process, trial vectors are merged with the current population to get the best $NP$ solutions from the merged solutions $2 \times NP$ in the next generation population. The merged solutions are sorted based on dominated and non-dominated concept and generate ranked solutions. As an example, the dominated and non-dominated sorting are shown in Figure 3. The non-dominated solutions are represented in the pareto-optimal surface. The non-dominated solutions are added to the next generation population until the number of solutions becomes equal to $NP$. If the number of solutions in a particular rank exceeds $NP$, then it is sorted based on crowding distance algorithm. The required number of solutions are added from the beginning of the sorted rank to make $NP$ number solutions in the next generation population. The selection process determines the best $NP$ number of solutions in the next generation population.

### 3.7 Termination Condition

Mutation, fitness computation, crossover and selection processes run for a maximum number of generations. At the end, we get a set of non-dominated solutions.

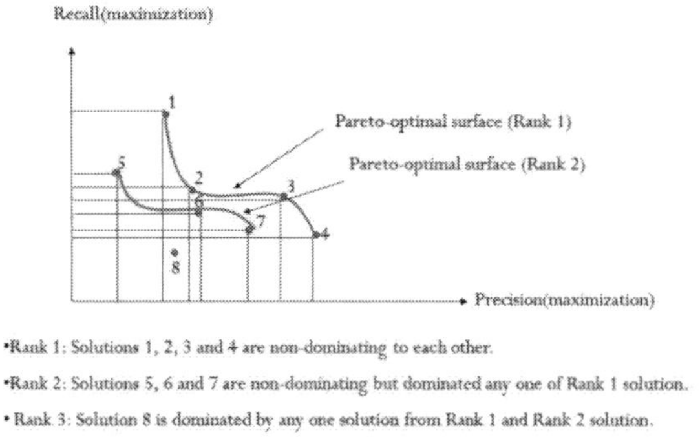


Figure 3: Representation of dominated and non-dominated solutions

### 3.8 Selecting the best solution

The multiobjective optimization (MOO) based algorithm yields a set of solutions on the Pareto optimal front at the end. None of these solutions is better compared to the others. However, we may often require to find out a solution at the end. Depending upon the user's requirements different criteria for selecting the best solutions can exist. Each feature vector of the final Pareto optimal front generates a classifier. We compute the F-measure value on the development set for each classifier. We select the solution which reports highest F-measure value. The features encoded in this chromosome is used to train a CRF and report the final evaluation on the test data.

### 3.9 Feature Set

In this section we describe the features that we implement for performing NER. The features are domain-independent and we implement these without using any external resources and/or tools.

1. **Local context:** We use local contextual information as the features of CRF. We use previous few and succeeding few words as the features for learning.

2. **Part-of-Speech information:** PoS information is one of the prominent features in identifying the NE. We have used CMU-ARK Twitter NLP tool[4] for extracting the PoS information. We use the PoS information of preceding and succeeding few tokens as the features.

3. **Word length:** From the given training data we observed that NEs generally become longer in lengths. We define a feature that is set to high if the length of the candidate token exceeds a predetermined threshold. In our case we assume the token to be a NE if if its length exceeds 5 characters.

4. **Suffix and Prefix:** Suffixes and prefixes of length upto 4 characters of the current word are used as the features.

5. **Word normalization:** We normalize the current token and use it as a feature. For normalization we map the capitalized letter to 'A', small letter to 'a' and numbers or symbols to 'x'.

6. **Previous word:** We prepare a list of most frequent words that appear before a NE in the training data. A binary valued feature is then defined that fires if the current word appears in this list.

7. **Stop word:** This checks whether the current word appears in the list of stop words or not. We obtain the list of stop words available at [5].

8. **Uppercase:** This feature checks whether the current word starts with a capital letter or contains a upper case letter inside the word or all the characters of the word are capitalized.

9. **All digit:** This feature checks whether the current token is consisting of only digits.

10. **AlphaDigit:** Tokens having combination of alphabet and digit have less probability of being a NE. This concept is used to define a binary feature in the proposed work which fires when the token is alphanumeric.

11. **First & last word:** Tweet level information are employed for defining two features i.e. if the current token is the first or last word of a particular tweet.

12. **Word frequency:** We observe that most frequently occurring words have a tendency of not being NE. We prepare a list of most frequent words from the training data. A binary

[4]http://www.ark.cs.cmu.edu/TweetNLP/

[5]http://ir.dcs.gla.ac.uk/resources/linguistic_utils/stop_words

valued feature is then defined that checks whether the current word appears in this list or not.

13. **Gazetteer:** We prepare a list of NEs from the training and development datasets. Along with the NE we also store the NE types. We define an integer-valued feature that takes the value that corresponds to the respective NE type.

## 4 Datasets and Experiments

In this section we firstly describe the datasets and then report the evaluation results.

### 4.1 Data Set

As discussed earlier, objective of the shared task was to identify both the coarse-grained and fine-grained NE from the tweets. Shared task organizers provided two separate versions of training ($train_{notype}$ and $train_{10type}$) datasets and four versions of development datasets ($dev_{notype}$, $dev2015_{notype}$, $dev_{10type}$ and $dev2015_{10type}$). The training dataset comprise of 1,795 tweets while development datasets comprises of 599 & 420 tweets for $dev$ and $dev2015$, respectively. A total of 1,768 NEs are present in the dataset, out of which 1,140 are present in the training set and rest 628 are present in the development set. Brief statistics of the datasets are shown in Table 1 and Table 2 for the coarse-grained NE tagged and fine-grained NE tagged datasets, respectively. Gold standard test datasets comprise of 1,000 tweets.

| Dataset | # Tweets | # Token | # NE |
|---|---|---|---|
| $train$ | 1795 | 34899 | 1140 |
| $dev$ | 599 | 11570 | 356 |
| $dev2015$ | 420 | 6789 | 272 |
| $test2015$ | 1000 | 16261 | - |

Table 1: Statistics of the coarse-grained dataset

### 4.2 Experimental Results

As a base learning algorithm we make use of Conditional Random Field (CRF)(Lafferty et al., 2001). We use the CRF++ [6] based package for our experiments. Evaluation of all the systems are performed in compliance with CoNLL 2002 evaluation script[7] as recommended in the shared task. For comparative analysis a baseline system was also provided by the organizers for both fine-grained and coarse-grained versions. We started our experiments by training the model on the features defined in Section 3.9. Iteratively we have trained, tested and evaluated the system in order to find out the best fitting feature sets. Afterwards we shifted our focus to DE for optimizing the feature set in terms of relevant features and its context information. DE was initialized with the population size equal to 100, and it was executed for 50 generations. We have carried out these experiments for both fine-grained and coarse-grained datasets. On termination, multiobjective differential evolution (MODE) reported optimized feature combinations for both the types of datasets. At the final step these optimized feature combinations were used to build the final system. We show the optimized feature sets as determined by MODE in Table 3.

| Types | ***train*** | ***dev*** | ***dev*2015** |
|---|---|---|---|
| person | 332 | 117 | 73 |
| product | 79 | 18 | 9 |
| company | 130 | 41 | 33 |
| geo-loc | 218 | 58 | 46 |
| movie | 31 | 3 | 3 |
| musicartist | 43 | 12 | 13 |
| tvshow | 26 | 8 | 6 |
| facility | 84 | 20 | 7 |
| sportsteam | 33 | 18 | 35 |
| other | 164 | 61 | 47 |

Table 2: Statistics of the fine-grained dataset.

Results of various models along with the baseline are reported in Table 4. The upper half of the table contains the experimental results for three systems. These three models correspond to the official baseline model, model developed with all the features and the model developed with the selected features of DE. The MODE based feature selection model yields the F-measure value of 56.81% for the $test2015$ dataset. It is evident that it performs well above the official baseline that showed the F-measure value of 49.88%. Similarly for the fine-grained NE types (lower half of the table) our system (39.84% F-measure) is convincingly ahead of the baseline model (31.97% F-measure) for the official test data ($test2015$).

[6] http://taku910.github.io/crfpp/

[7] http://www.cnts.ua.ac.be/conll2002/ner/bin/conlleval.txt

| Types | Dataset | Model | Precision | Recall | F-measure | Accuracy |
|---|---|---|---|---|---|---|
| notype | *dev* | Baseline | 65.25 | 55.90 | 60.21 | 96.95 |
| | | All features | 65.08 | 57.58 | 61.10 | 96.92 |
| | | MODE | 69.81 | 62.36 | 65.88 | 97.12 |
| | *dev*2015 | Baseline | 55.79 | 49.82 | 52.63 | 95.08 |
| | | All features | 51.49 | 50.92 | 51.21 | 94.31 |
| | | MODE | 60.97 | 53.51 | 57.43 | 95.60 |
| | *test*2015 | Baseline | 53.86 | 46.44 | 49.88 | 95.01 |
| | | All features | 52.37 | 56.32 | 54.27 | 95.55 |
| | | MODE | 63.43 | 51.44 | 56.81 | 95.50 |
| 10type | *dev* | Baseline | 57.04 | 44.38 | 49.92 | 96.44 |
| | | All features | 61.23 | 39.04 | 47.68 | 96.29 |
| | | MODE | 70.71 | 39.33 | 50.54 | 96.43 |
| | *dev*2015 | Baseline | 38.53 | 30.88 | 34.29 | 94.14 |
| | | All features | 37.14 | 23.90 | 29.08 | 93.50 |
| | | MODE | 48.33 | 24.26 | 32.35 | 94.33 |
| | *test*2015 | Baseline | 35.56 | 29.05 | 31.97 | 93.41 |
| | | All features | 42.41 | 30.00 | 35.14 | 94.94 |
| | | MODE | 60.68 | 29.65 | 39.84 | 94.54 |

Table 4: Results of various systems on different dataset. All values are in %.

| Features | *C-grained* | *F-grained* |
|---|---|---|
| POS | √ | √ |
| WordLength | √ | √ |
| Suffix | √ | √ |
| Prefix | √ | √ |
| WordNorm | √ | √ |
| PrevOccur | | √ |
| Stop word | | |
| InitCap | √ | |
| AllCap | | |
| InnerCap | | √ |
| AllDigit | | |
| AlphaDigit | √ | √ |
| First & last word | | |
| WordFreq | | |
| Gazetteer | | √ |

Table 3: Optimized feature sets.

## 5 Conclusion

In this paper we have presented our works that we carried out as part of our participation in the Twitter NER shared task. We have used a set of features which were implemented without using much domain specific resources and/or tools. We have considered various combinations of features and finally select the combination that yields the best result. We further apply MODE based feature selection on this feature set. Official evaluation shows F-measure of 39.84% for the fine-grained NE types and 56.81% F-measure for the coarse-grained NE type.

In future we would like to carry out more comprehensive analysis on the evaluation results. The features that we used here are very general in nature. In future we would like to investigate domain-specific features to improve the accuracy of the system.

## References


Daniel M. Bikel, Richard Schwartz, and Ralph M. Weischedel. 1999. An algorithm that learns what's in a name. *Mach. Learn.*, 34(1-3):211–231, February.

Leon Derczynski, Diana Maynard, Giuseppe Rizzo, Marieke van Erp, Genevieve Gorrell, Raphal Troncy, Johann Petrak, and Kalina Bontcheva. 2015. Analysis of named entity recognition and linking for tweets. *Information Processing & Management*, 51(2):32–49.

Asif Ekbal and Sivaji Bandyopadhyay. 2008a. Bengali named entity recognition using support vector machine. In *Third International Joint Conference on Natural Language Processing, IJCNLP 2008, Hyderabad, India, January 7-12, 2008*, pages 51–58.

Asif Ekbal and Sivaji Bandyopadhyay. 2008b. Named entity recognition in indian languages using maximum entropy approach. *Int. J. Comput. Proc. Oriental Lang.*, 21(3):205–237.

John D. Lafferty, Andrew McCallum, and Fernando C. N. Pereira. 2001. Conditional Random Fields: Probabilistic Models for Segmenting and Labeling Sequence Data. In *ICML*, pages 282–289.

Chenliang Li, Jianshu Weng, Qi He, Yuxia Yao, Anwitaman Datta, Aixin Sun, and Bu-Sung Lee. 2012. Twiner: Named entity recognition in targeted twitter stream. In *Proceedings of the 35th International ACM SIGIR Conference on Research and Development in Information Retrieval*, SIGIR '12, pages 721–730, New York, NY, USA. ACM.

Xiaohua Liu, Shaodian Zhang, Furu Wei, and Ming Zhou. 2011. Recognizing named entities in tweets. In *Proceedings of the 49th Annual Meeting of the Association for Computational Linguistics: Human Language Technologies - Volume 1*, HLT '11, pages 359–367, Stroudsburg, PA, USA. Association for Computational Linguistics.

B. Locke and J. Martin. 2009. Named entity recognition: Adapting to microblogging. *University of Colorado*.

Daniel Ramage, David Hall, Ramesh Nallapati, and Christopher D. Manning. 2009. Labeled lda: A supervised topic model for credit attribution in multilabeled corpora. In *Proceedings of the 2009 Conference on Empirical Methods in Natural Language Processing: Volume 1 - Volume 1*, EMNLP '09, pages 248–256, Stroudsburg, PA, USA. Association for Computational Linguistics.

Alan Ritter, Sam Clark, Mausam, and Oren Etzioni. 2011. Named entity recognition in tweets: An experimental study. In *Proceedings of the Conference on Empirical Methods in Natural Language Processing*, EMNLP '11, pages 1524–1534, Stroudsburg, PA, USA. Association for Computational Linguistics.

Utpal Kumar Sikdar, Asif Ekbal, and Sriparna Saha. 2012. Differential evolution based feature selection and classifier ensemble for named entity recognition. In *COLING 2012, 24th International Conference on Computational Linguistics, Proceedings of the Conference: Technical Papers, 8-15 December 2012, Mumbai, India*, pages 2475–2490.

Rainer Storn and Kenneth Price. 1997. Differential evolution a simple and efficient heuristic for global optimization over continuous spaces. *J. of Global Optimization*, 11(4):341–359, December.

# Lattice: Data Adaptation for Named Entity Recognition on Tweets with Features-Rich CRF

**Tian TIAN**
Lattice / 1 Maurice Arnoux
92120 MONTROUGE
tian.tian@live.cn

**Marco Dinarelli**
Lattice / 1 Maurice Arnoux
92120 MONTROUGE
marco.dinarelli@ens.fr

**Isabelle TELLIER**
Lattice / 1 Maurice Arnoux
92120 MONTROUGE
isabelle.tellier@univ-paris3.fr

## Abstract

This article describes our CRF named entity extractor for Twitter data. We first discuss some specificities of the task, with an example found in the training data. Then we present how we built our CRF model, especially the way features were defined. The results of these first experiments are given. We also tested our model with dev_2015 data and we describe the procedure we have used to adapt older Twitter data to the data available for this 2015 shared task. Our final results for the task are discussed.

## 1 Introduction

In this shared task, we have to extract 10 types of (or not typed) named entities in Twitter data. We have at our disposal two labelled corpora: train and dev. The first section shows some specificities of the data, from an example it contains. We then construct a CRF model for the task, using the software Wapiti. Our features for this CRF are chosen according to the state-of-the-art, they are described in the second section. The third section focuses on some experiments with train and dev and gives the obtained results. The fourth section is about the procedure we have used to build our final model, by applying a domain adaptation strategy. In the last section, we discuss some future work for this shared task.

## 2 Data Analysis

Although named entity recognition is a traditional task of natural language processing (NLP) which has given rise to a large body of works for written English (Finkel et al., 2005) or news wires in French (Stern and Sagot, 2010), the same task with Twitter data remains difficult (Ritter et al., 2011).

| |
|---|
| Today wasz Fun cusz anna Came juss for me <3: hahaha |

Figure 1: An example of tweet

This is not only because of the task itself, but also because of the way tweets are written.

Figure 1 shows an example of tweet. The correct sentence should be: Today was fun because Anna came just for me <3: hahaha. We can note the following phenomena:

- spelling mistakes: wasz (was), cusz (because), juss (just)
- confusion of upper/lower cases: Fun (fun), anna (Anna), Came (came)
- emoticon: <3
- interjection: hahaha

We remark here that the only name has no upper case letters whereas other words have upper cases (like "Fun", "Came"). So, it would be difficult for a named entity extractor to correctly detect this person name.

## 3 CRF Implementation and Features

### 3.1 CRF Features

We used the CRF implementation *Wapiti 1.5.0* [1] to create our CRF model. The optimization algorithm we chose was rprop+. The features for the tokens are all in unigrams and within a window of size 3 (previous token, current token and next token). The bigrams are only made of labels, characterizing label transitions. Table 1 shows the features we implemented. These templates have been chosen following (Suzuki and Isozaki, 2008), (Lavergne et al., 2010), (Nooralahzadeh et al., 2014) and (Constant et al., 2011)

[1] https://wapiti.limsi.fr



*Proceedings of the ACL 2015 Workshop on Noisy User-generated Text*, pages 68–71,
Beijing, China, July 31, 2015. ©2015 Association for Computational Linguistics

| token value |
|---|
| fstUpper<br>shortCap<br>longCap<br>mixCap<br>hasUpper<br>allUpper<br>capType: combination of 6 binary values<br>allLetter<br>singleLetter<br>tokenType: punctuation, 9, x or X |
| hasNumber<br>allNumber<br>isDecimal<br>onePunct<br>allPunct<br>hasPunct<br>longPunct<br>hasQuotation<br>hasAtLeast2periodes<br>finishedByPeriode<br>hasDash |
| lower<br>returnUnicodeVector |
| isEmal<br>isURL<br>isRT<br>isUSR<br>isHashTag<br>isDate<br>isTime<br>isAbbrev |
| prefixe_n, suffixe_n (n = 1..5) |
| postag in PTB: with binary values |
| category in Brown cluster: in binary tree |

Table 1: CRF features

The capType features regroup 6 binary features: allUpper, shortCap, longCap, allLower, fstUpper, mixCap. The tokenType feature transforms a token into a "skeleton": in this skeleton, all numbers are replaced by 9, all letters in lower case by x, all letters in upper case by X and the punctuations remain unchanged. The part-of-speech tags (postags) of the Penn Tree Bank (PTB) (Marcus et al., 1993) generate 45 distinct features. Each tag in the PTB becomes a feature with a binary value. The "category in Brown cluster" uses the result of Brown clustering (Brown et al., 1992) executed with 56,345,753 tweets available at `http://www.ark.cs.cmu.edu/TweetNLP/`. The class of each token is represented with 13 binary values. These values represent therefore a binary tree. Each value means one level in the binary tree. So we took the first value for each token, i.e. its category with only one level (two possible values).We then took the first two values of each token, resulting in the clustering of twitter tokens into four classes, etc. We took until all 13 values, to get the classes of the token at every level of the binary tree.

| | precision | recall | FB1 |
|---|---|---|---|
| dev | 69.01% | 33.15% | 44.78% |
| dev_2015 | 43.26% | 22.43% | 29.54% |

Table 2: Experiment results with model trained on train file

### 3.2 Use of Lexical Resources

As they were attached with the available baseline, we processed a set of entity dictionaries. We tried to associate these dictionaries with the 10 types of entities defined for the shared task. We deleted duplicated data (as we kept only cap.1000 but not cap.10 nor others, etc). Then we read every item of the lists. As some items (entities) contain more than one token, we extracted the first tokens (or the only token for one-token-entities) and the remaining ones before storing them into different lists. So, for every dictionary we had, we created 2 lists: a "B-dictionary" and a "I-dictionary", preparing the BIO labelings. Finally, we integrated these dictionaries into the model by binary values. For each token, if it is present in a dictionary (B-dictionary or I-dictionary), its value for the corresponding feature is set to 1, and 0 otherwise. And we could always try with other ressources like FreeBase `https://www.freebase.com/` and dbpedia `http://dbpedia.org/`.

## 4 Some Experiments and Results

With the templates defined in the previous section, we used rprop+ as optimization algorithm in Wapiti and we did some experiments (only with the 10 distinct types of entities) with models trained with "train" and tested on "dev", and later tested on "dev_2015". Table 2 shows some of these results.

## 5 CRF Model Training with Domain Data Adaptation

As we can see in the previous section, our first model performs poorly on dev_2105 data compared to dev. This suggests that the data in dev_2015 are very different from the data in dev and train. This intuition has indeed been confirmed by a quick data analysis.

As a consequence, we had the idea to perform a kind of domain data adaptation, inspired by the work of (Raymond and Fayolle, 2010). In this context, the data we want to adapt is called *source domain*. In our case, train and dev data play the role of this source domain. The role of *target domain* is played by the new version of tweet data provided for the shared task, that is dev_2105 data. The approach described in (Raymond and Fayolle, 2010) mixes together data from the source domain and from the target domain in order to train a CRF model. The originality of this approach consists in using more CRF features for the part of the data constituting the target domain than features for the data constituting the source domain. The consequence of this choice is that the CRF models learn word-label dependencies from both domains, but put much stronger importance (feature scores) on features in the target domain, since they are described by more information (features).

We annotated afterwards the training data, which we have already seen during the training phase, with such a model. If the model can apply stronger dependencies learned from the target-domain part of the training data, it will apply such dependencies performing thus the desired adaptation. Otherwise it will apply the dependencies learned from the source-domain part of the training data, thus keeping the old annotation.

We only applied an approximation of this domain adaptation procedure of (Raymond and Fayolle, 2010), because of a serious lack of time. In order to create our final model, we trained our first CRF model (with the templates mentioned in the previous section) with dev_2015. We then applied this first CRF model to train and dev to obtain train_crf and dev_crf. So, these data are labelled with our first CRF model. We got rid of the original labels for train and dev. And, in the end, we trained our final model (always with the same templates) with dev_2015, train_crf and dev_crf all together. We did the same procedure for the 10 types entities and for no typed data. Our results are described in Table 3.

| | precision | recall | FB1 |
|---|---|---|---|
| 10 types | 55.17% | 9.68% | 16.47% |
| no type | 58.42% | 25.72% | 35.71% |

Table 3: Results with model trained on dev_2015 then applied to train and dev files

Compared to results with dev_2015, we had a better precision, which confirms that the adaptation was worth doing. However we also had a much worse recall, which could be someway predicted since the dev_2015 data is much smaller than the training data. It thus creates a serious low covering problem. Such problem can be overcome by applying the exact adaptation procedure described in (Raymond and Fayolle, 2010), together with the use of more external resources (such as name lists).

## 6 Future work

In the future, we could do some proper experiments in cross validation with the training data, in order to find better templates, and find the best L1 and L2 regularization parameters of the CRF. We believe that correctly performing the adaptation procedure of (Raymond and Fayolle, 2010) and thus obtaining a better CRF model for our named entity extractor would lead to much better results.

## References

Peter F. Brown, Peter V. deSouza, Robert L. Mercer, Vincent J. Della Pietra, and Jenifer C. Lai. 1992. Class-based n-gram models of natural language. *Comput. Linguist.*, 18(4):467–479, December.

Matthieu Constant, Isabelle Tellier, Denys Duchier, Yoann Dupont, Anthony Sigogne, and Sylvie Billot. 2011. Intégrer des connaissances linguistiques dans un CRF : application à l'apprentissage d'un segmenteur-étiqueteur du français. In *TALN*, volume 1, page 321, Montpellier, France, June.

Jenny R. Finkel, Trond Grenager, and Christopher Manning. 2005. Incorporating non-local information into information extraction systems by Gibbs sampling. In *Proceedings of the 43rd Annual Meeting on Association for Computational Linguistics*, ACL '05, pages 363–370, Stroudsburg, PA, USA. Association for Computational Linguistics.

Thomas Lavergne, Olivier Cappé, and François Yvon. 2010. Practical very large scale crfs. In *Proceed-*

*ings of the 48th Annual Meeting of the Association for Computational Linguistics*, ACL '10, pages 504–513, Stroudsburg, PA, USA. Association for Computational Linguistics.

Mitchell P. Marcus, Beatrice Santorini, and Mary Ann Marcinkiewicz. 1993. Building a large annotated corpus of english: The penn treebank. *COMPUTATIONAL LINGUISTICS*, 19(2):313–330.

Farhad Nooralahzadeh, Caroline Brun, and Claude Roux. 2014. Part of speech tagging for french social media data. In *COLING 2014, 25th International Conference on Computational Linguistics, Proceedings of the Conference: Technical Papers, August 23-29, 2014, Dublin, Ireland*, pages 1764–1772.

Christian Raymond and Julien Fayolle. 2010. Reconnaissance robuste d'entités nommées sur de la parole transcrite automatiquement. In *Conférence Traitement automatique des langues naturelles, TALN'10*, Montréal, Québec, Canada, July. ATALA.

Alan Ritter, Sam Clark, Mausam, and Oren Etzioni. 2011. Named entity recognition in tweets: An experimental study. In *Proceedings of the Conference on Empirical Methods in Natural Language Processing*, EMNLP '11, pages 1524–1534, Stroudsburg, PA, USA. Association for Computational Linguistics.

Rosa Stern and Benoît Sagot. 2010. Resources for named entity recognition and resolution in news wires. In *Entity 2010 Workshop at LREC 2010*.

Jun Suzuki and Hideki Isozaki. 2008. Semi-supervised sequential labeling and segmentation using giga-word scale unlabeled data. In *In ACL*.

# Hallym: Named Entity Recognition on Twitter with Induced Word Representation

**Eun-Suk Yang**
Hallym University
esyang219@gmail.com

**Yu-Seop Kim**
Hallym University
yskim01@hallym.ac.kr

**Abstract**

Twitter is a type of social media that contains diverse user-generated texts. Traditional models are not applicable to tweet data because the text style is not as grammaticalized as that of newswire. In this paper, we construct word embeddings via canonical correlation analysis (CCA) on a considerable amount of tweet data and show the efficacy of word representation. Besides word embedding, we use part-of-speech (POS) tags, chunks, and brown clusters induced from Wikipedia as features. Here, we describe our system and present the final results along with their analysis. Our model achieves an F1 score of 37.21% with entity types and distinguishes 53.01% of the entity boundaries.

## 1 Introduction

Named entity recognition (NER) is a task of finding and classifying names of things, such as person, location, and organization, given a sequence of words. NER is a very important subtask of information extraction (IE).

With the development of the Internet, a huge amount of information has been generated by users. The information generated on the Internet, particularly on social media (e.g., Twitter and Facebook), includes very diverse and noisy texts. The volume of Twitter data has increased rapidly, and about 500 million tweets are sent per day[1]. In recent years, Twitter data have considered a new source in nature and researchers are paying increased attention to them (Bollen et al., 2011; Mathioudakis and Koudas, 2010).

Twitter is a type of microblogging service in which users are allowed to post contents such as small messages, individual images, or videos. There are a number of microblogging sites such as Twitter, Tumblr, Plurk and identi.ca. Each service has its own characteristics. For example, Plurk has a timeline view for videos and pictures, and Twitter has "status updates."

The characteristic of "status updates" is one of the features that makes the classification of named entities in Twitter difficult. In Twitter, there is a limit for the number of characters that people can post at once. People post their thoughts with a short sentence; this leads to the problem that tweets do not contain sufficient contextual information (Ritter et al., 2011).

The shared task of ACL W-NUT 2015 is to find named entities on Twitter. Here, we will focus on ten types of named entities: company, facility, geo-loc, movie, musicartist, other, person, product, sportsteam, and tvshow. We have the training and development data for Twitter and 53 gazetteers from the abovementioned shared task.

In this paper, we describe the datasets in Section 2 and present the model that we use in this study in Section 3. In Section 4, we discuss the features used and the methods used for generating these features. We present our final results along with their analysis in Section 5 and conclude this paper in Section 6.

## 2 Data and Labels

In this section, we introduce the considered datasets and describe the data format used. We also list the characteristics of each entity type with some examples.

### 2.1 Data

The datasets provided by shared task are raw tweets. Table 1 shows an overview of the sizes of these datasets. In a tweet, each line contains words and its label is separated by a tab and a blank line that forms a sentence boundary. All tokens follow the IOB format. The token with a B-prefix indi-

[1] See "http://www.internetlivestats.com/twitter-statistics/"



*Proceedings of the ACL 2015 Workshop on Noisy User-generated Text*, pages 72–77,
Beijing, China, July 31, 2015. ©2015 Association for Computational Linguistics

cates the beginning of a named entity and the token with an I-prefix indicates the inside of a named entity. An I-prefix only follows after a token with a B-prefix. An O tag indicates that a token does not belong to a specific named entity.

| Data | Tweets | Tokens |
|---|---|---|
| train | 1,795 | 37,899 |
| test | 1,000 | 16,261 |

Table 1: An overview of datasets.

### 2.2 Labels

In the system, we focus on the following ten types of named entities:

**company** The name of a company or a brand
e.g., Snapchat, Twitter, and Facebook

**facility** The name of an institution such as a museum, a center, or a restaurant
e.g., Iowa City schools and Disneyland

**geo-loc** The name of a city or country
e.g., Chicago and Russia

**movie** The title of a movie
e.g., Interstellar and Inception

**musicartist** The name of music groups or disc jockeys (DJs)
e.g., Taylor Swift and Lady Gaga

**other** A phrase that can be used generally such as the name of a ceremony or an anniversary, or the title of a song
e.g., X-mas and Murphy's law

**person** The name of a person; it can be the person's full name, last name, or first name
e.g., Steve King and Ellen

**product** The name of a product
e.g., Nokia 5800 and Coke

**sportsteam** The name of a sports team
e.g., Arsenal and West Ham

**tvshow** The title of a television (TV) show
e.g., The Persuaders and Pretty Little Liars

## 3 Model

Conditional Random Fields (CRFs) (Lafferty et al., 2001) and its variants have been successfully applied to various sequence labeling tasks (Maaten et al., 2011; Collins, 2002; McCallum and Li, 2003; Kim and Snyder, 2012; Kim et al., 2015b; Kim et al., 2015a; Kim and Snyder, 2013a; Kim and Snyder, 2013b). The NER task produces a sequence of named entity tags, $y = (y_1 \dots y_n)$, given a sequence of words, $x = (x_1 \dots x_n)$. We model the conditional probability $p(y|x;\theta)$ using linear-chain CRFs:

$$p(y|x;\theta) = \frac{\exp(\theta \cdot \Phi(x,y))}{\sum_{y' \in \mathcal{Y}(x)} \exp(\theta \cdot \Phi(x,y'))}$$

where $\theta$ denotes a set of model parameters. $\mathcal{Y}$ returns all possible label sequences of $x$, and $\Phi$ maps $(x,y)$ into a feature vector that is a linear sum of the local feature vectors: $\Phi(x,y) = \sum_{j=1}^{n} \phi(x,j,y_{j-1},y_j)$. Given the fully labeled sequences $\{(x^{(i)},y^{(i)})\}_{i=1}^{N}$, the objective of the training is to find $\theta$ that maximizes the log likelihood of the training data under the model with $l_2$-regularization:

$$\theta^* = \operatorname*{argmax}_{\theta} \sum_{i=1}^{N} \log p(y^{(i)}|x^{(i)};\theta) - \frac{\lambda}{2} ||\theta||^2 .$$

## 4 Features

In this section, we describe a variety of features that we have used in this study. We also used CRFsuite[2] because it makes the application of new features easy. Apart from the base features and gazetteer features provided by the organizers, we have used the following new features: POS tags, chunks, brown clustering, and word representation. Our model is composed of the following features:

### 4.1 Base features

Base features include the gazetteer features and orthographic features. In the NER task, a huge amount of unlabeled data is often used for identifying unseen entities. There are already 53 gazetteers in the baseline system. The maximum window size for gazetteer features is 6, and the model will learn the named entity type associated

[2] http://www.chokkan.org/software/crfsuite/

with a specific phrase, if it is in one or more of the gazetteer lexicons. Orthographic features can be divided into five types. The orthographic feature templates are as follows:

- $n$-gram: $w_i$ for $i$ in {-1,0,1}, conjunction of previous word and current word $w_{i-1}|w_i$ for $i$ in {-1,0}.

- Affixes: Prefixes and suffixes of $x_i$. The first and last $n$ characters ranging from 1 to 3.

- Capitalization: There are two patterns of capitalization: One is an indicator of capitalization for the first character, and the other is an indicator of capitalization for all characters.

- Digit: There are three patterns for numbers: i) Whether the current word has a digit, ii) whether the current word is a single digit, and iii) whether the current word has two digits.

- Non-alphabet: Whether the current word contains a hyphen and other punctuation marks. Among the other punctuation marks is the colon(:). In general, what follows right after a colon mark represents a feature weight. To make the model learn correctly, we normalize only the colon mark.

### 4.2 POS tags and chunks

In the NER task, POS tags and chunks contain very useful information for finding and classifying named entities. We predict POS tags and chunks by using a model trained with Twitter data. For POS tags, we use a model trained with the Penn Treebank-style tagset (Ritter et al., 2011). In a model, some Twitter-specific tags are added by Ritter et al. (2011): retweets, @usernames, #hashtags, and urls. For chunks, we use a named entity tagger[3] by Ritter et al. (2012). Predicted tags are used as features as follows:

- POS tag: a conjunction feature with the current word and the current POS tag $w_0|p_0$.

- Chunk tag: a unigram feature for chunk tag $c_0$ and a conjunction feature with the current word and the current chunk tag $w_0|c_0$.

[3]https://github.com/aritter/twitter_nlp

### 4.3 Brown clustering

Brown clustering is a hierarchical clustering method that groups words into a binary tree of classes (Brown et al., 1992). We downloaded a brown clustering[4] based on Wikipedia provided by Turian et al. (2010). We used whole bit string of the current word.

### 4.4 Word representation

As a new source, tweet data are not applicable to the traditional model because of the different text structure. For a new model, it is natural to use annotated data. However, it is difficult to create new labeled data for a rapid generation of tweets. Instead of constantly annotate new data, the general solution is creating induced word representations from a large body of unlabeled data (Mikolov et al., 2013; Pennington et al., 2014; Kim et al., 2014; Anastasakos et al., 2014). A lot of previous work have used CCA because of its simplicity and generality (Kim et al., 2015c; Kim et al., 2015d; Stratos et al., 2014; Kim et al., 2015b). We create a word representation by using the canonical correlation analysis (Hotelling, 1936). Furthermore, word embeddings are induced from 13 million tweets containing 270 million tokens. The dimension of word embeddings we used is 50 with words occurring more than twice in the data . The window size for the contextual information is 3: the current word and a word to the left and the right of the current word.

## 5 Results

### 5.1 Error analysis

Twitter contains noisy and informal style text, and most of the state-of-art applications show a weak performance on Twitter data (Ritter et al., 2011). In this section, we check the errors for noisy text from the baseline system and categorize them. The last two errors are related to user-generated texts such as Twitter data.

**Unseen word sequences:** The main cause of this error is in a previously unseen sequence. A huge number of tweets are posted on Twitter every day and they contain up-to-date information on events. The most recent information such as new product information can lead to the formation of unprecedented word sequences. These sequences do not appear in

[4]http://metaoptimize.com/projects/wordreprs/

| | $M_{noEmbedding}$ | | | $M_{Embedding}$ | | | +/- |
|---|---|---|---|---|---|---|---|
| **Type** | **P** | **R** | **F1** | **P** | **R** | **F1** | |
| **Overall** | 35.95 | 31.92 | 33.81 | 39.59 | 35.10 | 37.21 | + |
| **company** | 27.59 | 20.51 | 23.53 | 32.14 | 23.08 | 26.87 | + |
| **facility** | 24.14 | 18.42 | 20.90 | 32.00 | 21.05 | 25.40 | + |
| **geo-loc** | 42.66 | 52.59 | 47.10 | 46.00 | 59.48 | 51.88 | + |
| **movie** | 14.29 | 6.67 | 9.09 | 8.33 | 6.67 | 7.41 | - |
| **musicartist** | 0.00 | 0.00 | 0.00 | 7.69 | 2.44 | 3.70 | + |
| **other** | 18.33 | 16.67 | 17.46 | 20.49 | 18.94 | 19.69 | + |
| **person** | 53.27 | 61.99 | 57.30 | 56.99 | 64.33 | 60.44 | + |
| **product** | 3.57 | 2.70 | 3.08 | 14.29 | 8.11 | 10.34 | + |
| **sportsteam** | 62.50 | 7.14 | 12.82 | 54.55 | 8.57 | 14.81 | + |
| **tvshow** | 0.00 | 0.00 | 0.00 | 0.00 | 0.00 | 0.00 | . |

Table 2: Results for model with and without word embedding. $M_{noEmbedding}$ and $M_{Embedding}$ represent the model with and without word embedding, respectively. The rightmost column shows the decrease or increase in the F1 score with respect to the model without word embedding. $M_{Embedding}$ denotes our final model.

the training data and gazetteers, and thus, the model cannot learn them.

**Foreign languages:** This error is caused by tweets written in languages other than English. Words written in foreign languages are annotated by the O tag and not include a named entity. However, some words have the same spelling as an English word and thus, activate the gazetteer features. This problem leads to words with the O tag being predicted as a named entity type.

**Type disambiguation:** There are some words that have the same spelling but belong to different types according to the contextual information. This error is often observed for named entities such as *sportsteam* and *musicartist*. The word sequences with this error have a correctly distinguished entity boundary but predict the wrong entity type. For example, *Tampa Bay* in "Losing to the Penguins quasi-AHL lineup in December is a non-issue for *Tampa Bay*" is an entity for *sportsteam*, but the model classifies it as *geo-loc* instead of *sportsteam*. In another example, the names of two music artists in "Will *Shawn Mendez* be opening up for *Taylor Swift*" are predicted as *person* and not as *musicartist*.

**Informal name or abbreviations:** Twitter users compress what they want to say to meet the limit of 140 characters. This leads to informal texts unlike in news articles. Note that abbreviations do not indicate official full forms such as airports or countries. For example, *Southie* in "Proud that the 1st modern Olympic Champion is James Brendan Connolly of *#Southie* ." is an informal name of *South Boston*, and this word does not appear in the training set and gazetteers. With respect to abbreviations, people use abbreviattions for indicating a day or a month, such as *Mon* for Monday and *Jan* for January. These words are contained in gazetteers and activate the gazetteer features. A model makes errors by predicting them as named entities.

**Hashtag:** A hashtag is a combination of the "#" sign and some characters for organizing word sequences as searchable links in Twitter. The rule is to not use any space between the characters in the hashtag. For instance, the word *New Delhi* is transformed into *#NewDelhi* as a hashtag, so it is difficult to check the gazetteer lexicons for such text.

### 5.2 The effectiveness of word embedding

In this subsection, we describe the effectiveness of word embedding by analyzing the results obtained by using the model with and without word embedding. The only difference between both the models is the use of brown clustering and the word representation based on CCA.

In the NER task, the F1 score is a more appropriate metric than accuracy. Most of the labels in the NER data contain the O tag, indicating that they are not an entity. Since this leads to high accuracy, by using the F1 score, we obtain a more reasonable harmonic function of the precision and the recall.

Table 2 shows the results obtained by using models with and without word embedding. As shown in table 2, brown clustering and word embedding have a good effect on performance. All types of entities except *movie* show error reduction. For determining the efficacy of word embedding, we compare the errors between the models without word embedding and with word embedding. We find that word embedding plays an important role in resolving the problem of unseen word sequences and the problem of type disambiguation. First, the model without word embedding does not learn about an entity *ipad Mini Retina 2nd Generation 16GB wifi* because some of the words do not appear in the training data. In contrast, the model with embedding can learn unseen words from the induced word representation. This helps the model to predict that the abovementioned entity indicates a product name. The model without word embedding also has the problem of disambiguation of a word *Edison* because the model only learns that this word is a person's name from the gazetteers. However, in the word sequence "Edison #weather on January 16 , 2015", *Edison* indicates a town in New Jersey. The model with word embedding is provided additional information by the word embedding process and predicts the abovementioned word as *geo-loc* correctly.

## 6 Conclusion

In this paper, we described the data and features used for generating our model. Besides POS tags and chunk tags, we used a word representation based on CCA for improving the model's performance. Our final model shows an error reduction of 14.08% from the baseline system. We also presented some primary and Twitter-specific problems by categorizing errors.

## References


Tasos Anastasakos, Young-Bum Kim, and Anoop Deoras. 2014. Task specific continuous word representations for mono and multi-lingual spoken language understanding. In *ICASSP*, pages 3246–3250. IEEE.

Johan Bollen, Huina Mao, and Xiaojun Zeng. 2011. Twitter mood predicts the stock market. *Journal of Computational Science*, 2(1):1–8.

Peter F Brown, Peter V Desouza, Robert L Mercer, Vincent J Della Pietra, and Jenifer C Lai. 1992. Class-based n-gram models of natural language. *Computational linguistics*, 18(4):467–479.

Michael Collins. 2002. Discriminative training methods for hidden markov models: Theory and experiments with perceptron algorithms. In *Proceedings of the ACL-02 conference on Empirical methods in natural language processing-Volume 10*, pages 1–8. Association for Computational Linguistics.

Harold Hotelling. 1936. Relations between two sets of variates. *Biometrika*, pages 321–377.

Young-Bum Kim and Benjamin Snyder. 2012. Universal grapheme-to-phoneme prediction over latin alphabets. In *EMNLP*, pages 332–343. Association for Computational Linguistics.

Young-Bum Kim and Benjamin Snyder. 2013a. Optimal data set selection: An application to grapheme-to-phoneme conversion. In *HLT-NAACL*, pages 1196–1205. Association for Computational Linguistics.

Young-Bum Kim and Benjamin Snyder. 2013b. Unsupervised consonant-vowel prediction over hundreds of languages. In *ACL (1)*, pages 1527–1536.

Young-Bum Kim, Heemoon Chae, Benjamin Snyder, and Yu-Seop Kim. 2014. Training a korean srl system with rich morphological features. In *ACL*, pages 637–642. Association for Computational Linguistics.

Young-Bum Kim, Minwoo Jeong, Karl Stratos, and Ruhi Sarikaya. 2015a. Weakly supervised slot tagging with partially labeled sequences from web search click logs. In *HLT-NAACL*, pages 84–92. Association for Computational Linguistics.

Young-Bum Kim, Karl Stratos, Xiaohu Liu, and Ruhi Sarikaya. 2015b. Compact lexicon selection with spectral methods. In *ACL*. Association for Computational Linguistics.

Young-Bum Kim, Karl Stratos, and Ruhi Sarikaya. 2015c. Pre-training of hidden-unit crfs. In *ACL*. Association for Computational Linguistics.

Young-Bum Kim, Karl Stratos, Ruhi Sarikaya, and Minwoo Jeong. 2015d. New transfer learning techniques for disparate label sets. In *ACL*. Association for Computational Linguistics.

John Lafferty, Andrew McCallum, and Fernando CN Pereira. 2001. Conditional random fields: Probabilistic models for segmenting and labeling sequence data.

Laurens Maaten, Max Welling, and Lawrence K Saul. 2011. Hidden-unit conditional random fields. In *International Conference on Artificial Intelligence and Statistics*.

Michael Mathioudakis and Nick Koudas. 2010. Twittermonitor: trend detection over the twitter stream. In *Proceedings of the 2010 ACM SIGMOD International Conference on Management of data*, pages 1155–1158. ACM.

Andrew McCallum and Wei Li. 2003. Early results for named entity recognition with conditional random fields, feature induction and web-enhanced lexicons. In *HLT-NAACL*, pages 188–191. Association for Computational Linguistics.

Tomas Mikolov, Ilya Sutskever, Kai Chen, Greg S Corrado, and Jeff Dean. 2013. Distributed representations of words and phrases and their compositionality. In *Advances in neural information processing systems*, pages 3111–3119.

Jeffrey Pennington, Richard Socher, and Christopher D Manning. 2014. Glove: Global vectors for word representation. *Proceedings of the Empiricial Methods in Natural Language Processing (EMNLP 2014)*, 12:1532–1543.

Alan Ritter, Sam Clark, Oren Etzioni, et al. 2011. Named entity recognition in tweets: an experimental study. In *Proceedings of the Conference on Empirical Methods in Natural Language Processing*, pages 1524–1534. Association for Computational Linguistics.

Alan Ritter, Mausam, Oren Etzioni, and Sam Clark. 2012. Open domain event extraction from twitter. In *KDD*.

Karl Stratos, Do-kyum Kim, Michael Collins, and Daniel Hsu. 2014. A spectral algorithm for learning class-based $n$-gram models of natural language. In *UAI*.

Joseph Turian, Lev Ratinov, and Yoshua Bengio. 2010. Word representations: a simple and general method for semi-supervised learning. In *Proceedings of the 48th annual meeting of the association for computational linguistics*, pages 384–394. Association for Computational Linguistics.

# IHS_RD: Lexical Normalization for English Tweets

**Dmitry Supranovich**
IHS Inc. / IHS Global Belarus
131 Starovilenskaya St
220123, Minsk, Belarus
Dmitry.Supranovich@ihs.com

**Viachaslau Patsepnia**
IHS Inc.
55 Cambridge pkwy, Suite 601
Cambridge, MA 02142, USA
Slava.Patsepnia@ihs.com

**Abstract**

This paper describes the Twitter lexical normalization system submitted by IHS R&D Belarus team for the ACL 2015 workshop on noisy user-generated text. The proposed system consists of two components: a CRF-based approach to identify possible normalization candidates, and a post-processing step in an attempt to normalize words that do not have normalization variants in the lexicon. Evaluation on the test data set showed that our unconstrained system achieved the F-measure of 0.8272 (rank 1 out of 5 submissions for the unconstrained mode, rank 2 out of all 11 submissions).

## 1 Introduction

Social media texts found in such services as Twitter or Facebook have a great data-mining potential, as they offer real-time data that can be useful to monitor public opinion on brands, products, events, etc. However, current Natural Language Processing systems are usually optimized for clean data, which is not the type of data found in social media texts, as they are often noisy, containing a lot of slang, typos, and abbreviations.

Normalizing such text is challenging. We want to achieve high recall, making as many corrections as possible, but not at the expense of precision – words should not be incorrectly normalized.

Previous approaches to this task incorporated different tools and methods: dictionaries, language models, finite state transducers, and machine translation models. Some of the methods are unsupervised, though often requiring adjustment of parameters based on annotated data (Han and Baldwin (2011), Liu et al. (2011), and Gouws et al. (2011)). Some are supervised, like that in Chrupała (2014), making use of a Conditional Random Field (Lafferty et al., 2001) to learn the sequences of edit operations from labelled data.

In this paper, we present an approach based on the usage of normalization lexicons and a CRF model for identifying potential candidates.

## 2 Task Description

### 2.1 Dataset

The corpus provided by the organizers consists of 2950 annotated tweets. The annotations follow these guidelines (Baldwin et al., 2015):

- Non-standard words are normalized to one or more canonical English words based on a pre-defined lexicon. For instance, *l o v e* should be normalized to *love* (many-to-one normalization), *tmrw* to *tomorrow* (one-to-one normalization), and *cu* to *see you* (one-to-many normalization). Additionally, *IBM* should be left untouched as it is in the lexicon and it is in its canonical form, and the informal *lol* should be expanded to *laughing out loud.*
- Non-standard words may be either out-of-vocabulary (OOV) tokens (e.g., *tmrw* for *tomorrow*) or in-vocabulary (IV) tokens (e.g., *wit* for *with* in "I will come wit you").
- Only alphanumeric tokens (e.g., *2*, *4eva* and *tmrw*) and apostrophes used in contractions (e.g., *yoou've*) are considered for normalization. Tokens including hyphens, single quotes and other types of contractions should be ignored.
- Domain specific entities are ignored even if they are in non-standard forms, e.g., *#ttyl*, *@nyc*
- It is possible for a tweet to have no non-standard tokens but still require normalization (e.g., the example of *wit* above), and it is also possible for the tweet to require no normalization whatsoever.



*Proceedings of the ACL 2015 Workshop on Noisy User-generated Text*, pages 78–81,
Beijing, China, July 31, 2015. 

- Proper nouns should be left untouched, even if they are not in the given lexicon (e.g., *Twitter*).
- All normalizations should use the American spelling (e.g., *tokenize* rather than *tokenise*).

### 2.2 Evaluation

Evaluation was to be carried out according to Precision, Recall, and F1 metrics.

## 3 Experimental Setup

First, a normalization lexicon was generated from the given training data, enriched with the data from several sources:

- Word pairs extracted from the datasets used for lexical normalization (Han, 2011; Liu, 2011)
- The online social media abbreviation list of Beal (2015)[1]. Compared to the previous workshops with one-to-one normalizations, the current task also considers one-to-many normalizations, and obviously not all abbreviations are present in the training data, so the use of a list of social media abbreviations can be vital to the system.

At the current stage of development the system is unable to differentiate between several normalization variants; thus, entries with multiple possible variants were reviewed to make the most suitable variant first in the list (entries that are most frequent in datasets are placed first, any ties were manually reviewed).

Second, a CRF model was trained. The labels chosen were CAND and NOT_CAND, reflecting potential normalization candidates and words that should not be normalized, respectively. The following features were used:

**Token:** This feature represents the string of the current token.

**Context Feature:** The token to the left and the token to the right are used as two context features. The surrounding words usually convey useful information about a token which helps in predicting the correct tag for each token.

**Alphanumeric feature:** This feature checks whether the token adheres to the annotation guidelines and makes sure that non-adhering tokens are not marked as potential candidates.

**Normalization dictionary feature:** This feature checks whether the token is present in the generated normalization lexicon.

**Canonical lexicon feature**: This feature indicates whether or not the token is present in the canonical lexicon provided by the workshop organizers.

**Word length and number of vowels**: Two separate features as well as their correlation, allowing to tag words with uncommon length-vowel correlation, like *bcz, pls,* etc.

**Edit distance feature:** marks a token that is within an edit distance of 2 or less from any word in the canonical lexicon.

Third, the text is normalized:

- All tokens tagged as potential candidates by the CRF model are normalized to their lexicon variants.
- All alphanumeric words are normalized to the American spelling with the VarCon tool (Atkinson, 2015)[2]. This includes the tokens which are already normalized using the lexicon.
- We have also tried to improve the normalization results by using a did-you-mean (DYM) module that is currently being developed at IHS R&D team. The DYM module corrects user queries/sentences with misspellings by providing corrected variant(s) with a confidence measure (including no correction variant with the corresponding confidence measure). The DYM module is an SVM model trained on a set of features for each of the multiple candidates generated for an input query/sentence. We used the following features: error model score, Levenshtein distance, language model score, the ratio of common noun vocabulary words, the ratio of proper noun vocabulary words, and the number of changes in non-lowercase words. An error model score was obtained from an autocompletion and autocorrection module (AAM) for which an index was built from 12.4M documents (scientific papers - 42.1%, Wikipedia articles - 23.5%, patents - 19.4%, social texts - 8%, and news - 7%). The 2-gram language model was built from 177K patents (1.36G words and 2.6M vocabulary). Since we did not have enough time to tailor both DYM and AAM modules for social text processing, DYM and AAM modules were

[1]http://www.webopedia.com/quick_ref/textmessageabbreviations.asp

[2]http://wordlist.aspell.net/varcon/

used for this Twitter lexical normalization system as is, being actually tailored for technical and scientific texts.

### 3.1 Results and error analysis

Testing was performed on the provided corpus of 1967 tweets.

Table 1 shows the performance of our CRF candidate model with different features:

- A baseline model with only token, context and alphanumeric features.
- A baseline model with the normalization dictionary and the canonical lexicon features added.
- A model with all features enabled.

Table 2 reflects our submitted normalization result and a result without the DYM module described above.

| | *Precision (CRF \| Final)* | *Recall (CRF \| Final)* | *F1 (CRF \| Final)* |
|---|---|---|---|
| Tokens + Context + Alphanumeric | 0.991 \| 0.8782 | 0.57 \| 0.6013 | 0.7237 \| 0.7139 |
| Added dictionary features | 0.907 \| 0.8376 | 0.824 \| 0.8133 | 0.8635 \| 0.8253 |
| All features | 0.915 \| 0.8469 | 0.817 \| 0.8083 | 0.8632 \| **0.8272** |

Table 1. Result metrics of candidate CRF model with different features (and its impact on the result after normalization using a submitted system).

| | *Precision* | *Recall* | *F1* |
|---|---|---|---|
| Lexicon Normalization + DYM (submitted) | 0.8469 | 0.8083 | 0.8272 |
| Lexicon Normalization without DYM | 0.8765 | 0.7949 | **0.8337** |

Table 2. Result metrics of two normalization system configurations.

The DYM feature does a good job correcting typos and removing excessive duplicate letters (*beutiful* → *beautiful*, *tosee* → *to see*, and *smileeeeee* → *smile*). However, even with a high confidence threshold, quite a number of words are normalized excessively, mainly those in non-English (or partially English) tweets, e.g. *jeil* → *jail*, *hoje* → *hope*, and *wasan* → *was an*, in addition to some incorrect normalizations like *parkd* → *park* (instead of *parked*) or *hundread* → *hundreds* (instead of *hundred*). These mistakes are frequent, and an increase in recall does not outweigh a loss in precision; thus, the F-measure without the DYM feature in its current state is even a little bit higher than our submitted system with it. Lowering the confidence threshold brings more correct normalizations, but due to the nature of tweets even more incorrect ones, leading to an overall drop in F1 score. Nevertheless, we decided to use and submit the system with DYM, since we believe the text normalized this way is more suitable for further use.

Attempts were made to improve the performance of the DYM module as well as to select the correct candidate from a normalization lexicon if there is more than one variant present (ur → you're, your, you). For example, language detection works well on regular search queries and could potentially forbid the normalization of words in non-English tweets. However, it proved to be not helpful for tweets – the messages are short, some of them are a mixture of English and some other language (thus, if there is a normalization restriction on such tweets, potential English normalizations are lost), and slang- and abbreviation-rich tweets are hard to analyse. A language model was used in an attempt to select a correct normalization from multiple variants, but this did not prove to be effective, likely because the model used was not focused on social media texts.

We see room for potential improvement in tuning the DYM tool to social media texts, as well as in filtering non-English words from normalization candidates, experimenting with language models tailored to social media texts and further enriching the lexicon with new normalization data.

## 4 Conclusion

In this paper, we presented a system designed for participation in shared task #2 of the ACL 2015 workshop on noisy user-generated text. Our system makes use of CRF for identifying potential candidates, lexicons to normalize them and a DYM module as a post-processing step to further correct some of the misspelled words. Our system ranked second among all 11 submissions with 0.8272 F-measure and ranked first among 5 submissions for the unconstrained mode.

## References

Kevin Atkinson. VarCon. Vers. 2015.02.15. *Web.* 01 Apr. 2015. http://wordlist.aspell.net/varcon/

Timothy Baldwin, Marie-Catherine de Marneffe, Bo Han, Young-Bum Kim, Alan Ritter, and Wei Xu. 2015. Shared tasks of the 2015 workshop on noisy user-generated text: Twitter lexical normalization and named entity recognition. In *Proceedings of the Workshop on Noisy User-generated Text (WNUT 2015)*, Beijing, China.

Vangie Beal. Text messaging and online chat abbreviations. *Web.* 01 Apr. 2015. http://www.webopedia.com/quick_ref/textmessage abbreviations.asp

Grzegorz Chrupała. 2014. Normalizing tweets with edit scripts and recurrent neural embeddings. In *Proceedings of the 52nd Annual Meeting of the Association for Computational Linguistics (ACL 2014)*, pages 680–686, Baltimore, USA.

Stephan Gouws, Dirk Hovy, and Donald Metzler. 2011. Unsupervised mining of lexical variants from noisy text. In *Proceedings of the First workshop on Unsupervised Learning in NLP*, pages 82–90, Edinburgh, UK.

Bo Han and Timothy Baldwin. 2011. Lexical normalization of short text messages: Makn sens a #twitter. In *Proceedings of the 49th Annual Meeting of the Association for Computational Linguistics (ACL 2011)*, pages 368-378, Portland, USA.

John D. Lafferty, Andrew McCallum, and Fernando C. N. Pereira. 2001. Conditional Random Fields: Probabilistic models for segmenting and labeling sequence data. In *Proceedings of the Eighteenth International Conference on Machine Learning*, ICML'01, pages 282–289. Morgan Kaufmann Publishers Inc., San Francisco, CA, USA

Fei Liu, Fuliang Weng, Bingqing Wang, and Yang Liu. 2011. Insertion, deletion, or substitution? Normalizing text messages without precategorization nor supervision. In *Proceedings of the 49th Annual Meeting of the Association for Computational Linguistics (ACL 2011)*, pages 71-76, Portland, USA.

Fei Liu, Fuliang Weng, and Xiao Jiang. 2012. A broad-coverage normalization system for social media language. In *Proceedings of the 50th Annual Meeting of the Association for Computational Linguistics (ACL 2012)*, pages 1035-1044, Jeju Island, Korea.

Yi Yang and Jacob Eisenstein. 2013. A log-linear model for unsupervised text normalization. In *Proceedings of Conference on Empirical Methods in Natura Language Processing (EMNLP)*, pages 61-72, Seattle, USA.

# Bekli: A Simple Approach to Twitter Text Normalization

**Russell Beckley**
Oregon Health and Sciences University
Portland, Oregon
beckleyr@ohsu.edu

## Abstract

Every day, Twitter users generate vast quantities of potentially useful information in the form of written language. Due to Twitter's frequently informal tone, text normalization can be a crucial element for exploiting that information. This paper outlines our approach to text normalization used in the WNUT shared task. We show that a very simple solution, powered by a modestly sized, partially-curated wordlist—combined with a modest re-ranking scheme—can deliver respectable results.

## 1 Introduction

Twitter is an immense, living collection of written language from all over the world. Every day, Twitter publishes a staggering 500 million tweets[1]. The content of Twitter is virtually unlimited, and has proven useful for much research, including epidemiology: Chew and Eysenbach (2010); and sentiment analysis: Barbosa and Feng (2010), Bakliwal et al. (2013), Rosenthal et al. (2015), Li et al. (2014).

It would take many readers to keep up with Twitter's output, but, fortunately, we have natural language processing (NLP) methods that can automatically filter, condense, or extract information from text. However, NLP approaches are typically trained on formal edited text, and struggle with the informal, unedited text of Twitter. But there is a well-known way to mitigate this problem: *text normalization*, i.e. replacing non-standard tokens with their standard equivalents, yielding text that will be more agreeable to NLP.

[1]https://blog.twitter.com/2013/new-tweets-per-second-record-and-how

One flavor of non-standard writing—what I have previously focused on—is what I call "vernacular orthography" (VO). VO is spelling that indicates itentional non-standard pronunciation, such as when the string "dat" stands in for "that". While numerous papers offer solutions for text normalization (e.g. Han and Baldwin (2011), Yang and Eisenstein (2013), Zhang et al. (2013), Sproat et al. (2001), Li and Liu (2014)), and a few build models based on phonemic similarity (e.g. Kobus et al. (2008), Choudhury et al. (2007)), none to our knowledge have addressed VO in particular. This paper, too, addresses the general normalization problem, but uses lessons learned attempting to normalize VO.

## 2 System Architecture

The architecture of this system is very simple, consisting of three main parts: (1) a substitution list, (2) a couple of rule based components, and (3) a sentence level re-ranker. This provides for a fast per-token performance.

### 2.1 Substitution List

Most of the work is done by a semi-supervised substitution list consisting of ordered pairs. The first member of each pair is a string representing a non-standard word. The second member of each pair is a list of strings representing candidate replacements for the word. For example, one pair is ("n", ("and, in")). There are just over 45,000 pairs, where only the first 2000 are hand-curated.

To create the list, we use a collection of tweets (see "Resources Employed" section) and a derived dictionary, described presently. The dictionary has the 18,000 standard words most frequent in the tweet collection. For the construction of the dictionary, a



*Proceedings of the ACL 2015 Workshop on Noisy User-generated Text*, pages 82–86,
Beijing, China, July 31, 2015. 

word is considered to be standard if it has at least four characters, and is found in the CMU pronouncing dictionary, or, if it has fewer than three characters, it is found in the Norvig dictionary[2] and is sufficiently frequent (where sufficient frequency depends on the word length).

Now we want to find the most frequent OOVs that need to be normalized. We tokenize the twitter set and filter out all tokens that appear in our dictionary. We also filter out all tokens that do not match the format of normalizable tokens as specified by the shared task e.g. tokens that have non-alphanumeric characters other than an apostrophe('). Lastly, we filter out those tokens that could be normalized by our rule-based components (described in next subsection).

We count the occurrences of each OOV-candidate token type, sort by the count, and return the resulting list. This puts the most useful candidates first and provides for efficient use of annotation time. Suitable replacements require human judgement and occasional reference to outside sources. The outside sources were (1) Urban Dictionary, which is very useful for slang and acronyms (2) Twitter, which tells you how a word is most often used on Twitter, and (3) the training set provided for the shared task, which tells you how to normalize in ambiguous cases (e.g. "laughing out loud" v. "laugh out loud").[2]

In addition to these hand-curated entries, we added the Lexical normalization dictionaries, UniMelb and UTDallas, provided for the shared task. From these lists we took all entries not already in the hand-curated list.[2]

With this initial list in place, we ran it on the training set and analyzed the errors, looking specifically at false positives and false negatives. We sorted the tokens that caused these errors according to a formula that estimated what change would occur to the f-score if the token was to be removed or added to the list. If the token represented a false negative, we would estimate the change to f-score we would get by adding it to the list, assuming that it's substitution would always be the word most often associated with it in the training set. If it was false positive, we would estimate the change to f-score we would get by deleting it from the list.

This analysis revealed some weak spots in the list. First, there were a number of false positives caused by differing beliefs regarding what counts as non-standard. For example, there are several contractions (e.g. "gonna", "gotta", "wanna", and "ain't") that are not usually considered standard (rarely seen in The Wall Street Journal), and have straight forward normalizations, that are nonetheless considered to be in-vocabulary in the task. These words were removed from the substitution list, and added to a new list—a "do-not-normalize" list.

Furthermore, there were of course a number of false negatives. Many of these come from tokens that are in the dictionary, but that are often used in a non-standard way in informal speech. For example, "wit" is in standard dictionaries, referring to an intellectual feature; however it often appears in Twitter as a non-standard variation of "with", as in "you wit me hea?" Likewise on Twitter, "cause" almost always means "because". Such tokens were added to the substitution list.

It might be supposed that using the training set in this way could lead to severe over-fitting. To avoid this, we didn't make any adjustments for tokens appearing less than three times as a false positive, true positive, or false negative. The results show that any over-fitting was not severe, since the test f-score was just one point less than the training f-score.

### 2.2 Rule-based components

We also experimented with several rule-based components, two of which— because they applied in the greatest number of cases in the training set—were used in the final system. These components were the "ing" rule and the "coool" rule.

The "ing" rule looks for cases in which the verbal suffix "-ing" is altered to an "-in", "-en", or "-n", such as when "busting" becomes "bustin". If the test token is in the dictionary, the component generates no candidates. If the token is not in the dictionary, the component checks if the word ends with "-in", "-en", or "-n" proceeded by certain consonants, and if so, checks for the likelihood of additional syllables. If those conditions hold, it replaces the identified ending with "ing", and if the result is in the dictionary, it becomes a candidate.

The "coool" rule attempts to normalize text that,

[2]See "Resources Employed" section.

for emphasis, repeats characters, as in "Thaatt iss reallyyyyy neeeeat!" To generate candidates, the "coool" rule finds every run of more than two repeated characters and reduces the length of the run to two. For every one of these runs, we assume that the original had either one or two of that character in that place. We consider every string that can be created by reducing a subset of the two-character runs to one character each, and return only those strings that occur in the dictionary. For example, if the original token is "thaatt", we consider "thaatt", "thaat", "thatt", and "that", but return only "that", being in the dictionary.

When the system is run with only the "ing" and "coool" rules, plus the sentence level re-ranker, we get a precision of $.81$ and a recall of $.09$. However, when combined with the rest of the system, it's contribution is insignificant. It seems that the most frequent instances of these rules are already in the substitution list, so the rules do not generate enough true positives to offset their generated false positives.

Along with "ing" and "coool", we tried a number of similar rule-based components. For example, we looked for cases where "th" is replaced by either "d", "f", or "t". Another example is the "double consonant" rule, based on the idea that when a word ends with two consonants, and both are voiced or both are unvoiced, the second consonant is dropped. For example "wrist" becomes "wris". These are widespread phenomena, but not widespread enough on Twitter for the true positives to outweigh the false positives. A more sensitive rule or a better sentence-level re-ranker would be needed to make these components beneficial.

### 2.3 Sentence Level Reranker

The third major component of the system is the sentence level-re-ranker. This is, in short, a bigram Viterbi algorithm.

Bigrams were collected from our set of ten million tweets. Bigrams with any out-of-vocabulary tokens were ignored. From this set, for each bigram $(t_1, t_2)$, we computed $prob(t_2|t_1)$ with Laplacian smoothing. These became the transition probabilities in our Viterbi problem.

At test time, we generated candidates for each token. If the substitution list had an entry for an original token, all suggested substitutions in that entry became candidates. For each of these candidates, $c$, we initialize a weight, $w_c$, where $w_c = 2 \times (rank(c) + 1)$, and $rank(c)$ refers to $c$'s position in the list for the current token's entry in the substitution list. If the "ing" rule or the "coool" rule generated answers, those would also be candidates. For the "cool" rule, the weight was the number of deletions required to get the candidate from the original token. For the "ing" rule, the weight was, somewhat arbitrarily, 1. Finally, the original token is a candidate with a weight of $0$. These weights were the emission weights for Viterbi, and were treated as $-\log(prob(c))$. For each original token in the test set, we generated on average $.04$ other candidates.

The system then constructed a lattice from the tweet and all of its normalization candidates. With Viterbi dynamic programming it found the maximum probability path through the lattice. Words in the maximal path were taken to be the correct word for the corresponding token.

At the time of the shared task, I compared this approach to a simpler approach, in which, for any original token, the system ignored the context and selected the normalization with the greatest emission score (emission score as defined above). At first, the Viterbi method added 10 percentage points $f1$ over this method. However, after the the shared task was finished, I discovered that the greatest-emission method had an error. Having fixed that error, and re-running the system on the training data, I discovered that this greatest-emission rule, on the training data, gives better results than the Viterbi system used for the shared task: for $f1$ scores, the Viterbi approach gets a $.768$ while the greatest-emission score is $.816$. Note that, for the Viterbi approach, the test score, $.757$, is not much less than the training score. In summary, (1) the Viterbi approach, as implemented, is probably not the best, and (2) the overall normalization approach I describe in this paper is probably better than the shared task results suggest.

## 3 Resources Employed

The computations for training and testing were done on a MacBook. Required computational resources were minimal. Data resources are as follows:

A. **CMU pronouncing dictionary:** "an open-source machine-readable pronunciation dictio-

| Team Name | precision | recall | f1 |
|---|---|---|---|
| IHS_RD | 0.8469 | 0.8083 | 0.8272 |
| USZEGED | 0.8606 | 0.7564 | 0.8052 |
| bekli | 0.7732 | 0.7416 | 0.7571 |
| gigo | 0.7593 | 0.6963 | 0.7264 |
| lysgroup | 0.4592 | 0.6296 | 0.531 |

Table 1: Team Results for the unconstrained task.

nary for North American English that contains over 134,000 words and their pronunciations"[3]

B. **count_1w.txt from Peter Norvig**: "The 1/3 million most frequent words, all lowercase, with counts." [4]

C. **10 million tweets** collected by Steven Bedrick, of Oregon Health and Sciences University.

D. **WNUT Lexical normalisation dictionaries**[5]

   a. UniMelb

   b. UTDallas

E. **WNUT training set**.[6]

F. **Urban Dictionary:** a highly inclusive user-generated online dictionary.[7]

## 4 Results

Table 1 shows the results for the unconstrained task. The project described in the present work is named "bekli". The training set consisted of 2024 tweets with a total of 3928 tokens that needed to be normalized. The test set consisted of 1967 tweets with a total of 2738 tokens that needed to be normalized Baldwin et al. (2015).

## 5 Conclusion

The results show that a simple strategy with minimal computational resources can go along way. For example, the space required for the list and rule-based components is negligible. The only element that requires some heavy lifting is the sentence-level re-ranker with its long list of bigrams.

However, as I described above, selecting the token with the greatest-emission probability actually works better than my bigram approach, and requires far less computation. This leaves the question: what results could be achieved using a better re-ranker, one that successfully exploits context? Such a re-ranker would, among other benefits, make it feasible to use rules or substitutions that are not, without using context, capable of high precision.

Another question remaining is how much better can we do by expanding the curated segment of the list—if we, for example, double the size? This would would still allow a program to have a very small computational imprint, while doing nearly the work of a more sophisticated system.

[3]http://www.speech.cs.cmu.edu/cgi-bin/cmudict

[4]http://norvig.com/ngrams/count_1w.txt

[5]http://noisy-text.github.io/norm-shared-task.html

[6]http://noisy-text.github.io/norm-shared-task.html

[7]http://www.urbandictionary.com/

## References


Akshat Bakliwal, Jennifer Foster, Jennifer van der Puil, Ron O'Brien, Lamia Tounsi, and Mark Hughes. 2013. Sentiment analysis of political tweets: Towards an accurate classifier. In *Proceedings of the Workshop on Language Analysis in Social Media*, pages 49–58, Atlanta, Georgia, June. Association for Computational Linguistics.

Timothy Baldwin, Marie Catherine de Marneffe, Bo Han, Young-Bum Kim, Alan Ritter, and Wei Xu. 2015. Shared tasks of the 2015 workshop on noisy user-generated text: Twitter lexical normalization and named entity recognition. In *Proceedings of the Workshop on Noisy User-generated Text (WNUT 2015)*, Beijing, China.

Luciano Barbosa and Junlan Feng. 2010. Robust sentiment detection on twitter from biased and noisy data. In *Proceedings of the 23rd International Conference on Computational Linguistics: Posters*, pages 36–44.

Cynthia Chew and Gunther Eysenbach. 2010. Pandemics in the age of twitter: content analysis of tweets during the 2009 h1n1 outbreak. *PloS one*, 5(11):e14118.

Monojit Choudhury, Rahul Saraf, Vijit Jain, Animesh Mukherjee, Sudeshna Sarkar, and Anupam Basu.

2007. Investigation and modeling of the structure of texting language. *Int. J. Doc. Anal. Recognit.*, 10(3):157–174, December.

Bo Han and Timothy Baldwin. 2011. Lexical normalisation of short text messages: Makn sens a #twitter. In *Proceedings of the 49th Annual Meeting of the Association for Computational Linguistics: Human Language Technologies - Volume 1*, HLT '11, pages 368–378, Stroudsburg, PA, USA. Association for Computational Linguistics.

Catherine Kobus, François Yvon, and Géraldine Damnati. 2008. Normalizing sms: Are two metaphors better than one? In *Proceedings of the 22Nd International Conference on Computational Linguistics - Volume 1*, COLING '08, pages 441–448, Stroudsburg, PA, USA. Association for Computational Linguistics.

Chen Li and Yang Liu. 2014. Improving text normalization via unsupervised model and discriminative reranking. In *Proceedings of the ACL 2014 Student Research Workshop*, pages 86–93, Baltimore, Maryland, USA, June. Association for Computational Linguistics.

Jiwei Li, Alan Ritter, and Eduard H. Hovy. 2014. Weakly supervised user profile extraction from twitter. In *Proceedings of the 52nd Annual Meeting of the Association for Computational Linguistics, ACL 2014, June 22-27, 2014, Baltimore, MD, USA, Volume 1: Long Papers*, pages 165–174.

Sara Rosenthal, Preslav Nakov, Svetlana Kiritchenko, Saif M Mohammad, Alan Ritter, and Veselin Stoyanov. 2015. Semeval-2015 task 10: Sentiment analysis in twitter. In *Proceedings of the 9th International Workshop on Semantic Evaluation, SemEval*.

Richard Sproat, Alan W Black, Stanley Chen, Shankar Kumar, Mari Ostendorf, and Christopher Richards. 2001. Normalization of non-standard words. *Computer Speech & Language*, 15(3):287–333.

Yi Yang and Jacob Eisenstein. 2013. A log-linear model for unsupervised text normalization. In *EMNLP*, pages 61–72.

Congle Zhang, Tyler Baldwin, Howard Ho, Benny Kimelfeld, and Yunyao Li. 2013. Adaptive parser-centric text normalization. In *Proceedings of the 49th Annual Meeting of the Association for Computational Linguistics (1)*, pages 1159–1168.

# NCSU-SAS-Ning: Candidate Generation and Feature Engineering for Supervised Lexical Normalization

**Ning Jin**
Text Analytics R&D
SAS Institute, Inc.
Cary, NC, USA
Ning.Jin@sas.com

## Abstract

User generated content often contains non-standard words that hinder effective automatic text processing. In this paper, we present a system we developed to perform lexical normalization for English Twitter text. It first generates candidates based on past knowledge and a novel string similarity measurement and then selects a candidate using features learned from training data. The system has a constrained mode and an unconstrained mode. The constrained mode participated in the W-NUT noisy English text normalization competition (Baldwin et al., 2015) and achieved the best F1 score.

## 1 Introduction

User generated content, such as customer reviews, forum discussions, text messages and Twitter text, is of great value in applications like understanding users, trend discovery and crowdsourcing. For example, by reading the Twitter text posted by a user, a company can learn the user's preferences and connections and use the information for targeted advertising. For another example, by reading Amazon customer reviews about a certain product, a shopper can collect a lot of product information that is not available from manufacturers and retailers. Unfortunately, user generated content often contains ungrammatical sentence structures and non-standard words, which hinders automated text processing.

In this paper, we present a solution that attempts to perform lexical normalization (Han et al., 2011) for English Twitter text based on training text with human annotation (Baldwin et al., 2015). The solution has a constrained mode and an unconstrained mode. Both modes have the same architecture and components. Both use the annotated training data and CMU's *ark* POS tagger (Gimpel et al., 2011). The difference between them is parameter settings and the usage of a canonical lexicon dictionary by the unconstrained mode.

This paper is organized as follows: Section 2 describes the architecture and components shared by the constrained and unconstrained modes. Section 3 lists what resources are used by each system. In Section 4, we describe the different settings of the constrained and unconstrained modes and compare their performance. Section 5 concludes the paper and discusses future work.

## 2 Architecture and Components of the System

Given a tokenized English tweet $T = (t_1, t_2, \ldots, t_n)$, where $t_i$ is the $i$-th token and $n$ is the total number of tokens, our normalization system processes one token at a time and has two components: candidate generation and candidate evaluation. To normalize token $t_i$, the system first generates a small set of candidate canonical forms. Then it calculates a confidence score for each candidate and selects the one with the highest confidence score as the canonical form of token $t_i$. How to generate candidates and how to calculate confidence scores are learned from training data.

### 2.1 Candidate Generation

The candidates of a token $t_i$ include:

- The token itself



*Proceedings of the ACL 2015 Workshop on Noisy User-generated Text*, pages 87–92,
Beijing, China, July 31, 2015. ©2015 Association for Computational Linguistics

- All tokens that are considered canonical forms of $t_i$ in the training data (static mapping dictionary)
- A split into multiple canonical forms if the token $t_i$ is not a canonical form (for example, "loveyourcar" → "love your car")
- Top-$m$ most similar canonical forms found in training data (see subsection 2.2 for details of similarity measurement)

Figure 1 shows an example of training data and a new tweet for normalization. Table 1 shows a portion of the static mapping dictionary learned from the training data.

For token "ur" in the new tweet, the token itself is "ur". All of its possible canonical forms present in the training data are "you are" and "your". Let $m$ = 1, the most similar canonical form is "your". Therefore, the candidates of "ur" include "ur", "you are" and "your". For token "looove" in the new tweet, the token itself is "looove". It is absent in the training data, so it does not have its own canonical form available as candidates. Among all the canonical forms present in training data, canonical form "love" is most similar to "looove". Therefore, the candidates of "looove" include "looove" and "love".

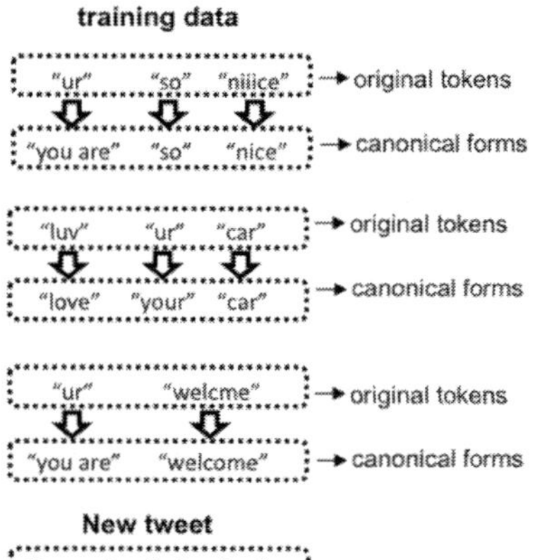


**Figure 1: An Example of Training Data and a New Tweet for Normalization**

| Key (token) | Value (canonical forms) |
|---|---|
| "ur" | "your", "you are" |
| "so" | "so" |
| "niiice" | "nice" |
| "luv" | "love" |
| "car" | "car" |
| "welcme" | "welcome" |

**Table 1: Static Mapping Dictionary Learned from Training Data**

## 2.2 Similarity Index

We measure similarity between two strings by first representing each string with a set of similarity features and then evaluating similarity with Jaccard Index (Levandowsky et al., 1971) of the two similarity feature sets.

The similarity features of a string $s$ include $n$-grams and $k$-skip-$n$-grams in $s$. In this paper, an $n$-gram in string $s$ is defined as a contiguous sequence of $n$ characters in $s$. A $k$-skip-$n$-gram in string $s$ is a generalization of $n$-gram with gaps between characters and is defined as a sequence of $n$ characters where the maximum distance between two characters is $k$. We prepend (append) a "$" to $n$-grams that appear at the beginning (end) of the string. We use "|" to indicate gaps in skip-grams. For example, Table 2 shows the similarity feature sets of "love", "looove", "car" and "cat", with $n$=2 and $k$=1.

| String | Similarity Feature Set |
|---|---|
| "love" | "$lo", "ov", "ve$", "l\|v", "o\|e" |
| "looove" | "$lo", "oo", "ov", "ve$", "l\|o", "o\|o", "o\|v", "o\|e" |
| "car" | "$ca", "ar$", "c\|r" |
| "cat" | "$ca", "at$", "c\|t" |

**Table 2: An Example of Similarity Features ($n$=2, $k$=1)**

Let the similarity feature set of a string $s$ be $f(s)$, then we measure string similarity between $s_1$ and $s_2$ by:

$$similarity(s_1, s_2) = JaccardIndex(f(s_1), f(s_2)) = \frac{|f(s_1) \cap f(s_2)|}{|f(s_1) \cup f(s_2)|}$$

For example, in Table 2, "love" and "looove" share similarity features {"$lo", "ov", "ve$", "o|e"}. The union of their similarity feature sets is {"$lo", "oo", "ov", "ve$", "l|v", "l|o", "o|o", "o|v", "o|e"}. The similarity score between "love" and "looove" is 4/9 = 0.44.

Different weights can be assigned to different similarity features when calculating similarity scores because $n$-grams at different positions have different importance for word recognition (White et al., 2008). For example, in the example shown in Table 2, we can assign weight 3 to bigrams at the beginning and end of strings and weight 1 to other features, and then the similarity score between "love" and "looove" becomes 8/13 = 0.615.

The similarity feature set calculation can use multiple ($n$, $k$) configurations instead of just one. For example, the similarity feature set can be composed of bigrams, trigrams, 1-skip-bigrams and 2-skip-bigrams together. If $k = 0$, it means no skip-gram is used.

This similarity measurement penalizes text edits such as insertion, deletion and substitution. Compared with Levenshtein distance (Levenshtein, 1966), one disadvantage of our similarity measurement is that two different strings may have 1.0 similarity score because the similarity feature set can only capture local character order information. For example, strings "aaabaa" and "aaaabaa" have exactly the same similarity feature set {"$aa", "ab", "ba", "aa$", "a|a", "a|b", "b|a"} and thus have 1.0 similarity score. Including skip-gram and using a larger $n$ in similarity feature calculation can mitigate this problem but cannot prevent it. Fortunately, this should be very rare when the similarity measurement is applied to two real world twitter tokens because such cases require the strings to be long and contain repetitive $n$-grams and skip-grams. One advantage of our similarity measurement over Levenshtein distance is that it takes into account the string length when penalizing text edits. The same text edit has a bigger impact when it occurs in a short string than in a long string because of the denominator in Jaccard Index. Another advantage of our similarity measurement is that it better handles repetition characters, which is commonly used in Twitter. For example, for our similarity measurement, both "looove" and "loooooove" are equally similar to "love". For Levenshtein distance, "loooooove" takes a much heavier penalty than "looove".[1] The biggest advantage of our similarity measurement over Levenshtein distance is the lower computational complexity. Let the length of a string $s$ be $l(s)$. The feature set size of $s$ is bounded by $O(l(s))$. Then the complexity of calculating Levenshtein distance between $s_1$ and $s_2$ is $O(l(s_1)l(s_2))$, which is quadratic when two strings have similar length. On the contrary, the complexity of calculating our similarity measurement is $O(l(s_1)+l(s_2))$, which is linear.[2]

We index all the canonical forms in the training data based on similarity features to facilitate finding top-$m$ canonical forms that are most similar to the query token. Given a query token, we can quickly narrow down our search space to canonical forms that share at least one similarity feature with the query token. Further efficiency improvement can be achieved by approximating the denominator in Jaccard Index based on string lengths or by imposing restrictions on the minimum number of similarity features to be shared by query token and results.

### 2.3 Candidate Evaluation

Given a tweet $T$, one of its token $t_i$ and one of the token's candidate $c$, we train a binary classifier that predicts whether $c$ is the correct canonical form of $t_i$ in the tweet $T$ and outputs a confidence score for the prediction. Among the candidates that the classifier predicts to be the correct canonical forms, we select the one with the highest confidence score as the canonical form of $t_i$. In our implementation of the system, we used a random forest classifier (Breiman, 2001) mainly because its training speed is faster and its performance is relatively insensitive to parameter values, but other binary classification algorithm should also work.

This step is mostly feature engineering and we used the following features:

- Support and confidence

  We calculate the support of token $t_i$ (number of times $t_i$ appears) and confidence of token $t_i$ being normalized to candidate $c$ (percentage of times $t_i$ is normalized to $c$) according to training data and use them as features for classification. For example, in the training data shown above, the support of token "ur" is 3 and the confidence of normalizing "ur" to "you are" is 2/3 = 0.67. The confidence of normalizing "ur" to "your" is 1/3 = 0.33. If the token $t_i$ is absent in the training data, e.g. "looove", then the support and confidence are both zero. If the token $t_i$ is present but the normalization from $t_i$ to $c$ is absent in training data, then only the confidence is zero. These features are context free and the intuition is that the higher the support and confidence are (high support is necessary in case of small sample), the more likely that $c$ is the correct canonical form of $t_i$.

- String information

  We calculate the string similarity score (Jaccard Index of feature sets) between token $t_i$ and candidate $c$ and use it as a feature for

[1] Certain preprocessing can mitigate this problem for Levenshtein distance. For example, all single character repetitions get reduced to two before Levenshtein distance is calculated. But it does not handle repetition of multiple characters, e.g. "lolol".

[2] The linear complexity depends on using hash table to calculate set union and intersection. Another implementation is sorting the similarity features first and then calculating union and intersection, which has $O(l*log(l))$ complexity ($l$ is the longer string length of the two strings) and is still better than quadratic complexity of Levenshtein distance.

classification. String similarity score is a good feature for difference between token and its canonical form caused by misspelling (for example, "seperate" → "separate"), but it is not a good feature for difference caused by abbreviation (for example, "lol" → "laughing out loud"). Therefore, we also add string length and difference in string length between $t_i$ and $c$ so that classifier can choose to ignore string similarity score when necessary.

All string information features are context free.

- POS tagging information

One of the motivations of text normalization is to facilitate subsequent tasks, such as part-of-speech tagging and named entity recognition. Therefore, good text normalization should make the subsequent tasks easier. We observed that in the training data, in 90% of the cases where a token is normalized to another token, the canonical form has higher POS tagging confidence, based on the *ark* POS tagger (Gimpel et al., 2011), than the original. Therefore we use change in POS tagging confidence at position $i$ in tweet $T$ before and after normalizing $t_i$ to $c$ as a feature for classification.

We also include change in mean POS tagging confidence in tweet $T$ because changing one token can affect the confidence of tagging other tokens. In addition to change in POS tagging confidence, we use POS tags of tokens $t_{i-1}$ and $t_i$ as features (tag is empty if $t_i$ is the first token) because there can be patterns of consecutive POS tags and some patterns are much more frequent than others.

All POS tagging features use context information.

The importance of these classification features are evaluated in Section 4.

To train the classifier, we generate candidates for each token in training data and label each pair according to human annotation. If the candidate is the correct canonical form of the token in the tweet, then the pair is labeled as class 1; otherwise the pair is labeled as class 0. Feature vectors with features described above are calculated for each pair. Then a random forest binary classifier is learned. When the classifier is learned, the class (label) weights are adjusted inversely proportional to class frequencies in the data because the data is imbalanced and majority of the observations are in class 0.

## 3 Resources Employed

We implemented two modes for our normalization system: a constrained mode and an unconstrained mode.[3] The constrained mode uses only the training data *train_data_20150430.json* and the *ark* twitter POS tagger (Gimpel et al., 2011). The unconstrained mode uses the canonical English lexicon dictionary *scowl.american.70*, in addition to all resources used by the constrained mode.

## 4 Settings and Evaluation

For both the constrained and unconstrained modes, we use only bigrams and 1-skip-bigrams as similarity features. The differences between the two modes are listed below.

For the constrained mode:

- It uses best-scoring canonical forms from the similarity index as candidates.
- It uses similarity index for candidate generation only when the token contains repetitive characters (same character occupying consecutive positions).[4]
- It builds a similarity index based on all canonical forms present in the training data.
- Dictionary and feature learning and classifier training are based on the same data set.

For the Unconstrained mode:

- It uses *top-3* best-scoring canonical forms from the similarity index as candidates.
- It builds a similarity index based on all canonical forms in the training data and all lexicons in the dictionary *scowl.american.70*.
- It always uses the similarity index for candidate generation.

---

[3] The unconstrained mode was developed when we were writing this paper, after the annotation for the test data set was revealed. Only the constrained mode was submitted for the competition.

[4] This is because a similarity index based on smaller vocabulary leads to less reliable candidates. For example, in the example shown in Figure 1, the similarity index returns "car" as a candidate of "cat" because "car" is the most similar canonical form in training data. In a larger vocabulary, "cat" itself should be the most similar canonical form.

- Dictionary and feature learning and classifier training are based on different data sets.

For the constrained mode, dictionaries (including static mapping dictionary and similarity index), classification feature calculation and classifier training are based on the same data set. It causes overfitting because the dictionaries and the support and confidence features leak label information. However, our cross-validation results show that learning dictionaries, support and confidence features, and classifier on the same data set generates better generalization as well. It leads to better F1 score than splitting the data set into two parts and learning dictionaries and features on one part and learning the classifier on the other part. This is because having large dictionaries is crucial for candidate generation and the correct canonical form cannot be found if it is not among the candidates. Using all the available data instead of splitting it allows the system to learn larger dictionaries and more than makes up for the overfitting problem.

For the unconstrained mode, dictionaries and features are learned on 67% of the available data and the classifier is learned on 33% of the available data (random split). This is different from constrained mode because the unconstrained mode already has a very large canonical form dictionary in *scowl.american.70* and the accuracy of selecting the correct canonical form becomes the bottleneck.

We used the data sets provided by the WNUT 2015 lexical normalization competition (described in (Baldwin et al., 2015)) for evaluation. During our development of the systems, only the training data file *train_data_20150430.json* was used for any parameter selection and design decisions. We used cross-validation to estimate system performance. The constrained and unconstrained modes have separate classifier training.

Table 3 shows the performance of the constrained mode with different sets of classification features based on the test data file *test_truth.json* concealed from development. It can be seen that the support and confidence features are the most important for achieving high F1 score. Without the support and confidence features, the F1 score of the constrained mode decreases by 0.0521. The POS tagging features constitute the second most important feature set. Without POS tagging features, the F1 score goes down by 0.0129. The string features are the least important set of features as they lead to very marginal improvement in F1 score.

| | **Precision** | **Recall** | **F1 Score** |
|---|---|---|---|
| Constrained w/ all features | 0.9061 | 0.7865 | 0.8421 |
| Constrained w/o support and confidence features | 0.9423 | 0.6803 | 0.7901 |
| Constrained w/o POS tagging features | 0.902 | 0.7673 | 0.8292 |
| Constrained w/o string features | 0.9102 | 0.7825 | 0.8416 |

**Table 3: Importance of Classification Features**

In Table 4, we report the evaluation results based on the test data file *test_truth.json* concealed from development. For constrained mode, we list the top-two results by teams NCSU_SAS_NING (Ning.cm) and NCSU_SAS_WOOKHEE (Wookhee.cm). For unconstrained mode, we list the top result by team IHS_RD (IHS_RD.um) and the result by our own unconstrained mode (Ning.um), which was developed after the competition ended.

| Performance | Constrained Mode | | Unconstrained Mode | |
|---|---|---|---|---|
| | Ning.cm | Wookhee.cm | Ning.um | IHS_RD.um |
| Precision | 0.9061 | 0.9136 | **0.9339** | 0.8469 |
| Recall | 0.7865 | 0.7398 | 0.7582 | **0.8083** |
| F1 Score | **0.8421** | 0.8175 | 0.837 | 0.8272 |

**Table 4: Competition Evaluation Results**

It can be seen that our normalization system has the best F1 score in both constrained mode and unconstrained mode. In fact, our constrained mode has the best F1 score overall, better than our unconstrained mode, which seems counterintuitive. Besides, the unconstrained mode is expected to achieve higher recall than the constrained mode because of its much larger dictionary, but the evaluation results show that the unconstrained mode has lower recall and higher precision than the constrained mode. The following three factors lead to the inferior F1 score and recall by our unconstrained mode:

The much larger canonical form dictionary used by the unconstrained mode contains many rarely used words and having such words as candidates causes the candidate evaluation component to be more conservative in selecting candidates other than the original tokens (higher precision and lower recall). A potential solution is to use a smaller dictionary of most frequently used words instead of a large dictionary or to use a dictionary with word frequency based on a large corpus.

Even if we exclude the rare words, the mere increase in number of candidates per token makes selecting the correct candidate more challenging. For example, our unconstrained mode successfully suggests "Brooklyn" as a candidate for token "Brklyn", which our constrained mode is incapable of, but the candidate evaluation component fails to select "Brooklyn" as the correct canonical form. A potential solution is to include more context information for candidate evaluation. For example, text likelihood estimated by a CRF model before and after normalization can be added as classification features. Having word frequency as a feature can also be helpful.

The binary class labeling in the candidate evaluation component does not differentiate normalization without change (e.g. "car" → "car") from normalization with change (e.g. "ur" → "your"). As a result, we are unable to tune parameters to favor normalization with change in order to achieve a better trade-off between precision and recall (higher recall and slightly lower precision), which means higher F1 score. A potential solution is to change the candidate evaluation component into a two-level classification. The first level classifies whether the normalization needs any change. If no, then the token itself is output as the normalization result. If yes, then the second level classification assigns a confidence score to each candidate that is different from the token and outputs the one with the highest score as the result.

## 5 Conclusions and Future Work

In this paper, we present a system to perform lexical normalization for English Twitter text, with a constrained mode and an unconstrained mode. Our constrained mode achieves the top F1 score in the W-NUT noisy text normalization competition and outperforms other participants' unconstrained modes. Our unconstrained mode currently has slightly lower recall and F1 score than the constrained mode, but it has a lot more room for improvement as discussed in the evaluation section. Future work includes implementing the ideas to improve the unconstrained mode and exploring semi-supervised and unsupervised text normalization. One potential solution for unsupervised text normalization is first clustering tokens based on context (e.g. Brown clustering (Brown et al., 1992)) and then choosing the most frequent token in each cluster as the canonical form for all tokens in that cluster.

## Reference


T. Baldwin, M. Catherine, B. Han, Y.B. Kim, A. Ritter and W. Xu. 2015. *Shared Tasks of the 2015 Workshop on Noisy User-generated Text: Twitter Lexical Normalization and Named Entity Recognition. In Proc. of WNUT.*

L. Breiman. 2001. *Random Forests*. Machine Learning, 45(1), 5-32.

P. Brown, P. deSouza, R. Mercer, V. Della Pietra, J. Lai. 1992. *Class-Based n-gram Models of Natural Language. Computational Linguistics*, vol. 18, pp. 467–479.

K. Gimpel, N. Schneider, B. O'Connor, D. Das, D. Mills, J. Eisenstein, M. Heilman, D. Yogatama, J. Flanigan, and N. A. Smith. 2011. *Part-of-speech tagging for Twitter: Annotation, features, and experiments*. In *Proc. of ACL*.

B. Han and T. Baldwin. 2011. "Lexical normalisation of short text messages: Makn sens a #twitter". In *Proc. of ACL*.

M. Levandowsky and D. Winter. 1971. *Distance between sets. Nature* 234 (5): 34–35.

V. Levenshtein. 1966. *Binary codes capable of correcting deletions, insertions, and reversals. Soviet Physics Doklady* 10 (8): 707–710.

S. White, R. Johnson, S. Liversedge, K. Rayner. 2008. *Eye Movements When Reading Transposed Text: The Importance of Word-Beginning Letters. Journal of experimental psychology Human perception and performance.*

# DCU-ADAPT: Learning Edit Operations for Microblog Normalisation with the Generalised Perceptron

**Joachim Wagner** and **Jennifer Foster**
ADAPT Centre
School of Computing
Dublin City University
Dublin, Ireland
{jwagner|jfoster}@computing.dcu.ie

## Abstract

We describe the work carried out by the DCU-ADAPT team on the Lexical Normalisation shared task at W-NUT 2015. We train a generalised perceptron to annotate noisy text with edit operations that normalise the text when executed. Features are character $n$-grams, recurrent neural network language model hidden layer activations, character class and eligibility for editing according to the task rules. We combine predictions from 25 models trained on subsets of the training data by selecting the most-likely normalisation according to a character language model. We compare the use of a generalised perceptron to the use of conditional random fields restricted to smaller amounts of training data due to memory constraints. Furthermore, we make a first attempt to verify Chrupała (2014)'s hypothesis that the noisy channel model would not be useful due to the limited amount of training data for the source language model, i.e. the language model on normalised text.

## 1 Introduction

The W-NUT Lexical Normalisation for English Tweets shared task is to normalise spelling and to expand contractions in English microblog messages (Baldwin et al., 2015). This includes one-to-many and many-to-one replacements as in "we're" and "l o v e". Tokens containing characters other than alphanumeric characters and the apostrophe are excluded from the task, as well as proper nouns and acronyms that would be acceptable in well-edited text. (The input, however, does not identify such tokens and unnecessarily modifying them is penalised in the evaluation.)

To make evaluation easier, participants are further required to align output tokens to input tokens, e.g. when the four tokens "l", "o", "v" and "e" are amalgamated to the single token "love", three empty tokens must follow in the output. This is easy for approaches that process the input token by token but may require extra work if the input string is processed differently.

We participate in the constrained mode that allows off-the-shelf tools but no normalisation lexicons and additional data to be used. Furthermore, we do not use any lexicon of canonical English but learn our normalisation model purely from the provided training data.

Our approach follows previous work by Chrupała (2014) in that we train a sequence labeller to annotate edit operations that are intended to normalise the text when applied to the input text. However, while Chrupała uses conditional random fields for sequence labelling, we further experiment with using a generalised Perceptron and with using a simple noisy channel model with character $n$-gram language models trained on the normalised side of the training data to select the final normalisation from a set of candidate normalisation generated from an ensemble of sequence labellers and from selectively ignoring some of the proposed edit operations.

## 2 Experimental Setup

### 2.1 Data Set and Cross-validation

The microblog data set of the shared task contains 2,950 tweets for training and 1,967 tweets for final testing. Each tweet is tokenised and the tokens of the normalised tweets are aligned to the input, allowing for one-to-one, many-to-one and one-to-many alignments.

For five-fold cross-validation, we sort the training data by tweet ID and split it into 5 sets of roughly the same number of tokens. (The number of tweets varies from 579 to 606.) Systems are trained on four sets and tested on the remain-



*Proceedings of the ACL 2015 Workshop on Noisy User-generated Text*, pages 93–98,
Beijing, China, July 31, 2015. 

ing set. Since the sequence labellers require a development set, we split the union of the four sets again into 5 sets to carry out nested cross-validation, training 25 models in total for each system.

### 2.2 Feature Extraction

For extracting recurrent neural network language model features, we use Elman[1] (Chrupała, 2014), a modification of the RNNLM toolkit[2] (Mikolov et al., 2010; Mikolov, 2012) that outputs hidden layer activations. We use the off-the-shelf model from Chrupała (2014)[3]. The input are the characters of the tweet[4] in one-hot encoding. The network has a hidden layer with 400 neurons and it predicts the next byte. Following Chrupała (2014), we reduce the 400 activations to 10 binary features: We select the 10 most active neurons in order and apply a threshold (0.5) to the activation. The value of the $i$-th feature expresses which neuron was $i$-th active and whether its activation was below 0.5, e.g. the first feature states which neuron is most active and whether or not its activation is below 0.5. As there are 400 neurons and 2 possible binarised activations, there are 800 possible values.[5]

Edit operations are extracted from the parallel training data searching for the lowest edit distance and recording the edit operations with dynamic programming. We customise the edit costs function to always postpone insertions to after deleting characters so that each input character can be assigned exactly one edit operation from the set {do nothing, delete character, insert string before character}. To capture insertions at the end of the tweet, we append a NULL byte to all tweets.

The above setup, features and edit operations are identical to Chrupała (2014) to the best of our knowledge. We further add a character class feature {NULL, control, space, apostrophe, punctuation, digit, quote, bracket, lowercase letter, uppercase letter, non-ASCII, other} and a feature indicating whether the character is part of a token that is eligible for editing according to the shared task rules, i.e. whether or not the characters encountered since the last space or start of tweet only are letters, digits, apostrophes and spaces.

### 2.3 Sequence Labelling

For character-level sequence labelling, we try *(a)* Sequor[6] (Chrupała and Klakow, 2010), an implementation of the generalised perceptron (Collins, 2002),[7] with 10 iterations, and *(b)* Wapiti[8] (Lavergne et al., 2010)'s implementation of conditional random fields (Lafferty et al., 2001) using l-bfgs optimisation with a history of 5 steps, elastic net regularisation ($\rho_1 = 0.333$ and $\rho_2 = 0.001$) and no hard limit on the number of iterations. We extend the feature templates of Chrupała (2014)[9] by including our additional two features. The template generates unigram, bigram and trigram character features within a +/- 2 window. All remaining features are included as unigrams of the current value.

Due to the nested cross-validation (see above), Sequor is trained on $64\%$ $(0.8^2)$ of the training data, $16\%$ $(0.8 \times 0.2)$ is used as development set and 20% (1/5) for testing. For Wapiti, we use only $16\%$ for training (and the remaining $64\%$ for development set) in each cross-validation fold due to memory constraints.[10]

### 2.4 Generating Candidates

We produce candidate normalisations from the edit operations proposed by the sequence model. However, if we allowed each insert and delete operation to be either realised or not, we would produce up to $2^N$ candidates, where $N$ is the number of edit operations. With $N = 140$ (maximum lengths of a tweet), handling these many candidates is not feasible. Instead, we recursively split the sequence of edit operations produced by the sequence labeller into up to eight sections. To find good split points, we propose to minimise

$$\sqrt{|e_L - e_R|} + \max(\{0, 10 - s\})/2 \qquad (1)$$

[1] https://bitbucket.org/gchrupala/elman

[2] http://rnnlm.org/

[3] https://bitbucket.org/gchrupala/codeswitch/overview

[4] More precisely, we process UTF-8 bytes. For the training data, this is the same as characters as the training set does not contain any multi-byte UTF-8 characters.

[5] These RNN-LM hidden layer activation features have been used successfully in text segmentation and word-level language identification (Chrupała, 2013; Barman et al., 2014).

[6] https://bitbucket.org/gchrupala/sequor

[7] The generalised perceptron has been shown to match performance of state-of-the-art methods in word segmentation, POS tagging, dependency parsing and phrase-structure parsing (Zhang and Clark, 2011).

[8] https://wapiti.limsi.fr/

[9] We thank Grzegorz Chrupała for providing his template and for translating it to the Sequor template format.

[10] With 64%, memory usage grew to over 400 GB over night, causing heavy swap activity on our machines with 256 GB RAM (and 410 GB swap space).

where $e_L$ and $e_R$ are the number of insert or delete operations to the left and right respectively, and $s$ is the number of consecutive no-operations to the left. The first term tries to balance the number of edit operations on each side while the second term introduces a preference to not split clusters of edit operations.

For each section, we either use the edit operations produced by the sequence labeller or do not edit the section. As we split each sequence into no more than eight sections, we produce up to $2^8 = 256$ candidates.[11] Only one candidate, identical to the input, will be produced if there are no delete or insert operations and two candidates will be produced if there is just one delete or insert operation.

In training, we may potentially produce up to $5 \times 256 = 1{,}280$ candidates per tweet as the nested cross-validation gives us five sequence labellers per cross-validation run. During testing, up to $25 \times 256 = 6{,}400$ candidates may be produced. (The actual maximum number of candidates may be lower when labellers agree on the edit operations.)

### 2.5 Applying Edit Operations

After producing candidate edit operation sequences that use subsets of the edit operations predicted by a sequence model, the edit operations are executed to produce candidates strings for the normalised tweets. As the shared task asks for tokenised output aligned to the input tokens, we apply the edit operations to each token in the following sequence:

1. Apply all edit operations at character positions that correspond to input tokens.
2. Apply insert operations recorded at the space between tokens and at the end of the tweet to the preceding token.
3. Apply delete operations at the space between tokens, moving the contents of the token to the right to the end of the token to the left, leaving behind an empty token. (Delete operations at the end-of-tweet marker are ignored.)

Due to time constraints, we do not attempt to improve the alignment of output tokens to input tokens.

[11] Splitting the eight sections again would produce $2^{16} =$ 65,536 candidates.

### 2.6 Language Modelling

For language modelling, we train SRILM (Stolcke, 2002) on the normalised tweets of the training data. As we want to build character $n$-gram models and SRILM has no direct support for this, we re-format the candidate strings to make each character a token. To distinguish space characters from token separators, we represent them with double underscores.

### 2.7 Candidate Selection

We use the noisy channel model[12] to select the most plausible source $\hat{s}$ for the observed target $t$ from the set of candidates $S(t)$:

$$\arg\max_{s \in S(t)} P(t|s)P(s) \tag{2}$$

$P(s)$ is provided by the language model (Section 2.6). Standard models give high probability to making few or no edits. However, we trust our sequence models as Chrupała (2014) reported encouraging results. Therefore, we give high probability to using the predicted edit operations. We consider two models for $P(t|s)$:

$$P_1(t|s) = \begin{cases} 0.979 & \text{if all edit operations are used} \\ 0.020 & \text{if } \; s = t \\ 0.001 & \text{otherwise} \end{cases} \tag{3}$$

and

$$P_2(t|s) = \begin{cases} 1 & \text{if all edit operations are used} \\ 0 & \text{otherwise} \end{cases} \tag{4}$$

Note that $P_1$ is not a proper probability model as there is never exactly one "otherwise" case but $2^i - 2$ cases where $i$ is the number of sections considered in candidate generation, causing the total to be either $0.999$ or between $1.001$ and $0.999 + 0.001 \times (2^8 - 2) = 1.253$. $P_2$ effectively excludes the original input and all candidates that use only some but not all of the edit operations suggested by the sequence labellers. Since there are five sequence labellers per cross-validation fold due to nested cross-validation and 25 sequence labellers during testing, $P_2$ effectively selects between 5 or 25 candidates.[13]

[12] The noisy channel model has been applied successfully to spelling correction (Kernighan et al., 1990; Wilcox-O'Hearn et al., 2008) and machine translation (Way, 2010), among other areas.

[13] Han et al. (2013) also use a trigram language model for normalisation, but only to reduce a larger candidate set to an

| | 2 | 3 | 4 | 5 | 6 |
|---|---|---|---|---|---|
| WB | 14.70 | 9.97 | 7.91 | 7.31 | **7.19** |
| KN | 14.73 | 9.83 | 7.81 | 7.33 | 7.43 |
| GT | 14.63 | 9.88 | 7.91 | 7.45 | 7.44 |

Table 1: Average language model perplexity over the five cross-validation runs for $n$-gram sizes $n = 2, ..., 6$ and smoothing methods WB = Witten-Bell, KN = Keyser-Ney and GT = Good-Turing. Standard deviation $\sigma \leq 0.23$ for all configurations.

### 2.8 Evaluation Measures

We evaluate our best systems using the evalution script provided by the shared task organisers. It counts:

- The number of correctly modified tokens, i.e. tokens that need to be replaced by a new non-empty token and the system correctly predicts this token.
- Number of tokens needing normalisation, i.e. tokens that are modified in the gold output. However, again, tokens that are to be deleted are ignored, e.g. "l o v e" to "love" counts as one event only despite the replacement of three tokens with empty tokens.
- The number of tokens modified by system, i.e. tokens for which a substitution with a non-empty token is proposed by the system.

Based on these numbers, precision, recall and F1-score are calculated and we select the system and configuration to be used on the test set based on highest average F1-score over the 5 cross-validation runs.

## 3 Results

We use character $n$-gram language models in the noisy channel model for candidate selection. To address sparsity of data that arises when test sentences contain $n$-grams that are rare or unseen in the training data, we try Witten-Bell, Keyser-Ney and Good-Turing smoothing. Table 1 shows average cross-validation perplexity for these three smoothing methods and $n = 2, ..., 6$. Over all five cross-validation folds, the language model that gives the lowest perplexity when trained on the training data and applied to the internal test set is the 6-gram model with Witten-Bell smoothing. This confirms the recommendations in the SRILM documentation to use Witten-Bell smoothing when the vocabulary is small such as when building a character language model.

$n$-best list before applying more complex models to token-level candidate selection.

| | | P | R | F1 |
|---|---|---|---|---|
| $P_1$ | W | 83.2% | 37.7% | 51.9% |
| $P_1$ | S | 83.2% | 41.0% | 54.9% |
| $P_2$ | W | **85.9%** | 47.7% | 61.4% |
| $P_2$ | S | 85.7% | **56.1%** | **67.8%** |

Table 2: Average cross-validation results over the five cross-validation runs for transition models $P_1$ and $P_2$, W = Wapiti CRF sequence labeller (trained on only 16% of the training data), S = Sequor generalised perceptron sequence labeller (trained on 64% of the training data), P = precision, R = recall, F1 = F1 measure. Standard deviation $\sigma \leq 0.03$ for all cells.

Table 2 shows cross-validation results for the four systems resulting from the choices between transition models $P_1$ and $P_2$ and using the Wapiti CRF or the Sequor generalised perceptron sequence labeller. The differences are not large in precision but for recall, the model $P_1$ performs poorly. Also the CRF consistently has lower recall than the respective perceptron model. Interestingly, the CRF achieves best precision. On F1-score, the best result is obtained with model $P_2$, which reduces the noisy channel model to selection between sequence modeller hypotheses, together with the Sequor sequence modeller.

On the final test set, our best system using $P_2$ and Sequor has precision 81.90%, recall 55.09% and F1 65.87%, placing it fifth out of six submissions in the "constrained" category.

## 4 Discussion

A possible explanation for the low recall obtained with the $P_1$ model is that this noise model cannot counter the effect that shorter sentences generally receive higher language model probability scores and therefore there is a tendency to reject edit operations that insert additional characters.

Furthermore, we observe that our system often assigns inserted text to the wrong evaluation units, e.g. inserting the string " laughing out" before the space before "lol" and then replacing second "L" of "lol" with "ud". This is not wrong on the string level, but in the token-level evaluation, we make two errors: wrongly appending " laughing out" to the previous token and wrongly normalising "lol" to just "loud" instead of "laughing out loud".

Since the model $P_1$ did not come out best, we cannot reject Chrupała (2014)'s hypothesis that the noisy channel model would not be useful. However, our observations also do not provide much support for this hypothesis as we did not include standard models from previous work (Cook and Stevenson, 2009; Han et al., 2013) in our experiment.

## 5 Conclusions

We trained two sequence modellers to predict edit operations that normalise input text when executed and experimented with applying the noisy channel model to selecting candidate normalisation strings.

Future work should:

- Train the CRF on the full training data, either using a more memory-friendly (but possibly slower) optimisation method or using an even larger machine.
- Experiment with LSTM sequence modelling (Hochreiter and Schmidhuber, 1997; Gers, 2001), which has been applied successfully to speech recognition and caption generation (Graves and Jaitly, 2014; Vinyals et al., 2015).
- Combine models with voting rather than language model score.
- For the noisy channel model, try standard models from previous work (Cook and Stevenson, 2009; Han et al., 2013).
- To better understand the selection preferences of the noisy channel model, compare the F1-score obtained when evaluating against the gold data to the F1-score obtained when evaluating the system output against its own input, i.e. are we biased towards doing nothing?
- Introduce a brevity penalty to counter the effect of selecting short candidate normalisations in the noisy channel model.
- Automatically revise the alignment to input token according to global co-occurrence statistics.
- Carry out a full error analysis of what the system does well and where it fails.

## Acknowledgments

This research is supported by Science Foundation Ireland through the CNGL Programme (Grant 12/CE/I2267) in the ADAPT Centre (www.adaptcentre.ie) at Dublin City University. We thank the anonymous reviewers for their comments on this paper. Furthermore, we thank Grzegorz Chrupała for sharing his feature templates and for his suggestion to try Sequor.

## References

Timothy Baldwin, Marie Catherine de Marneffe, Bo Han, Young-Bum Kim, Alan Ritter, and Wei Xu. 2015. Shared tasks of the 2015 workshop on noisy user-generated text: Twitter lexical normalization and named entity recognition. In *Proceedings of the Workshop on Noisy User-generated Text (WNUT 2015)*, Beijing, China.

Utsab Barman, Joachim Wagner, Grzegorz Chrupała, and Jennifer Foster. 2014. DCU-UVT: Word-level language classification with code-mixed data. In *Proceedings of the First Workshop on Computational Approaches to Code Switching. EMNLP 2014, Conference on Empirical Methods in Natural Language Processing*, pages 127–132, Doha, Qatar, October. Association for Computational Linguistics.

Grzegorz Chrupała and Dietrich Klakow. 2010. A named entity labeler for German: Exploiting Wikipedia and distributional clusters. In Nicoletta Calzolari (Conference Chair), Khalid Choukri, Bente Maegaard, Joseph Mariani, Jan Odijk, Stelios Piperidis, Mike Rosner, and Daniel Tapias, editors, *Proceedings of the Seventh conference on International Language Resources and Evaluation (LREC'10)*, Valletta, Malta, May. European Language Resources Association (ELRA).

Grzegorz Chrupała. 2013. Text segmentation with character-level text embeddings. In *Proceedings of the ICML 2013 Workshop on Deep Learning for Audio, Speech and Language Processing*, Atlanta, GA, USA. `https://sites.google.com/site/deeplearningicml2013/accepted_papers`.

Grzegorz Chrupała. 2014. Normalizing tweets with edit scripts and recurrent neural embeddings. In *Proceedings of the 52nd Annual Meeting of the Association for Computational Linguistics (Volume 2: Short Papers)*, pages 680–686, Baltimore, Maryland, June. Association for Computational Linguistics.

Michael Collins. 2002. Discriminative training methods for hidden Markov models: Theory and experiments with perceptron algorithms. In *Proceedings of the 2002 Conference on Empirical Methods in Natural Language Processing (EMNLP'02)*, pages 1–8, Morristown, NJ, USA, July. Association for Computational Linguistics.

Paul Cook and Suzanne Stevenson. 2009. An unsupervised model for text message normalization. In *Proceedings of the Workshop on Computational Approaches to Linguistic Creativity*, pages 71–78, Boulder, Colorado, June. Association for Computational Linguistics.

Felix Gers. 2001. *Long Short-Term Memory in Recurrent Neural Networks*. Ph.D. thesis, École Polytechnique Fédérale de Lausanne, Département d'Informatique, Lausanne. Switzerland. http://www.felixgers.de/papers/phd.pdf.

Alex Graves and Navdeep Jaitly. 2014. Towards end-to-end speech recognition with recurrent neural networks. In Eric P. Xing and Tony Jebara, editors, *Proceedings of The 31st International Conference on Machine Learning*, volume 32 of *JMLR Workshop and Conference Proceedings*. http://jmlr.org/proceedings/papers/v32/.

Bo Han, Paul Cook, and Timothy Baldwin. 2013. Lexical normalization for social media text. *ACM Transactions on Intelligent Systems and Technology (TIST) - Special section on twitter and microblogging services, social recommender systems, and CAMRa2010: Movie recommendation in context archive*, 4(1):5:1–5:27. doi 10.1145/2414425.2414430.

Sepp Hochreiter and Jürgen Schmidhuber. 1997. Long short-term memory. *Neural Computation*, 9(8):1735–1780. doi:10.1162/neco.1997.9.8.1735.

Mark D. Kemighan, Kenneth W. Church, and William A. Gale. 1990. A spelling correction program based on a noisy channel model. In Hans Karlgren, editor, *COLING-90: Papers presented to the 13th International Conference on Computational Linguistics on the occasion of the 25th Anniversary of COLING and the 350th Anniversary of Helsinki University, Volume 2*. http://www.aclweb.org/anthology/C/C90/.

John Lafferty, Andrew McCallum, and Fernando CN Pereira. 2001. Conditional random fields: Probabilistic models for segmenting and labeling sequence data. pages 282–289.

Thomas Lavergne, Olivier Cappé, and François Yvon. 2010. Practical very large scale crfs. In *Proceedings of the 48th Annual Meeting of the Association for Computational Linguistics*, pages 504–513, Uppsala, Sweden, July. Association for Computational Linguistics.

T. Mikolov, M. Karafiát, L. Burget, J. Černocký, and S. Khudanpur. 2010. Recurrent neural network based language model. In *Proceedings of the 11th Annual Conference of the International Speech Communication Association (INTERSPEECH 2010)*, Makuhari, Chiba, Japan. International Speech Communication Association (ICSA). http://www.fit.vutbr.cz/research/groups/speech/publi/2010/mikolov_interspeech2010_IS100722.pdf.

Tomáš Mikolov. 2012. *Statistical Language Models based on Neural Networks*. Ph.D. thesis, Brno University of Technology, Faculty of Information Technology, Department of Computer Graphics and Multimedia, Brno, Czech Republic. http://www.fit.vutbr.cz/~imikolov/rnnlm/thesis.pdf.

Andreas Stolcke. 2002. SRILM — an extensible language modeling toolkit. In John H. L. Hansen and Bryan Pellom, editors, *Proceedings of the 7th International Conference on Spoken Language Processing (ICSLP2002)*, volume 2, pages 901–904, Baixas, France. International Speech Communication Association (ISCA).

Oriol Vinyals, Alexander Toshev, Samy Bengio, and Dumitru Erhan. 2015. Show and tell: A neural image caption generator. http://arxiv.org/abs/1411.4555, to appear in Computer Vision and Pattern Recognition.

Andy Way. 2010. Machine translation. In Alexander Clark, Chris Fox, and Shalom Lappin, editors, *The Handbook of Computational Linguistics and Natural Language Processing*, pages 531–573. Wiley Blackwell, Chichester, UK, July.

Amber Wilcox-O'Hearn, Graeme Hirst, and Alexander Budanitsky. 2008. Real-word spelling correction with trigrams: A reconsideration of the Mays, Damerau, and Mercer model. In Alexander Gelbukh, editor, *Computational Linguistics and Intelligent Text Processing - 9th International Conference, CICLing 2008, Haifa, Isarael, February 17–23, 2008 - Proceedings*, volume 4919/2008, pages 605–616. Springer Berlin/Heidelberg, Germany. 2006 draft version available on http://ftp.cs.toronto.edu/pub/gh/WilcoxOHearn-etal-2006.pdf.

Yue Zhang and Stephen Clark. 2011. Syntactic processing using the generalized perceptron and beam search. *Computational Linguistics*, 37(1):105–151.

# LYSGROUP: Adapting a Spanish microtext normalization system to English.

**Yerai Doval, Jesús Vilares, Carlos Gómez-Rodríguez**
LYS group, Departamento de Computación, Facultade de Informática,
Universidade da Coruña, Campus de Elviña, 15071 A Coruña, Spain
{yerai.doval, jvilares, cgomezr}@udc.es – www.grupolys.org

## Abstract

In this article we describe the microtext normalization system we have used to participate in the Normalization of Noisy Text Task of the ACL W-NUT 2015 Workshop. Our normalization system was originally developed for text mining tasks on Spanish tweets. Our main goals during its development were flexibility, scalability and maintainability, in order to test a wide variety of approximations to the problem at hand with minimum effort. We will pay special attention to the process of adapting the components of our system to deal with English tweets which, as we will show, was achieved without major modifications of its base structure.

## 1 Introduction

The value of Twitter and other *microblogging* services as information sources in domains like marketing, business intelligence, journalism, etc. is obvious nowadays. Nevertheless, such amount of information can only be appropriately exploited through *text mining* techniques.

However, there are notable differences between "standard" language and the so-called *texting* used in those *microtexts*. In this kind of writings, it is important to reduce the number of characters used to fit their length restrictions while maintaining the readability of the message to some extent. To achieve this, most of the techniques applied rely on phonetics, thus being language-specific (López Rúa, 2007). For example: intentionally ignoring orthographic and grammar rules, as in "be like" for "am/is/are/was/were like" in the case of English or "asique" for "así que" in the case of Spanish; the usage of shortenings, contractions and abbreviations such as "c u" for "see you" in English or "ksa" for "casa" in Spanish; or the employment of *smileys* to express emotions, for instance `:)` to express happiness. These resulting terms are called *lexical variants* (Han et al., 2013).

The problem is that, in general, text mining tools are very sensitive to those phenomena, as they are designed for dealing with standard texts. Therefore, it is necessary to *normalize* these texts before their processing, that is, to transform them into standard language. This way "c u nxt week", for example, would be transformed into "see you next week". This is the goal of the W-NUT 2015 Normalization Task (Baldwin et al., 2015).

The rest of this paper is organized as follows: Section 2 describes the core architecture of our system, and how it was adapted to fit this shared task, and Section 3 presents the resources used. Next, Section 4 evaluates the system and discusses the results obtained. Finally, Section 5 presents our conclusions and considers some possible future improvements for our system.

## 2 Architecture

Our tweet normalization system was developed taking as basic premises its flexibility, scalability and maintainability. As a starting point, we took a previous prototype for Spanish tweet normalization (Vilares et al., 2013) which, although fully functional, did not turn out to be as flexible and maintainable as expected. This could have become a problem for future developments, since the adaptation effort needed to integrate new techniques would have been too large, so we decided to refactor the whole system to solve this.

The general scheme of the original system mimics that of Han and Baldwin (2011) and comprises three stages:

1. Tweet preprocessing.

2. In-vocabulary word identification (IV), based on the lexicon of the system, obtaining as



*Proceedings of the ACL 2015 Workshop on Noisy User-generated Text*, pages 99–105,
Beijing, China, July 31, 2015. ©2015 Association for Computational Linguistics

a result an initial set of out-of-vocabulary words (OOV).

3. OOV set processing in order to distinguish between correct words which are out of the system lexicon and proper *lexical variants*, obtaining for each one of the latter a normalized form. This last step can be in turn decomposed into two: the first one, which generates a set of possible normalization candidates based on the application of certain normalization techniques; and the second one, which selects one of these candidates as the normalized form (in our case, in a score-driven process).

As for the particular normalization techniques employed throughout our system, we decided to try first a combination of two of the traditional approximations to this task (Kobus et al., 2008): the spell checking and the automatic speech recognition metaphors.

### 2.1 The pipeline

We decided to give our system an *object oriented* approach (using JAVA) as opposed to the *imperative* approach of the original prototype (in PERL). The new system is structured in *processors*, formerly known as *modules* in the prototype, whose goal is to apply a certain process to the input tweets so that we can obtain the normalization candidates of their terms at its output.

The core component of our system is the pipeline, consisting of a classic cascade structure where we can insert an arbitrary number of processors and have their inputs and outputs automatically linked. In this way, the original input of the system becomes the input of the first processor, the output of the first processor is the input of the second one, the output of this second processor is the input of the third one, and so on, until reaching the last processor, whose output becomes the output of the system.

Regarding its design, we have followed good engineering practices and made extensive use of *design patterns*. Among them, it should be noted the use of the *decorator* pattern which, in our context, represents a simple pipeline, allowing us to dynamically stack an arbitrary number of processors. Its combination with the *composition* pattern lets us group them into *stages*, which enable the definition of particular processor sequences while still sharing the same basic processor interface, thus preserving the flexibility of the *decorator*. Thereby, the resulting structure allows for the dynamic construction of different pipeline configurations of varying complexity and different levels of abstraction, not being restricted to the original settings.

The application of the *template* pattern allowed us to factorize great part of the common processes of the components, such as the sequential iteration through all the input tweets, which most of the processors perform. This resulted in a great homogenization of the code, thus simplifying maintenance and allowing us to focus our efforts on the specific implementation of the processing methods in each case.

Moreover, some processors make use of external tools capable of being changed even at runtime — something of special interest in multilingual environments. It should also be possible to integrate them into other external components, so that their logic can be reused by others. All this involves decoupling the processors from the specific implementations of the external components employed, which we have achieved through the use of the *inversion of control* pattern.

Furthermore, communication between the components of the pipeline is done through structured text files, allowing us to gain flexibility as we can integrate and exchange with ease new processing modules regardless of their particular implementation (Vilares et al., 2013). In this case we have used XML along with an implementation of the *abstract factory* pattern for its construction and parsing. This also facilitates possible future migrations to other data representation languages, such as JSON.

Finally, we have created a *dynamic configuration subsystem* based on XML files that allows us to define and instantiate the particular structure of the pipeline on which we want to process the tweets. The advantages of such a subsystem are clear, both for system maintainability and testing:

1. It improves the multilingual support of the system by enabling the definition of configurations that use processors and resources designed for a particular language.

2. It allows for experimentation in a simple, agile and documented (the configuration file itself also serves as documentation) manner.

3. It avoids the necessity of modifying the system source code.

### 2.2 Configuration before W-NUT 2015

The current processor configuration for Spanish tweet normalization derives from that one used by the initial prototype for its participation in the TweetNorm 2013 task (Alegría et al., 2013). The general procedure works like this: firstly, using processors to prepare the input (preprocessing); secondly, employing those whose purpose is to obtain new normalization forms (candidates generation); thirdly, using those in charge of selecting or filtering the best normalization forms (candidate filtering/selection); and lastly, employing those which prepare the final output of the system (postprocessing). Such setup includes the following processors:

- `FreelingProcessor`, which reads the input data in the TweetNorm 2013 format and uses `Freeling` (Padró and Stanilovsky, 2012) to perform the tokenization, lemmatization and POS tagging (although these tags are not currently in use) of the text of the tweet.

- `MentionProcessor`, `HashtagProcessor`, `URLProcessor` and `SmileyProcessor`, which act as filters for OOVs we do not want to consider for normalization.

- `LaughESProcessor`, which normalizes laugh string representations, as in "ja" for "jajaja".

- `PhoneticProcessor`, which uses a phonetic table to map characters to their phonetic equivalent strings, such as "x" to "por".[1]

- `SMSDictionaryProcessor`, which looks for normalization candidates in an SMS dictionary, for example "también" (too/also) for "tb".

- `AspellProcessor`, which obtains normalization candidates using the spell checker `aspell` (Aspell, 2011), as in "polémica" (controversy) for "polemik". It should be noted that this tool has been customised with a new phonetic table for Spanish, based on the Metaphone algorithm (Philips, 1990) and a new Spanish dictionary extracted from Wikimedia resources.[2]

- `AffixESProcessor`, which identifies and normalizes affix-derived Spanish forms of base words, also supporting phonetical writing, as in the case of "chikiyo" for "chiquillo" (little boy), obtained from "chico" with the suffix "-illo" (little/small).

- `NGramProcessor`, which calculates the scores of those most likely normalization candidates according to the Viterbi algorithm (Manning and Schütze, 1999, Ch. 9) taking as reference the Web 1T 5-gram v1 (Brants and Franz, 2006) Spanish language model.

- `CandidateProcessor`, which selects the top-scoring candidate for each word.

- `ResultProcessor`, which dumps the tweet data obtained by the system to a file using the required format.

### 2.3 Adaptation for W-NUT 2015

In general, the adaptation process revolved around implementing new processors and integrating new resources to account for the requirements of this new task, such as the use of English instead of Spanish on the new I/O data format, while leaving the base structure of the system untouched. This was precisely the main goal during the refactoring process at the beginning of this project.

The resulting configuration includes the following new processors (see Section 3 for a description of the resources they use):

- `WNUTTweetProcessor`, which parses the structured input (now in JSON format instead of plain text) and obtains the system representation of the tweets.

- `ArkTweetProcessor`, which uses the `ark-tweet-nlp` POS tagger to obtain the morphosyntactic information of the input tweet tokens.

- `WNUTFilterProcessor`, which filters out all those terms that should not be normalized according to the task rules (mentions, hashtags, URLs, etc.) using regular expressions.

[1]The character "x" resembles the multiplication (times) sign ×, which in Spanish is read as "por".

[2]http://wikimediafoundation.org

- LowerCaseProcessor, which takes all the candidate forms of a token and lowercases them; AspellCProcessor, a constrained version of the original AspellProcessor described in Section 2.2 (see Section 3 for further details).

- WNUTNgramProcessor, which is similar to the previous NGramProcessor but with some added modifications to fit the particularities of our new custom language model.

- WNUTResultProcessor, which dumps all tweet data generated by the system in the required output format (JSON).

We show in Figure 1 a graphical representation of the architecture of the system both before (left side) and after (right side) the adaptation.

Unfortunately, time limitations prevented us from implementing an English phonetic table for the PhoneticProcessor, which would have provided us with mappings such as "two", "too" or "to" for "2". To alleviate this, we did extend the SMS dictionary to cover some of these cases.

It should be noted that because of those limitations we did not address those cases were multiple contiguous tokens of the input tweet should be normalized into a single output token (i.e. the so called "n-1 mappings"). Moreover, since that phenomenon was rare (it appeared in just 11 tweets out of 2950 of the training dataset) we considered that leaving this feature behind would have little impact on the final performance of the system.

## 3 Integrated resources

The base resources we have used for this task, and on which most of the system processors rely, are the following:

- aspell (Aspell, 2011), the well-known spell-checker together with its default English dictionary.

- ark-tweet-nlp (Owoputi et al., 2013), a Twitter-focused NLP toolkit from which we have used its POS tagger.

- BerkeleyLM (Pauls and Klein, 2011), a Java library and toolset focused on language modeling.

- Redis,[3] a noSQL key-value datastore; and the SMS normalization dictionaries, canonical lexicon and training dataset provided by the organizers of the task.

As a result of processing the previous resources, we have obtained the following additional ones:

- A global SMS normalization dictionary implemented as a Redis datastore, whose entries were extracted from the two normalization dictionaries and the training dataset provided by the organizers.

- A Kneser-Ney language model (Kneser and Ney, 1995) of the target domain (standard tweet text) obtained with the BerkeleyLM tools taking as input tweets of the training dataset.

- A new English dictionary for aspell built on the canonical lexicon.

With respect to the differences existing between the configurations of the system for constrained and unconstrained runs, there is only one. In the case of the *constrained* run, since only *off-the-shelf* tools are permitted, the aspell spell-checker was employed using its default dictionary but filtering its retrieved candidate corrections taking as reference the canonical lexicon; i.e. only those candidates that could be found on this lexicon were taken into account. On the other hand, in the case of the *unconstrained* run, aspell was used instead with the dictionary obtained from the canonical lexicon. The rest of the processors and their parameters remained the same.

Moreover, although we also considered the use of the Web 1T 5-gram v1 language model in the unconstrained run, our preliminary tests showed that the results obtained were very poor in this case, as we further comment in Section 4.

## 4 Evaluation

Table 1 shows the results obtained for the *training* corpus. It should be noted that these correspond to a slightly *overfitted* system, since we inadvertently used a language model built using the whole training dataset (for candidate selection) in our 10-fold cross-validation framework. Nevertheless, this also gave us an interesting clue to the main performance bottleneck of our system, as we will discuss below.

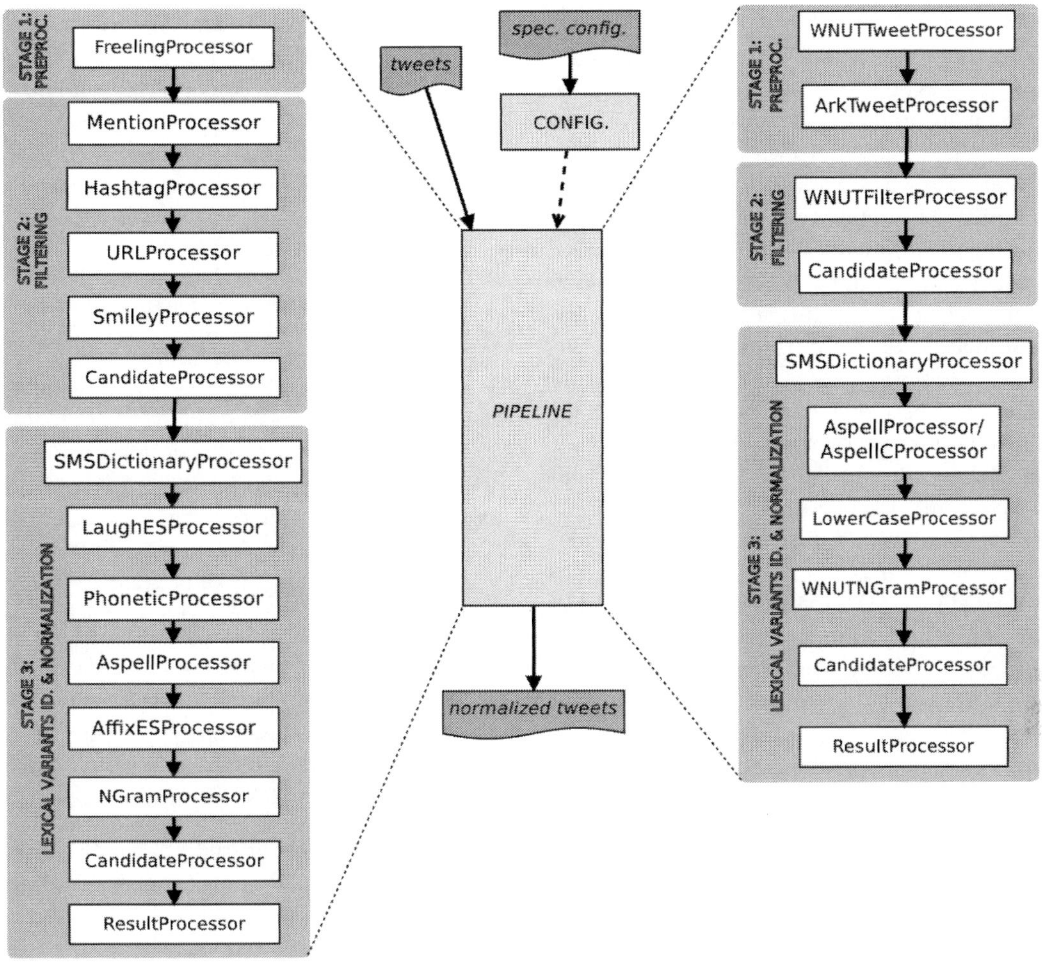


Figure 1: Original pipeline (left) and pipeline adapted for W-NUT 2015 (right) integrated into the architecture of the system.

| | precision | recall | F1 |
|---|---|---|---|
| constrained | 0.8956 | 0.8746 | 0.8850 |
| unconstrained | 0.8914 | 0.8739 | 0.8825 |

Table 1: Training results.

| | precision | recall | F1 |
|---|---|---|---|
| constrained | 0.4646 | 0.6281 | 0.5341 |
| unconstrained | 0.4592 | 0.6296 | 0.5310 |

Table 2: Testing results.

Table 2 shows the results obtained for the *test* corpus. At the sight of these figures, which differ considerably from the previous ones, we decided to analyse them in more detail. For this purpose, we obtained a recall metric on the scope of the candidates proposed by the system; in other words, we wanted to see how many times the correct candidate corresponding to a token of the dataset was among the ones considered by the system. The resulting ratio came to `0.87`, which means that most of the times we had had the chance to select the correct normalization form for a given non-standard token but the system failed to make the selection, and is also a consistent figure with respect to those shown on Table 1. This was not a big surprise for us, mainly because it is a well-known problem we have been aware of since we started working on (Spanish) tweet normalization. Therefore, we can conclude that the performance bottleneck of our system is still the candidate selection process, which is heavily influenced by the

[3] `http://redis.io/`

language model in use.

In this respect, tuning experiments were also made by extending our unconstrained configuration through the addition of the Web 1T 5-gram v1 English language model as a knowledge source. Only unigrams and bigrams could be used because of unsolved memory limitations. However, in contrast with previous experiments performed for Spanish, the resulting performance was unsatisfactory. Because of this, the use of these language models for our final submission was dismissed. According to our analysis, the cause for this seems to be the great differences, at both the lexical and syntactical levels, between the texts used to build this model, which could be considered as "regular" texts, and those corresponding to tweets, which agrees with the observations of Chrupała (2014). As illustrative examples of this type of expressions we can take "I like them girls" and "Why you no do that?", which are lexically correct but not syntactically valid, so language models built using regular texts will not recognize them. In the case of our previous experiments on Spanish, this difference was not so clear.

## 5 Conclusions and Future work

We have presented in this work the tweet normalization system used by our group to participate in the W-NUT 2015 Normalization Task which, in turn, is an adaptation of another existing Spanish tweet normalization system.

Within the scope of this task, it became clear that most of the normalization mistakes made by our system occurred during the candidate selection stage, as it was unable to determine the correct normalization term obtained in previous stages from the set of candidates available. The reason for it is that we do not have at this very moment enough training data to build a representative language model of the target domain (normalized text of English tweets).

Furthermore, there is another type of normalization phenomena which, at this moment, cannot be correctly handled by our system: n-1 mappings. This is due to the initial approach we took for this system, which only considered 1-1 and 1-n mappings, but not n-1 mappings, together with our time limitations.

All that being said, as future lines of work we are considering the following improvements to our system:

- Obtaining a representative language model of the target domain by using a larger normalized tweet corpus. This corpus will be comprised of tweets without non-standard words, so we can still capture the morphosyntactic structure of these texts (Yang and Eisenstein, 2013).
- Using POS tags and syntactic information to improve the candidate selection process.
- Integrating a classifier in the extraction process of the final normalization candidates, taking as features aspects such as the syntactic and morphosyntactic information obtained, their probability according to the language model, whether they were selected or not by the Viterbi algorithm, their string and phonetic differences with respect to the original form, etc.
- Keeping the canonical lexicon updated using resources like Wikipedia, since the language model construction process relies heavily upon a good lexical reference in order to correctly discard non-standard words.

Moreover, we intend to study the application of tweet normalization, for both Spanish and English tweets, in *opinion mining* tasks (Vilares et al., 2015).

## Acknowledgments

This research has been partially funded by the Spanish Ministry of Economy and Competitiveness and FEDER (through project FFI2014-51978-C2-2-R) and by the Autonomous Government of Galicia (through grant R2014/034).

## References

Iñaki Alegría, Nora Aranberri, Víctor Fresno, Pablo Gamallo, Lluís Padró, Iñaki San Vicente, Jordi Turmo, and Arkaitz Zubiaga. 2013. Introducción a la tarea compartida Tweet-Norm 2013: Normalización léxica de tuits en español. In *Tweet-Norm 2013. Tweet Normalization Workshop 2013*, volume 1086 of *CEUR Workshop Proceedings*, pages 1–9. CEUR-WS.org.

GNU ASPELL (rel. 0.60). 2011. Available at: `http://aspell.net` (visited on May 2015).

Timothy Baldwin, Marie Catherine de Marneffe, Bo Han, Young-Bum Kim, Alan Ritter, and Wei Xu. 2015. Shared tasks of the 2015 workshop on noisy user-generated text: Twitter lexical normalization and named entity recognition. In *Proceedings of the Workshop on Noisy User-generated Text (WNUT 2015)*, Beijing, China.

Thorsten Brants and Alex Franz. 2006. Web 1T 5-gram Version 1 (ref. LDC2006T13). DVD. Distributed by Linguistic Data Consortium.

Grzegorz Chrupała. 2014. Normalizing tweets with edit scripts and recurrent neural embeddings. In *Proc. of the 52nd Annual Meeting of the Association for Computational Linguistics (Volume 2: Short Papers)*, pages 680–686. ACL.

Bo Han and Timothy Baldwin. 2011. Lexical normalisation of short text messages: makn sens a #twitter. In *Proc. of the 49th Annual Meeting of the Association for Computational Linguistics: Human Language Technologies (ACL-HLT 2011) - Volume 1*, pages 368–378. ACL.

Bo Han, Paul Cook, and Timothy Baldwin. 2013. Lexical normalization for social media text. *ACM Transactions on Intelligent Systems and Technology (TIST)*, 4(1):5:1–5:27.

Reinhard Kneser and Hermann Ney. 1995. Improved backing-off for M-gram language modeling. In *Proc. of the IEEE International Conference on Acoustics, Speech and Signal Processing (ICASSP-95)*, volume 1, pages 181–184. IEEE.

Catherine Kobus, François Yvon, and Géraldine Damnati. 2008. Normalizing SMS: Are Two Metaphors Better Than One? In *Proc. of the 22nd International Conference on Computational Linguistics (COLING'08) - Volume 1*, pages 441–448. ACL.

Paula López Rúa. 2007. Teaching L2 vocabulary through SMS language: Some didactic guidelines. *Estudios de lingüística inglesa aplicada*, 7:165–188.

Christopher D. Manning and Hinrich Schütze. 1999. *Foundations of Statistical Natural Language Processing*. The MIT Press, Cambridge (Massachusetts) and London (England).

Olutobi Owoputi, Brendan O'Connor, Chris Dyer, Kevin Gimpel, Nathan Schneider, and Noah A. Smith. 2013. Improved part-of-speech tagging for online conversational text with word clusters. In *Proc. of the 2013 Conference of the North American Chapter of the Association for Computational Linguistics: Human Language Technologies (NAACL-HLT 2013)*, pages 380–390. ACL. Toolkit available at: `http://www.ark.cs.cmu.edu/TweetNLP/` (visited on May 2015).

Lluís Padró and Evgeny Stanilovsky. 2012. Freeling 3.0: Towards Wider Multilinguality. In *Proceedings of the Eight International Conference on Language Resources and Evaluation (LREC'12)*. European Language Resources Association (ELRA). Toolkit available at: `http://nlp.lsi.upc.edu/freeling/` (visited on May 2015).

Adam Pauls and Dan Klein. 2011. Faster and Smaller N-gram Language Models. In *Proc. of the 49th Annual Meeting of the Association for Computational Linguistics: Human Language Technologies (ACL-HLT 2011) - Volume 1*, pages 258–267. ACL. BerkeleyLM source code available at `https://code.google.com/p/berkeleylm/` (visited on May 2015).

Lawrence Philips. 1990. Hanging on the metaphone. *Computer Language*, 7(12):39–43.

Jesús Vilares, Miguel A. Alonso, and David Vilares. 2013. Prototipado rápido de un sistema de normalización de tuits: Una aproximación léxica. In *Tweet-Norm 2013. Tweet Normalization Workshop 2013*, volume 1086 of *CEUR Workshop Proceedings*, pages 39–43. CEUR-WS.org.

David Vilares, Miguel A. Alonso, and Carlos Gómez-Rodríguez. 2015. On the usefulness of lexical and syntactic processing in polarity classification of Twitter messages. Accepted for publication in *Journal of the Association for Information Science and Technology (JASIST)*. DOI 10.1002/asi.23284.

Yi Yang and Jacob Eisenstein. 2013. A Log-Linear Model for Unsupervised Text Normalization. In *Proc. of the 2013 Conference on Empirical Methods in Natural Language Processing (EMNLP 2013)*, pages 61–72. ACL.

# IITP: Hybrid Approach for Text Normalization in Twitter

**Md Shad Akhtar, Utpal Kumar Sikdar and Asif Ekbal**
Dept of Computer Science and Engineering
IIT Patna
Patna, India
(shad.pcs15,utpal.sikdar,asif)@iitp.ac.in

## Abstract

In this paper we report our work for normalization of noisy text in Twitter data. The method we propose is hybrid in nature that combines machine learning with rules. In the first step, supervised approach based on conditional random field is developed, and in the second step a set of heuristics rules is applied to the candidate wordforms for the normalization. The classifier is trained with a set of features which were are derived without the use of any domain-specific feature and/or resource. The overall system yields the precision, recall and F-measure values of 90.26%, 71.91% and 80.05% respectively for the test dataset.

## 1 Introduction

Twitter has seen a phenomenal growth in the number of users during the last few years. Over 500 million user accounts have been registered with it with approx 302 million active users [1]. Amount of user generated contents over the web would be unarguably enormous i.e. almost 500 million tweets per day [2]. The fact that Twitter data (*or tweets*) are typically noisy and unstructured in nature are due to several grammatical & spelling mistakes it contain. The size limitation (constitute upto 140 characters only) is the another prominent reason. It confines a user to devise different short forms (*e.g. 'c u ltr.'* for *'see you later.'*) of a valid word. Interpreting such forms may be an easier task for a human being but, is very difficult to build an accurate system for solving any problem related to natural language processing (NLP). At times, user puts extra emphasis by stretching/elongating a valid word to express their feelings. For example, they often use word like '*yeeessss*' to show their happiness, which is a stretched form of '*yes*'.

Normalization of noisy text is an important and necessary pre-processing task for building different applications related to text processing. It is pretty obvious from various studies (Liu et al., 2011; Foster et al., 2011) that presence of noisy texts makes any natural language processing (NLP) task very tedious to achieve good accuracy levels. The goal of normalization is twofold, i.e. a) identification of candidates for normalization and b) converting the candidate wordforms to the normalized form. Unlike the general well-formatted corpus, like newswire, it does not always contain noisy text. Its main sources are normally those platforms on which users have complete freedom to express themselves. Therefore, user generated tweets are one of the major sources of noisy texts. In the last couples of years researchers across worldwide are actively working for the normalization of noisy contents of twitter (Han and Baldwin, 2011; Liu et al., 2012; Wang and Ng, 2013; Porta and Sancho, 2013; Chrupala, 2014). In (Han and Baldwin, 2011), a linear Support Vector Machine (SVM) classifier was trained for detecting ill-formed words, and then performed normalization based on morphophonemic similarity. Application of edit operations and recurrent neural embedding can be found in (Chrupala, 2014) for text normalization. Their method learns sequence of edit operations using conditional random field (CRF). In another work, (Liu et al., 2012) investigated the human perspectives of enhanced letter transformation, visual priming and the phonetic similarity for the text normalization. The use of beam search decoder and finite-state transducers can be seen in (Wang and Ng, 2013; Porta and Sancho, 2013) for the word normalization. These existing works are based on different setups and datasets.

[1] http://en.wikipedia.org/wiki/Twitter

[2] http://www.cnet.com/news/report-twitter-hits-half-a-billion-tweets-a-day/



*Proceedings of the ACL 2015 Workshop on Noisy User-generated Text*, pages 106–110,
Beijing, China, July 31, 2015. ©2015 Association for Computational Linguistics

For further advancement of research on text normalization and to provide a common benchmark setup for evaluation, a shared task "ACL2015 W-NUT: Normalization of Noisy Text in Twitter"[3] was organized. The shared task had two variants: constrained mode and unconstrained mode. We participated only for the constrained mode which did not permit us to use any external resources and/or tools except few that were recommended by the organizers. In this paper we report our work for normalization. We implemented a hybrid system where machine learning along with rules are utilized to perform the task. We have exploited lexical and syntactic properties of a tweet as discussed in section 3.1 to derive a feature set for identification of noisy text in the first step. We train Conditional Random Field (CRF) (Lafferty et al., 2001) as a machine learning algorithm to identify the candidate wordforms that need to be normalized. In second step, we apply some rule based methods (as defined in section 3.2) in order to normalize the wordforms which were identified in first step.

The organization of the paper is as follows. A brief theoretical discussion on CRF is presented in section 2. Section 3 discuss about the feature set and methodology used in the proposed work. Experimental result and analysis can be found in section 4. We conclude the paper in section 5.

## 2 Conditional Random Field (CRF)

Conditional Random Field, introduced by (Lafferty et al., 2001), is a robust sequence learning algorithm based on the conditional probability. Let an observation sequence $O =< o_1, o_2, ..., o_T >$ is given, then the conditional probability of a state sequence $S =< s_1, s_2, ..., s_T >$ can be formulated as:

$$P(S|O) = \frac{1}{Z_0} exp(\sum_{t=1}^{T} \sum_{k=1}^{K} \lambda_k \times f_k(s_{t-1}, s_t, o, t)) \quad (1)$$

where $\lambda_k$ is the weight of the feature function $f_k(s_{t-1}, s_t, o, t)$, that is to be learned via training. In general, feature functions takes binary value but at times it may range between $-\infty$ to $+\infty$. The output of this function relies on certain state sequence i.e. $s_{t-1}, s_t$ and observation properties. The normalization factor $Z_o$, define in equation 2, is used to make all conditional probabilities sum up to unity and can be calculated efficiently using dynamic programming.

$$Z_0 = \sum_{s} exp(\sum_{t=1}^{T} \sum_{k=1}^{K} \lambda_k \times f_k(s_{t-1}, s_t, o, t)) \quad (2)$$

## 3 Methods

After discussing theoretical aspect of CRF, we now describe our methodology that we use to perform text normalization. It comprises of two steps. First step consists of training a supervised machine learning model for the identification of noisy text. We implement a set of features that were mostly derived without using any deep domain-specific resources and/or tools. We perform 3-fold cross validation on the training data to determine the best feature combination. In the second step, potential candidates identified to be noisy were analysed and subsequently processed using various heuristic based rules for normalization. Figure 1 depicts schematic diagram of the proposed system.

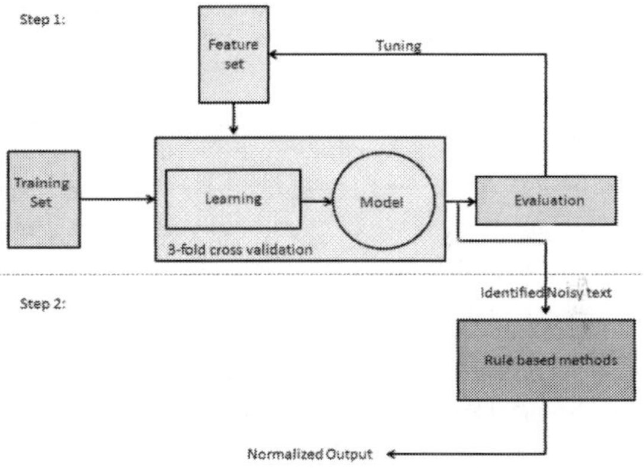


Figure 1: Proposed methodology. Dotted horizontal line separates two steps.

### 3.1 Feature Set

This section describes the feature set that was implemented for identifying the potential candidates that need to be normalized. All the features defined are domain-independent in nature. No other external resources and/or tools, with the exception of vocabulary of words [4], were used in the proposed work. Following are the brief descriptions of the implemented features.

[3] http://noisy-text.github.io/

[4] http://noisy-text.github.io/files/scowl.american.70

1. **Local context:** Local contextual information in the forms of surrounding words are used as the feature.

2. **Vocabulary word:** Noisy word can not be a part of valid vocabulary. Therefore, all out-of-vocabulary (OOV) are the potential candidates that should be normalized. We define a feature that fires if the current is OOV.

3. **Part-of-Speech (PoS) information:** We use CMU-Tweet PoS tagger [5] for extracting the PoS information. This is used as a feature of CRF.

4. **Word length:** From the given training data we observed that noisy texts are generally shorter in lengths. We define a binary valued feature that is set to high if the length of the candidate token exceeds a predetermined threshold. In our case we assume the token to be a noisy text if its length is less than 4 characters.

5. **Suffix and Prefix:** Suffixes and prefixes of length upto 4 characters of the current word are used as the features.

6. **Only digit:** This feature checks whether the current token is consisting of only digits or not. The word has a low probability of being noisy if it contains only the digits. Few exceptions are *2*(to), *4*(for) etc.

7. **AlphaDigit:** An alphanumeric token have a high probability of being a noisy text. A binary valued feature is thus defined in the proposed work which fires when the token is alphanumeric.

8. **Consecutive characters:** This feature fires when a token consists of more than 2 consecutive characters is found. This feature helps in identifying the stretched/elongated words.

9. **Compact word form:** Apostrophe mark (') is used to indicate the omission of one or more letters from a word (e.g. *i'm, you're* etc.). A binary feature is defined which identifies the missing apostrophe mark in a word.

10. **Present participle (*a.k.a* ing-form) of a verb:** From the analysis of training data we observed that people tends to skip 'i' or 'g' from the present participle, i.e. *ing* form, of a verb. For example, they use *goin* in place of *going*. Thus a feature is defined and set to 'on' if a token is found with the above pattern.

11. **Single character:** This feature fires when the token consists of a single character only with the exception of two characters i.e. 'I' and 'a'.

12. **Hash tag & Username:** Hash tags and usernames in tweets, which starts with # & @ respectively, are not considered as noisy text in the training data. Therefore this feature is set to false if a token starts with # or @.

### 3.2 Heuristic rules for normalization

Once the noisy text was identified in the first step, we devise a set of rules for normalization. These rules are heuristic in nature and based on the facts & analysis on the training data. Below is the list of rules implemented according to their application in the proposed work.

1. **Frequent abbreviation:** This is the first rule that we apply on the noisy text. We make use of a list of frequent abbreviations used in twitter and its normal form. The list was compiled from the Web [6,7] and training data. If the token identified as a potential candidate in the first step is present in the list we simply replace it with the normal text, otherwise, we move onto the next rule.

2. **Present participle of a verb:** A rule is defined for a misspelled present participle verb as discussed in section 3.1. We identify and cross check its PoS tag (i.e. *VERB*) in order to retrieve its valid equivalent form.

3. **Missing apostrophe('):** Twitter users normally drops apostrophe mark in tweets. We define a rule to identify and insert a apostrophe mark at proper place. This rule was employed for handling following variants: *'m, 'll, 've, 're, n't, 's* etc.

[5] http://www.ark.cs.cmu.edu/TweetNLP/

[6] http://www.webopedia.com/quick_ref/Twitter_Dictionary_Guide.asp

[7] http://marketing.wtwhmedia.com/30-must-know-twitter-abbreviations-and-acronyms/

4. **Elongated form:** Noisy word in its elongated form (i.e. *yeeeeesss* for *yes*) are identified and translated into valid word by iteratively stripping off consecutive characters.

5. **Split two merged words:** This rule splits a noisy word, if it is a concatenation of two valid words. For example 'thankyou' is concatenation of two separate words i.e. 'thank' and 'you'. We find out word pair at each split point and applied this rule for the pair that has both valid word. Token 'thankyou' has following word pair for 7 spit point: i.e. (1: 't', 'hankyou'; 2: 'th', 'ankyou'; 3: 'tha', 'nkyou'; 4: 'than', 'kyou'; 5: 'thank, 'you'; 6: 'thanky', 'ou'; and 7: 'thankyo', 'u';). Word pair ('thank, 'you') at split point 5 is chosen for the normalization. Before applying this rule a threshold for word length was heuristically set to 6 characters.

6. **British to American standard:** American standard was preferred as an official English language standard for the shared task. We define a rule which identifies British standard word and convert it to corresponding American standard counterpart. Notable differences between the two standards that we have incorporated in the work are 'our' to 'or' (e.g. *labour* to *labor*), 'ise' to 'ize' (e.g. *realise* to *realize*), 're' to 'er' (e.g. *centre* to *center*) etc.

## 4 Datasets and Experiments

In subsequent subsections we discuss the dataset used in the system and evaluation results, respectively.

### 4.1 Data Set

Objective of the shared task was to identify and normalize the noisy text in tweets. Only training dataset was provided by the shared task organizers. The training dataset comprise of 2,950 tweets and a total of 3,942 noisy tokens were present in the dataset. In absence of the development dataset, we use 3-fold cross validation for training the model. Gold standard test datasets contains 1,967 tweets. Table 1 list the statistics of the datasets.

### 4.2 Experimental Results

Conditional Random Field (CRF)(Lafferty et al., 2001) was used as a base learning algorithm in the proposed work. We use the CRF++ [8] based package for training and testing. To evaluate the performance of the system, an evaluation script along with the dataset was provided by the organizers. We perform 3-fold cross-validation technique to fine-tune the system, and identify the best fitting feature combination. The performance of 3-fold cross validation experiment yields the F-measure of 92.21% for identification problem (i.e. denoting only the candidates for normalization). For the test set it shows the F-measure of 86.63%. After identifying the candidates of normalization we apply heuristics to perform normalization. Rules were applied according to their appearance. We have tried various combination of rule sequences and found that the listed sequence is the one which gives us better performance. While we perform 3-fold cross validation we obtain the precision, recall and F-measure values of 88.59%, 74.92% and 81.19%, respectively. Finally we obtain the precision, recall and F-measure values of 90.26%, 71.91% and 80.05%, respectively. Results of these experiments are shown in Table 2.

| Dataset | # Tweets | # Tokens | # Noisy |
|---|---|---|---|
| *train* | 2950 | 44385 | 3942 |
| *test* | 1967 | 29421 | 2776 |

Table 1: Statistics of the dataset

We closely analyze the errors encountered by our system. We observed that many errors were due to the incorrect identification of the candidates that need to be normalized. The jumbled words, e.g. *'liek', 'whta'* etc. were not properly recognized. With more accurate identification system we would have achieved better result. For example in case of 100% noisy text identification, we obtained an increase of 3.75% in our final F-measure. For normalization error, our method arguably lags behind in two fronts: a) ambiguities in normalization and b) many-to-one mapping cases. Many of these may be reduced by careful design of the heuristic rules.

## 5 Conclusion

In this paper we have reported our works that we carried out as part of our participation in the Twitter text normalization shared task. We have developed a hybrid system where in the first step

[8]http://taku910.github.io/crfpp/

| Task | Dataset | Precision | Recall | F-measure | Accuracy |
|---|---|---|---|---|---|
| Identification | *3-fold cv* | 89.51 | 95.08 | 92.21 | 98.70 |
| | *test* | 93.08 | 81.01 | 86.63 | 97.64 |
| Normalization | *3-fold cv* | 88.59 | 74.92 | 81.19 | - |
| | *test* | 90.26 | 71.91 | 80.05 | - |

Table 2: Result of the proposed system. All values are in %.

we identify the candidates for normalization using a CRF based approach, and in the second step we employed several heuristics for converting the wordforms into the normalized form. We have implemented the features which are mostly domain-independent in the sense that we did not make use of any domain specific resources and/or tools for their extraction. Official evaluation shows that our system achieves the F-measure of 80.05%.

In future we would like to carry out more comprehensive analysis on the evaluation results. The features and rules that we used here are very general and straightforward in nature. In future we would like to modify the system into a fully machine learning based approach and put extra emphasis on errors.

## References


Grzegorz Chrupala. 2014. Normalizing tweets with edit scripts and recurrent neural embeddings. In *Proceedings of the 52nd Annual Meeting of the Association for Computational Linguistics, ACL 2014, June 22-27, 2014, Baltimore, MD, USA, Volume 2: Short Papers*, pages 680–686.

Jennifer Foster, Özlem Çetinoglu, Joachim Wagner, Joseph Le Roux, Stephen Hogan, Joakim Nivre, Deirdre Hogan, and Josef van Genabith. 2011. #hardtoparse: POS tagging and parsing the twitterverse. In *Analyzing Microtext, Papers from the 2011 AAAI Workshop, San Francisco, California, USA, August 8, 2011*.

Bo Han and Timothy Baldwin. 2011. Lexical normalisation of short text messages: Makn sens a #twitter. In *Proceedings of the 49th Annual Meeting of the Association for Computational Linguistics: Human Language Technologies - Volume 1*, HLT '11, pages 368–378, Stroudsburg, PA, USA. Association for Computational Linguistics.

John D. Lafferty, Andrew McCallum, and Fernando C. N. Pereira. 2001. Conditional Random Fields: Probabilistic Models for Segmenting and Labeling Sequence Data. In *ICML*, pages 282–289.

Xiaohua Liu, Shaodian Zhang, Furu Wei, and Ming Zhou. 2011. Recognizing named entities in tweets. In *Proceedings of the 49th Annual Meeting of the Association for Computational Linguistics: Human Language Technologies - Volume 1*, HLT '11, pages 359–367, Stroudsburg, PA, USA. Association for Computational Linguistics.

Fei Liu, Fuliang Weng, and Xiao Jiang. 2012. A broad-coverage normalization system for social media language. In *Proceedings of the 50th Annual Meeting of the Association for Computational Linguistics: Long Papers - Volume 1*, ACL '12, pages 1035–1044, Stroudsburg, PA, USA. Association for Computational Linguistics.

Jordi Porta and José-Luis Sancho. 2013. Word normalization in twitter using finite-state transducers. In *Proceedings of the Tweet Normalization Workshop co-located with 29th Conference of the Spanish Society for Natural Language Processing (SEPLN 2013), Madrid, Spain, September 20th, 2013.*, pages 49–53.

Pidong Wang and Hwee Tou Ng. 2013. A beam-search decoder for normalization of social media text with application to machine translation. In *Human Language Technologies: Conference of the North American Chapter of the Association of Computational Linguistics, Proceedings, June 9-14, 2013, Westin Peachtree Plaza Hotel, Atlanta, Georgia, USA*, pages 471–481.

# NCSU_SAS_WOOKHEE: A Deep Contextual Long-Short Term Memory Model for Text Normalization

**Wookhee Min** **Bradford W. Mott**
Center for Educational Informatics
North Carolina State University
Raleigh, NC, USA
{wmin, bwmott}@ncsu.edu

## Abstract

To address the challenges of normalizing online conversational texts prevalent in social media, we propose a contextual long-short term memory (LSTM) recurrent neural network based approach, augmented with a self-generated dictionary normalization technique. Our approach utilizes a sequence of characters as well as the part-of-speech associated with words without harnessing any external lexical resources. This work is evaluated on the English Tweet data set provided by the ACL 2015 W-NUT Normalization of Noisy Text shared task. The results, by achieving second place (F1 score: 81.75%) in the constrained track of the competition, indicate that the proposed LSTM-based approach is a promising tool for normalizing non-standard language.

## 1 Introduction

Recent years have seen increasing use of online social media such as Twitter and Facebook that has generated a growing body of text where non-standard language is prevalent. These non-standard lexical items take many different forms, including unintentional errors based on users' cognitive misconceptions and typographical errors, and intentional non-canonical language such as abbreviations, word lengthening by duplication of characters, Internet slang, phonetic substitutions, and creative use of language (Chrupała, 2014; Owoputi et al., 2013).

A key challenge posed by these non-standard texts is the negative impact on traditional natural language processing (NLP) pipeline processes, evidenced by noticeable underperformance of their predictive accuracy in various domains such as part-of-speech tagging (Gimpel et al., 2011) and named entity recognition (Ritter et al., 2011) compared to more standard text. As an approach to addressing this challenge, text normalization techniques have been widely investigated, ranging from extracting domain specific lexical variants (Gouws et al., 2011), unified letter transformation (Liu et al., 2011), dictionary based methods using string substitution (Han et al., 2012) in an unsupervised manner, to character-level edit operation predictions utilizing conditional random fields in a supervised manner (Chrupała, 2014).

Because language data consists of sequential information, such as streams of characters and sequences of words, many NLP approaches leverage computational models that can effectively deal with temporal data, such as hidden Markov models and conditional random fields (Täckström, 2013; Chrupała, 2014). More recently, deep learning models (e.g., multi-layer feed-forward neural networks, recurrent neural networks, recursive neural networks) have been used in NLP to achieve state-of-the-art performance in areas such as speech recognition (Hinton et al., 2012) and sentiment analysis (Socher et al., 2013). The success of deep learning has been attainable with the emergence of effective training methods for deep networks, such as pre-training (Vincent et al., 2010) and optimization techniques (Zeiler, 2010; Martens and Sutskever, 2011) that significantly diminish problems associated with vanishing and exploding gradient that



*Proceedings of the ACL 2015 Workshop on Noisy User-generated Text*, pages 111–119,
Beijing, China, July 31, 2015. 

are often observed in multi-layer neural network training.

In this work, we leverage long-short term memory models (LSTMs) (Hochreiter and Schmidhuber, 1997; Graves, 2012), a variant of recurrent neural networks, to conduct text normalization on the data set given from the W-NUT English lexical normalization shared task (Baldwin et al., 2015). We additionally harness the part-of-speech tagger created by Noah's Ark research team (Owoputi et al., 2013), a free resource to the constrained task. Similar to Chrupała's work that predicts Levenshtein edit operations between canonical and non-canonical forms of words (Chrupała, 2014), this proposed approach predicts word-level edit operations based on character-level inputs. The proposed approach is novel compared to previous work from four perspectives: (1) it utilizes LSTMs to predict the word-level edit operations, along with a dictionary induced from the training set, (2) it takes as input the surrounding words as well as the current word to capture contextual information of the predicted word, while any additional contextual information (e.g., part-of-speech tags) is treated as heading characters of the word, (3) character and part-of-speech embeddings are learned on the fly in the normalization task instead of having them trained in a separate model, and (4) the self-generated dictionary based normalization as an antecedent step provides statistically significant F1 gains over the standalone computational model.

## 2 System Architecture

Our proposed system consists of three steps. In the first step, it filters out domain-specific entities such as tokens beginning with @, hash-tags, and URLs. Next, the system searches for words contained in a dictionary generated solely from the training data and normalizes them when appropriate. If words are not normalized in the previous steps, they are passed to the third step, where an LSTM model predicts the canonical form of the word, utilizing the word itself and surrounding words (the previous and following word). In the next sub-sections, we detail how each of the three steps collaboratively operate and explain how the LSTM model is learned based on the training set along with a high-level illustration of the architecture.

### 2.1 Sequence Flow

The proposed model operates in three primary phases: (1) domain-specific entity filtering, (2) dictionary-based normalization, and (3) LSTM-based normalization.

The first step performs a simple preprocessing of input words. First, every word is converted to the corresponding lowercase word. Second, words that are hash-tags, at-mentions, or URLs are filtered out and left as-is. This preprocessing is useful since the W-NUT normalization task guideline suggests not changing domain-specific entities, and including them could possibly inject noise into predictive models for non-filtered word prediction.

Second, to conduct the dictionary-based normalization, a dictionary is generated from the training set as an index of raw tokens with a list of their normalized forms. For instance, words such as "*ur*" and "*no*" are multiple mapped words, where multiple canonical forms are observed in the training set such as ["*your*", "*you are*"] and ["*no*", "*know*", "*not*"], respectively. This is mainly because they are normalized differently depending on the context used in tweets. On the other hand, words that have a single mapped word are unique in terms of post-normalization form. We denote the first type of words (multiple mapping) as *ambiguous words*, and the second type of words (single mapping) as *unique words*. We use this mapping information as a criterion to decide whether to normalize words based on the dictionary or pass the decision over to the LSTM model in the third step. If a word in the test set turns out to be a unique word, we label the word with the corresponding mapping as defined in the dictionary; otherwise, we pass the word to the LSTM model. This is based on the assumption that these unique words are more likely to have the same unique form in unseen texts.

Finally, once the second normalization step is completed, only words that are either ambiguous or out-of-vocabulary determined by the training set-based dictionary are left and sent to the LSTM model. For ambiguous words, it is important that the model accurately identify the right usage of the words considering context in the tweets. Additionally, it is necessary to capture common patterns of standard words, so that the model can predict canonical forms of words

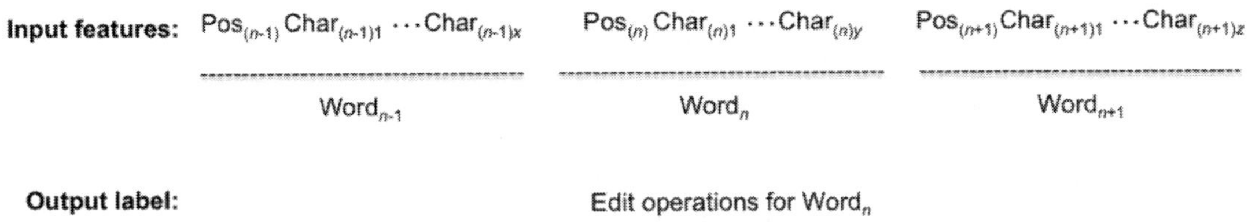


Figure 1: The input features based on characters and POSs and output label (edit operations) used to find the normalized form of $n$th word ($Word_n$). The preceding word ($Word_{n-1}$) and the following word ($Word_{n+1}$)'s POS and constituting characters are combined with the current word ($Word_n$) as input features, where $Word_{n-1}$, $Word_n$, and $Word_{n+1}$ has $x$, $y$, and $z$ characters, respectively.

even when they are not seen in the training set. In this work, we formulate an LSTM model to predict an integrated list of edit operations of a word to become a standard word, leveraging its contextual information.

## 2.2 Data Set Encoding for LSTM

A preliminary step to induce an LSTM model is to encode the data set in a trainable format (i.e., specification of input features and output labels). We define the input format as a list of sequential, lowercased characters that compose the previous word, current word, and following word. Each character is mapped to a unique index (0–66), since there are a total of 67 different characters in the training data after the preprocessing step described in 2.1. If the current word does not have a previous or next word (e.g., the first or last word in a tweet), a padding character is assigned for the previous or following word to have a consistent format. In this work, we additionally consider a word's part-of-speech (POS) as extra input to the model, as previous literature (e.g., Yarowsky, 1997; Täckström, 2013) indicates POS tags can improve performance in other natural language processing tasks, such as text-to-speech synthesis and NLP parsers. We use an off-the-shelf POS tagger that features Brown clustering: the CMU Twitter Part-of-Speech Tagger, which achieves a state-of-the-art tagging result of 93% on a Twitter benchmark data set (Owoputi et al., 2013). The extracted POS information is added as a distinct heading character to each word, so that they are leveraged in the LSTM models. Similar to the character padding, we apply a POS padding for missing previous or next words. Note that leveraging POSs about words is extendable to utilize any other meta-information, and we examine the feasibility of applying this technique with POS tags in the context of text normalization. The input encoding for predicting edit operations of the current word ($Word_n$) is described in Figure 1. To summarize, the number of inputs in a sequence is $3 + x + y + z$, where $x$, $y$ and $z$ are the number of characters of the previous, current, and following word, respectively, while 3 is derived from the POS tags of all three words.

Encoding the output is based on the Levenshtein distance algorithm (Levenshtein, 1966) that supports three operations: *insert*, *replace*, and *delete*, inspired by Chrupała's text normalization work (Chrupała, 2014). In this work, we reformulate his approach to predict word-level edit operations instead of character-level edit operations, by which the model predicts a label for an individual token. In the character-level prediction, to correctly normalize a token, it requires all correction predictions on every character that belongs to a word (i.e., probabilities get multiplied), whereas the word-level prediction requires one prediction per token.

Once a training sample is given, the Levenshtein distance algorithm calculates the required edit operations to convert the possibly non-standard word into the corresponding canonical form. For example, "*dese*" and "*dey*" with the canonical forms of "these" and "they", respectively, have edit operations of "*insert_t_replace_h, none, none, none, none*" and "*insert_t_replace_h, none, none, none*" (a comma is used as a delimiter for characters). Note that the insert operation only supports inserting a character before the current character, so to support insertions at the end of a word, every input word (e.g., "*doin*") is concatenated with an empty character (e.g., "*doin* "), and edit operations are applied on the empty character (e.g., "*none, none, none, none, insert_g*"). Since more class labels make this multi-class classification task more challenging, it is important to have an optimized set of edit operation labels, while the model should be still capable of converting to canonical words based on the given edit operation. For the preceding example, a way to shrink the label size is omitting repeated *none* operations at the end of the string. With this optimization applied, both "*dese*" and "*dey*" have the same edit operation of "*insert_t_replace_h*" ignoring all following "*none*"s. From this, the model can successfully decode the operation by replacing the first character of "*d*" with "*th*" and appending following stream of characters from each example, thereby constructing "*these*" and "*they*", respectively. A more pronounced benefit of this technique can be found when there is no change required in terms of the edit operations. No change examples will have a single common label of *nothing*; otherwise, a series of *none* operations will be generated as independent labels based on the length of the word.

Another challenge in the edit operation approach lies in dealing with variants of repeated occurrence of the same character (e.g., "*sooo*", "*soooo*") often used to emphasize the word, since all required edit operations will be treated as different labels (e.g., "*none, none, delete, delete*", "*none, none, delete, delete, delete*") in spite of similar forms of edits (note that we omit the last *none* due to the previously-mentioned optimization). To address this challenge, we attempt to replace characters that subsequently occur more than two times with a single character or double characters, and see if the converted word exists in the dictionary (in this work, the double character conversions have a higher priority over the single character conversion, if both exist in the dictionary). If it appears in the dictionary, we use the word as an input word and calculate the edit operations based on the converted word setting; otherwise, we use the original word as the input word. We expect this would reduce the number of possible labels (e.g., both "*sooo*" and "*soooo*" are converted to "*so*", as "*so*" is defined as a canonical form in the dictionary while "*soo*" is not, and so both of them have edit operations of nothing). As a result, the total number of labels obtained form the training set is reduced from 706 to 694.

Training examples for LSTMs are built upon all words except for hash-tags, at-mentions, and URLs that are filtered in the first step, regardless of whether a word is ambiguous or unique. In this manner, we expect that LSTMs can capture context information from every three-word example and thus utilize all available contextual dependencies when ambiguous or out-of-vocabulary words appear in the test set.

### 2.3 Long-Short Term Memory (LSTM) for Text Normalization

An LSTM (Hochreiter and Schmidhuber, 1997) is a variant of recurrent neural networks (RNNs) that is specifically designed for sequence labeling on temporal data. LSTM has been extended to have a longer term memory compared to traditional RNNs by introducing a memory block that features one or more self-connected memory cells along with three gating units: input gate, forget gate and output gate (Graves, 2012). Traditional RNNs often suffer from vanishing and exploding gradient problems when training deep networks using the backpropagation-through-time method, and thus prevent RNNs from storing long-term dependencies from previous time steps in the sequential data. In LSTMs, the input and output gate modulate the incoming and outgoing signals on the memory cell, and the forget gate controls the previous state of the memory cell whether to remember or forget; this structure allows it to preserve gradient information over long periods of time, and thus effectively address vanishing/exploding gradients that make training difficult in standard RNNs (Graves, 2012).

We use an LSTM as our base model, as described in Figure 2. Note that in the figure, the previous word ($Word_{t-1}$) and the following word ($Word_{t+1}$) are omitted due to the space limitations; it is important to note that they have the same structure as in the current word ($Word_t$). For a word's edit operation prediction, three words and their associated POSs are fed into the model in the form of a sequence of characters for each word. As noted above, the POS of each word is inserted before the first character of that word, regarded as a heading character that provides extra information for the associated word.

When a deep learning model takes words or characters as input, an approach to obtaining their representation is using *one-hot-encoding*, which is a bit vector whose length is the size of the vocabulary of words or characters, where only the associated word/character bit is on (i.e., 1) while all other bits are off (i.e., 0). Another popular approach is utilizing word/character embeddings, where their representations are learned in the context of unsupervised language modeling (Mikolov et al., 2013; Pennington et al., 2014) or supervised tasks of interest (Mesnil et al., 2013). We choose the latter approach and learn character embeddings using a linear projection layer while training the text normalization LSTM model in a supervised manner. We set

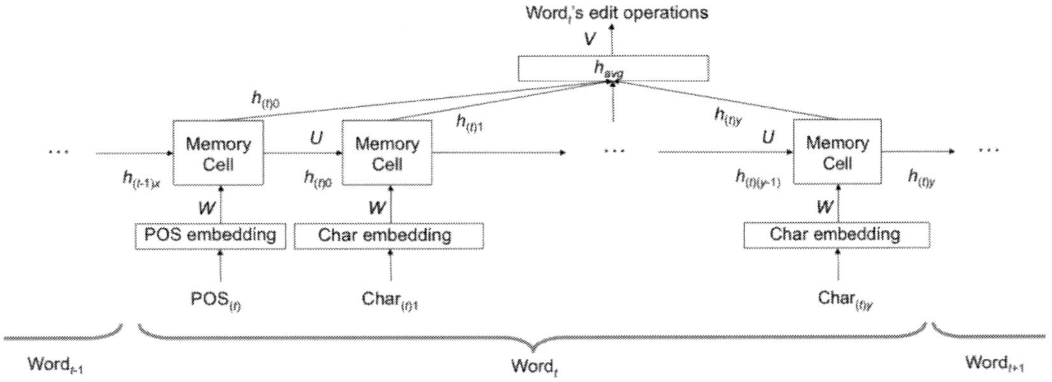


Figure 2: An illustration of the LSTM-based text normalization model

both the character and POS embedding size to 256 for this task based on preliminary analyses using a grid search.

For our base code, we utilized a Theano-based (Bastien et al., 2012) LSTM implementation[1] with a single-cell memory block per time, which was implemented targeting a sentiment analysis task on an IMDB data set.

In this implementation, the input gate ($i_t$), forget gate ($f_t$), and candidate value of the memory content ($\tilde{c_t}$) at time $t$ are computed by Equation (1), (2), and (3), respectively, in which $W$ and $U$ are weight matrices for the input ($x_t$) at time $t$ and the cell output ($h_{t-1}$) at time $t$-1, $b$ is the bias vector of each unit, and $\sigma$ and tanh are the logistic sigmoid and hyperbolic tangent function, respectively:

$$i_t = \sigma(W_i x_t + U_i h_{t-1} + b_i) \quad (1)$$
$$f_t = \sigma(W_f x_t + U_f h_{t-1} + b_f) \quad (2)$$
$$\tilde{c_t} = \tanh(W_c x_t + U_c h_{t-1} + b_c) \quad (3)$$

Once the three vectors are computed, the current memory cell's state is updated to a new state ($c_t$), by modulating the current memory candidate value ($\tilde{c_t}$) via the input gate ($i_t$) and the previous memory cell state ($c_{t-1}$) via the forget gate ($f_t$). Through this process, a memory cell decides whether to keep or forget the previous memory state and regulates the candidate of the current memory state via the input gate. This step is described in Equation (4):

$$c_t = i_t \tilde{c_t} + f_t c_{t-1} \quad (4)$$

In Equation (5), the output gate ($o_t$), similarly calculated as in Equation (1) and (2), is utilized to compute the cell activation ($h_t$) of the LSTM block, based on the new memory state ($c_t$) (Equation 6):

$$o_t = \sigma(W_o x_t + U_o h_{t-1} + b_o) \quad (5)$$
$$h_t = o_t \tanh(c_t) \quad (6)$$

In this model, as a variant of the LSTM proposed by Graves (2012), the input and forget gates do not take as input the previous memory cell's state, and the output gate does not utilize the current memory cell's state, to take advantage of a computational benefit when training models; rather, the current memory cell's state is only utilized to calculate the cell's output representation, along with the computed vector from the output gate (Equation 6).

As illustrated in Figure 2, a character or POS is fed into the model at each time step, inducing a cell output ($h$) and a cell state ($c$). To predict the label (i.e., edit operations of a word), the model performs an average pooling ($h_{avg}$) on a sequence of computed cell output representations ($h_{(t-1)0}$ to $h_{(t+1)z}$) on the training example with the three word input sequence, calculates posterior probabilities of all candidate labels using the averaged representation ($h_{avg}$) in a softmax layer, and chooses the label with the highest posterior probability value as prediction.

[1] http://deeplearning.net/tutorial/lstm.html

| | Without Dictionary Normalization | | | With Dictionary Normalization | | |
|---|---|---|---|---|---|---|
| | Precision | Recall | F1 | Precision | Recall | F1 |
| Fold 1 | 0.8777 | 0.6735 | 0.7622 | 0.8803 | 0.7185 | 0.7912 |
| Fold 2 | 0.9036 | 0.6546 | 0.7592 | 0.9134 | 0.7232 | 0.8072 |
| Fold 3 | 0.8737 | 0.6352 | 0.7356 | 0.8797 | 0.6805 | 0.7674 |
| Fold 4 | 0.8671 | 0.6501 | 0.7431 | 0.9107 | 0.6986 | 0.7907 |
| Fold 5 | 0.8388 | 0.6867 | 0.7551 | 0.8859 | 0.7347 | 0.8032 |
| Averaged score | **0.8722** | **0.6600** | **0.7510** | **0.8940** | **0.7111** | **0.7919** |

Table 1: 5-fold cross validation results of LSTMs without dictionary normalization and with dictionary normalization.

| | Non-contextual Model | | | Contextual Model | | |
|---|---|---|---|---|---|---|
| | Precision | Recall | F1 | Precision | Recall | F1 |
| Fold 1 | 0.9032 | 0.6838 | 0.7783 | 0.8803 | 0.7185 | 0.7912 |
| Fold 2 | 0.8776 | 0.7419 | 0.8041 | 0.9134 | 0.7232 | 0.8072 |
| Fold 3 | 0.8988 | 0.6704 | 0.7680 | 0.8797 | 0.6805 | 0.7674 |
| Fold 4 | 0.9209 | 0.6961 | 0.7929 | 0.9107 | 0.6986 | 0.7907 |
| Fold 5 | 0.8589 | 0.7387 | 0.7943 | 0.8859 | 0.7347 | 0.8032 |
| Averaged score | **0.8919** | **0.7062** | **0.7875** | **0.8940** | **0.7111** | **0.7919** |

Table 2: 5-fold cross validation results of LSTMs: non-contextual model vs. contextual model.

For other parameter settings in this experiment, we used 256 hidden units, 25% drop-out rate (Srivastava et al., 2014), ADADELTA (Zeiler, 2012) for the network optimization, negative log-likelihood for the cost function, and mini-batch based gradient descent with the batch size set to 16. To avoid overfitting, we set aside a separate validation set, and let the training process repeat until there is no progress within the last ten iterations in terms of performance on the validation set.

## 3 Empirical Evaluation

Before submitting our test set result to the W-NUT English lexical normalization shared task, we ran a 5-fold cross validation on the training set to evaluate the proposed approach. To conduct the experiment, we split the training set into 5 partitions based on a Tweet-level separation, and trained an LSTM model, iteratively using 4 out of the 5 partitions in each fold.

In the first evaluation, we examine two variations of our approach to measure the impact of dictionary-based normalization as an intermediate step: (1) applying phase 1 and phase 3, in which we do not leverage dictionary-based normalization but predict labels based on an LSTM model after at-mention and hash-tag and URL filtering, and (2) applying all three phases. The evaluation is conducted on contextual models that take three word inputs.

Table 1 describes the result of these two approaches for each fold. For pairwise comparison of the two approaches, we conduct a Wilcoxon signed-rank test on F1 rates. The result indicates that there is a statistically significant improvement in F1 rates (79.19% by achieving 5.4% marginal improvement) for "with dictionary normalization" over "without dictionary normalization" ($Z$=-2.023, $p$=0.043). To examine the effects of the LSTM-based model, we further evaluated a without-LSTM approach (phase 1 and 2 only), in which all out-of-vocabulary words are left unchanged, and the most often observed canonical form in the dictionary is used as the label for ambiguous words (if the frequency is tied, the first form in the hash table is used). The average F1 score of this dictionary only model is 0.7786; the LSTM model with the dictionary statistically outperforms the dictionary only model ($Z$=-2.023, $p$=0.043).

In the second evaluation, we additionally compare another set of two variations: contextual model (taking surrounding words as well as the current word) vs. non-contextual model (only taking the current word). Table 2 summarizes the comparison on the two approaches enriched with the dictionary normalization. The contextual model outperforms the non-contextual model in terms of the F1 score, but the difference does not elicit a statistically significant difference ($Z$=-1.214, $p$=0.225).

To construct a final model for the test set prediction, we utilize an ensemble method on contextual LSTM models with dictionary normalization. Given a test set, we calculate the prediction probability from each of the 5 models induced from the five-fold cross validation, multiply the probability values from the softmax layer, and choose the label with the highest resulting probability. In the evaluation through the W-NUT competition, this approach (NCSU_SAS_WOOKHEE.cm) achieved a precision score of 91.36%, recall score of 73.98%, and F1 score of 81.75%, placing second in the constrained text normalization track.

## 4 Conclusion and Future Work

Text normalization is a key capability for addressing the challenges posed by noisy text. This paper presents a contextual long-short term memory based normalization method, augmented with a dictionary-based normalization technique. Evaluations with the training set indicate that the dictionary-based normalization significantly outperforms the without-dictionary model. This method was evaluated on the English Tweet test set offered by the W-NUT shared task, and shows promise as a lexical normalizer for noisy texts by achieving an F1 score of 81.75%. We conclude that inputs encoded with a sequence of characters are a natural fit for the LSTM's temporal structure when normalizing non-standard language.

In the future, it will be important to investigate if including more surrounding words as context contributes to the model's performance, and examine possibilities of using different types of word-level meta-data as additional heading characters in the model. Another direction for future work is to investigate adaptations of the LSTM model with a self-generated dictionary. For example, when a word is an ambiguous word, the LSTM's prediction is not necessarily part of the normalization candidates given by the dictionary for the word. A tight coupling between the LSTM model and the candidate list or building a separate model targeted to only ambiguous words may significantly increase performance.

## References

Timothy Baldwin, Marie Catherine de Marneffe, Bo Han, Young-Bum Kim, Alan Ritter, and Wei Xu. 2015. Shared Tasks of the 2015 Workshop on Noisy User-generated Text: Twitter Lexical Normalization and Named Entity Recognition. In *Proceedings of the Workshop on Noisy User-generated Text (WNUT 2015)*, Beijing, China.

Frédéric Bastien, Pascal Lamblin, Razvan Pascanu, James Bergstra, Ian Goodfellow, Arnaud Bergeron, Nicolas Bouchard, David Warde-Farley, and Yoshua Bengio. 2012. Theano: new features and speed improvements. *arXiv preprint arXiv:1211.5590*.

Grzegorz Chrupała. Normalizing tweets with edit scripts and recurrent neural embeddings. 2014. In *Proceedings of the 52nd Annual Meeting of the Association for Computational Linguistics*, pages 680–686. Association for Computational Linguistics.

Kevin Gimpel, Nathan Schneider, Brendan O'Connor, Dipanjan Das, Daniel Mills, Jacob Eisenstein, Michael Heilman, Dani Yogatama, Jeffrey Flanigan, and Noah A. Smith. 2011. Part-of-speech tagging for Twitter: Annotation, features, and experiments. In *Proceedings of the 49th Annual Meeting of the Association for Computational Linguistics: Human Language Technologies: short papers-Volume 2*, pages 42–47. Association for Computational Linguistics.

Stephan Gouws, Dirk Hovy, and Donald Metzler. 2011. Unsupervised mining of lexical variants from noisy text. In *Proceedings of the First workshop on Unsupervised Learning in NLP*, pages 82–90. Association for Computational Linguistics.

Alex Graves. 2012. *Supervised sequence labelling with recurrent neural networks*. Heidelberg: Springer.

Bo Han, Paul Cook, and Timothy Baldwin. 2012. Automatically constructing a normalisation dictionary for microblogs. In *Proceedings of the 2012 joint conference on empirical methods in natural language processing and computational natural language learning*, pages 421–432. Association for Computational Linguistics.

Geoffrey Hinton, Li Deng, Dong Yu, George E. Dahl, Abdel-rahman Mohamed, Navdeep Jaitly, Andrew Senior et al. 2012. Deep neural networks for acoustic modeling in speech recognition: The shared views of four research groups. *Signal Processing Magazine, IEEE*, 29(6): 82–97.

Sepp Hochreiter, and Jürgen Schmidhuber. 1997. Long short-term memory. *Neural computation*, 9(8): 1735–1780.

V. I. Levenshtein. 1966. Binary codes capable of correcting deletions, insertions, and reversals. *Soviet physics doklady*, 10(8): 707–710.

Fei Liu, Fuliang Weng, Bingqing Wang, and Yang Liu. 2011. Insertion, deletion, or substitution?: normalizing text messages without pre-categorization nor supervision. In *Proceedings of the 49th Annual Meeting of the Association for Computational Linguistics: Human Language Technologies: short papers-Volume 2*, pages 71–76. Association for Computational Linguistics.

James Martens and Ilya Sutskever. 2011. Learning recurrent neural networks with hessian-free optimization. In *Proceedings of the 28th International Conference on Machine Learning (ICML-11)*, pages 1033–1040.

Grégoire Mesnil, Xiaodong He, Li Deng, and Yoshua Bengio. 2013. Investigation of recurrent-neural-network architectures and learning methods for spoken language understanding. In *Proceedings of the 14th Annual Conference of the International Speech Communication Association*, pages 3771–3775.

Tomas Mikolov, Ilya Sutskever, Kai Chen, Greg S. Corrado, and Jeff Dean. 2013. Distributed representations of words and phrases and their compositionality. In *Advances in Neural Information Processing Systems*, pages 3111–3119.

Olutobi Owoputi, Brendan O'Connor, Chris Dyer, Kevin Gimpel, Nathan Schneider, and Noah A. Smith. 2013. Improved Part-of-Speech Tagging for Online Conversational Text with Word Clusters. In *Proceedings of the 2013 Conference of the North American Chapter of the Association for Computational Linguistics: Human Language Technologies*, pages 380–390.

Jeffrey Pennington, Richard Socher, and Christopher D. Manning. Glove: Global vectors for word representation. 2014. In *Proceedings of the Empiricial Methods in Natural Language Processing (EMNLP 2014)*.

Alan Ritter, Sam Clark, and Oren Etzioni. Named entity recognition in tweets: an experimental study. 2011. In *Proceedings of the Conference on Empirical Methods in Natural Language Processing*, pp. 1524–1534. Association for Computational Linguistics.

Richard Socher, Alex Perelygin, Jean Wu, Jason Chuang, Christopher D. Manning, Andrew Y. Ng, and Christopher Potts. 2013. Recursive deep models for semantic compositionality over a sentiment treebank. In *Proceedings of the 2013 Conference on Empirical Methods in Natural Language Processing*, pages 1631–1642, Stroudsburg, PA, October. Association for Computational Linguistics.

Nitish Srivastava, Geoffrey Hinton, Alex Krizhevsky, Ilya Sutskever, and Ruslan Salakhutdinov. 2014. Dropout: A simple way to prevent neural networks from overfitting. *The Journal of Machine Learning Research*, 15 (1): 1929–1958.

Oscar Täckström, Dipanjan Das, Slav Petrov, Ryan McDonald, and Joakim Nivre. 2013. Token and type constraints for cross-lingual part-of-speech tagging. *Transactions of the Association for Computational Linguistics*, 1: 1–12.

Pascal Vincent, Hugo Larochelle, Isabelle Lajoie, Yoshua Bengio, and Pierre-Antoine Manzagol. 2010. Stacked denoising autoencoders: Learning useful representations in a deep network with a local denoising criterion.

*The Journal of Machine Learning Research*, 11: 3371–3408.

David Yarowsky. 1997. Homograph disambiguation in text-to-speech synthesis. In *Progress in speech synthesis*, pages 157–172. Springer, New York.

Matthew D. Zeiler. 2012. ADADELTA: an adaptive learning rate method. *arXiv preprint arXiv:1212.5701*

# USZEGED: Correction Type-sensitive Normalization of English Tweets Using Efficiently Indexed n-gram Statistics

**Gábor Berend**
University of Szeged
Department of Informatics
Árpád tér 2., 6720 Szeged, Hungary
berendg@inf.u-szeged.hu

**Ervin Tasnádi**
University of Szeged
Department of Informatics
Árpád tér 2., 6720 Szeged, Hungary
Tasnadi.Ervin@stud.u-szeged.hu

### Abstract

This paper describes the framework applied by team USZEGED at the "Lexical Normalisation for English Tweets" shared task. Our approach first employs a CRF-based sequence labeling framework to decide the kind of corrections the individual tokens require, then performs the necessary modifications relying on external lexicons and a massive collection of efficiently indexed n-gram statistics from English tweets. Our solution is based on the assumption that from the context of the OOV words, it is possible to reconstruct its IV equivalent, as there are users who use the standard English form of the OOV word within the same context. Our approach achieved an F-score of 0.8052, being the second best one among the unconstrained submissions, the category our submission also belongs to.

## 1 Introduction

Social media is a rich source of information which has been proven to be useful to a variety of applications, such as event extraction (Sakaki et al., 2010; Ritter et al., 2012; Ritter et al., 2015) or trend detection, including the tracking of epidemics (Lamb et al., 2013). Analyzing tweets in general, however, can pose several difficulties. From an engineering point of view, the streaming nature of tweets requires that special attention is paid to the scalability of the algorithms applied and from an NLP point of view, the often substandard characteristics of social media utterances has to be addressed. The fact that tweets are often written on mobile devices and are informal makes the misspelling and abbreviations of words and expressions, as well as the use of creative informal language prevalent, giving rise to a higher number of out-of-vocabulary (OOV) words than in other genres.

## 2 Related Work

The informal language of social media, including Twitter, is extremely heterogeneous, making its grammatical analysis more difficult compared to standard genres such as newswire. It has been shown previously, that the performance of linguistic analyzers trained on standard text types degrade severely once they are applied to texts found in social media, especially tweets (Ritter et al., 2011; Derczynski et al., 2013).

In order to build taggers that perform more reliable on social media texts, one possible way is to augment the training data by including texts originating from social media (Derczynski et al., 2013). Such approaches, however, require considerable human effort, so one possible alternative can be to normalize the social media texts first, then apply standard analyzers on these normalized texts. Recently, a number of approaches have been proposed for the lexical normalization of informal (mostly social media and SMS) texts (Liu et al., 2011; Liu et al., 2012; Han et al., 2013; Yang and Eisenstein, 2013).

Han and Baldwin (2011) rely on the identification of the words that require correction, then define a confusion set containing the candidate IV correction forms for such words. Finally, a ranking scheme, taking multiple factors into consideration, is applied which selects the most likely correction for an OOV word. In their subsequent work, Han et al. (2012) propose an automated method to construct accurate normalization dictionaries.

Liu et al. (2011; 2012) propose a character-level sequence model to predict insertions, deletions and substitutions. They first collect a large set of noisy `(OOV, IV)` training pairs from the Web. These pairs are then aligned at the character level



*Proceedings of the ACL 2015 Workshop on Noisy User-generated Text*, pages 120–125,
Beijing, China, July 31, 2015. ©2015 Association for Computational Linguistics

and provided as training data for a CRF classifier. The authors also released their 3,802-element normalization dictionary that our work also relies at.

Yang and Eisenstein (2013) introduce an unsupervised log-linear model for the task of text normalization. Besides the features that can be derived from pairs of words (e.g. edit distance), features considering the context are also employed in their model. As the number of class labels in that model is equal to the size of the IV words an OOV word could possibly be corrected to (typically on the order of $10^4$-$10^5$, which is far beyond the typical label size of classification tasks), the authors propose the use of Sequential Monte Carlo training approach for learning the appropriate feature weights.

## 3 The Task of Lexical Normalization

Formally, given an $m$-long sequence of words in the $i^{th}$ tweet, $T_i = [t_{i,1}, t_{i,2}, \ldots, t_{i,m}]$, participants of the shared task had to return a sequence of normalized in-vocabulary (IV) words, i.e. $S_i = [s_{i,1}, s_{i,2}, \ldots, s_{i,m}]$. The training set of the shared task consisted of 2,950 tweets comprising 44,385 tokens, while the test set had 1,967 tweets which included a total of 29,421 tokens. According to the dataset, most of the words did not require any kind of corrections, i.e. the proportion of unmodified words was 91.12% and 90.57% for the training and test set, respectively. Further details with respect the shared task can be found in the paper (Baldwin et al., 2015).

As a consequence, we first built a sequence model to decide *which* tokens need to be corrected and *in what way*. A typical distinction of the correction types would be based on the number of tokens a noisy token and its corrected form comprises of. According to this approach, one could distinguish between one-to-one, one-to-many and many-to-one corrections on the per token basis. However, instead of applying the above types of corrections, we identified a more detailed categorization of the correction types and trained a linear chain CRF utilizing CRFsuite (Okazaki, 2007). The correction types a token could be classified as were the following:

- $MissingApos$, standing for tokens that only differ from their corrected version in the absence of an apostrophe (e.g. *youll* → *you'll*),
- $MissingWS$, standing for tokens that only differ from their corrected version in the absence of one or more whitespace characters (e.g. *whataburger* → *what a burger*),
- $1to1_{ED\leq2}$, standing for corrections where no whitespace characters had to be inserted and the augmented edit distance (introduced in Section 4.2) between the noisy token and its normalized form was at most 2 (e.g. *tmrw*→*tomorrow*),
- $1to1_{ED\geq3}$, standing for corrections where no whitespace characters had to be inserted and the augmented edit distance was at least 3 (e.g. *plz*→*please*),
- $1toM_{ABB}$, standing for corrections where both whitespace and alphanumeric characters had to be inserted to obtain a tokens corrected variant (e.g. *lol* → *laugh out loud*).

| | Training | Test |
|---|---|---|
| $MissingApos$ | 507 | 369 |
| $MissingWS$ | 126 | 76 |
| $1to1_{ED\leq2}$ | 1,979 | 1,405 |
| $1to1_{ED\geq3}$ | 413 | 292 |
| $1toM_{ABB}$ | 917 | 634 |
| $Subtotal$ | 3,942 | 2,776 |
| $O$ | 40,443 | 26,645 |
| $Total$ | 44,385 | 29,421 |

Table 1: Distribution of the correction types in the training and test sets

For the sake of completeness, we should add that a further class label ($O$) was employed. This, however, corresponded to the case when there was no correction required to be performed for a token. As mentioned above, more than 90% of the words in both the training and test sets belonged to this category. Table 1 shows the distribution of the correction types on both the training and test sets.

## 4 Proposed Approach

Our approach consists of a sequence labeling module and relies on lookups from an efficiently indexed n-gram corpus of English tweets. Subsequently, we describe the details of these modules.

### 4.1 Sequence Labeling for Determining Correction Types

As already mentioned in Section 3, the first component in our pipeline was a linear chain CRF

(Lafferty et al., 2001). Besides the common word surface forms, such as the capitalization pattern, the first letter or character suffixes, we relied on the following dictionary resources upon determining the features for the individual words:

- the SCOWL dictionary being part of the `aspell` spell checker project containing canonical English dictionary entries,
- the normalization dictionaries of Han et al. (2012) and Liu et al. (2012),
- the 5,307-element normalization dictionary derived from the portal `noslang.com`, which map common social media abbreviations to their complete forms.

For each token, word type features were generated along with the word types of its neighboring tokens. The POS tags assigned to each token and its neighboring tokens by the Twitter POS tagger (Gimpel et al., 2011) were also utilized as features in the CRF model. The Twitter POS tag set was useful to us, as it contains a separate tag (**G**) for multi-word abbreviations (e.g. *ily* for *I love you*), which was expected to be highly indicative for the correction type $1toM_{ABB}$.

In order to be able to discriminate the $MissingWS$ class, we introduced a feature which indicates for a token $t$ originating from a tweet whether the relation

$$\max_{s \in split(t)} freq_{1T}(s) \geq \tau$$

holds, where $\tau$ is a threshold calibrated to $10^6$ based on the training set, $freq_{1T}(s)$ is a function which returns the frequency value associated with a string $s$ according to the Google 1T 5-gram corpus and the function $split(t)$ returns the set of all the possible splits of token $t$ such that its components are all contained in the SCOWL dictionary. For instance $split(\text{“}whataburger\text{”})$ returns a set of splits including “*what a burger*”, “*what a burg er*” and “*what ab urger*”. As there is a split (i.e. “*what a burger*”) that is sufficiently frequent according to the n-gram corpus, we take it as an indication that the original token omitted some whitespace characters that we need to inserted.

A CRF model with the above feature set was trained using L-BFGS training method and L1 regularization using CRFsuite (Okazaki, 2007). The overall token accuracy this model achieved was

| | Precision | Recall | F-score |
|---|---|---|---|
| $MissingApos$ | 0.9686 | 0.9744 | 0.9715 |
| $MissingWS$ | 0.8795 | 0.5794 | 0.6986 |
| $1to1_{ED\leq2}$ | 0.9078 | 0.8504 | 0.8782 |
| $1to1_{ED\geq3}$ | 0.9593 | 0.6852 | 0.7994 |
| $1toM_{ABB}$ | 0.9624 | 0.8942 | 0.9271 |
| $O$ | 0.9874 | 0.9959 | 0.9916 |
| macro average | 0.9442 | 0.8299 | 0.8777 |

Table 2: Results of predicting the correction types for tokens on the training set

| | Precision | Recall | F-score |
|---|---|---|---|
| $MissingApos$ | 0.9755 | 0.9702 | 0.9728 |
| $MissingWS$ | 0.7674 | 0.4342 | 0.5546 |
| $1to1_{ED\leq2}$ | 0.8619 | 0.7950 | 0.8271 |
| $1to1_{ED\geq3}$ | 0.8793 | 0.5240 | 0.6567 |
| $1toM_{ABB}$ | 0.9449 | 0.8659 | 0.9037 |
| $O$ | 0.9816 | 0.9932 | 0.9874 |
| macro average | 0.9018 | 0.7638 | 0.8171 |

Table 3: Results of predicting the correction types for tokens on the test set

0.9830 and 0.9746 and the proportion of tweets for which all the tokens were tagged properly was 0.7902 and 0.7143 for the training and test sets, respectively. A more detailed breakdown of the classification performances of the sequence model on the training and test sets are included in Table 2 and Table 3. These tables reveal that the most difficult error type to identify was the one where a word missed some whitespace characters (row $MissingWS$). This class happens to be the least frequent and one of the most heterogeneous class as well, which might be an explanation for the lower results on that class.

### 4.2 Augmented Edit Distance

When determining a set of candidate IV words that an OOV might be rewritten for, it is a common practice to place an upper bound on the edit distance between the IV candidates and the OOV word. In order to measure edit distance between tokens originating from tweets and their corrected forms, we implemented a modification of the standard edit distance algorithm that is especially tailored to measuring the difference of OOV tokens originating from social media to IV ones.

The edit distance we employed is asymmetric as insertions of characters into OOV tokens have no costs. For instance, for the words *tmrw* and *to-*

*morrow*, the edit distance is regarded as 0 if the former is considered to be the substandard OOV token and the latter one as the standard IV one. Note, however, if the role of the two tokens was changed (i.e if *tmrw* was treated as IV and *tomorrow* as OOV), their edit distance would become 4. A further relaxation to the standard edit distance is that we assign 0 cost to the following kinds of phonetically motivated transcriptions:

- $z \to s$ located at the end of words (e.g. in $cat\underline{z} \to cat\underline{s}$),
- $a \to er$ located at the end of words (e.g. in $bigg\underline{a} \to bigg\underline{er}$).

By making the above relaxations to the definition of the standard edit distance, we could obtain larger candidate sets for a given edit distance threshold for tokens with higher recall, as we could reduce the edit distance between the OOV words and their appropriate IV equivalent in many cases. Obviously, as the candidate set grows, it might get increasingly difficult to choose the correct normalization from it. However, at this stage of our pipeline, we were more interested in having the correct IV word in the set of candidate normalization, rather than reducing its size.

### 4.3 Making Use of Twitter n-gram Statistics

Our basic assumption was that from the context of an OOV word, it is possible to reconstruct its IV equivalent, as there are users who use the correct IV English form of the OOV word within the same context, e.g. *see you tomorrow* instead of *see u tmrw*. The Twitter n-gram frequencies we made use of were the ones that we aggregated over the Twitter n-gram corpus augmented with demographic metadata described in (Herdadelen, 2013).

For a given token $t_i$ at position $i$ in a tweet, we chose the most probable corrected form according to the formula

$$\arg\max_{t' \in C(t_i, ct(t_i))} P(t'|t_{i-1})P(t_{i+1}|t'), \qquad (1)$$

where the function $C(t_i, ct(t_i))$ returns a set of IV candidates for the token $t_i$, according to $ct(t_i)$, which is the correction type determined for that token by the sequence model introduced in Section 4.1. We indexed the Twitter n-gram corpus with the highly effective LIT indexer (Ceylan and Mihalcea, 2011), which made fast queries of the form $\mathtt{t_{i-1}} * \mathtt{t_{i+1}}$ possible, the symbol $\star$ being a placeholder for any token at the given position. The only case when we did not choose the normalization of an OOV word according to (1) was when there was a unique suggestion for an IV word in the normalization dictionaries we listed in Section 4.1.

| Correction | Precision | Recall | F-score |
|---|---|---|---|
| $MissingApos$ | 0.9972 | 0.9972 | 0.9972 |
| $MissingWS$ | 0.8684 | 0.4177 | 0.5641 |
| $1to1$ | 0.9191 | 0.9219 | 0.9205 |
| $1toM_{ABB}$ | 0.8861 | 0.9533 | 0.9185 |

Table 4: Detailed performance on the different correction types on the training dataset

| Correction | Precision | Recall | F-score |
|---|---|---|---|
| $MissingApos$ | 1.0000 | 0.9841 | 0.992 |
| $MissingWS$ | 0.9737 | 0.4458 | 0.6116 |
| $1to1$ | 0.9141 | 0.9127 | 0.9134 |
| $1toM_{ABB}$ | 0.8523 | 0.9699 | 0.9073 |

Table 5: Detailed performance on the different correction types on the test dataset

The performance of the normalization on the training and test sets, according to the correction types we defined can be found in Table 4 and Table 5, respectively. From these tables, one can see that the worst results were obtained for the correction type when spaces were required to be inserted to a OOV word.

This is in accordance with the fact that our sequence model obtained the lowest scores exactly on this kind of corrections. However, due to the fact that this error category is the least frequent, the lower scores on that category does not harm that much our overall performance as can be seen in Table 6 for both the training and test corpora. The results shown in Table 6 also illustrate that our approach seems to generalize well, as there is a small gap between the performances observed on the training and test sets of the shared task.

| | Training | Test |
|---|---|---|
| precision | 0.8703 | 0.8606 |
| recall | 0.7673 | 0.7564 |
| F1 | **0.8156** | **0.8052** |

Table 6: Overall performance of our system on the training and test sets

## 5 Conclusion

In this paper, we introduced our approach to the lexical normalization of English tweets that ranked second at the shared task among the unconstrained submissions. Our framework first performs sequence labeling over the tokens of a tweet to predict *which* tokens need to be corrected and in *what way*. This step is followed by correction type-sensitive candidate set generation, from which set the most likely IV normalization of an OOV word is selected by querying an efficiently indexed large n-gram dataset of English tweets.

## References


Timothy Baldwin, Marie Catherine de Marneffe, Bo Han, Young-Bum Kim, Alan Ritter, and Wei Xu. 2015. Shared tasks of the 2015 workshop on noisy user-generated text: Twitter lexical normalization and named entity recognition. In *Proceedings of the Workshop on Noisy User-generated Text (WNUT 2015)*, Beijing, China.

Hakan Ceylan and Rada Mihalcea. 2011. An efficient indexer for large n-gram corpora. In *Proceedings of the 49th Annual Meeting of the Association for Computational Linguistics: Human Language Technologies: Systems Demonstrations*, HLT '11, pages 103–108, Stroudsburg, PA, USA. Association for Computational Linguistics.

Leon Derczynski, Alan Ritter, Sam Clark, and Kalina Bontcheva. 2013. Twitter part-of-speech tagging for all: Overcoming sparse and noisy data. In *Proceedings of the International Conference on Recent Advances in Natural Language Processing*. Association for Computational Linguistics.

Kevin Gimpel, Nathan Schneider, Brendan O'Connor, Dipanjan Das, Daniel Mills, Jacob Eisenstein, Michael Heilman, Dani Yogatama, Jeffrey Flanigan, and Noah A. Smith. 2011. Part-of-speech tagging for twitter: Annotation, features, and experiments. In *Proceedings of the 49th Annual Meeting of the Association for Computational Linguistics: Human Language Technologies: Short Papers - Volume 2*, HLT '11, pages 42–47, Stroudsburg, PA, USA. Association for Computational Linguistics.

Bo Han and Timothy Baldwin. 2011. Lexical normalisation of short text messages: Makn sens a #twitter. In *Proceedings of the 49th Annual Meeting of the Association for Computational Linguistics: Human Language Technologies - Volume 1*, HLT '11, pages 368–378, Stroudsburg, PA, USA. Association for Computational Linguistics.

Bo Han, Paul Cook, and Timothy Baldwin. 2012. Automatically constructing a normalisation dictionary for microblogs. In *Proceedings of the 2012 Joint Conference on Empirical Methods in Natural Language Processing and Computational Natural Language Learning (EMNLP-CoNLL 2012)*, pages 421–432, Jeju Island, Korea.

Bo Han, Paul Cook, and Timothy Baldwin. 2013. Lexical normalization for social media text. *ACM Trans. Intell. Syst. Technol.*, 4(1):5:1–5:27, February.

Ama Herdadelen. 2013. Twitter n-gram corpus with demographic metadata. *Language Resources and Evaluation*, 47(4):1127–1147.

John D. Lafferty, Andrew McCallum, and Fernando C. N. Pereira. 2001. Conditional random fields: Probabilistic models for segmenting and labeling sequence data. In *Proceedings of the Eighteenth International Conference on Machine Learning*, ICML '01, pages 282–289, San Francisco, CA, USA. Morgan Kaufmann Publishers Inc.

Alex Lamb, Michael J. Paul, and Mark Dredze. 2013. Separating fact from fear: Tracking flu infections on twitter. In *In NAACL*.

Fei Liu, Fuliang Weng, Bingqing Wang, and Yang Liu. 2011. Insertion, Deletion, or Substitution? Normalizing Text Messages without Pre-categorization nor Supervision. In *Proceedings of the 49$^{th}$ Annual Meeting of the Association for Computational Linguistics: Human Language Technologies*, pages 71–76, Stroudsburg, PA, USA. Association for Computational Linguistics.

Fei Liu, Fuliang Weng, and Xiao Jiang. 2012. A Broad-Coverage Normalization System for Social Media Language. *Proceedings of the 50th Annual Meeting of the Association for Computational Linguistics: Long Papers-Volume 1*, pages 1035–1044.

Naoaki Okazaki. 2007. Crfsuite: a fast implementation of conditional random fields (crfs).

Alan Ritter, Sam Clark, Mausam, and Oren Etzioni. 2011. Named entity recognition in tweets: An experimental study. In *Proceedings of the Conference on Empirical Methods in Natural Language Processing*, EMNLP '11, pages 1524–1534, Stroudsburg, PA, USA. Association for Computational Linguistics.

Alan Ritter, Mausam, Oren Etzioni, and Sam Clark. 2012. Open domain event extraction from twitter. In *Proceedings of the 18th ACM SIGKDD International Conference on Knowledge Discovery and Data Mining*, KDD '12, pages 1104–1112, New York, NY, USA. ACM.

Alan Ritter, Evan Wright, William Casey, and Tom Mitchell. 2015. Weakly supervised extraction of computer security events from twitter. In *Proceedings of the 24th International Conference on World Wide Web*, WWW '15, pages 896–905, Republic and Canton of Geneva, Switzerland. International World Wide Web Conferences Steering Committee.

Takeshi Sakaki, Makoto Okazaki, and Yutaka Matsuo. 2010. Earthquake shakes twitter users: Real-time event detection by social sensors. In *Proceedings of the 19th International Conference on World Wide Web*, WWW '10, pages 851–860, New York, NY, USA. ACM.

Yi Yang and Jacob Eisenstein. 2013. A Log-Linear Model for Unsupervised Text Normalization. *Proceedings of the Empirical Methods on Natural Language Processing (EMNLP)*, pages 61–72.

# Shared Tasks of the 2015 Workshop on Noisy User-generated Text: Twitter Lexical Normalization and Named Entity Recognition

**Timothy Baldwin**
University of Melbourne
tb@ldwin.net

**Marie Catherine de Marneffe**
The Ohio State University
demarneffe.1@osu.edu

**Bo Han**
IBM Research
bohan.ibm@aul.ibm.com

**Young-Bum Kim**
University of Wisconsin
ybkim@cs.wisc.edu

**Alan Ritter**
The Ohio State University
ritter.1492@osu.edu

**Wei Xu**
University of Pennsylvania
xwe@cis.upenn.edu

## Abstract

This paper presents the results of the two shared tasks associated with W-NUT 2015: (1) a text normalization task with 10 participants; and (2) a named entity tagging task with 8 participants. We outline the task, annotation process and dataset statistics, and provide a high-level overview of the participating systems for each shared task.

## 1 Introduction

As part of the 2015 ACL-IJCNLP Workshop on Noisy User-generated Text (W-NUT), we organized two shared tasks: (1) a text normalization task (Section 2); and (2) a named entity tagging task (Section 3).

In the text normalization task, participants were asked to convert non-standard words to their standard forms for English tweets. Participating systems were classified by their use of resources, into a constrained and an unconstrained category: constrained systems were permitted to use only the provided training data and off-the-shelf tools; unconstrained systems, on the other hand, were free to use any public tools and resources. There were 6 official submissions in the constrained category, and 5 official submissions in the unconstrained category. Overall, deep learning methods and methods based on lexicon-augmented conditional random fields (CRFs) achieved the best results. The winning team achieved a precision of 0.9061 precision, recall of 0.7865, and F1 of 0.8421.

The named entity recognition task attracted 8 participants. The majority of teams built their systems using linear-chain conditional random fields (Lafferty et al., 2001), and many teams also used brown clusters and word embedding features (Turian et al., 2010). Notable new techniques for named entity recognition in Twitter include a semi-Markov MIRA trained tagger (nrc), an end-to-end neural network using no hand-engineered features (multimedialab), an approach that weights training data to compensate for concept drift (USFD), and a differential evolution approach to feature selection (iitp). The submission from the winning team (ousia) achieved suprisingly good performance on this difficult task, near the level of inter-rater agreement.

## 2 Text Normalization Shared Task

In this section, we outline the Twitter Text Normalization Shared Task, describing the data and annotation process, and outlining the approaches adopted by participants.

### 2.1 Background

Non-standard words are present in many text genres, including advertisements, professional forums, and SMS messages. They can be the cause of reading and understanding problems for humans, and degrade the accuracy of text processing tools (Han et al., 2013; Plank et al., 2014a; Kong et al., 2014). Text normalization aims to transform non-standard words to their canonical forms (Sproat et al., 2001; Han and Baldwin, 2011) as shown in Figure 1. Common examples of non-standard words include abbreviations (e.g., *u* "you"), and non-standard spellings (e.g., *cuming* "coming" or *2mr* "tomorrow"). The prevalence of non-standard words in social media text results in markedly higher out-of-vocabulary (OOV) rates; normalizing the text brings OOV rates down to more conventional levels and makes the text more amenable to automatic processing with off-the-shelf tools which have been trained on edited text.

Text normalization over Twitter data has been addressed at different granularities. For instance, non-standard words can be considered as spelling errors at the character (Liu et al., 2011) or word level (Wang and Ng, 2013). Text normalization can also be approached as a machine



*Proceedings of the ACL 2015 Workshop on Noisy User-generated Text*, pages 126–135,
Beijing, China, July 31, 2015. 

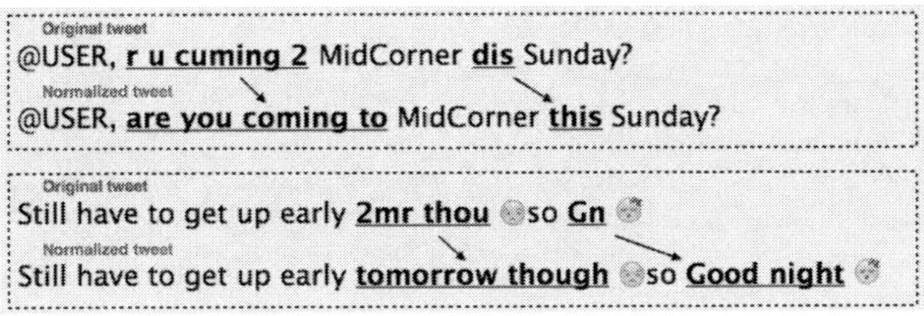


Figure 1: Normalization examples

translation task, whereby non-standard words are mapped to more canonical expressions (Aw et al., 2006). Other approaches have involved deep learning (Chrupała, 2014), cognitively-inspired approaches (Liu et al., 2012), random walks (Hassan and Menezes, 2013), and supervision using automatically-mined parallel data (Ling et al., 2013).

One major challenge in text normalization research has been the lack of annotated data for training and evaluating methods. As a result, most Twitter text normalization methods have been unsupervised or semi-supervised (Cook and Stevenson, 2009; Han et al., 2012; Yang and Eisenstein, 2013), and evaluated over small-scale hand-annotated datasets. This has hampered analysis of the strengths and weaknesses of individual methods, and was our motivation in organizing the lexical normalization shared task.

## 2.2 Shared Task Design

This lexical normalization shared task is focused exclusively on English, and was designed with three primary desiderata in mind: (1) to construct a much larger dataset than existing resources; (2) to allow all of 1:1, 1:$N$ and $N$:1 word $n$-gramm appings; and (3) to cover not just OOV non-standard words but also non-standard words that happen to coincide in spelling with standard words. In all three regards, the shared task expands upon the scope of the de facto evaluation datasets of Han and Baldwin (2011) and Liu et al. (2011).

One constraint that was placed on candidate tokens for normalization was that they should be all-alphanumeric. For normalization, we adopted American spelling.

In order to establish a more level playing field for participants, but also encourage the use of a wide range of resources, participants were required to nominate their system categories:

- **Constrained:** participants could not use any data other than the provided training data to perform the text normalization task. They were allowed to use pre-trained tools (e.g., Twitter POS taggers), but no normalization lexicons or extra tweet data.
- **Unconstrained:** participants could use any publicly accessible data or tools to perform the text normalization task.

Evaluation was based on token-level precision, recall and F-score.

### 2.2.1 Preprocessing

We first collected tweets using the Twitter Streaming API over the period 23–29 May, 2014, and then used `langid.py` (Lui and Baldwin, 2012)[1] to remove all non-English tweets. Tokenization was performed with `CMU-ARK tokeniser`.[2] To ensure that tweets had a high likelihood of requiring lexical normalization, we filtered out tweets with less than 2 non-standard words (i.e. words not occurring in our dictionary — see Section 2.2.3). While this biases the sample of tweets, the decision was made at a pragmatic level to ensure a reasonable level of lexical normalization and "annotation density". This was based on a pilot study over a random sample of English tweets, in which we found that many non-standard words were actually unknown named entities which did not require normalization. In all, 5,200 randomly-sampled English tweets were annotated for the shared task dataset.

### 2.2.2 Annotation

12 interns and employees at IBM Research Australia were involved in the data annotation. All

[1] `https://github.com/saffsd/langid.py`

[2] `https://github.com/myleott/ark-twokenize-py`

annotators had a high level of English proficiency (IELTS $\geq$ 6.0) and were reasonably familiar with Twitter data. Each annotator labeled at least 200 tweets, and each tweet was independently labeled by two annotators based on the annotation guidelines.[3] As part of this, any non-English tweets misclassified by `langid.py` were manually removed from the dataset. This resulted in the final size of the annotated dataset dropping to 4,917 tweets. All annotations were completed within two weeks, and achieved an average Cohen's $\kappa$ of 0.5854.

For all instances of annotator disagreement, an annotator who was not involved in the first-pass annotation process was asked to adjudicate in the following week. During the course of the shared task, we additionally examined and incorporated a small number of annotation corrections reported by participants.

#### 2.2.3 English Lexicon

It is impossible to reach consensus on the dividing line between standard words and non-standard words (e.g. are *footie*, *y'all* and *youse* non-standard or standard words?). We artificially arrive at such a dividing line via membership in a prescribed lexicon of English. Specifically, we use the `SCOWL` database with American spellings as the default English lexicon.[4] The `SCOWL` database integrates words from multiple sources and also contains valid word spelling variations, which makes it an excellent English lexicon for this shared task. As suggested in the database guidelines, we used a dictionary size of 70%, such that the lexicon contains words found in most dictionaries, but also many high-frequency proper nouns such as *Obama* and *Facebook*.

The overall English lexicon (after de-duplication) contains 165,458 words. This lexicon was used: (a) to pre-filter data, i.e., tweets with less than two tokens not in this lexicon are dropped from our annotations; and (b) as the basis of the standard words for normalization.

#### 2.2.4 Dataset Statistics

The dataset was randomly split 60:40, into 2,950 tweets for the training data and 1,967 tweets for the test data. Table 1 details the number of (possibly multi-word) tokens in each of the training and test data that were normalized based on a 1:1, 1:$N$ or $N$:1 mapping. We additionally include the proportion of tokens in each category that were contained in the test data, to confirm that the dataset is relatively balanced in composition between the training and test partitions.

Overall, 373 non-standard word types were found in the intersection of the training and test data. The number of non-standard word types unique to the training and test partitions was 777 and 488, respectively. We further show the top-10 most frequent non-standard words and their token frequencies in the training, test and combined datasets in Table 2. Despite the large number of unique non-standard word in the training and test partitions, there is relatively strong agreement in the high-frequency non-standard words across the dataset partitions.

| Category | 1:1 | 1:$N$ | $N$:1 | Overall |
|---|---|---|---|---|
| Training | 2,875 | 1,043 | 10 | 3,928 |
| Test | 2,024 | 704 | 10 | 2,738 |
| Training ratio | 0.587 | 0.597 | 0.500 | 0.589 |

Table 1: Numbers of non-standard words in the training and test datasets for the lexical normalization task, broken down into 1:1, 1:$N$ and $N$:1 mappings from non-standard words to standard words. "Training ratio" represents the number of non-standard words in the training data divided by the overall non-standard words in that category.

| Rank | Training | | Test | | Combined | |
|---|---|---|---|---|---|---|
| 1 | u | 333 | u | 236 | u | 569 |
| 2 | lol | 272 | lol | 197 | lol | 469 |
| 3 | im | 182 | im | 154 | im | 336 |
| 4 | dont | 92 | nigga | 60 | dont | 149 |
| 5 | omg | 67 | dont | 57 | nigga | 117 |
| 6 | nigga | 57 | lmao | 45 | omg | 101 |
| 7 | niggas | 52 | n | 43 | lmao | 96 |
| 8 | lmao | 51 | niggas | 42 | niggas | 94 |
| 9 | n | 49 | omg | 34 | n | 92 |
| 10 | ur | 46 | ur | 28 | ur | 74 |

Table 2: Top-10 most frequent non-standard words in each partition of the lexical normalization dataset.

[3] http://noisy-text.github.io/files/annotation_guideline_v1.1.pdf

[4] Version 2014.11.17 was used.

### 2.3 Normalization Approaches and Discussion

Overall, 10 teams submitted official runs to the shared task: 6 teams participated in the constrained category, 5 teams in the unconstrained category, and 1 team in both categories.[5] The normalization results for each category are shown in Tables 3 and 4. Overall, common approaches were lexicon-based methods, CRFs, and neural network-based approaches. Among the constrained systems, neural networks achieved strong results, even without off-the-shelf tools. In contrast, CRF- and lexicon-based approaches were shown to be effective in the unconstrained category. Surprisingly, the best overall result was achieved by a constrained system, suggesting that the relative advantage in accessing additional datasets or resources has less impact than the quality of the underlying model that is used to model the task.

**NCSU_SAS_NING (Jin, 2015)** Normalization candidates were generated based on the training data, and scored based on Jaccard index over character $n$-gram[ s]. Candidates were evaluated using random forest classifiers to offset parameter sensitivity, using features including normalization statistics, string similarity and POS.

**NCSU_SAS_WOOKHEE (Min et al., 2015)** Word-level edits are predicted based on long-short term memory (LSTM) recurrent neural networks (RNN), using character sequences and POS tags as features. The LSTM is further complemented with a normalization lexicon induced from the training data.

**NCSU_SAS_SAM (Leeman-Munk et al., 2015)** Two forward feed neural networks are used to predict: (1) the normalized token given an input token; and (2) whether a word should be normalized or left intact. Normalized tokens are further edited by a "conformer" which down-weights rare words as normalization candidates.

**IITP (Akhtar et al., 2015b)** A CRF model is trained over the training data, with features including word sequences, POS tags and morphology features. Post-processing heuristics are used to post-edit the output of the CRF.

[5] One team (GIGO) didn't submit a description paper.

**DCU-ADAPT (Wagner and Foster, 2015)** A generalized perceptron method is used generate word edit operations, with features including character $n$-gram[ s], character classes, and RNN language model hidden layer activation features. The final normalization word is selected based on the noisy channel model with a character language model.

**IHD_RD (Supranovich and Patsepnia, 2015)** non-standard words are identified using a CRF tagger, using features such as token-level features, contextual tokens, dictionary lookup, and edit distance. Multiple lexicons are combined to generate normalization candidates. A query misspelling correction module (i.e., DidYouMean) is used to post-process the output.

**USZEGED (Berend and Tasnádi, 2015)** A CRF model is used to identify tokens requiring normalization, and determine the type of normalization required. Normalization candidates are then proposed based on revised edit distance. The final normalization candidate is selected on the basis of $n$-grams tatistics.

**BEKLI (Beckley, 2015)** A substitution dictionary is constructed in which keys are non-standard words and values are lists of potential normalizations. Frequent morphology errors are captured by hand-crafted rules. Finally, the Viterbi algorithm is applied to bigram sequences to decode the normalized sentence with maximum probability.

**LYSGROUP (Mosquera et al., 2015)** A system originally developed for Spanish text normalization was adapted to English text normalization. The method consists of a cascaded pipeline of several data adaptors and processors, such as a Twitter POS tagger and a spell checker.

## 3 Named Entity Recognition over Twitter

The second shared task of WNUT2015 is named entity recognition over Twitter data. Named entity recognition is a crucial component in many information extraction pipelines, however the majority of available NER tools were developed for newswire text and perform poorly on informal text genres such as Twitter. While performance on named entity recognition in newswire is quite high (Tjong Kim Sang and De Meulder, 2003), state-

| Team name | Precision | Recall | F1 | Method highlights |
|---|---|---|---|---|
| NCSU_SAS_NING | 0.9061 | 0.7865 | 0.8421 | Random Forest |
| NCSU_SAS_WOOKHEE | 0.9136 | 0.7398 | 0.8175 | Lexicon + LSTM |
| NCSU_SAS_SAM | 0.9012 | 0.7437 | 0.8149 | ANN |
| IITP | 0.9026 | 0.7191 | 0.8005 | CRF + Rule |
| DCU-ADAPT | 0.8190 | 0.5509 | 0.6587 | Generalized Perceptron |
| LYSGROUP | 0.4646 | 0.6281 | 0.5341 | Spanish Normalization Adaption |

Table 3: Results of the constrained systems for the lexical normalization shared task

| Team name | Precision | Recall | F1 | Method highlights |
|---|---|---|---|---|
| IHS_RD | 0.8469 | 0.8083 | 0.8272 | Lexicon + CRF + DidYouMean |
| USZEGED | 0.8606 | 0.7564 | 0.8052 | CRF + *n*-gram[ s] |
| BEKLI | 0.7743 | 0.7416 | 0.7571 | Lexicon + Rule + Ranker |
| GIGO | 0.7593 | 0.6963 | 0.7264 | N/A |
| LYSGROUP | 0.4592 | 0.6296 | 0.5310 | Spanish Normalization Adaption |

Table 4: Results of the unconstrained systems for the lexical normalization shared task

of-the-art performance on Twitter data lags far behind.

The diverse and noisy style of user-generated content presents serious challenges. For instance tweets, unlike edited newswire text, contain numerous nonstandard spellings, abbreviations, unreliable capitalization, etc.

Another challenge is concept drift (Dredze et al., 2010; Fromreide et al., 2014); the distribution of language and topics on Twitter is constantly shifting leading to degraded performance of NLP tools over time. To evaluate the effect of drift in a realistic scenario, the current evaluation uses a test set from a separate time period, which was not announced to participants until the (unannotated) test data was released at the beginning of the evaluation period.

To address these challenges, there has been an increasing body of work on adapting named entity recognition tools to noisy social media text (Derczynski et al., 2015b; Plank et al., 2014a; Cherry and Guo, 2015; Ritter et al., 2011; Plank et al., 2014b), however different research groups have made use of different evaluation setups (e.g. training / test splits) making it challenging to perform direct comparisons across systems. By organizing a shared evaluation we hope to help establish a common evaluation methodology (for at least one dataset) and also promote research and development of NLP tools for user-generated social media text genres.

### 3.1 Training and Development Data

The training and development data for our task was taken from previous work on Twitter NER (Ritter et al., 2011), which distinguishes 10 different named entity types (see Table 5 for the set of types). The data was split into 1,795 annotated tweets for training (`train`) and 599 as a development set (`dev`). Participants were allowed to use the development data for training purposes in their final submissions. This data was gathered in September 2010 and annotated by the 5th author.

### 3.2 Test Data Annotation

The test data was randomly sampled from December 2014 through February 2015. Two native English speakers were recruited to independently annotate the test data. The annotators were presented with a set of simple guidelines[6] that cover common ambiguous cases and also instructed to refer to the September 2010 data for reference. The BRAT tool[7] was used for annotation. A screenshot of the interface presented to annotators is shown in Figure 2. During an initial training period, both annotators independently labeled a set of 200 tweets after which disagreements were discussed and resolved before moving on to annotate the final test set. This initial annotation was only done

[6]`http://bit.ly/1FSP6i2`
[7]`http://brat.nlplab.org/`

for the purpose of training the annotators and the resulting data was discarded.

The annotators then went on to double-annotate a set of 1,425 messages. An adjudicator, the annotator of the training and dev sets, went through each message and resolved disagreements. The dataset was randomly split into 425 messages as an additional development set (`dev2015`) which was released to participants at the beginning of the evaluation period. The remaining 1,000 messages (`test`) were used for the final evaluation; annotations on the test data were withheld from participants until the end of the evaluation period.

Table 5 presents precision and recall for each of the 10 categories treating one annotator's labels as gold and the other's as predicted. This exposes the challenging nature of this annotation task and can be viewed as a kind of human upper bound on possible system performance, though we believe the consistency of the final annotations to be somewhat higher due to the second pass made by the adjudicator. The value of Cohen's $\kappa$ as measured on word-level annotations is 0.607.

A baseline system was provided to participants which takes a simple approach based on CRFsuite[8] using a standard set of features which include contextual, orthographic and gazetteers generated from Freebase (Bollacker et al., 2008). The evaluation consisted of 2 sub-tasks: one in which participants' systems were required to segment and classify 10 named entity types and one where the task is only to predict entity segmentation (no types).

### 3.3 Approaches

Eight teams (Table 6) participated in the named entity recognition shared task. A wide variety of approaches were taken to tackle this task. Table 7 summarizes the features used by each team and the machine learning approach taken. Many teams made use of word embeddings and Brown clusters as features. One team (multimedialab) used absolutely no hand-engineered features, relying entirely on word embeddings and a feed-forward neural-network (FFNN) architecture (Godin et al., 2015). Other new approaches to Twitter NER include a semi-Markov MIRA trained tagger developed by the NRC team (Cherry and Guo, 2015) and the use of entity-linking based features by ousia (Yamada et al., 2015). All the other teams used CRFs. On top of a CRF, the iitp team used a differential evolution based technique to obtain an optimal feature set.

Most systems used the training data as well as both dev sets provided to train their system, except multimedialab which did not use `dev2015` as training data and NRC which only used `train`. [9]

Tables 8 and 9 report the results obtained by each team for segmentation and classification of the 10 named entity types and for segmentation only, respectively.

### 3.4 System Descriptions

Following is a brief description of the approach taken by each team:

| | Precision | Recall | $F_{\beta=1}$ |
|---|---|---|---|
| company | 41.46 | 33.33 | 36.96 |
| facility | 50.00 | 66.67 | 57.14 |
| geo-loc | 63.57 | 70.09 | 66.67 |
| movie | 35.71 | 35.71 | 35.71 |
| musicartist | 60.98 | 47.17 | 53.19 |
| other | 48.21 | 50.00 | 49.09 |
| person | 60.42 | 80.56 | 69.05 |
| product | 44.83 | 19.12 | 26.80 |
| sportsteam | 75.00 | 71.74 | 73.33 |
| tvshow | 55.56 | 50.00 | 52.63 |
| Overall | 56.64 | 57.52 | 57.07 |

Table 5: Precision and recall comparing one annotator against the other. Cohen's kappa between the annotators was 0.607. Disagreements between the annotators resolved by a 3rd adjudicator for the final datasets.

| Team ID | Affiliation |
|---|---|
| Hallym | Hallym University |
| iitp | Indian Institute of Technology Patna |
| lattice | University Paris 3 |
| multimedialab | UGent - iMinds |
| NLANGP | Institute for Infocomm Research |
| nrc | National Research Council Canada |
| ousia | Studio Ousia |
| USFD | University of Sheffield |

Table 6: Team ID and affiliation of the named entity recognition shared task participants.

[8] `http://www.chokkan.org/software/crfsuite/`

[9] A post-competition analysis of the effect of training on development sets is presented in the NRC system description paper (Cherry et al., 2015).

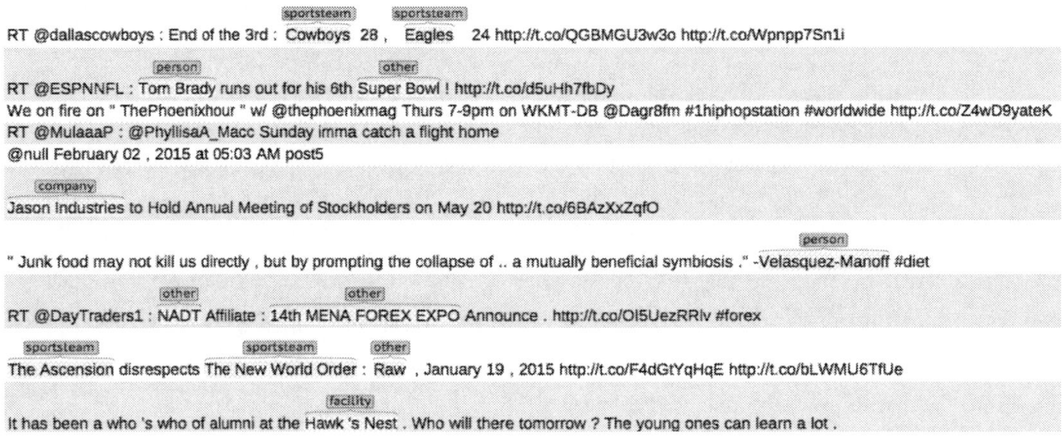


Figure 2: Annotation interface.

| | POS | Orthographic | Gazetteers | Brown clustering | Word embedding | ML |
|---|---|---|---|---|---|---|
| BASELINE | – | ✓ | ✓ | – | – | CRFsuite |
| Hallym | ✓ | – | – | ✓ | correlation analysis | CRFsuite |
| iitp | ✓ | ✓ | ✓ | – | – | CRF++ |
| lattice | ✓ | ✓ | – | ✓ | – | CRF wapiti |
| multimedialab | – | – | – | – | word2vec | FFNN |
| NLANGP | – | ✓ | ✓ | ✓ | word2vec & GloVe | CRF++ |
| nrc | – | – | ✓ | ✓ | word2vec | semi-Markov MIRA |
| ousia | ✓ | ✓ | ✓ | – | ✓ | entity linking |
| USFD | ✓ | ✓ | ✓ | ✓ | – | CRF L-BFGS |

Table 7: Features and machine learning approach taken by each team.

| | Precision | Recall | $F_{\beta=1}$ |
|---|---|---|---|
| ousia | 57.66 | 55.22 | 56.41 |
| NLANGP | 63.62 | 43.12 | 51.40 |
| nrc | 53.24 | 38.58 | 44.74 |
| multimedialab | 49.52 | 39.18 | 43.75 |
| USFD | 45.72 | 39.64 | 42.46 |
| iitp | 60.68 | 29.65 | 39.84 |
| Hallym | 39.59 | 35.10 | 37.21 |
| lattice | 55.17 | 9.68 | 16.47 |
| BASELINE | 35.56 | 29.05 | 31.97 |

Table 8: Results segmenting and categorizing entities into 10 types.

| | Precision | Recall | $F_{\beta=1}$ |
|---|---|---|---|
| ousia | 72.20 | 69.14 | 70.63 |
| NLANGP | 67.74 | 54.31 | 60.29 |
| USFD | 63.81 | 56.28 | 59.81 |
| multimedialab | 62.93 | 55.22 | 58.82 |
| nrc | 62.13 | 54.61 | 58.13 |
| iitp | 63.43 | 51.44 | 56.81 |
| Hallym | 58.36 | 48.5 | 53.01 |
| lattice | 58.42 | 25.72 | 35.71 |
| BASELINE | 53.86 | 46.44 | 49.88 |

Table 9: Results on segmentation only (no types).

**Hallym (Yang and Kim, 2015)** The Hallym team used an approach based on CRFs using both Brown clusters and word embeddings trained using Canonical Correlation Analysis as features.

**iitp (Akhtar et al., 2015a)** The iitp team proposed a multi-objective differential evolution based technique for feature selection in twitter named entity recognition.

**lattice (Tian, 2015)** Lattice employed a CRF model using Wapiti. The feature templates consisted of standard features used in state-of-the-art. They trained first a model with dev_2015 and evaluated this model on train and dev.

**multimedialab (Godin et al., 2015)** The goal of the multimedia lab system was to only use neural networks and word embeddings to show the power of automatic feature learning and semi-supervised methods. A Feed-Forward Neural Network was first trained, that used only word2vec word embeddings as input. Word embeddings were trained on 400 million unlabeled tweets. Leaky ReLUs were used as activation function in combination with dropout to prevent overfitting. A context window of 5 words was used As input (2 words left and right). The output is a single tag of the middle word. Afterwards, a rule-based post-processing step was executed to ensure every I-tag has a B-tag in front of it and that all tags within a single span are of the same type. Train and dev were used as training data and used dev_2015 as validation set.

**NLANGP (Toh et al., 2015)** The NLANGP team modeled the problem as a sequential labeling task and used Conditional Random Fields. Several post-processing steps (e.g. rule-based matching) were applied to refine the system output. Besides Brown clusters, K-means clusters were also used; the K-means clusters were generated based on word embeddings.

**nrc (Cherry et al., 2015)** NRC applied a MIRA-trained semi-Markov tagger with Gazetteer, Brown cluster and Word Embedding features. The Word Embeddings were built over phrases using Word2Vec's phrase finder tool, and were modified using an auto-encoder to be predictive of Gazetteer membership.

**ousia (Yamada et al., 2015)** The main characteristics of the ousia method is enhancing the performance of Twitter named entity recognition using entity linking. Once entity mentions are disambiguated to the knowledge base entries, high-quality knowledge can be easily extracted from a knowledge base such as the popularity of the entity, the classes of the entity, and the likelihood that the entity appears in the given context. They adopted supervised machine-learning with features including the results of NER and various information of the entity in knowledge bases. We use Stanford NER was used for the NER and in-house end-to-end entity linking software was applied for entity linking.

**USFD (Derczynski et al., 2015a)** Feature extraction was based on large Brown clusters, gazetteers tuned to the input data, and distant supervision from Freebase. The representation was tuned for drift by down-weighting temporally distant training examples. The classifier was a linear chain CRF with hyperparameters tuned for Twitter.

## 4 Summary

In this paper, we presented two shared tasks on Twitter text processing: Lexical Normalization and Named Entity Recognition. We detailed the task setup and datasets used in the respective shared tasks, and also outlined the approach taken by the participating systems. Both shared tasks were of a scale substantially larger than what had previously been attempted in the literature, with two primary benefits. First, we are able to draw stronger conclusions about the true potential of different approaches. Second, through analyzing the results of the participating systems, we are able to suggest potential research directions for both future shared tasks and noisy text processing in general.

## Acknowledgments

We would like to thank Svitlana Volkova and Junming Xu for feedback on a previous draft of this paper. We also thank Javier Angel and Gabriella Talvy for annotating the test data for the named entity recognition shared task, and IBM Research Australia for the generous support in doing the annotation for the lexical normalization shared task.

## References

Md Shad Akhtar, Utpal Kumar Sikdar, and Asif Ekbal. 2015a. Iitp: Multiobjective differential evolution based twitter named entity recognition. In *proceedings of WNUT*.

Md Shad Akhtar, Utpal Kumar Sikdar, and Asif Ekbal. 2015b. Iitp: Hybrid approach for text normalization in twitter. In *proceedings of WNUT*, Beijing, China.

AiTi Aw, Min Zhang, Juan Xiao, and Jian Su. 2006. A phrase-based statistical model for SMS text normalization. In *Proceedings of COLING/ACL 2006*, pages 33–40, Sydney, Australia.

Russell Beckley. 2015. Bekli:a simple approach to twitter text normalization. In *proceedings of WNUT*, Beijing, China.

Gabor Berend and Ervin Tasnádi. 2015. Uszeged: Correction type-sensitive normalization of english tweets using efficiently indexed n-gram statistics. In *proceedings of WNUT*, Beijing, China.

Kurt Bollacker, Colin Evans, Praveen Paritosh, Tim Sturge, and Jamie Taylor. 2008. Freebase: a collaboratively created graph database for structuring human knowledge. In *Proceedings of the 2008 ACM SIGMOD international conference on Management of data*, pages 1247–1250. ACM.

Colin Cherry and Hongyu Guo. 2015. The unreasonable effectiveness of word representations for twitter named entity recognition. NAACL.

Colin Cherry, Hongyu Guo, and Chengbi Dai. 2015. Nrc: Infused phrase vectors and updated gazetteers for named entity recognition in twitter. In *proceedings of WNUT*.

Grzegorz Chrupała. 2014. Normalizing tweets with edit scripts and recurrent neural embeddings. In *Proceedings of the 52nd Annual Meeting of the Association for Computational Linguistics (ACL 2014)*, pages 680–686, Baltimore, USA, June.

Paul Cook and Suzanne Stevenson. 2009. An unsupervised model for text message normalization. In *Proceedings of the Workshop on Computational Approaches to Linguistic Creativity (CALC '09)*, pages 71–78, Boulder, USA.

Leon Derczynski, Isabelle Augenstein, and Kalina Bontcheva. 2015a. Usfd: Twitter ner with drift compensation and linked data. In *proceedings of WNUT*.

Leon Derczynski, Diana Maynard, Giuseppe Rizzo, Marieke van Erp, Genevieve Gorrell, Raphaël Troncy, Johann Petrak, and Kalina Bontcheva. 2015b. Analysis of named entity recognition and linking for tweets. *Information Processing & Management*, 51(2):32–49.

Mark Dredze, Tim Oates, and Christine Piatko. 2010. We're not in kansas anymore: detecting domain changes in streams. In *Proceedings of the 2010 Conference on Empirical Methods in Natural Language Processing*, pages 585–595. Association for Computational Linguistics.

Hege Fromreide, Dirk Hovy, and Anders Søgaard. 2014. Crowdsourcing and annotating ner for twitter# drift. *European language resources distribution agency*.

Fréderic Godin, Baptist Vandersmissen, Wesley De Neve, and Rik Van de Walle. 2015. multimedialab @ acl wnut ner shared task: Named entity recognition for twitter microposts using distributed word representations. In *proceedings of WNUT*.

Bo Han and Timothy Baldwin. 2011. Lexical normalisation of short text messages: Makn sens a #twitter. In *Proceedings of the 49th Annual Meeting of the Association for Computational Linguistics: Human Language Technologies (ACL HLT 2011)*, pages 368–378, Portland, USA.

Bo Han, Paul Cook, and Timothy Baldwin. 2012. Automatically constructing a normalisation dictionary for microblogs. In *Proceedings of the Joint Conference on Empirical Methods in Natural Language Processing and Computational Natural Language Learning 2012 (EMNLP-CoNLL 2012)*, pages 421–432, Jeju Island, Korea, July.

Bo Han, Paul Cook, and Timothy Baldwin. 2013. Lexical normalisation for social media text. *ACM Transactions on Intelligent Systems and Technology*, 4(1):5:1–5:27.

Hany Hassan and Arul Menezes. 2013. Social text normalization using contextual graph random walks. In *Proceedings of the 51st Annual Meeting of the Association for Computational Linguistics (ACL 2013)*, pages 1577–1586, Sofia, Bulgaria, August.

Ning Jin. 2015. Ncsu-sas-ning: Candidate generation and feature engineering for supervised lexical normalization. In *proceedings of WNUT*, Beijing, China.

Lingpeng Kong, Nathan Schneider, Swabha Swayamdipta, Archna Bhatia, Chris Dyer, and A. Noah Smith. 2014. A dependency parser for tweets. In *Proceedings of the 2014 Conference on Empirical Methods in Natural Language Processing (EMNLP)*, pages 1001–1012.

John D. Lafferty, Andrew McCallum, and Fernando C. N. Pereira. 2001. Conditional random fields: Probabilistic models for segmenting and labeling sequence data. In *Proceedings of the Eighteenth International Conference on Machine Learning*.

Samuel Leeman-Munk, James Lester, and James Cox. 2015. Ncsu_sas_sam: Deep encoding and reconstruction for normalization of noisy text. In *proceedings of WNUT*, Beijing, China.

Wang Ling, Chris Dyer, Alan W Black, and Isabel Trancoso. 2013. Paraphrasing 4 microblog normalization. In *Proceedings of the 2013 Conference on Empirical Methods in Natural Language Processing (EMNLP 2013)*, pages 73–84, Seattle, USA, October.

Fei Liu, Fuliang Weng, Bingqing Wang, and Yang Liu. 2011. Insertion, deletion, or substitution? Normalizing text messages without pre-categorization nor supervision. In *Proceedings of the 49th Annual*

*Meeting of the Association for Computational Linguistics: Human Language Technologies (ACL HLT 2011)*, pages 71–76, Portland, USA.

Fei Liu, Fuliang Weng, and Xiao Jiang. 2012. A broad-coverage normalization system for social media language. In *Proceedings of the 50th Annual Meeting of the Association for Computational Linguistics (ACL 2012)*, pages 1035–1044, Jeju Island, Korea, July.

Marco Lui and Timothy Baldwin. 2012. langid.py: An off-the-shelf language identification tool. In *Proceedings of the 50th Annual Meeting of the Association for Computational Linguistics (ACL 2012) Demo Session*, pages 25–30, Jeju, Republic of Korea.

Wookhee Min, Bradford Mott, James Lester, and James Cox. 2015. Ncsu_sas_wookhee: A deep contextual long-short term memory model for text normalization. In *proceedings of WNUT*, Beijing, China.

Yerai Doval Mosquera, Jesús Vilares, and Carlos Gómez-Rodríguez. 2015. Lysgroup: Adapting a spanish microtext normalization system to english. In *proceedings of WNUT*, Beijing, China.

Barbara Plank, Dirk Hovy, Ryan McDonald, and Anders Søgaard. 2014a. Adapting taggers to twitter with not-so-distant supervision. In *Proceedings of COLING 2014, the 25th International Conference on Computational Linguistics: Technical Papers*, pages 1783–1792.

Barbara Plank, Dirk Hovy, and Anders Søgaard. 2014b. Learning part-of-speech taggers with inter-annotator agreement loss. In *Proceedings of EACL*.

Alan Ritter, Sam Clark, Oren Etzioni, et al. 2011. Named entity recognition in tweets: an experimental study. In *Proceedings of the Conference on Empirical Methods in Natural Language Processing*, pages 1524–1534. Association for Computational Linguistics.

Richard Sproat, Alan W. Black, Stanley Chen, Shankar Kumar, Mari Ostendorf, and Christopher Richards. 2001. Normalization of non-standard words. *Computer Speech and Language*, 15(3):287–333.

Dmitry Supranovich and Viachaslau Patsepnia. 2015. Ihs_rd: Lexical normalization for english tweets. In *proceedings of WNUT*, Beijing, China.

Tian Tian. 2015. Data adaptation for named entity recognition on tweets with features-rich crf. In *proceedings of WNUT*.

Erik F Tjong Kim Sang and Fien De Meulder. 2003. Introduction to the conll-2003 shared task: Language-independent named entity recognition. In *Proceedings of the seventh conference on Natural language learning at HLT-NAACL 2003-Volume 4*, pages 142–147. Association for Computational Linguistics.

Zhiqiang Toh, Bin Chen, and Jian Su. 2015. Improving twitter named entity recognition using word representations. In *proceedings of WNUT*.

Joseph Turian, Lev Ratinov, and Yoshua Bengio. 2010. Word representations: a simple and general method for semi-supervised learning. In *Proceedings of the 48th annual meeting of the association for computational linguistics*, pages 384–394. Association for Computational Linguistics.

Joachim Wagner and Jennifer Foster. 2015. Dcu-adapt: Learning edit operations for microblog normalisation with the generalised perceptron. In *proceedings of WNUT*, Beijing, China.

Pidong Wang and Hwee Tou Ng. 2013. A beam-search decoder for normalization of social media text with application to machine translation. In *Proceedings of the 2013 Conference of the North American Chapter of the Association for Computational Linguistics: Human Language Technologies (NAACL HLT 2013)*, pages 471–481, Atlanta, USA, June.

Ikuya Yamada, Hideaki Takeda, and Takefuji Yoshiyasu. 2015. Enhancing named entity recognition in twitter messages using entity linking. In *proceedings of WNUT*.

Yi Yang and Jacob Eisenstein. 2013. A log-linear model for unsupervised text normalization. In *Proceedings of the 2013 Conference on Empirical Methods in Natural Language Processing (EMNLP 2013)*, pages 61–72, Seattle, USA, October.

Eun-Suk Yang and Yu-Seop Kim. 2015. Hallym: Named entity recognition on twitter. In *proceedings of WNUT*.

# Enhancing Named Entity Recognition in Twitter Messages Using Entity Linking

**Ikuya Yamada**[1 2 3] **Hideaki Takeda**[2] **Yoshiyasu Takefuji**[3]
ikuya@ousia.jp takeda@nii.ac.jp takefuji@sfc.keio.ac.jp
[1]Studio Ousia, 4489-105-221 Endo, Fujisawa, Kanagawa, Japan
[2]National Institute of Informatics, 2-1-2 Hitotsubashi, Chiyoda, Tokyo, Japan
[3]Keio University, 5322 Endo, Fujisawa, Kanagawa, Japan

### Abstract

In this paper, we describe our approach for *Named Entity Recognition in Twitter*, a shared task for ACL 2015 Workshop on Noisy User-generated Text (Baldwin et al., 2015). Because of the noisy, short, and colloquial nature of Twitter, the performance of Named Entity Recognition (NER) degrades significantly. To address this problem, we propose a novel method to enhance the performance of the Twitter NER task by using *Entity Linking* which is a method for detecting entity mentions in text and resolving them to corresponding entries in knowledge bases such as Wikipedia. Our method is based on supervised machine-learning and uses the high-quality knowledge obtained from several open knowledge bases. In comparison with the other systems proposed for this shared task, our method achieved the best performance.

## 1 Introduction

Named Entity Recognition (NER) refers to the task of identifying mentions of entities (e.g., persons, locations, organizations) within text. Because of the noisy, short, and colloquial nature of Twitter messages (or *tweets*), the performance of standard NER software significantly suffers. For example, Derczynski et al. (Derczynski et al., 2015) recently demonstrated that the performance of various state-of-the-art NER software (e.g., Stanford NER and ANNIE) is typically lower than 50% F1[1] for tweets.

Entity Linking (EL) refers to the task of detecting textual entity mentions and linking them to corresponding entries within knowledge bases (e.g., Wikipedia, DBpedia (Auer et al., 2007), Freebase (Bollacker et al., 2008)). Because of the recent emergence of large online knowledge bases (KB), EL has recently gained significant attention. It is evident that the performance of EL also degrades when analyzing tweets (Derczynski et al., 2015; Meij et al., 2012). However, Guo et al. (Guo et al., 2013) recently revealed that the main failures of Twitter EL are caused while detecting entity mentions from text, because existing EL methods usually address the mention detection task by using external NER software whose performance is unreliable when processing tweets. Consequently, several approaches (Guo et al., 2013; Yamada et al., 2015) have been proposed with enhanced abilities that address the task in an *end-to-end* manner without completely depending on NER software.

The main objective of this study is to investigate the possibility of enhancing the performance of Twitter NER by using an end-to-end EL. Although EL is typically performed *after* NER in most of the existing methods, our approach performs EL *before* NER and uses the EL results to enhance the NER performance. Resolving the entity mentions to the KB entries enables us to use the high-quality knowledge in KB for enhancing the NER performance. This knowledge includes things such as the popularity of the entity, the classes of the entity, and the likelihood that the entity appears in the given context.

We begin by briefly introducing our end-to-end EL method that specifically focuses on tweets. Our EL method is based on supervised machine-learning and addresses the task in an end-to-end manner. It considers every possible n-gram as a candidate entity mention and detects the mention with a corresponding link to a KB entry if the mention exists in the KB. Furthermore, it can handle mentions that appear as irregular forms (e.g., *misspellings*, *abbreviations*, *acronyms)* using several approximate string matching algorithms.

[1]The harmonic mean of precision and recall.



*Proceedings of the ACL 2015 Workshop on Noisy User-generated Text*, pages 136–140,
Beijing, China, July 31, 2015. 

The NER task is split into two separate subtasks: *segmentation* and *classification*. During segmentation, the entity mentions are detected from tweets. Then, the entity mentions are classified into the predefined entity types. Both tasks involve supervised machine-learning with various features.

For the segmentation task, we use data obtained from the KB of the corresponding entity mention detected by the EL and the output of a NER software as the main machine-learning features. Furthermore, we include several common features used in traditional NER methods.

For the classification task, the following three types of features are used as primary features: 1) the KB types of the entity detected by the EL, 2) the entity types detected by the NER software, and 3) the vector representation of the entity mention derived from word embeddings. The entity's KB types are extracted from the corresponding entries in DBpedia and Freebase. Furthermore, the vector representation of the entity mention is derived using GloVe word embeddings (Pennington et al., 2014).

To train and evaluate our system, we used the dataset given by the *Named Entity Recognition in Twitter* shared task. Our proposed method significantly outperformed the second ranked system by a wide margin; *10.3% F1* at the segmentation task, and *5.0% F1* at the end-to-end (both the segmentation and the classification) task.

## 2 The Proposed System

### 2.1 Preprocessing

The system first assigns part-of-speech tags to the resulting tokens using ARK Twitter Part-of-Speech Tagger (Gimpel et al., 2011). It also tokenizes Twitter hashtags using our enhanced implementation of the hashtag tokenization.

### 2.2 Entity Linking

We formalize our EL task as follows: Given a tweet, our goal is to recognize a set of entity mentions (e.g., *Obama*, *President Obama*, *Barack Obama*) that appear in a tweet, and then resolve the mentions into entities (e.g., Barack Obama) in Wikipedia if they exist.

Our EL system addresses the task using the following two steps; *mention candidate generation* and *mention detection and disambiguation*.

#### 2.2.1 Mention Candidate Generation

Our system first generates a set of candidate entity mentions with the set of corresponding referent entities. The system takes all the n-grams of $n \leq 10$ and looks up each n-gram in a dictionary, treats an n-gram as a candidate mention if it exists in the dictionary, and finally, generates an output of pairs of mentions and their associated possible referent entities.

**Mention-Entity Dictionary:** The system uses a *mention-entity* dictionary that maps a mention surface (e.g., *apple*) to the possible referent entities (e.g., Apple Inc., Apple (food)). The possible mention surfaces of an entity are extracted from the corresponding Wikipedia page title, the page titles of the Wikipedia pages that redirect to the page of the entity, and anchor texts in Wikipedia articles that point to the page of the entity. We constructed this dictionary using the January 2015 dump of Wikipedia.

**Approximate Candidate Generation:** One major problem of the mention candidate generation task is that many entity mentions in tweets cannot be detected because they appear as irregular forms (e.g., *misspellings, abbreviations*). In order to address this problem, we introduce the following three approximate string-matching methods to improve the ability of this task:

- *Fuzzy match* searches the mention candidates that have text surfaces within a certain distance of the surface of the n-gram measured by edit distance.
- *Approximate token search* obtains mention candidates whose text surfaces have a significant ratio of words in common with the surface of the n-gram.
- *Acronym search* retrieves mention candidates with possible acronyms[2] that include the surface of the n-gram.

When using the above methods, we observed that the number of mention candidates becomes very large. To deal with this, we use a simple filtering method based on *soft tf-idf* (Cohen et al., 2003); we simply use only the mention candidates that have a similarity greater than a threshold measured by the soft tf-idf. We use 0.9 as the threshold

[2]We generate acronyms by tokenizing the mention surface and simply taking the first characters of the resulting tokens.

because this achieves the best performance in our experiments of EL.

#### 2.2.2 Mention Detection and Disambiguation

Given a pair of a mention and its possible referent entity, it needs to be determined if the possible referent entity is indeed the correct one for its associated mention.

In this system, we use a supervised machine-learning algorithm to assign a relevance score to each of the pairs and select the entity mention with the highest score. We use *random forest* as the machine-learning algorithm.

Here, we use machine-learning features that are mostly identical to the method proposed previously (Yamada et al., 2015). Basically, we use various features that are commonly observed in EL studies and enhance the performance further by introducing two new features: 1) the entity popularity knowledge extracted from Wikipedia page views[3], and 2) the contextual similarity between the entity and the tweet measured by word embeddings.

### 2.3 Named Entity Recognition

We address the NER task by performing two subtasks: *segmentation* and *classification*.

#### 2.3.1 Segmentation of Named Entities

In this step, entity mentions are detected from tweets. We formalize this task as follows. Given an n-gram in a tweet, the goal of this task is assigning a binary label that represents whether the n-gram should be detected as an entity mention. Note that in order to enable the straightforward integration of EL and this task, we formalize this task as simply classifying n-grams instead of the commonly-used IOB labeling approach (Ramshaw and Marcus, 1995).

The basic strategy that we adopt here is to combine the output of NER software and the KB knowledge of the corresponding entity mention detected by the EL using supervised machine-learning. We again use *random forest* as the machine-learning algorithm.

We use Stanford NER[4] as the NER software that achieves relatively better performance in the Twitter NER task in a recent study (Derczynski et al., 2015). Here, we adopt two models of Stanford NER to enhance the performance: 1) the standard three-class model which is included in the software and 2) a model that does not use capitalization as a feature, in order to deal with the unreliability of capitalization in tweets.

The results of the NER and the KB knowledge of the corresponding entity mention detected by the EL are used as the primary machine-learning features. We also include features that are traditionally used in NER such as part-of-speech tags and the capitalization features. Furthermore, the ratio of the capitalized words in the tweet is also used as an indicator of the reliability of the capitalization.

The machine-learning features for this step include:

- *EL relevance score**: The relevance score of the entity mention assigned by the previous EL step.
- *Link probability**: The probability of the entity mention appearing as an anchor text in Wikipedia.
- *Capitalization probability**: The probability of the entity mention being capitalized in Wikipedia.
- *The number of inbound links**: The number of inbound links of the corresponding entity in Wikipedia.
- *The average page view**: The average page view of the corresponding entity in Wikipedia.
- *NER span match*: Binary values that represent whether the n-gram is detected by NER models.
- *Part-of-speech tags*: Part-of-speech tags of the previous, first, last, and next words of the n-gram.
- *Context capitalization*: Binary values that represent whether the previous, first, last, and next words of the n-gram are capitalized.
- *Character length*: The number of characters read in the surface of the n-gram.
- *Token length*: The number of tokens read in the n-gram.

Note that some features (marked with *) are based on an entity mention detected by EL, thus

[3]http://dumps.wikimedia.org/other/pagecounts-raw/

[4]http://nlp.stanford.edu/software/CRF-NER.shtml

these features can be missing if there is no corresponding entity mention detected by the EL.

We also resolve overlaps of mentions by iteratively selecting the longest entity mention from the beginning of a tweet.

#### 2.3.2 Classification of Named Entities

In this step, detected entity mentions are classified into the predefined types (i.e., person, geo-loc, facility, product, company, movie, sportsteam, musicartist, tvshow, and other) using supervised machine-learning. Here, linear support vector machine is used as the machine-learning model.

One main machine-learning feature of this step is the corresponding entity types retrieved from KBs. We obtain KB entity types from the corresponding entries in DBpedia[5] and Freebase[6].

One problem in this step is that there are several entity mentions that cannot be detected by EL because of various reasons (e.g., a non-existent entity in the KB, an error performing EL). In addition, some minor entities might not have entity types in the KBs. In order to deal with this problem, we first include the entity types predicted by Stanford NER as features. However, because the target entity types of our task do not directly correspond to the ones given in Stanford NER (i.e., location, person, and organization), the effectiveness of these features is obviously limited. Therefore, we introduce another type of feature based on word embeddings. For this, we use GloVe word embeddings[7] to calculate an average vector of vectors of words in n-gram text.

We also include the relevance score assigned by the previous EL step that indicates the reliability of the KB entity types to the model. The number of words and the number of characters in the n-gram text are also included as features to enhance the expressiveness of our model even further.

The machine-learning features for this step include:

- *KB entity types*: The entity types in KBs. The KBs used include DBpedia and Freebase.
- *NER detected type*: The detected entity types of the NER model. As mentioned in Section 2.3.1, we use two different models of Stanford NER.
- *N-gram vector*: The vector representation of the n-gram derived using the method explained above and includes each dimension of the vector as a separate feature.
- *EL relevance score*: The relevance score assigned by the previous EL step.
- *Character length*: The number of characters read in the n-gram text.
- *Token length*: The number of tokens read in the n-gram.

| System Name | Precision | Recall | F1 |
|---|---|---|---|
| Our Method | **72.20%** | **69.14%** | **70.63%** |
| NLANGP | 67.74% | 54.31% | 60.29% |
| USFD | 63.81% | 56.28% | 59.81% |
| multimedialab | 62.93% | 55.22% | 58.82% |
| nrc | 62.13% | 54.61% | 58.13% |

Table 1: Performances of the proposed systems at segmenting entities

## 3 Experiments

### 3.1 Experimental Setup

To train our proposed EL method, we used the #Microposts 2015 EL dataset (Rizzo et al., 2015) that contains *3,998* tweets and *3,993* annotations of entities.[8] The performance of our EL method using this particular dataset is reported in (Yamada et al., 2015).

For this shared task, we trained and evaluated our proposed Twitter NER using the dataset provided by the workshop.[9]

### 3.2 Results

Table 1 shows the results of the segmentation task of the five top-ranking systems. Our proposed method significantly outperforms the second ranked method by 10.3% F1.

The end-to-end results (both segmentation and classification tasks) of the five top-ranking systems are shown in Table 2. Here, our method significantly outperforms the second ranked method by 5.0% F1. Table 3 also presents detailed scores broken down by entity types.

[5] `http://mappings.dbpedia.org/server/ontology/classes/`

[6] `http://wiki.freebase.com/wiki/Type`

[7] We use the 300-dimensional model generated using 840B tokens obtained from CommonCrawl corpus. `http://nlp.stanford.edu/projects/glove/`

[8] We use the *training* and the *dev* set of the #Microposts 2015 dataset as the training data.

[9] We use the *train*, the *dev*, and the *dev_2015* set for training the NER model.

| System Name | Precision | Recall | F1 |
|---|---|---|---|
| Our Method | 57.66% | **55.22%** | **56.41%** |
| NLANGP | **63.62%** | 41.12% | 51.40% |
| nrc | 53.24% | 38.58% | 44.74% |
| multimedialab | 49.52% | 39.18% | 43.75% |
| USFD | 45.72% | 39.64% | 42.46% |

Table 2: Performances of the proposed systems at both segmentation and classification tasks

| Entity Type | Precision | Recall | F1 |
|---|---|---|---|
| company | 41.82% | 58.97% | 48.94% |
| facility | 50.00% | 26.32% | 34.48% |
| geo-loc | 57.59% | 78.45% | 66.42% |
| movie | 66.67% | 40.00% | 50.00% |
| musicartist | 70.00% | 34.15% | 45.90% |
| other | 47.06% | 42.42% | 44.62% |
| person | 70.97% | 77.19% | 73.95% |
| product | 34.78% | 21.62% | 26.67% |
| sportsteam | 66.67% | 34.29% | 45.28% |
| tvshow | 14.29% | 50.00% | 22.22% |

Table 3: Performance of our system at both segmentation and classification tasks broken down by entity types

## 4 Conclusions

In this paper, we proposed a novel method for the Twitter NER task. We showed that the data retrieved from open knowledge bases (i.e., Wikipedia, DBpedia, Freebase) can be naturally leveraged to enhance NER using *entity linking*. Furthermore, this data appears to be highly effective for both the *segmentation* and the *classification* tasks.

## References

Sören Auer, Christian Bizer, Georgi Kobilarov, Jens Lehmann, Richard Cyganiak, and Zachary Ives. 2007. DBpedia: a nucleus for a web of open data. *The Semantic Web*, pages 722–735.

Timothy Baldwin, Marie Catherine de Marneffe, Bo Han, Young-Bum Kim, Alan Ritter, and Wei Xu. 2015. Shared tasks of the 2015 workshop on noisy user-generated text: Twitter lexical normalization and named entity recognition. In *Proceedings of the Workshop on Noisy User-generated Text (WNUT 2015)*.

Kurt Bollacker, Colin Evans, Praveen Paritosh, Tim Sturge, and Jamie Taylor. 2008. Freebase: a collaboratively created graph database for structuring human knowledge. In *Proceedings of the 2008 ACM SIGMOD International Conference on Management of Data (SIGMOD '08)*, pages 1247–1250.

William W. Cohen, Pradeep D. Ravikumar, and Stephen E. Fienberg. 2003. A comparison of string distance metrics for name-matching tasks. In *Proceedings of IJCAI-03 Workshop on Information Integration on the Web*, pages 73–78.

Leon Derczynski, Diana Maynard, Giuseppe Rizzo, Marieke van Erp, Genevieve Gorrell, Raphaël Troncy, Johann Petrak, and Kalina Bontcheva. 2015. Analysis of named entity recognition and linking for tweets. *Information Processing & Management*, 51(2):32–49.

Kevin Gimpel, Nathan Schneider, Brendan O'Connor, Dipanjan Das, Daniel Mills, Jacob Eisenstein, Michael Heilman, Dani Yogatama, Jeffrey Flanigan, and Noah A Smith. 2011. Part-of-speech tagging for Twitter: annotation, features, and experiments. In *Proceedings of the 49th Annual Meeting of the Association for Computational Linguistics: Human Language Technologies (HLT '11)*, pages 42–47.

Stephen Guo, Ming-Wei Chang, and Emre Kiciman. 2013. To link or not to link? a study on end-to-end Tweet entity linking. In *Proceedings of the 2013 Conference of the North American Chapter of the Association for Computational Linguistics: Human Language Technologies (NAACL-HLT '13)*, pages 1020–1030.

Edgar Meij, Wouter Weerkamp, and Maarten de Rijke. 2012. Adding semantics to microblog posts. In *Proceedings of the Fifth ACM International Conference on Web Search and Data Mining (WSDM '12)*, pages 563–572.

Jeffrey Pennington, Richard Socher, and Christopher D Manning. 2014. GloVe: Global vectors for word representation. In *Proceedings of the 2014 Conference on Empirical Methods in Natural Language Processing (EMNLP '14)*, pages 1532–1543.

Lance A. Ramshaw and Mitchell P. Marcus. 1995. Text chunking using transformation-based learning. In *Proceedings of ACL Third Workshop on Very Large Corpora*, pages 82–94.

Giuseppe Rizzo, Amparo Elizabeth Cano Basave, Bianca Pereira, Andrea Varga, Matthew Rowe, Milan Stankovic, and Aba-Sah Dadzie. 2015. Making sense of microposts (#Microposts2015) named entity recognition and linking (NEEL) challenge. In *5th Workshop on Making Sense of Microposts (#Microposts2015)*.

Ikuya Yamada, Hideaki Takeda, and Yoshiyasu Takefuji. 2015. An end-to-end entity linking approach for Tweets. In *5th Workshop on Making Sense of Microposts (#Microposts 2015)*.

# Improving Twitter Named Entity Recognition using Word Representations

**Zhiqiang Toh, Bin Chen and Jian Su**
Institute for Infocomm Research
1 Fusionopolis Way
Singapore 138632
{ztoh,bchen,sujian}@i2r.a-star.edu.sg

## Abstract

This paper describes our system used in the ACL 2015 Workshop on Noisy User-generated Text Shared Task for Named Entity Recognition (NER) in Twitter. Our system uses Conditional Random Fields to train two separate classifiers for the two evaluations: predicting 10 fine-grained types, and segmenting named entities. We focus our efforts on generating word representations from large amount of unlabeled newswire data and tweets. Our experiment results show that cluster features derived from word representations significantly improve Twitter NER performances. Our system is ranked 2nd for both evaluations.

## 1 Introduction

Named Entity Recognition (NER) is the task of identifying and categorizing the various mentions of people, organizations and other named entities within the text. NER has been an essential analysis component in many Natural Language Processing (NLP) systems, especially information extraction and question answering.

Traditionally, the NER system is trained and applied on long and formal text such as the newswire. From the beginning of the new millennium, user-generated content from the social media websites such as Twitter and Weibo presents a huge compilation of informative but noisy and informal text. This rapidly growing text collection becomes more and more important for NLP tasks such as sentiment analysis and emerging topic detection.

However, standard NER system trained on formal text does not work well on this new and challenging style of text. Therefore, adapting the NER system to the new and challenging Twitter domain has attracted increasing attention of researchers. The ACL 2015 Workshop on Noisy User-generated Text (W-NUT) Shared Task for NER in Twitter is organized in response to these new changes (Tim Baldwin, 2015).

We participated in the above Shared Task, which consists of two separate evaluations: one where the task is to predict 10 fine-grained types (10types) and the other in which only named entity segments are predicted (notypes).

For both evaluations, we model the problem as a sequential labeling task, using Conditional Random Fields (CRF) as the training algorithm. An additional postprocessing step is applied to further refine the system output.

The remainder of this paper is structured as follows. In Section 2, we report on the external resources used by our system and how they are obtained and processed. In Section 3, the features used are described in details. In Section 4, the experiment and official results are presented. Finally, Section 5 summarizes our work.

## 2 External Resources

External resources have shown to improve the performances of Twitter NER (Ritter et al., 2011). Our system uses a variety of external resources, either publicly available, or collected and preprocessed by us.

### 2.1 Freebase Entity Lists

We use the Freebase entity lists provided by the task organizers. For some of the lists that are not provided (e.g. a list of sports facilities), we manually collect them by calling the appropriate Freebase API.

### 2.2 Unlabeled Corpora

We gather unlabeled corpora from three different sources: (1) Pre-trained word vectors generated using the GloVe tool (Pennington et al.,



*Proceedings of the ACL 2015 Workshop on Noisy User-generated Text*, pages 141–145,
Beijing, China, July 31, 2015. ©2015 Association for Computational Linguistics

2014)[1], (2) English Gigaword Fifth Edition[2], and (3) raw tweets collected between the period of March 2015 and April 2015.

For English Gigaword, all articles of *story* type are collected and tokenized. Further preprocessing is performed by following the cleaning step described in Turian et al. (2010). This results in a corpus consisting of 76 million sentences.

The collected raw tweets are tokenized[3] and non-English tweets are removed using `langid.py` (Lui and Baldwin, 2012), resulting in a total of 14 million tweets.

## 3 Features

This section briefly describes the features used in our system. Besides the features commonly used in traditional NER systems, we focus on the use of word cluster features that have shown to be effective in previous work (Ratinov and Roth, 2009; Turian et al., 2010; Cherry and Guo, 2015).

### 3.1 Word Feature

The current word and its lowercase format are used as features. To provide additional context information, the previous word and next word (in original format) are also used.

### 3.2 Orthographic Features

Orthographic features based on regular expressions are often used in NER systems. We only use the following two orthographic features: InitialCap (`[A-Z][a-z].*`) and AllCaps (`[A-Z]+`). In addition, the first character and last two characters of each word are used as features.

### 3.3 Gazetteer Feature

The current word is matched with entries in the Freebase entity lists and the feature value is the type of entity list matched.

### 3.4 Word Cluster Features

Unsupervised word representations (e.g. Brown clustering) have shown to improve the performance of NER. Besides brown clusters, we also use clusters generated using the K-means algorithm. These two kinds of clusters are generated from the processed Gigaword and tweet corpora (Section 2.2).

Brown clusters are generated using the implementation by Percy Liang[4]. We experiment with different cluster sizes ($\{100, 200, 500, 1000\}$), resulting in different cluster files for each of the corpora. For each cluster file, different minimum occurrences ($\{5, 10, 20\}$) and binary prefix lengths ($\{4, 6, \cdots, 14, 16\}$) are tested. For each word in the tweet, its corresponding binary prefix string representation is used as the feature value.

K-means clusters are generated using two different methods. The first method uses the `word2vec` tool (Mikolov et al., 2013)[5]. By varying the minimum occurrences ($\{5, 10, 20\}$), word vector size ($\{50, 100, 200, 500, 1000\}$), cluster size ($\{50, 100, 200, 500, 1000\}$) and sub-sampling threshold ($\{0.00001, 0.001\}$), different cluster files are generated and tested. Similar to the Brown cluster feature, the name of the cluster that each word belongs to is used as the feature value.

The second method uses the GloVe tool to generate global vectors for word representation[6]. As the GloVe tool does not output any form of clusters, K-mean clusters are generated from the global vectors using the K-means implementation from Apache Spark MLlib[7]. Similarly, by varying the minimum count ($\{5, 10, 20, 50, 100\}$), window size ($\{5, 10, 15, 20\}$), vector size ($\{50, 100, 200, 500, 1000\}$), and cluster size ($\{50, 100, 200, 500, 1000\}$), different cluster files are generated and tested.

We also generate K-mean cluster files using the pre-trained GloVe word vectors (trained from Wikipedia 2014 and Gigaword Fifth Edition, Common Crawl and Twitter data) in the same manner.

We create a cluster feature for each cluster file that is found to improve the 5-fold cross validation performance. As there are over 800 cluster files, we only test a random subset of cluster files each time and select the best cluster file from the subset to create a new cluster feature. The procedure is repeated for a new subset of cluster files, until no (or negligible) improvement is obtained. Our final settings use one Brown cluster feature and six K-means cluster features (for both 10types and notypes settings).

[1] http://nlp.stanford.edu/projects/glove/

[2] https://catalog.ldc.upenn.edu/LDC2011T07

[3] The tweet tokenization script can be found at https://github.com/myleott/ark-twokenize-py

[4] https://github.com/percyliang/brown-cluster/

[5] https://code.google.com/p/word2vec/

[6] Due to memory constraints, only the tweet corpus is used to generate global vectors.

[7] https://spark.apache.org/mllib/

| | 10types | | | | | |
|---|---|---|---|---|---|---|
| Feature | Fold 1 | Fold 2 | Fold 3 | Fold 4 | Fold 5 | Overall |
| Word Feature | 25.76 | 23.93 | 27.59 | 28.01 | 9.69 | 23.94 |
| + Orthographic Features | 36.48 | 35.64 | 41.20 | 43.27 | 25.34 | 37.03 |
| + Gazetteer Feature | 44.36 | 43.94 | 48.22 | 44.84 | 30.35 | 42.94 |
| + Word Cluster Features | 55.85 | 57.49 | 60.07 | 58.35 | 44.99 | 55.95 |
| + Postprocessing | 56.09 | 57.82 | 60.07 | 58.88 | 45.78 | 56.31 |

Table 1: 5-fold cross-validation F1 performances for the 10types evaluation. Each row uses all features added in the previous rows.

| | notypes | | | | | |
|---|---|---|---|---|---|---|
| Feature | Fold 1 | Fold 2 | Fold 3 | Fold 4 | Fold 5 | Overall |
| Word Feature | 30.91 | 30.08 | 33.41 | 36.99 | 20.69 | 31.09 |
| + Orthographic Features | 52.06 | 54.29 | 52.22 | 53.11 | 44.49 | 51.62 |
| + Gazetteer Feature | 52.26 | 56.70 | 58.78 | 56.74 | 47.45 | 54.77 |
| + Word Cluster Features | 65.14 | 65.57 | 66.77 | 68.13 | 55.31 | 64.66 |
| + Postprocessing | 65.44 | 65.85 | 67.30 | 68.70 | 56.00 | 65.13 |

Table 2: 5-fold cross-validation F1 performances for the notypes evaluation. Each row uses all features added in the previous rows.

## 4 Experiments and Results

Our system is trained using the CRF++ tool[8]. We trained separate classifiers for the two different evaluations (10types and notypes).

To select the optimum settings, we make use of all available training data (`train`, `dev`, `dev_2015`) and conduct 5-fold cross validation experiments. For easier comparisons with other systems, the 5 folds are split such that `dev` is the test set for Fold 1, while `dev_2015` is the test set for Fold 5.

### 4.1 Preliminary Results on Training Data

Table 1 and Table 2 shows the 5-fold cross validation performances after adding each feature group for the 10types and notypes evaluations respectively. The use of word clusters significantly improves the performances for both evaluations. There is an overall improvement of 13% and 9% for the 10types and notypes evaluation respectively when word cluster features are added. This demonstrates the usefulness of word vectors in improving the accuracy of a Twitter NER system.

Comparing the performances of Fold 1 (tested on `dev`) and Fold 5 (tested on `dev_2015`), we observe a significant performance difference. Similar observations can also be seen for the other three folds (tested on a subset of `train`) when compared with Fold 5. This suggests that there are notable differences between the data provided during the training period (`train` and `dev`) and evaluation period (`dev_2015`), probably because the two sets of data are collected in different time periods.

### 4.2 Postprocessing

We also experiment with a postprocessing step based on heuristic rules to further refine the system output (last row of Table 1 and Table 2). The heuristic rules are based on string matching of words with name list entries. To prevent false positives, we require entries in some of the name lists to contain at least two words and should not contain common words/stop words. For certain name lists where single-word entries are common but ambiguous (e.g. name of sports clubs), we check for the presence of cue words in the tweet before matching. For example, for single-word sport team names that are common in tweets, we check for the presence of cue words such as "vs". Examples of name lists used include names of professional athletes, music composers and sport facilities.

[8] http://taku910.github.io/crfpp/

| | 10types | | | | notypes | | | |
|---|---|---|---|---|---|---|---|---|
| System | Rank | Precision | Recall | F1 | Rank | Precision | Recall | F1 |
| NLANGP | 2 | 63.62 | 43.12 | 51.40 | 2 | 67.74 | 54.31 | 60.29 |
| 1st | 1 | 57.66 | 55.22 | 56.41 | 1 | 72.20 | 69.14 | 70.63 |
| 2nd | 2 | 63.62 | 43.12 | 51.40 | 2 | 67.74 | 54.31 | 60.29 |
| 3rd | 3 | 53.24 | 38.58 | 44.74 | 3 | 63.81 | 56.28 | 59.81 |
| Baseline | – | 35.56 | 29.05 | 31.97 | – | 53.86 | 46.44 | 49.88 |

Table 3: Comparison of our system (NLANGP) with the top three participating systems and official baselines for the 10types and notypes evaluations.

| | 10types | | | notypes | | |
|---|---|---|---|---|---|---|
| System | Precision | Recall | F1 | Precision | Recall | F1 |
| NLANGP | 63.62 | 43.12 | 51.40 | 67.74 | 54.31 | 60.29 |
| - Word Cluster Features | 57.99 | 25.26 | 35.19 | 62.56 | 38.43 | 47.61 |

Table 4: System performances on the test data when word cluster features are not used.

### 4.3 Evaluation Results

Table 3 presents the official results of our 10types and notypes submissions. We also include the results of the top three participating systems and official baselines for comparison.

As shown from the table, our system (NLANGP) is ranked 2nd for both evaluations. Based on our preliminary Fold 5 performances, our system performances on the test data (`test_2015`, collected in the same period as `dev_2015`) are within expectation. In general, the fine-grained evaluation is a more challenging task, as seen from the huge performance difference between the F1 score of 10types and notypes.

| Type | Precision | Recall | F1 |
|---|---|---|---|
| COMPANY | 80.00 | 41.03 | 54.24 |
| FACILITY | 52.17 | 31.58 | 39.34 |
| GEO-LOC | 63.81 | 57.76 | 60.63 |
| MOVIE | 100.00 | 33.33 | 50.00 |
| MUSICARTIST | 50.00 | 9.76 | 16.33 |
| OTHER | 50.00 | 30.30 | 37.74 |
| PERSON | 70.70 | 64.91 | 67.68 |
| PRODUCT | 20.00 | 8.11 | 11.54 |
| SPORTSTEAM | 79.41 | 38.57 | 51.92 |
| TVSHOW | 0.00 | 0.00 | 0.00 |
| Overall | 63.62 | 43.12 | 51.40 |

Table 5: Performance of each fine-grained type of our system.

Table 5 shows the performance of each fine-grained type of our system. Unlike traditional NER where state-of-the-art systems can achieve performances over 90 F1 for the 3 MUC types (PERSON, LOCATION and ORGANIZATION), Twitter NER poses new challenges in accurately extracting entity information in such genre that does not exist in the past.

We are interested to know the performance contribution of the word clusters on the test data. Table 4 shows the performances on the test data when word cluster features are not used. Similarly to the observations observed in the training data, word clusters are important features for our system: a performance drop greater than 16% and 12% is observed for the 10types and notypes evaluation respectively.

## 5 Conclusion

In this paper, we describe our system used in the W-NUT Shared Task for NER in Twitter. We focus our efforts on improving Twitter NER using word representations, namely, Brown clusters and K-means clusters, that are generated from large amount of unlabeled newswire data and tweets. Our experiments and evaluation results show that cluster features derived from word representations are effective in improving Twitter NER performances. In future, we hope to investigate on the use of distant supervision learning technique to build better system that can perform more robustly across tweets from different time periods. We also like to perform an error analysis to help us understand which other problems persist so as to address them in future.

## References


Colin Cherry and Hongyu Guo. 2015. The Unreasonable Effectiveness of Word Representations for Twitter Named Entity Recognition. In *Proceedings of the 2015 Conference of the North American Chapter of the Association for Computational Linguistics: Human Language Technologies*, pages 735–745, Denver, Colorado, May–June. Association for Computational Linguistics.

Marco Lui and Timothy Baldwin. 2012. langid.py: An Off-the-shelf Language Identification Tool. In *Proceedings of the ACL 2012 System Demonstrations*, pages 25–30, Jeju Island, Korea, July. Association for Computational Linguistics.

Tomas Mikolov, Wen-tau Yih, and Geoffrey Zweig. 2013. Linguistic Regularities in Continuous Space Word Representations. In *Proceedings of the 2013 Conference of the North American Chapter of the Association for Computational Linguistics: Human Language Technologies*, pages 746–751, Atlanta, Georgia, June. Association for Computational Linguistics.

Jeffrey Pennington, Richard Socher, and Christopher Manning. 2014. Glove: Global Vectors for Word Representation. In *Proceedings of the 2014 Conference on Empirical Methods in Natural Language Processing (EMNLP)*, pages 1532–1543, Doha, Qatar, October. Association for Computational Linguistics.

Lev Ratinov and Dan Roth. 2009. Design Challenges and Misconceptions in Named Entity Recognition. In *Proceedings of the Thirteenth Conference on Computational Natural Language Learning (CoNLL-2009)*, pages 147–155, Boulder, Colorado, June. Association for Computational Linguistics.

Alan Ritter, Sam Clark, Mausam, and Oren Etzioni. 2011. Named Entity Recognition in Tweets: An Experimental Study. In *Proceedings of the 2011 Conference on Empirical Methods in Natural Language Processing*, pages 1524–1534, Edinburgh, Scotland, UK., July. Association for Computational Linguistics.

Marie Marie Catherine de Marneffe Young-Bum Kim Alan Ritter Wei Xu Tim Baldwin, Bo Han. 2015. Findings of the 2015 Workshop on Noisy User-generated Text. In *Proceedings of the Workshop on Noisy User-generated Text (WNUT 2015)*. Association for Computational Linguistics.

Joseph Turian, Lev-Arie Ratinov, and Yoshua Bengio. 2010. Word Representations: A Simple and General Method for Semi-Supervised Learning. In *Proceedings of the 48th Annual Meeting of the Association for Computational Linguistics*, pages 384–394, Uppsala, Sweden, July. Association for Computational Linguistics.

# Multimedia Lab @ ACL W-NUT NER Shared Task: Named Entity Recognition for Twitter Microposts using Distributed Word Representations

**Fréderic Godin**
Multimedia Lab
Ghent University - iMinds
Ghent, Belgium
frederic.godin@ugent.be

**Baptist Vandersmissen**
Multimedia Lab
Ghent University - iMinds
Ghent, Belgium
baptist.vandersmissen@ugent.be

**Wesley De Neve**
Multimedia Lab & IVY Lab
Ghent University - iMinds & KAIST
Ghent, Belgium & Daejeon, South-Korea
wesley.deneve@ugent.be

**Rik Van de Walle**
Multimedia Lab
Ghent University - iMinds
Ghent, Belgium
rik.vandewalle@ugent.be

## Abstract

Due to the short and noisy nature of Twitter microposts, detecting named entities is often a cumbersome task. As part of the ACL2015 Named Entity Recognition (NER) shared task, we present a semi-supervised system that detects 10 types of named entities. To that end, we leverage 400 million Twitter microposts to generate powerful word embeddings as input features and use a neural network to execute the classification. To further boost the performance, we employ dropout to train the network and leaky Rectified Linear Units (ReLUs). Our system achieved the fourth position in the final ranking, without using any kind of hand-crafted features such as lexical features or gazetteers.

## 1 Introduction

Users on Online Social Networks such as Facebook and Twitter have the ability to share microposts with their friends or followers. These microposts are short and noisy, and are therefore much more difficult to process for existing Natural Language Processing (NLP) pipelines. Moreover, due to the informal and contemporary nature of these microposts, they often contain Named Entities (NEs) that are not part of any gazetteer.

In this challenge, we tackled Named Entity Recognition (NER) in microposts. The goal was to detect named entities and classify them in one of the following 10 categories: company, facility, geolocation, music artist, movie, person, product, sports team, tv show and other entities. To do so, we *only* used word embeddings that were automatically inferred from 400 million Twitter microposts as input features. Next, these word embeddings were used as input to a neural network to classify the words in the microposts. Finally, a post-processing step was executed to check for inconsistencies, given that we classified on a word-per-word basis and that a named entity can span multiple words. An overview of the task can be found in Baldwin et al. (2015).

The challenge consisted of two subtasks. For the first subtask, the participants only needed to detect NEs without categorizing them. For the second subtask, the NEs also needed to be categorized into one of the 10 categories listed above. Throughout the remainder of this paper, only the latter subtask will be considered, given that solving subtask two makes subtask one trivial.

## 2 Related Work

NER in news articles gained substantial popularity with the CoNLL 2003 shared task, where the challenge was to classify four types of NEs: persons, locations, companies and a set of miscellaneous entities (Tjong Kim Sang and De Meulder, 2003). However, all systems used hand-crafted features such as lexical features, look-up tables and corpus-related features. These systems provide good performance at a high engineering cost and need a lot of annotated training data (Nadeau and Sekine, 2007). Therefore, a lot of effort is needed to adapt them to other types of corpora.

More recently, semi-supervised systems



*Proceedings of the ACL 2015 Workshop on Noisy User-generated Text*, pages 146–153,
Beijing, China, July 31, 2015. 

showed to achieve near state-of-the-art results with much less effort (Turian et al., 2010; Collobert et al., 2011). These systems first learn word representations from large corpera in an unsupervised way and use these word representations as input features for supervised training instead of using hand-crafted input features. There exist three major types of word representations: distributional, clustering-based and distributed word representations, and where the last type of representation is also known as a word embedding. A very popular and fast to train word embedding is the word2vec word representation of Mikolov et al. (2013). When complemented with traditional hand-crafted features, word representations can yield F1-scores of up to 91% (Tkachenko and Simanovsky, 2012).

However, when applied to Twitter microposts, the F1-score drops significantly. For example, Liu et al. (2011) report a F1 score of 45.8% when applying the Stanford NER tagger to Twitter microposts and Ritter et al. (2011) even report a F1-score of 29% on their Twitter micropost dataset. Therefore, many researchers (Cano et al., 2013; Cano et al., 2014) trained new systems on Twitter microposts, but mainly relied on cost-intensive hand-crafted features, sometimes complemented with cluster-based features.

Therefore, in this paper, we will investigate the power of word embeddings for NER applied to microposts. Although adding hand-crafted features such as lexical features or gazetteers would probably improve our F1-score, we will only focus on word embeddings, given that this approach can be easily applied to different corpora, thus quickly leading to good results.

## 3 System Overview

The system proposed for tackling this challenge consists of three steps. First, the individual words are converted into word representations. For this, only the word embeddings of Mikolov et al. (2013) are used. Next, we feed the word representations to a Feed-Forward Neural Network (FFNN) to classify the individual words with a matching tag. Finally, we execute a simple, rule-based post-processing step in which we check the coherence of individual tags within a Named Entity (NE).

### 3.1 Creating Feature Representations

Recently, Mikolov et al. (2013) introduced an efficient way for inferring word embeddings that are effective in capturing syntactic and semantic relationships in natural language. In general, a word embedding of a particular word is inferred by using the previous or future words within a number of microposts/sentences. Mikolov et al. (2013) proposed two architectures for doing this: the Continuous Bag Of Words (CBOW) model and the Skip-gram model.

To infer the word embeddings, a large dataset of microposts is used. The algorithm iterates a number of times over this dataset while updating the word embeddings of the words within the vocabulary of the dataset. The final result is a look-up table which can be used to convert every word $w(t)$ in a feature vector $w_e(t)$. If the word is not in the vocabulary, a vector only containing zeros is used.

### 3.2 Neural Network Architecture

Based on the successful application of Feed-Forward Neural Networks (FFNN) using word embeddings as input features for both recognizing NEs in news articles (Turian et al., 2010; Collobert et al., 2011) and Part-of-Speech tagging of Twitter microposts (Godin et al., 2014), a FFNN is used as the underlying classification algorithm. Because a NE can consist of multiple words, the BIO (Begin, Inside, Outside NE) notation is used to classify the words. Given that there are 10 different NE categories that each have a Begin and Inside tag, the FFNN will assign a $tag(t)$ to every word $w(t)$ out of 21 different tags.

Because the tag $tag(t)$ of a word $w(t)$ is also determined by the surrounding words, a context window centered around $w(t)$ that contains an odd number of words, is used. As shown in Figure 1, the corresponding word embeddings $w_e(t)$ are concatenated and used as input to the FFNN. This is the input layer of the neural network.

The main design parameters of the neural network are the type of activation function, the number of hidden units and the number of hidden layers. We considered two types of activation functions, the classic *tanh* activation function and the newer (leaky) Rectified Linear Units (ReLUs). The output layer is a standard softmax function.

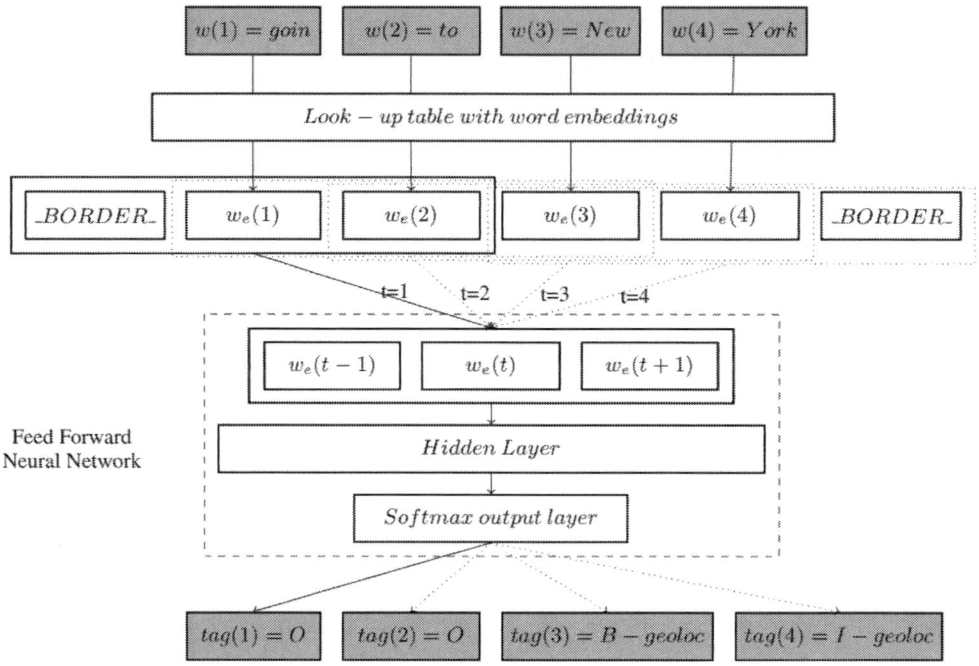


Figure 1: High-level illustration of the FFNN that classifies each word as part of one of the 10 named entity classes. At the input, a micropost containing four words is given. The different words $w(t)$ are first converted in feature representations $w_e(t)$ using a look-up table of word embeddings. Next, a feature vector is constructed for each word by concatenating all the feature representations $w_e(t)$ of the other words within the context window. In this example, a context window of size three is used. One-by-one, these concatenated vectors are fed to the FFNN. In this example, a one-hidden layer FFNN is used. The output of the FFNN is the tag $tag(t)$ of the corresponding word $w(t)$.

### 3.3 Postprocessing the Neural Network Output

Given that NEs can span multiple words and given that the FFNN classifies individual words, we apply a postprocessing step after a micropost is completely classified to correct inconsistencies. The tags of the words are changed according to the following two rules:

- If the NE does not start with a word that has a B(egin)-tag, we select the word before the word with the I(nside)-tag and replace the O(utside)-tag with a B-tag and copy the category of the I-tag.
- If the individual words of a NE have different categories, we select the most frequently occurring category. If it is a tie, we select the category of the last word within the NE.

## 4 Experimental Setup

### 4.1 Dataset

The challenge provided us with three different datasets: train, dev and dev_2015. These datasets have 1795, 599 and 420 microposts, respectively, also containing 1140, 356 and 272 NEs, respectively. The train and dev datasets came from the same period and therefore have some overlap in NEs. Moreover, they contained the complete dataset of Ritter et al. (2011). The microposts within dev_2015, however, were sampled more recently and resembled the test set of this challenge. The test set consisted of 1000 microposts, having 661 NEs. The train and dev dataset will be used as training set throughout the experiments and the dev_2015 dataset will be used as development set.

For inferring the word embeddings, a set of raw Twitter microposts was used, collected during 300 days using the Twitter Streaming API, from

1/3/2013 till 28/2/2014. After removing all non-English microposts using the micropost language classifier of Godin et al. (2013), 400 million raw English Twitter microposts were left.

### 4.2 Preprocessing the Data

For preprocessing the 400 million microposts, we used the same tokenizer as Ritter et al. (2011). Additionally, we used replacement tokens for URLs, mentions and numbers on both the challenge dataset and the 400 million microposts we collected. However, we did not replace hashtags as doing so experimentally demonstrated to decrease the accuracy.

### 4.3 Training the Model

The model was trained in two phases. First, the look-up table containing per-word feature vectors was constructed. To that end, we applied the word2vec software (v0.1c) of Mikolov et al. (2013) on our preprocessed dataset of 400 million Twitter microposts to generate word embeddings. Next, we trained the neural network. To that end, we used the Theano library (v0.6) (Bastien et al., 2012), which easily effectuated the use of our NVIDIA Titan Black GPU. We used mini-batch stochastic gradient descent with a batch size of 20, a learning rate of 0.01 and a momentum of 0.5. We used the standard negative log-likelihood cost function to update the weights. We used dropout on both the input and hidden layers to prevent overfitting and used (Leaky) Rectified Linear Units (ReLUs) as hidden units (Srivastava et al., 2014). To do so, we used the implementation of the Lasagne[1] library. We trained the neural network on both the train and dev dataset and iterated until the accuracy on the dev_2015 set did not improve anymore.

### 4.4 Baseline

To evaluate our system, we made use of two different baselines. The word embeddings and the neural network architecture were evaluated in terms of word level accuracy. For these components, the baseline system simply assigned the O-tag to every word, yielding an accuracy of 93.53%. For the postprocessing step and the overall system evaluation, we made use of the baseline provided by the challenge, which performs an evaluation at the level of NEs. This baseline system uses lexical features and gazetteers, yielding an F1-score of 34.29%. Note that we only report the performance for subtask two (i.e., categorizing the NEs), except for the final evaluation.

[1]https://github.com/Lasagne/Lasagne

Table 1: Evaluation of the influence of the context window size of the word embeddings on the accuracy of predicting NER tags using a neural network with an input window of five words, 500 hidden Leaky ReLU units and dropout. All word embeddings are inferred using negative sampling and a Skip-gram architecture, and have a vector size of 400. The baseline accuracy is achieved when tagging all words of a micropost with the O-tag.

| Context Window | Accuracy | Error Rate Reduction |
|---|---|---|
| Baseline | 93.53% | |
| 1 | **95.64%** | **-32.57%** |
| 3 | 95.57% | -31.44% |
| 5 | 95.52% | -30.72% |

## 5 Experiments

### 5.1 Word Embeddings

For inferring the word embeddings of the 400 million microposts, we mainly followed the suggestions of Godin et al. (2014), namely, the best word embeddings are inferred using a Skip-gram architecture and negative sampling. We used the default parameter settings of the word2vec software, except for the context window.

As noted by Bansal et al. (2014), the type of word embedding created depends on the size of the context window. In particular, a bigger context window creates topic-oriented embeddings while a smaller context window creates syntax-oriented embeddings. Therefore, we trained an initial version of our neural network using an input window of five words and 300 hidden nodes, and evaluate the quality of the word embeddings based on the classification accuracy on the dev_2015 dataset. The results of this evaluation are shown in Table 1. Although the difference is small, a smaller context window consistently gave a better result.

Additionally, we evaluated the vector size. As a general rule of thumb, the larger the word embeddings, the better the classification (Mikolov et al., 2013). However, too many parameters and too few training examples will lead to suboptimal results and poor generalization. We chose word embeddings of size 400 because smaller embeddings experimentally showed to capture not as much detail and resulted in a lower accuracy. Larger word embeddings, on the other hand, made the model too complex to train.

The final word2vec word embeddings model has a vocabulary of 3,039,345 words and word representations of dimensionality 400. The model was trained using the Skip-gram architecture and negative sampling ($k = 5$) for five iterations, with a context window of one and subsampling with a factor of 0.001. Additionally, to be part of the vocabulary, words should occur at least five times in the corpus.

### 5.2 The Neural Network Architecture

The next step is to evaluate the Neural Network Architecture. The most important parameters are the size of the input layer, the size of the hidden layers and the type of hidden units. Although we experimented with multiple hidden layers, the accuracy did not improve. We surmise that (1) the training set is too small and that (2) the word embeddings already contain a fixed summary of the information and therefore limit the feature learning capabilities of the neural network. Note that the word embeddings at the input layer can also be seen as a (fixed) hidden layer.

First, we will evaluate the activation function and the effectiveness of dropout ($p = 0.5$). We compared the classic *tanh* function and the leaky ReLU with a leak rate of 0.01[2]. As can be seen in Table 2, both activation functions perform equally good when no dropout is applied during training. However, when dropout is applied, the gap between the two configurations becomes larger. The combination of ReLUs and dropout seems to be the best one, compared to the classic configuration of a neural network[3].

Next, we will evaluate a number of neural network configurations for which we varied the input layer size and the hidden layer size. The results are depicted in Table 3. Although the differences are small, the best configuration seems to be a neural network with five input words and 500 hidden nodes.

[2]This is the default value in Lasagne and showed to work the best for us

[3]Given that dropout also acts as a regularization technique, a comparison with other regularization techniques should be conducted to be complete (e.g., L2 regularization)

Table 2: Evaluation of the influence of the activation function and dropout on the accuracy of predicting NE tags. A fixed neural network with an input window of five, word embeddings of size 400 and 500 hidden units is used. The baseline accuracy is achieved when tagging all words of a micropost with the O-tag.

| Activ. Function | Dropout | Accuracy | Error Rate Reduction |
|---|---|---|---|
| Baseline | | 93.53% | |
| Tanh | No | 95.01% | -22.78% |
| | Yes | 95.49% | -30.30% |
| L. ReLU | No | 95.02% | -23.01% |
| | Yes | **95.64%** | **-32.57%** |

Finally, we evaluate our best model on the NE level instead of on the word level. To that end, we calculated the F1-score of our best model using the provided evaluation script. The F1-score of our best model on dev_2015 is 45.15%, which is an absolute improvement of almost 11% and an error reduction of 16.52% over the baseline (34.29%) provided by the challenge.

### 5.3 Postprocessing

As a last step, we corrected the output of the neural network for inconsistencies because our classifier does not see the labels of the neighbouring words. As can be seen in Table 4, the postprocessing causes a significant error reduction, yielding a final F1-score of 49.09% on the dev_2015 development set, and an error reduction of 22.52% over the baseline.

Additionally, we also report the F1-score on the dev_2015 development set for subtask one, where the task was to only detect the NEs but not to categorize them into the 10 different categories. For this, we retrained the model with the best parameters of subtask two. The results are shown in Table 5.

If we compare both subtasks, we see that the neural network has a similar error reduction for both subtasks but that the postprocessing step effectuates a larger error reduction for subtask two. In other words, a common mistake of the neural network is to assign different categories to different words within one NE. These mistakes are easily corrected by the postprocessing step.

Table 3: Evaluation of the influence of the input layer and hidden layer size on the accuracy/error reduction when predicting NE tags. The fixed neural network is trained with dropout, word embeddings of size 400 and ReLUs. The error reduction values are calculated using the baseline which tags all words with an O-tag.

| Window | Number of hidden units | | |
|---|---|---|---|
| | 300 | 500 | 1000 |
| Three | 95.63% / -32.35% | 95.58% / -31.66% | 95.55% / -31.21% |
| Five | 95.57% / -31.44% | **95.64% / -32.57%** | 95.61% / -32.12% |

Table 4: Evaluation of the postprocessing step for detecting named entities. The baseline was provided by the challenge.

| Configuration | F1 | Error Rate Reduction |
|---|---|---|
| Baseline | 34.29% | |
| Without postprocessing | 45.15% | -16.52% |
| With postprocessing | **49.09%** | **-22.52%** |

Table 5: Evaluation of the postprocessing step for detecting named entities without categorizing them. The baseline was provided by the challenge.

| Configuration | F1 | Error Rate Reduction |
|---|---|---|
| Baseline | 52.63% | |
| Without postprocessing | 60.04% | -15.64% |
| With postprocessing | **60.80%** | **-17.24%** |

## 6 Evaluation on the Test Set

Our best model realized a F1-score of 58.82% on subtask one (no categories), hereby realizing an error reduction of 17.84% over the baseline (49.88%). On subtask two (10 categories), an F1-score of 43.75% was realized, yielding an error reduction of 17.32% over the baseline (31.97%). A break-down of the results on the different NE categories can be found in Table 6. Our system ranked fourth in both subtasks.

## 7 Conclusion

In this paper, we presented a system to apply Named Entity Recognition (NER) to microposts. Given that microposts are short and noisy compared to news articles, we did not want to invest time in crafting new features that would improve NER for microposts. Instead, we implemented the semi-supervised architecture of Collobert et al. (2011) for NER in news articles. This architecture only relies on good word embeddings inferred from a large corpus and a simple neural network.

To realize this system, we used the word2vec software to quickly generate powerful word embeddings over 400 million Twitter microposts. Additionally, we employed a state-of-the-art neural network for classification purposes, using leaky Rectified Linear Units (ReLUs) and dropout to train the network, showing a significant benefit over classic neural networks. Finally, we checked the output for inconsistencies when categorizing the named entities.

Our word2vec word embeddings trained on 400 million microposts are released to the community and can be downloaded at http://www.fredericgodin.com/software/.

## Acknowledgments

The research activities described in this paper were funded by Ghent University, iMinds, the Institute for the Promotion of Innovation by Science and Technology in Flanders (IWT), the Fund for Scientific Research-Flanders (FWO-Flanders), and the European Union.

## References

[Baldwin et al.2015] Timothy Baldwin, Marie Catherine de Marneffe, Bo Han, Young-Bum Kim, Alan Ritter, and Wei Xu. 2015. Shared tasks of the 2015 workshop on noisy user-generated text: Twitter lexical normalization and named entity recognition. In *Proceedings of the Workshop on Noisy User-generated Text (WNUT 2015)*, Beijing, China.

[Bansal et al.2014] Mohit Bansal, Kevin Gimpel, and

Table 6: Break-down of the results on the test set. The test set contains 661 NEs. Our system detected 523 NEs of which 259 NEs were correct.

| Category | Precision | Recall | F1 | #Entities |
|---|---|---|---|---|
| company | 57.89% | 28.21% | 37.93% | 19 |
| facility | 30.77% | 21.05% | 25.00% | 26 |
| geo-loc | 55.24% | 68.10% | 61.00% | 143 |
| movie | 37.50% | 20.00% | 26.09% | 8 |
| musicartist | 16.67% | 2.44% | 4.26% | 6 |
| other | 20.78% | 12.12% | 15.31% | 77 |
| person | 60.89% | 63.74% | 62.29% | 179 |
| product | 22.58% | 18.92% | 20.59% | 31 |
| sportsteam | 77.42% | 34.29% | 47.52% | 31 |
| tvshow | 33.33% | 50.00% | 40.00% | 3 |
| **Total** | **49.52 %** | **39.18%** | **43.75%** | **523** |


Karen Livescu. 2014. Tailoring continuous word representations for dependency parsing. In *Proceedings of the 52nd Annual Meeting of the Association for Computational Linguistics, ACL 2014, June 22-27, 2014, Baltimore, MD, USA, Volume 2: Short Papers*, pages 809–815. The Association for Computer Linguistics.

[Bastien et al.2012] Frédéric Bastien, Pascal Lamblin, Razvan Pascanu, James Bergstra, Ian J. Goodfellow, Arnaud Bergeron, Nicolas Bouchard, and Yoshua Bengio. 2012. Theano: new features and speed improvements. Deep Learning and Unsupervised Feature Learning NIPS 2012 Workshop.

[Cano et al.2013] Amparo Elizabeth Cano, Andrea Varga, Matthew Rowe, Milan Stankovic, and Aba-Sah Dadzie. 2013. Making sense of microposts (#msm2013) concept extraction challenge. In *Making Sense of Microposts (#MSM2013) Concept Extraction Challenge*.

[Cano et al.2014] Amparo E Cano, Giuseppe Rizzo, Andrea Varga, Matthew Rowe, Stankovic Milan, and Aba-Sah Dadzie. 2014. Making sense of microposts (#Microposts2014) named entity extraction & linking challenge. In *WWW 2014, 23rd International World Wide Web Conference, Making Sense of Microposts 2014*, Seoul, South Korea.

[Collobert et al.2011] Ronan Collobert, Jason Weston, Léon Bottou, Michael Karlen, Koray Kavukcuoglu, and Pavel Kuksa. 2011. Natural language processing (almost) from scratch. *Journal of Machine Learning Research*, 12:2493–2537.

[Godin et al.2013] Fréderic Godin, Viktor Slavkovikj, Wesley De Neve, Benjamin Schrauwen, and Rik Van de Walle. 2013. Using topic models for twitter hashtag recommendation. In *Proceedings of the 22Nd International Conference on World Wide Web Companion*, WWW '13 Companion, pages 593–596, Republic and Canton of Geneva, Switzerland. International World Wide Web Conferences Steering Committee.

[Godin et al.2014] Fréderic Godin, Baptist Vandersmissen, Azarakhsh Jalalvand, Wesley De Neve, and Rik Van de Walle. 2014. Alleviating manual feature engineering for part-of-speech tagging of twitter microposts using distributed word representations. In *Workshop on Modern Machine Learning and Natural Language Processing (NIPS 2014)*.

[Liu et al.2011] Xiaohua Liu, Shaodian Zhang, Furu Wei, and Ming Zhou. 2011. Recognizing named entities in tweets. In *Proceedings of the 49th Annual Meeting of the Association for Computational Linguistics: Human Language Technologies - Volume 1*, HLT '11, pages 359–367, Stroudsburg, PA, USA. Association for Computational Linguistics.

[Mikolov et al.2013] Tomas Mikolov, Kai Chen, Greg Corrado, and Jeffrey Dean. 2013. Efficient estimation of word representations in vector space. *CoRR*, abs/1301.3781.

[Nadeau and Sekine2007] David Nadeau and Satoshi Sekine. 2007. A survey of named entity recognition and classification. *Linguisticae Investigationes*, 30(1):3–26, January. Publisher: John Benjamins Publishing Company.

[Ritter et al.2011] Alan Ritter, Sam Clark, Mausam, and Oren Etzioni. 2011. Named entity recognition in tweets: An experimental study. In *Proceedings of the Conference on Empirical Methods in Natural Language Processing*, EMNLP '11, pages 1524–1534, Stroudsburg, PA, USA. Association for Computational Linguistics.

[Srivastava et al.2014] Nitish Srivastava, Geoffrey Hinton, Alex Krizhevsky, Ilya Sutskever, and Ruslan

Salakhutdinov. 2014. Dropout: A simple way to prevent neural networks from overfitting. *Journal of Machine Learning Research*, 15:1929–1958.

[Tjong Kim Sang and De Meulder2003] Erik F. Tjong Kim Sang and Fien De Meulder. 2003. Introduction to the conll-2003 shared task: Language-independent named entity recognition. In Walter Daelemans and Miles Osborne, editors, *Proceedings of CoNLL-2003*, pages 142–147. Edmonton, Canada.

[Tkachenko and Simanovsky2012] Maksim Tkachenko and Andrey Simanovsky. 2012. Named entity recognition: Exploring features. In *11th Conference on Natural Language Processing, KONVENS 2012, Empirical Methods in Natural Language Processing, Vienna, Austria, September 19-21, 2012*, pages 118–127.

[Turian et al.2010] Joseph Turian, Lev Ratinov, and Yoshua Bengio. 2010. Word representations: A simple and general method for semi-supervised learning. In *Proceedings of the 48th Annual Meeting of the Association for Computational Linguistics*, ACL '10, pages 384–394, Stroudsburg, PA, USA. Association for Computational Linguistics.

# NCSU_SAS_SAM: Deep Encoding and Reconstruction for Normalization of Noisy Text

**Samuel P. Leeman-Munk** **James C. Lester**
Center for Educational Informatics
North Carolina State University
Raleigh, NC, USA
{spleeman, lester}@ncsu.edu

**James A. Cox**
Text Analytics R&D
SAS Institute Inc.
Cary, NC, USA
james.cox@sas.com

## Abstract

As a participant in the W-NUT Lexical Normalization for English Tweets challenge, we use deep learning to address the constrained task. Specifically, we use a combination of two augmented feed forward neural networks, a flagger that identifies words to be normalized and a normalizer, to take in a single token at a time and output a corrected version of that token. Despite avoiding off-the-shelf tools trained on external data and being an entirely context-free model, our system still achieved an F1-score of 81.49%, comfortably surpassing the next runner up by 1.5% and trailing the second place model by only 0.26%.

## 1 Introduction

The phenomenal growth of social media, web forums, and online reviews has spurred a growing interest in automated analysis of user-generated text. User-generated text presents significant computational challenges because it is often highly disfluent. To address these challenges, we have begun to see a growing demand for tools and techniques to transform noisy user-generated text into a canonical form, most recently in the Workshop on Noisy User Text at the Association for Computational Linguistics. This work describes a submission to the Lexical Normalization for English Tweets challenge as part of this workshop (Baldwin et al., 2015)

Motivated by the success of prior deep neural network architectures, particularly denoising autoencoders, we have developed an approach to transform noisy user-generated text into a canonical form with a feed-forward neural network augmented with a projection layer (Collobert et al., 2011; Kalchbrenner, Grefenstette, & Blunsom, 2014; Vincent, Larochelle, Bengio, & Manzagol, 2008). The model performs a character-level analysis on each word of the input. The absence of hand-engineered features and the avoidance of direct and indirect external data make this model unique among the three top-performing models in the constrained task.

This paper is organized as follows. In Section 2 we describe each component of our model. In Section 3 we describe the specific instantiation of our model, and in Section 4 we present and discuss results.

## 2 Architecture and Components

Our model consists of three components: a *Normalizer* that encodes the input and then reconstructs it in normalized form, a *Flagger* that determines whether the Normalizer should be used or if the word should be taken as-is, and a *Conformer* that attempts to smooth out simple errors introduced by quirks in the Normalizer.

In this section we will use the simple example transformation of "u" to "you" where "u" is the input text and "you" is the gold standard normalization. In our example we use a maximum word size of three. Figure 1 shows the flow of our example through the model. In broad overview, the input is preprocessed and sent to both the Nor-



*Proceedings of the ACL 2015 Workshop on Noisy User-generated Text*, pages 154–161,
Beijing, China, July 31, 2015. ©2015 Association for Computational Linguistics

malizer and the Flagger. The Normalizer computes a candidate normalization, and the Flagger determines whether to use that candidate or the original word. The Normalizer's output is passed to the Conformer, which conforms it to a word in the vocabulary list, and then the candidate, the flag, and the original input word are passed to a simple decision component that either keeps the original word or uses the normalized version based on the output of the Flagger. While it may seem inefficient that the normalized version is always computed, even if it is not used, this approach is used so that the Normalizer and Flagger can be run in parallel on many inputs at once.

### 2.1 Deep Feed-Forward Neural Networks

As the central element of the Flagger and the Normalizer, the deep feed-forward neural network forms the basis of our model. A deep feed-forward neural network takes a vector of numbers as input. This vector is known as a *layer* and each value within it is a *neuron*. The network multiplies the input layer by a matrix of weights to return another vector. This new vector is then transformed by a non-linearity. A number of functions can serve as the non-linearity, including the sigmoid and the hyperbolic tangent, but our model uses a rectified linear unit, given by the following expression.

$$y = \max(x, 0)$$

The rectified linear unit has been successful in a number of natural language tasks such as speech processing (Zeiler et al., 2013), and it was effective in an unpublished part-of-speech tagging model we developed.

The transformed vector is referred to as a *hidden* layer because its values are never directly observed in the normal functioning of the model. A deep feed-forward neural network can contain any number of hidden layers, each going through the same process, multiplying by a matrix of weights and transforming via a non-linearity. Hidden layers may also be of any size. Multiple applications of learnable weight matrices and non-linear transformations together allow a deep neural network to represent complex relationships between input and output (Bengio, 2009).

Deep feed-forward neural networks are trained by *backpropagation*. Backpropagation is a training method by which the gradient of any given weight in a network can be calculated from the error between the output of the network and a gold standard. It is described in more detail in (Rumelhart, Hinton, & Williams, 1986).

### 2.2 The Normalizer

Our use of deep feed-forward neural networks for the task of normalization is inspired by the success of denoising autoencoders. (Vincent et al., 2008). Denoising autoencoders are neural networks whose output is the same as their input. That is, they specialize in developing a robust encoding of an input such that the input can be reconstructed from the encoding alone. The denoising aspect refers to the fact that to encourage robustness, denoising autoencoders are given inputs that have been deliberately corrupted, or "noised" and are expected to reconstruct them without the noise. It is this "denoising" aspect that makes denoising autoencoders so interesting for text normalization.

The main component of our model, the Normalizer, uses a feed-forward neural network that functions on a similar principle to that of a denoising autoencoder. It reads the character sequence that describes the word and encodes it

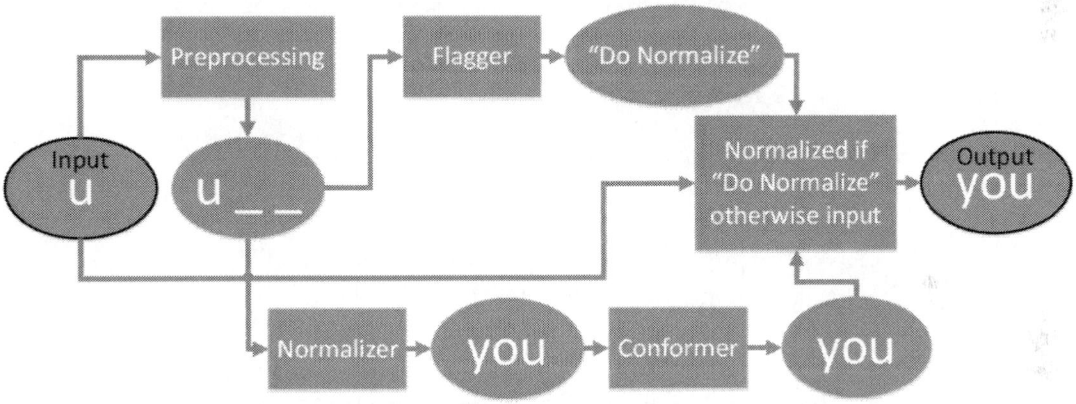


Figure 1: A flowchart detailing the process of normalizing a word. Information flows from left to right and ellipses represent data objects while rectangles represent processes.

internally, outputting the denoised (normalized) version. It accomplishes this in three sets of layers. First the character projection layer takes a string and represents it as a fixed-length numeric vector. Next, a feed-forward neural network converts the data into its internal representation and, with a special output layer, into a denoised version of the input. Figure 2 shows a diagram of the Normalizer's architecture.

The first step of the Normalizer is performed by the character projection layer (Collobert et al., 2011). The character projection layer learns floating point vector representations of characters, which it concatenates into one large floating point vector word representation. In our example, the letter "u" is represented by $n$ floating point numbers. For example, if $n = 3$ the representation for "u" might be [0.1, -1.2, -0.3]. This vector was chosen arbitrarily, but in the actual model, values are learned in training. The representations allow more information to be associated with a character than a simple numeric index.

In this simple example, the word "u" is composed of one character, but if it were longer, each letter would be separately represented. A key challenge at this point is that a feed-forward neural network cannot handle an arbitrary number of inputs. Because each position in the vector is a neuron matched directly to a set of weights, changing the size of the vector would require changing the size of the learned weights, and the model would have to be retrained.

To accommodate this, we use a fixed window. Before we send our input to the Normalizer, we preprocess it to meet a specified length, filling in unused spaces with a sentinel padding "character" that projects to its own set of learned weights like the other characters. Since the maximum word size in our example is 3, we use a window of size 3. Therefore, our input "u" becomes [u, _, _] and then is projected and concatenated and becomes something like [0.1, -1.2, -0.3, 1.3, 0.0, -1.1, 1.3, 0.0, -1.1]. Notice that we have nine values now in our input. That is the three values from "u" and then the three values for "_" ([1.3, 0.0, -1.1]) twice, once for each "_". After this step, the system has a numeric vector representation of a word that is always the same length. It now sends it to the first layer of the feed-forward neural network. We deliberately select a large enough window that only in a small minority of cases does a word have to be reduced to fit into the window.

The last hidden layer's values go through one final matrix multiplication to output a list of values $wv$ in size, where $w$ is the size of the window and $v$ is the number of possible characters including the padding character, that is, the number of characters in the alphabet, which is shared between the input and output layers. In this last layer the nonlinear transformation is a special version of the softmax operation.

The softmax operation transforms a vector such that each of its values is between zero and one and the new vector sums to one. Mathematically, it is given as:

$$\sigma(z)_j = \frac{e^{zj}}{\sum_{k=1}^{K} e^{zk}}$$

Where K is the number of values in the vector. In our model, K = v, the size of the alphabet. These individual values can alternately be considered posterior probabilities for each of the possible decisions. If each value is mapped to a character, one can simply take the highest value to select the most likely character. In this case, we are predicting a window of $w$ characters rather than a single character, so we perform softmax separately on each of the $w$ sets of $v$ values in the layer. In prediction, we simply take the index of the

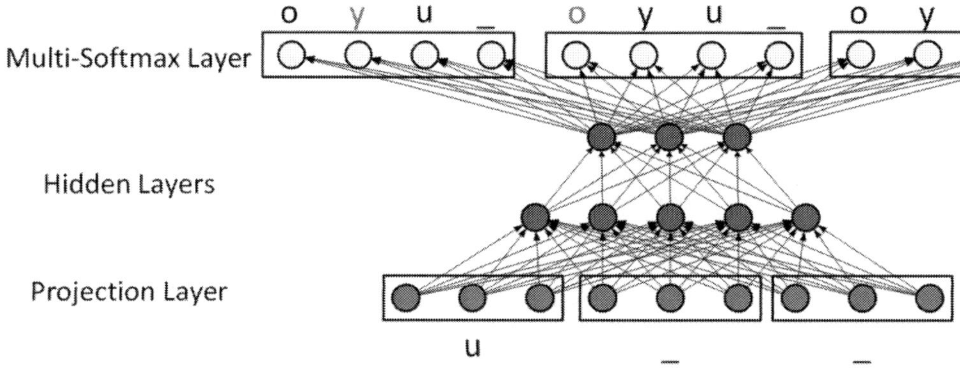


Figure 2: A diagram of the Normalizer correcting "u" to "you." The circles represent values, the lines weights.

highest value in each of the *w* sets, but in training we take the whole prediction distribution and try to maximize the likelihood of each correct letter. We do not attempt to predict character embeddings because we are learning them, and the model would be likely to learn a trivial function with character embeddings that are all equal.

Training the Normalizer as a whole relies on generating posterior distributions and attempting to minimize the total negative log likelihood of the gold standard. Mathematically, our objective function is

$$\text{cost} = -\sum_{p \in P} ln(p)$$

Where $p$ is an element in $P$, the vector of the probabilities of each gold standard letter. So, if our model predicts "y" as 75% likely for character 1, "o" as 95% likely for character 2, and "u" as 89% likely for character 3 in our window of size 3, the negative log likelihoods calculated as (.29, .05, .12) are summed to get the error. This sum error gives a simple measurement of performance to optimize, which backpropagates through the model to learn all the weights described above (Rumelhart et al., 1986).

### 2.3 The Flagger

The Flagger identifies what does and does not require normalization. The vast majority of the training data (91%) does not require normalization, so returning the reconstructed encoding of every word would risk incorrectly regenerating an already canonical token.

The Flagger has the same general structure as the Normalizer itself except for the final layer. Instead of generating text at the last layer, a softmax layer predicts whether the token should be normalized at all. Thus, the Flagger's output layer is two neurons in size, one representing the flag "Do Normalize," and another representing the flag "Do Not Normalize." In the construction of the gold standard for the task, there were three reasons a token would not be normalized: firstly, the token is already correct, second, the token is in a protected category (hashtags or foreign words), or third, it was simply unrecognizable such that the human normalizer could not find the correct form. The Flagger accounts for but does not distinguish between these three possibilities.

### 2.4 The Conformer

Even when a token should be corrected, it is possible that the normalizer will come very close to correcting it without succeeding. Reconstructing the word "laughing," for instance, the normalizer can fail completely if it predicts even one letter wrong. An early analysis of validation data found that the normalizer had predicted "laugling" instead of laughing. These off-by-one errors are a frequent enough occurrence to merit a module to deal with them. The Conformer is also useful for correctly normalizing rare words whose correct normalization is too long for the window to represent. In particular "lmfao" expands to an impressive 27 characters, but if the Normalizer predicts only the first 25 characters, the Conformer can easily select the correct token.

To correct these small normalizer errors we construct the Conformer by collecting a dictionary from the gold standard training data. The dictionary is simply a list of all the unique words in the gold standard data. Then at runtime, whenever the Normalizer runs and predicts a word that is not present in the dictionary, we replace it with the closest word in the dictionary according to Levenshtein distance (Levenshtein, 1966). Ties are resolved based on which word comes first in the dictionary. Because Python's set function, which does not guarantee a specific order of its contents, is used to construct the dictionary, the dictionary's order is not predictable and thus ties are resolved unpredictably.

## 3 Settings and Evaluation

The model was implemented in Theano, a Python library for fast evaluation of multi-dimensional arrays using matrix operations (Bastien et al., 2012; Bergstra et al., 2010). We used Theano's implementation of backpropagation to train our model. For our window size, we selected 25 characters, which is large enough to completely represent 99.9% of the tokens in the training data while remaining computationally feasible. There are also a number of hyper-parameters: the number and size of hidden layers, the size of character embeddings, and the dropout rate. We tried various combinations of values between 50 and 6000 for the size and 1 and 4 for the number of hidden layers in both our Normalizer and Flagger. Some combinations we tried can be seen in the results section. Especially large sizes and numbers of layers proved to require more memory than our GPU could support, and training them on our CPU was exceptionally slow. We also tried 50% and 75% dropout, meaning that during training we randomly excluded hidden nodes from consideration at each layer. Dropout has been shown to improve performance by discouraging overfitting on the training data, and 50% and 75% are common dropout rates (Hinton, 2014).

We found the highest F1 score on the validation data for the Normalizer with two hidden layers of size 2000 each and 50% dropout. This was close to the maximum size our GPU could support without reducing the batch size to be too small to take advantage of the parallelism. The Flagger's highest score was found at two hidden layers of size 1000 each and 75% dropout. Attempts to provide hidden layers of different sizes consistently found inferior results. For the size of each embedding in the character projection layer, 10 had proven effective earlier in a simpler unpublished Twitter part-of-speech task. We selected 25 for our character embedding size to account for the greater complexity of a normalization task.

We separated the provided training data into 90% training data, 5% validation data and 5% was held out as test data. In order to construct a useful model on the small amount of available data, we iterate training over the same data many times. Our model stopped training after 150 training iterations in which there was no improvement on the validation set. We chose 150 iterations as the smallest value that did not lead to ending the training at a clearly suboptimal value. The training also stops at 5,000 iterations but in practice it converged before reaching this value.

Early in development we found that the Normalizer had exceptional trouble reconstructing twitter-specific objects, that is, hash-tags (#goodday), at-mentions (@marysue) and URLs (http://blahblah.com). Generally its behavior in all three cases was to follow the standard marker characters (@, #, http://) with a string of gibberish unrelated to the word itself. Because these are protected categories that should not be changed, we removed them from the training data and rely on the Flagger to flag them as not to be corrected.

We used layer-wise pre-training, meaning we first trained with zero hidden layers (going directly from the character projection to the softmax layer) to initialize the character embeddings, then we trained with one hidden layer, initializing the character embeddings with their previously trained values. When we trained the full model using two hidden layers, we initialized both the character projection layer and the weights from the projected input to the first hidden layer with the values learned before. The model continued to learn all the weights it used. Pretrained weights continued to be trained in the full model, although "freezing" some pretrained weights after pretraining and only training later weights in the full model has shown success when working with large amounts of unsupervised data and may be worthwhile to consider in future work (Yosinski, Clune, Bengio, & Lipson, 2014).

Running on an NVIDIA GeForce GTX 680 GPU with 2 GB of onboard memory, training the Normalizer took about six hours. We do not include CPU and RAM specifications because they were not heavily utilized in the GPU implementation. The Flagger was considerably faster to train than the Normalizer, taking only a little over half an hour.

## 4 Results and Discussion

The model earned third place in the competition, with scores very close to the second place model. The model's results in the competition compared to the first, second, and fourth place models is shown in Table 1. The precision scores are much higher than the recall scores for all models because in this task precision measures the capability of the model to not normalize what does not need normalizing while recall requires that a model both correctly identify what needs to be normalized and correctly normalize it.

In addition to the challenge results, we performed a more in-depth analysis on our own held-out validation and test data. Our analysis of the scores is shown in Table 2.

Initial data on the Flagger is in Table 3. We further analyzed the different errors made on the validation data. Our findings can be found in Table 4. Given the large proportion of errors mistakenly marked "Do Not Normalize," we looked at these errors. A few examples can be found in Table 5. Although the Flagger was not trained with Normalizer confidence in mind, it does an impressive job of only cancelling a normalization when the normalization is either unnecessary or would fail. In no case did the Flagger prevent the Normalizer from making a correct normalization.

An analysis in Figure 3 shows some early results from using only the Normalizer without a Conformer or Flagger. To fit this many runs in a reasonable time span, we used only ten percent of the training data. In this analysis, error rate is measured by token. To put the error rates in perspective, our final error rate was close to three percent. We show this graph to illustrate a number of points. Particularly, we wish to illustrate the challenge of encoding and reconstructing every item in a massive vocabulary, the value of additional iterations of layer-wise pre-training, and the large spikes in the error rates at certain points in the model.

| Model | Precision | Recall | F1-Score |
|---|---|---|---|
| NCSU_SAS _NING | 0.9061 | **0.7865** | **0.8421** |
| NCSU_SAS _WOOKHEE | **0.9136** | 0.7398 | 0.8175 |
| NCSU_SAS _SAM | 0.9012 | 0.7437 | 0.8149 |
| Iitp | 0.9026 | 0.7191 | 0.8005 |

Table 1: Results of the constrained task

| Data | Precision | Recall | F1-Score | Accuracy |
|---|---|---|---|---|
| Validation | 0.8942 | 0.7752 | 0.8305 | 0.9740 |
| Test | 0.8229 | 0.6870 | 0.7488 | 0.9656 |

Table 2: Model Scores on Validation and Test Data

| Data | Precision | Recall | F1-Score | Accuracy |
|---|---|---|---|---|
| Validation | 0.9818 | 0.9939 | 0.9878 | 0.9776 |
| Test | 0.9783 | 0.9930 | 0.9856 | 0.9736 |

Table 3: Flagger scores on Validation and Test Data

| Error | Percentage Occurrence |
|---|---|
| Correctly flagged, misnormalized | 13.85% |
| Mistakenly flagged "Do Not Normalize" | 66.15% |
| Mistakenly flagged "Do Normalize" | 20.00% |

Table 4: Analysis of errors. Percentages given are out of the total error count.

| Original | Gold Standard | Normalized |
|---|---|---|
| FB | Facebook | fabol |
| Fuhh | f*** | fuhh |
| OPENFOLLOW | open follow | openffolow |
| Feela | Feels | feela |
| Bkuz | because | bkuze |
| Kin | kind of | kin |
| Bruuh | brother | bruuhr |

Table 5: Examples of tokens that were mistakenly flagged "Do Not Normalize." The "Normalized" column is what the model would have produced if the Flagger had produced the flag "Do Normalize"

The Normalizer demands much more representational power when not assisted by the Flagger. Before we added the Flagger, we saw continual improvement of results going up to four layers of six thousand nodes each. We saw greater improvements from adding more nodes per layer than from adding more layers. The cluster of three lines near the top all have layers of 1500 or 2000 nodes each, and the next cluster down is the models we tried with 4500 and 6000 nodes. Incidentally, all but the smallest of these models were too large for our GPU's 2GB of onboard memory. As a reminder, after we added the flagger, we only required two layers of 2000 nodes each to get competitive results. In each case we used a dropout rate of 50%.

The default models pre-trained each layer for 250 iterations and we also trained models with the same structure for 500 iterations. We find a noticeable improvement in the error rate for the models that were pre-trained for more iterations. In the graph, the models with more pre-training make up the cluster of lines near the bottom of the graph.

Looking at the graphs, one may notice that some lines have brief spikes multiple percentage points in size. Because it only takes a one-letter mistake for a word to be misnormalized, we expect that at these times a small error arose that affected a large number of words. It is worth pointing out that each model continues to improve while in its spike, eventually dropping back to pre-spike levels.

The model is unique among the three top-performing models in that it avoids external data both directly and through indirect sources. The constrained task does not allow external data, but it does allow the use of off-the-shelf tools trained on external data. Our model does not use any such tools. Without the assistance of tools such as part-of-speech taggers, attempts to use context proved ineffective, likely because of increased sparsity. A given word that appears in the training set three hundred times may only appear three times after another particular word, and may not occur more than once with a particular prior word and following word, so it is more difficult to find patterns in limited data. Future work could either attempt to use tools to provide additional information or could simply take advantage of large amounts of data to learn directly the relationships such tools traditionally abstract for the benefit of conventional machine learning.

There is one other point: the human graders often made different decisions about whether or what a term should be normalized to. For example, sometimes the word "pics" used to refer to pictures was normalized to "pictures" but other times it was left as "pics". These inconsistencies in the gold standard make it difficult to accurately judge the quality of the models submitted. Occasionally when we examined mistakes the model made, we found that the model's prediction was correct according to the gold standard, but that the gold standard was wrong. An inter-rater reliability measure would help us to gauge not only how well our models compare to each other but how they compare to agreement between human coders.

this happened much less often than having the system normalize incorrectly. A model that predicts words from a vocabulary instead of reconstructing them would be faster to train and would not require a Conformer, and, considering the top two models were vocabulary based, might outperform our reconstruction-based model.

A second direction for future work centers on leveraging external data. With more time and greater computing power, it may be the case that it is possible to learn sophisticated language models in an unsupervised fashion from both standard conversational text and twitter data.

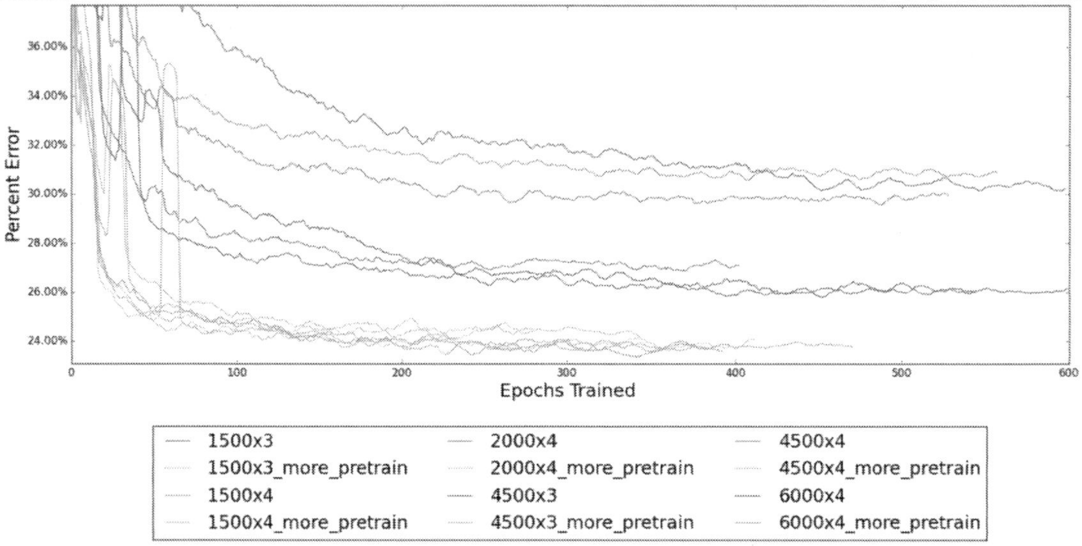


Figure 3: The Normalizer component validation scores by epoch. Model structures are given by "LxN" where L is the size of each layer and N is the number of layers and more_pretrain indicates that pretraining has continued for 500 instead of 250 iterations, and they cluster at the bottom with the lowest error. To smooth the graphs and make them more interpretable, values at each epoch are the average of a 10-epoch window.

## 5 Conclusions and Future Work

Normalization of Twitter text is a challenging task. With a direct application of simple deep learning techniques and without relying on any sources of external data, direct or indirect, we built a model that performed competitively with the other models in the task. Our method shows the ability of deep learning to tackle complex tasks without labor-intensive hand-engineering of features.

An important direction for future work is simplifying the normalization pipeline. The need for a Conformer in particular suggests that there is room for improvement in the model. Although constructing the normalized form rather than selecting from a list leaves the possibility open that a system could normalize to a correct word that did not appear in the training data, in practice

With this additional data, a model may be able to effectively use context in distinguishing between multiple possible normalizations of a word. Denoising autoencoders in particular are known to make good use of unsupervised data.

A third direction for future work is to investigate more challenging normalization tasks that include correction of syntax and do not present the text already tokenized. These will give us an opportunity to attempt tasks closer to the challenges our normalization systems will face in the real world.

Finally, it will be important to investigate the overall utility of normalization of text as a preprocessing step for other analysis. While many tasks will only benefit from cleaning the data, it is not clear that the canonical forms of words retain the same connotations that the original "noisy" versions held. For a simple example, if we were to normalize "coooooooool" to "cool" we would lose the emphasis implied by the elongation of the vowel. For some tasks, it may be important to retain the information contained in such non-canonical forms.

## References

Baldwin, Timothy, Catherine, Marie, Han, Bo, Kim, Young-Bum, Ritter, Alan, & Xu, Wei. (2015). Shared Tasks of the 2015 Workshop on Noisy User-generated Text : Twitter Lexical Normalization and Named Entity Recognition. In *Proceedings of the Workshop on Noisy User-generated Text (WNUT 2015)*. Beijing, China.

Bastien, Frédéric, Lamblin, Pascal, Pascanu, Razvan, Bergstra, James, Goodfellow, Ian, Bergeron, Arnaud, … Bengio, Yoshua. (2012). Theano: New Features and Speed Improvements. In *Deep Learning and Unsupervised Feature Learning NIPS 2012 Workshop* (pp. 1–10). Retrieved from http://arxiv.org/abs/1211.5590v1

Bengio, Yoshua. (2009). Learning Deep Architectures for AI. *Foundations and Trends® in Machine Learning*, *2*(1), 1–127. http://doi.org/10.1561/2200000006

Bergstra, James, Breuleux, Olivier, Bastien, Frédéric, Lamblin, Pascal, Pascanu, Razvan, Desjardins, Guillaume, … Bengio, Yoshua. (2010). Theano: A CPU and GPU Math Compiler in Python. In *Proceedings of the 9th Python in Science Conference* (pp. 3–10). Austin, Texas.

Collobert, Ronan, Weston, Jason, Bottou, Leon, Karlen, Michael, Kavukcuoglu, Koray, & Kuksa, Pavel. (2011). Natural Language Processing (almost) from Scratch. *The Journal of Machine Learning Research*, *12*, 2493–2537. Retrieved from http://dl.acm.org/citation.cfm?id=2078186

Hinton, Geoffrey. (2014). Dropout : A Simple Way to Prevent Neural Networks from Overfitting. *The Journal of Machine Learning Research*, *15*, 1929–1958.

Kalchbrenner, Nal, Grefenstette, Edward, & Blunsom, Phil. (2014). A Convolutional Neural Network for Modelling Sentences. *ACL*, 655–665.

Levenshtein, Vladimir. (1966). Binary Codes Capable of Correcting Deletions, Insertions, and Reversals. *Soviet Physics Doklady*, *10*(8), 707–710.

Rumelhart, David, Hinton, Geoffrey, & Williams, Ronald. (1986). Learning Representations by Back-propagating Errors. *Nature*, *323*(9), 533–536. Retrieved from http://books.google.com/books?hl=en&lr=&id=FJblV_iOPjIC&oi=fnd&pg=PA213&dq=learning+representations+by+back-propagating+errors&ots=zZEk5hHYWU&sig=B86wdYsAvCWVEN3aA-RCmw8_IJ8

Vincent, Pascal, Larochelle, Hugo, Bengio, Yoshua, & Manzagol, Pierre-antoine. (2008). Extracting and Composing Robust Features with Denoising Autoencoders. *Proceedings of the 25th International Conference on Machine Learning - ICML '08*, (July), 1096–1103. http://doi.org/10.1145/1390156.1390294

Yosinski, Jason, Clune, Jeff, Bengio, Yoshua, & Lipson, Hod. (2014). How Transferable are Features in Deep Neural Networks? In *Advances in Neural Information Processing Systems 27* (pp. 1–9).

Zeiler, M. D., Ranzato, M., Monga, R., Mao, M., Yang, K., Le, Q. V., … Hinton, G. E. (2013). On Rectified Linear Units for Speech Processing. *ICASSP, IEEE International Conference on Acoustics, Speech and Signal Processing - Proceedings*, 3517–3521. http://doi.org/10.1109/ICASSP.2013.6638312

# Author Index

**Association for Computational Linguistics**
209 N. Eighth Street
Stroudsburg, Pennsylvania 18360

ISBN 978-1-5108-0953-6

9 781510 809536

CURRAN ASSOCIATES INC.
proceedings.com